RAMAN'S
One Hundred and Ten-Year Ephemeris
of
PLANETARY POSITIONS
(1891 to 2000 A.D.)

Books on Astrology by Dr. B. V. Raman

Astrology for Beginners
A Manual of Hindu Astrology
A Catechism of Astrology
Hindu Predictive Astrology
How to Judge a Horoscope Vol. I
How to Judge a Horoscope Vol. II
Three Hundred Important Combinations
Prasna Marga Vol. I
Prasna Marga Vol. II
Prasna Tantra
Notable Horoscopes
My Experiments with Astrology
Nirayana Tables of Houses
Bhavartha Ratnakara
Ashtakavarga System of Prediction
Graha and Bhava Balas
Hindu Astrology and the West
Planetary Influences on Human Affairs
Muhurta or Electional Astrology
Studies in Jaimini Astrology
Klachakra Dasa
Raman's One Hundred Ten Years Ephemeris (1891-2000

RAMAN'S
One Hundred and Ten-Year Ephemeris of

Planetary Positions
(1891 to 2000 A.D.)

REVISED & ENLARGED EDITION

BANGALORE VENKATA RAMAN

Editor : THE ASTROLOGICAL MAGAZINE

📖 UBSPD
UBS Publishers' Distributors Ltd.
New Delhi Bangalore Chennai
Calcutta Patna Kanpur London

UBS Publishers' Distributors Ltd.

5 Ansari Road, New Delhi-110 002

Phones: 3273601, 3266646 ✫ *Cable*: ALLBOOKS ✫
Fax: 3276593, 3274261
e-mail: ubspd.del@smy.sprintrpg.ems.vsnl.net.in
Internet: www.ubspd.com

10 First Main Road, Gandhi Nagar, Bangalore-560 009

Phones: 2263901, 2263902, 2253903 ✫ *Cable*: ALLBOOKS ✫
Fax: 2263904

6, Sivaganga Road, Nungambakkam, Chennai-600 034

Phones : 8276355, 8270189 ✫ *Cable* : UBSIPUB ✫ *Fax* : 8278920

8/1-B, Chowringhee Lane, Calcutta-700 016

Phones: 2441821, 2442910, 2449473 ✫ *Cable*: UBSIPUBS ✫
Fax : 2450027

5 A, Rajendra Nagar, Patna-800 016

Phones: 672856, 673973, 656170 ✫ *Cable* : UBSPUB ✫ *Fax*: 656169

80, Noronha Road, Cantonment, Kanpur-208 004

Phones : 369124, 362665, 357488 ✫ *Fax* : 315122

Distributors for Western India:
M/s Preface Books
Shivali Apartments, Plot No. 1, S. No. 25/4, Chintamani Society,
Karve Nagar, Pune 411052 ✫ Phone: 349491

Overseas Contact
475 North Circular Road, Neasden, London NW2 7QG
Tele : 081-450-8667 ✫ *Fax* : 0181-452-6612 Attn: UBS

Copyright © Dr. B.V. Raman

Tenth Edition	1992
Reprint	1999

All rights reserved. No part of this publication may be reproduced or transmitted in any form or by any means, electronic or mechanical including photocopying, recording, or any information storage and retrieval system, without permission in writing from the publisher.

Printed at Taj Press, A 35/4 Mayapuri Industrial Area
Phase-I, New Delhi

PREFACE TO FIRST EDITION

The idea to bring out an Ephemeris covering not only our time but also the last decade of the last century, had persisted for a long time. However, it began to take concrete shape a decade ago largely due to the pressure brought to bear upon me by the innumerable readers of THE ASTROLOGICAL MAGAZINE and my other publications.

Ephemerides published in foreign countries were available till about 10 years ago though at exhorbitant prices. Hence the need for a publication of this type became all the more necessary.

It seemed highly desirable that an ephemeris capable of meeting the demands of astrological students and savants and those interested in the study of astrology all over the world irrespective of their preference — Sayana (tropical,) or Nirayana (Sidereal) — and reasonably accurate and easy to consult should be made available.

RAMAN'S NINETY-YEAR EPHEMERIS covers a period of 90 years (1891 to 1980) so that the birth dates of most of the persons alive today are covered. The ephemeris covering the coming few years will be of much use to astrological practitioners for timing events on the basis of transits.

In compiling this Ephemeris, no originality can be claimed. Full use has been made of astronomical facts, tables and mathematical results already computed by others. Acknowledgement courtesies are due to:

Astrologische Ephemeriden, American Astrology Tables of Houses, Baumgartner's Ephemeriden (1850–2000), *Positions Planetaires* (1840 to 2000), *the Deutsche Ephemerides* and *Stallman's Solar and Planetary Longitudes for Years* —2000 to +2000.

This Ephemeris can be used universally, as planetary positions given are Sayana (tropical). Students of Hindu astrology will be able to use it not only for casting horoscopes according to the Nirayana sidereal) system but also for finding the *thithi* (lunar day), the *nakshatra* (constellation) and the *yoga* which are necessary elements of Hindu astrology.

The use of this ephemeris with an Example has been discussed in the Introduction.

While a copy each of the (a) Ninety–Year Ephemeris, (b) *A Manual of Hindu Astrology* and (c) *Nirayana Tables of Houses* will place in the hands of a student of astrology all the information needed to correctly compute the horoscope for any date between the years 1891 to 1980 A. D. one can also cast a horoscope fairly correctly even without (b) and (c) as Condensed Tables of Houses given in Table II cover ascendant and tenth house longitudes for ten degree intervals of latitude and 16m intervals of Sidereal Time.

Appreciation is extended to Sri T. S. Kalyanaraman and to my children Gayatri Devi Raman, B. Niranjan Babu and B. Satchidananda Babu for their assistance in making the calculations.

Finally I wish to thank Mr. P.N. Kamat and Mr. G.K. Anantharam of IBH Prakashana for having readily come forward to publish the book in an attractive form.

BANGALORE :   B. V. RAMAN
24-12-1973.

PREFACE TO THE TENTH EDITION

THE tenth edition appearing so soon after the tenth edition is testimony of the popularity of the ephemeris with its users. This combined edition of the Ninety Year Ephemeris and the Twenty Year Ephemeris contains information for 110 years in one volume from 1891 to 2000 A.D.

The demand for this Ephemeris has been exceedingly high.

UBS Publishers' Distributors Ltd., New Delhi, deserves to be thanks for their promptness in bringing out quickly this combined enlarghed edition.

                                             B.V. RAMAN

"Sri Rajeswari"
Bangalore-560 020
1st February, 1992

INTRODUCTION

The computation of this Ephemeris has been done for 5-30 p.m. Indian Standard Time (I.S.T.) or Greenwich Mean Noon.

As already indicated, all planetary positions are Sayana or tropical ; and to get the Hindu or Nirayana positions, the Ayanamsa for the year in question is to be deducted.

The positions of the Sun, Mars, Jupiter, Venus, Saturn and Rahu are given at ten-day intervals. The Moon's position is given for every alternate day. The position of Mercury is given at five-day intervals. The positions of Uranus, Neptune and Pluto are given for the first of every month.

The planetary positions for any given date and time can be ascertained by interpolation, as per the example given below :

AYANAMSA

The Ayanamsa for the beginning of each year adopted by THE ASTROLOGICAL MAGAZINE is given at the foot of each year's ephemeris and also in Table IX.

For astrological purposes, it is enough if the Ayanamsa given in the Ephemeris is deducted from the Sayana positions. If greater accuracy is desired, the precessional value for the number of months passed from the beginning of the year can be ascertained by dividing the difference between the two values of the two years by 12.

The Table of longitudes and latitudes covers important places all the world over.

TIME CORRECTIONS

In India, Standard Time, now observed, was introduced on 1-1-1906. Before this date, local mean time was in vogue. Or the births used to be recorded in terms of ghatis (or pals or naligais) and vighatis (or vipals or vinadis), each ghati being equal to 24 minutes and each vighati being equal to 24 seconds. By converting the ghatis and *vighatis* into hours and minutes and adding the same to the time of sunrise, we can get the birth time in hours and minutes.

Subsequently the old railway time was in vogue. This was local time of Madras. Therefore the old railway time can be converted into I.S.T. by merely adding 9 minutes to it.

Advanced Standard Time was observed from 1-9-1942 to 15-10-1945 for war purposes. Therefore times of birth recorded during this period should be reduced by one hour.

SUMMER TIME

In recent years in some countries in Europe and America, Daylight Saving or Summer Time is used during certain periods of the year. This Summer Time is generally one hour ahead of the standard time. Countries in which Summer Time is used can be ascertained from other authoritative sources.

Calculating the Geo-centric Positions of Planets

Let us erect the horoscope of a person born on August 8, 1895 at 4h. 30m. p.m. (I.S.T.) at Bangalore, Long. 77° 35′ (or 5h. 10m. 20s.) E and Lat. 13° N.

(a) Since the time of birth is given in *Standard Time, convert it into Local Mean Time. Bangalore is located 4° 55′ West of Standard Time longitude *viz.*, 82° 30′. Hence we have to deduct from the time of birth 19m. 40s. (the difference between standard longitude and local longitude being 4° 55′, the time equivalent will be 19m. 40s, at the rate of 4 minutes of time per 1° longitude).

The local mean time of birth will be 4h. 10m. 20s. p.m.

The Ephemeris is calculated for 5-30 p.m. (I.S.T.) or 12 noon (G.M.T.)

This means the positions are correct for 5h. 10m. 20s. L.M.T. Bangalore, or 4h. 51m, 16s. p.m. (L.M.T.) at Bombay or 12h. 58m. p.m. (L.M.T.) Berlin and so on.

In actual practice, for getting planetary positions, no conversion to L.M.T. is needed for births in India. Simply take the difference between the time of birth (I.S.T.) and 5-30 p.m. For births recorded before I.S.T. was introduced, the L.M.T. may be converted into I.S.T. Or in the alternative, the L.M.T. equal to 5-30 p.m. (I.S.T.) can be taken and the difference between this and the time of birth found out.

The positions required are for 4th. 10m. 20s. p.m. (L.M.T.) 8-8-1895 :

Required : *The Position of the Sun :*

From Ephemeris :	13th August :	140° 27'
	3rd August :	130° 51'
	Motion in 10 days :	9° 36'
	Motion in 1 day	0° 57' 36"
	Motion in 1 hour	0° 2' 24"

Ephemeris position on 3rd August :
(5-30 p.m. I.S.T.)   130° 51' 0"

For 5 days from 3rd Aug. to 8th Aug :   4° 48'

∴ Position on 8th August :   135° 39'

Less motion in 1 hour   0° 2' 24"

Position at birth time   =   135° 36' 36"

   =   Leo   15° 36' 36"

This is the Sayana of Western position.   135° 36' 36"

Deducting the year's Ayanamsa :   20° 56' 39"

The Hindu or Nirayana position   114° 39' 57"

   =   Cancer   24° 40'

The Position of the Moon :

From Ephemeris :	9th August	359° 13'
	7th August	335° 38'
	Motion in 2 days.	23° 35'
	Motion in 1 day	11° 47' 30"
	Motion in 1 hour	29' 29"

Moon's position on 7th August   335° 38'

Add 1, day's motion   11° 47' 30"

Moon's position on 8th August   347° 25' 30"
(at 5-30 p.m. I.S.T.)

Since the birth time is at 4h. 10m. 20s. p.m. and the Ephemeris is given for 5th. 10m. 20s. p.m. (L.M.T.) or 5-30 p.m. (I.S.T.) deduct from the above

1 hourly motion :   0° 29' 29"

Moon's position at birth   346° 56' 01"

   =   Pisces   16° 56' 01"

This is the Sayana or Western position.

Deduct the year's Ayanamsa to get the Nirayana or Hindu position.

Sayana position	Pisces	16° 56' 01"	
Ayanamsa		20° 56' 39"	

The Moon's Nirayana position is Aquarius
(Kumbha)   25° 59' 22"

Reference to the table of Nakshatras (Table IV) reveals that Aquarius 20° to Pisces 3° 20' falls in Poorvabhadrapada.

The ecliptic is divided into 27 constellations of 13° 20' (or 800' of arc) each. Reduce the longitude of the Moon (or any planet) to minutes and divide the same by 800. The quotient is the number of constellations already passed : and the remainder, the part covered in the current asterism the Moon is in.   In this example:

Aquarius	25° 59' 22"	
=	10 signs 25° 59' 22"	
=	325° 59' 2''	
=	19559' 22"	

$$\text{Dividing this by 800:} \quad \frac{19559'\ 22"}{800}$$

= Quotient 24
remainder 359' 22"

The ruling star is the 25th, *viz.*, Poorvabhadra. 359' 22" have been covered in this star and the balance to be traversed is (800'-359' 22")

= 440' 38" or 440' or X.

Corresponding to this balance (X) the period of the Planet (i.e., the lord of the ruling star) remaining at the time of birth can be ascertained thus: (See Table V).

$$\frac{\text{X} \times \text{Dasa years of the lord of the ruling star}}{800}$$

In this case the lord of the ruling star being Jupiter and his total period being 16 years, the period remaining at the time of birth will be

$$\frac{440'\ 38" \times 16}{800} = \text{Yrs.}\ 8\text{-}9\text{-}25$$

Reference to Table V gives the ruling Dasa and the balance at the time of birth on the basis of the Moon's position. The Moon here is in Aquarius 25° 59′ 22″. For this Table V gives:

Balance of Jupiter's Dasa as yrs. 8–9–25.

Thithi (Lunar Day)

Each thithi or lunar day is equal to .9483 of a day so that a lunar month is equal to about 29.53 days. The ending time of a thithi is the moment at which the Moon is removed from the Sun by multiples of 12°. Thus when the Moon is 12° away from the Sun, the first lunar day or Prathami ends; when 24° Dwitiya and so on; when in conjunction the Amavasya (New Moon)., and when in opposition (180°) Pournimasya, (full Moon) ends.

It is enough for astrological purposes to know what thithi rules at the time of birth.

To find the lunar date or thithi deduct the longitude of the Sun from that of the Moon. If the difference is less than 180 , it is the bright half or Sukla Paksha ; if it is more than 180°, it is dark half or Krishna Paksha.

Divide the balance (Moon–Sun) by 12° (or 720′). The quotient represents the number of thithis elapsed and the remainder the part of the of the next (i.e., current) thithi that has elapsed.

Thus to know the thithi ruling on 8-8-1895 at the given time: First we deduct the longitude of the Sun (114° 40′ or 6880′) from that of the Moon (326° or 19560′). The remainder is 211° 20′ (12680′). It is more than 180° and hence it is the dark half (Krishna Paksha). day is the 18th (or 3rd lunar day of the dark half). 440′ (7° 20′) of its portion has been traversed, leaving 280′ (4° 40′) yet to be traversed. If portion has been traversed, leaving 300′ (5°) yet to be traversed. If the remainder is multiplied by 24 and divided by the difference of the daily motions of the Sun and the Moon, we get the number of hours (from the time of birth) still covering the thithi in question.

The daily motion of the Moon on the day of birth	11° 47′
*Daily motion of the Sun	57′
	10° 50′
Difference : =	650′

* For convenience sake more than 30″ are taken as 1′ and less than 30″ rejected.

Multiplying 280 by 24 and dividing the product by 650 we get

$$\frac{280 \times 24}{650} = 10h.\ 20m.$$

which added to the time of birth gives 2-30 a.m. (L.M.T.) (on 9th August) which will be the ending moment of the thithi (3rd lunar day of the dark half).

YOGA

There are 27 Yogas.

Yoga is the period during which the joint motion in longitude of the Sun and the Moon amounts to 13° 20′ of arc. The following formula is according to Suryasiddhanta.

$$\frac{Sun's\ longitude\ +\ Moon's\ longitude}{13°\ 20'\ (or\ 800')}$$

Taking the axample :

Sun's longitude	114°–40′
Moon's longitude	326°– 0′
Total	440°–40′
=	80°–40′
=	4840′

Dividing 4840′ by 800 we get quotient 6 and remainder 40.6 Yogas have transpired and the 7th viz., Sukarman is ruling. 40′ is the part of the current (Sukarman) yoga that has elapsed. Yet to be covered in this yoga is 760′. To ascertain the time at which the current yoga ends, divide the remainder (40′) by the sum of the daily motions of the Sun and the Moon (0° 57′ + 11° 47′ = 12° 44′ or 764′) and multiply by 24 to reduce the results to hours :

$$\frac{760 \times 24}{764} = 23h\ 52m$$

The Sukarman Yoga ends at 23h. 52m. from the time of birth.

The Table of Yogas (Table VI) enables one to ascertain the Yoga on the basis of the joint motion of the Sun and the Moon.

Thus in the example the sum of the Sun's and the Moon's longitude is 80° 40′. According to Table VI Sukarman commences at 80° and extends till 93° 20′.

ANOTHER EXAMPLE

Let us erect the horoscope of a person born on 22-9-1951 at 9-35 p.m. (I.S.T.) at Bangalore, Lat. 13° N, Long. 77° 30′ E. (or 5h. 10m. 20s. E.)

Two steps are involved, viz., (a) Determining planetary positions and (b) Determining the Lagna.

PLANETARY POSITIONS

As the positions of planets are given at 5-30 p.m. I.S.T. (or Greenwich Mean Noon) take the difference between 5-30 p.m. and time of birth (I.S.T.)

Time of Birth	=	9–35 p.m.	(I.S.T.)
Positions given for	=	5–30 p.m.	(I.S.T.)
Difference		4h. 5m.	

This can also be termed Interval.

*THE SUN

From Ephemeris : 2nd October 1951	=	188° 30′
22nd September	=	178° 41′
Motion in 10 days		9° 49′
Motion in 1 day (24 hours)	=	59′
Motion in 1 hour		2′ 27″ 5‴
Ephemeris position on 22nd September		178° 41′
Motion in 4h. 5m.		0 10′
Position (Sayana) at birth		178° 51′ 0″
*Less Ayanamsa for 1951		21·44
Sun's Hindu or Nirayana Position		157° 7′
	=	Virgo 7° 7′

---

* In reckoning daily motion or Ayanamsa, less than 30′ is rejected and more than 31′ considered as 1°.

THE MOON

Moon's Position on 21st September	69° 15'
Motion in 1 day	11 58
Motion in 4h. 5m.	2' 2' 10"
Moon's (Sayana) Position on 22nd September at birth time	83 15 10
Less Ayanamsa	21 43 37
Hindu or Nirayana Position	61 31 33
= Gemini 1° 31' 33'

Reference Table: The Moon is in Mrigasira 3.

MARS

October 2nd	=	148° 28'
September 22nd	=	142 15
Motion in 10 days		6° 13'
Motion in 1 day		37'
Motion in 4h. 05m.	=	6'
∴ Sayana position of Mars at birth	=	142° 21'
Nirayana position of Mars	=	120° 37'
= Leo 0° 37' = Makha 1

MERCURY

October 2nd	=	179° 49'
September 22nd	=	162 37
Motion in 10 days	=	17° 12'
Motion in 1 day	=	1° 43'
Motion in 4h. 05m.	=	0° 17'
∴ Sayana position at birth	=	162° 37'
	+	17'
		162° 54'
Nirayana position of Mercury	=	141° 10'
= Leo 21° 10' = Pubba 3

* JUPITER

October 2nd	=	9° 14′
September 22nd	=	10° 33′
Motion (R) in 10 days	=	1° 19′
Motion (R) in 1 day	=	0° 8′
Motion (R) in 4h. 05m.	=	0° 1′

∴ Sayana position of Jupiter (R) at birth = 10° 32′ = 370° 32′

Nirayana position of Jupiter (R) at birth = 348° 48′

= Pisces 18° 48′ = Revati 1

VENUS

October 2nd	=	153° 9′
September 22nd	=	152° 15′
Motion in 10 days	=	0° 54′
Motion in 1 day	=	0° 5′
Motion in 4h. 05m.	=	0° 1′
∴ Sayana position of Venus (R) at birth	=	152° 14′
Nirayana position of Venus (R)	=	130° 30′

= Leo 10° 30′ = Makha 1

SATURN

October 2nd	=	185° 52′
September 22nd	=	184° 37′
Motion in 10 days	=	1° 15′
Motion in 1 day	=	0° 8′
Motion in 4h. 05m.	=	0° 1′
∴ Sayana position of Saturn at birth	=	184° 38′
Nirayana position of Saturn	=	162° 54′

= Virgo 12° 54′ = Hasta 1

URANUS

October 1st	=	103° 50′
September 1st	=	102° 57′
Motion in 30 days	=	0° 53′

---

* Jupiter is retrograde and hence the backward motion.

Motion in 1 day	= 0° 1′ 46″
Motion in 21 days	= 0° 37′ 6″
Sayana position of Urunus at birth	= 103° 34′ 6″
Nirayana position of Uranus at birth	= 81° 50′ 29″
	= Gemini 21° 49′ 24″
	= Aslesha 2

NEPTUNE

October 1st	= 198° 52′
September 1st	= 197° 49′
Motion in 30 days	= 1° 3′
Motion in 21 days	= 0° 44′
∴ Sayana position of Neptune at birth	= 198° 33′
Nirayana position of Neptune at birth	= 176° 49′
	= Virgo 26° 49′
	= Chitta 2

*RAHU

October 2nd	= 338° 16′
September 22nd	= 338° 47′
Motion in 10 days	= — 31′
Motion in 1 day	= — 3′
∴ Sayana position of Rahu at birth	= 338° 47′
Nirayana position of Rahu at birth	= 217° 03′
	= Aquarius 17° 03′ = Satabhisha 4

DETERMINING LAGNA OR ASCENDANT

The Condensed Tables of Houses (Table III) and the Table of Sidereal Time (Tables I and II) should enable one to calculate the Lagna or the ascendant point fairly accurately.

The Table of Sidereal Time is for Ujjain local noon.

This can generally be used for all places in India without much difference and hence without any correction.

By adding 50 ⅘ seconds to this, the Sidereal Time for G.M.N. (Greenwich Mean Noon) is obtained.

Greenwich is 75° 50′ (or 5h. 3m, and 20s.) West of Ujjain. The longitudinal correction of 50 ⅘s. (at the rate of approximately 10

---

* Rahu's motion is always backward. Add 180° to Rahu to get Kethu's position.

seconds per hour or 15° of longitude) is positive. Therefore the Sidereal Time for Greenwich Mean Noon is obtained by simply adding 50 ⅚s. (or round figure 51 seconds) to the Sidereal Time given in Table I.

For example according to Table No. I Sidereal Time at local Ujjain Mean Noon on 1-1-1900 is 18h. 41m. 53s. Adding correction of 51s. we get the S. T. at Greenwich Mean Noon as 18h. 42m. and 44s. *(The Die Dueutsche Ephemeride* for 1900 gives the same value).

It is very necessary that the time of birth (generally given in Standard Time) should be converted into its equivalent local mean time.

1. From Table I find the figure corresponding to the year in question. Let it be denoted by Y.

2. From Table II take the figure corresponding to the date in question. Let it be denoted by D.

(In the case of a leap year, if the date concerned lies between March 1 and December 31, take the next date.)

3. Find I = Interval of time between the Mean Noon and the required moment given in Local Mean Time. This is positive or negative according as the given moment is after or before Mean Noon.

4. Find K, the motion of Sidereal Time corresponding to "I", to be calculated at the rate of 9.86 seconds (roughly 10 seconds) per mean solar hour or 10 seconds per hour. This is + if the time of birth is after the noon and − if before noon.

5. Find C the longitudinal correction in the Sidereal Time for the place. It is negative or positive according as the place is to the East or to the West of Ujjain, which is 75° 50′ East of Greenwich.

The required Sidereal Time = Y + D ± I ± K ± C

In the above example: Since the time of birth is given as 9-35 p.m. i.e., (I.S.T.) its equivalent L.M.T. — (difference in time between standard longitude and local longitude to be deducted from or added to I.S.T. according as the place of birth is west or east of the standard longitude, *viz.*, 82° 30′ or 5h. 30m.) — is 9h. 15m. 20s, which for convenience sake can be taken as 9h. 15m. p.m.

The Sidereal Time of Birth in the example horoscope will be :

		h	m	s
Y	=	18	40	27
D	=	17	20	51
I	=	09	15	00
K	=	00	01	30
		45	17	48

Expunging multiples of 24 from this sum, we get S.T. of birth = 21h. 17m. 48s. or 21h. 18m.

We proceed thus :

(a) Place of birth   13° N Lat.

(b) Sidereal Time of birth   21h. 18m.

FIRST STEP

(a) Lagna at 10° N Lat. for S.T. 21h. 04m = Taurus 21° 45′

                                                  (Table III)

(b)   –do–   21h. 20m =   ,,   25° 51′

(c) Increase in Lagna for a rise in 16m. S.T. = 4° 6′

(d) S.T. time at birth (21h. 18m.) is ahead of S.T. of (a) by 14m.

(e) Therefore increase in Lagna for 14m. is $\dfrac{4° 6′ \times 14}{16} = 3° 35′$

(f) Lagna at 10° N Lat. to S.T. 21h. 18m.   =   21° 45′

                                                        3° 35′

                        Taurus   25° 10′

SECOND STEP

(g) Lagna at 20° N for 21h. 04m.   =   25° 36″

(h) Lagna at 20° N for 21h. 20m.   =   29° 51′

(i) Increase in Lagna for a rise in 16m. S.T.   =   4° 15′

Repeating (d) and (f) increase in Lagna for 14m.

                                         = $\dfrac{4° 15′ \times 14}{16}$

                                         =   3° 43°

∴ Lagna at 20° N at 21h. 18m.   =   29° 19′

THIRD STEP

(a) Lagna at 10° N Lat. S.T. 21h. 18m.   = Taurus 25° 20′

(b) Lagna at 20° N.S.T. 21h. 18m.   =   29° 19′

Change in Lagna for change of 10° in latitude = 3° 59′

Change in Lagna for change of 3° in latitude

$$= \frac{3° \ 59′ \times 3}{10}$$

$$= 1° \ 11′$$

∴ Lagna at 13°, at S.T. 21h. 18m.   = 25° 20′ Taurus

                                 +   1° 11′

                                    26° 31′ Taurus

This is Sayana or tropical. To obtain the Nirayana Lagna (Hindu system) deduct the Ayanamsa for 1951 from the Sayana Lagna.

Sayana Lagna   Taurus   26° 31′

Ayanamsa for 1951   21° 43′ 38″

                                4° 47′ 22″ Taurus

Lagna at birth = 4° 47′ 22″ Taurus or Vrishabha

TENTH HOUSE

The longitude of the 10th house for a given sidereal time is the same for all latitudes. Therefore by simply entering the tenth house column and following the same procedure as given in Step II for ascendant determination, the tenth house longitude can be obtained.

In the example horoscope :

(a) Tenth House longitude (Sayana) for S.T.

                      21h. 04m. Aquarius 13° 32′

       –do–   21h. 20m.   ,,   17° 33′

(b) Increase in longitude for a rise

            in 16m. S.T.   =   4° 1′

Sidereal Time at birth (21h. 18m.) is ahead of S.T. of (a) by 14 minutes.

Therefore increase in tenth house longitude for 14m. is

$$\frac{4°}{16} \times 14 = 3° \ 31′$$

Tenth house longitude at S.T. 21h. 4m. is Aquarius   13° 33′
Increase in 14m.   3° 31′

Tenth house longitude at birth (*i.e.*, S.T.
                  21h. 18m.)   Aquarius   17° 4′
                         Less Ayanamsa   21° 44′
                                Capricorn   25° 20′

All these calculations can be eliminated and the longitudes of the Ascendant, 10th and other houses can be easily and quickly obtained by reference to *Nirayana Tables of Houses.*

Another Example : Let us cast the chart for a future epoch *viz.*, 8-8-1992 at 7-30 p.m. (IST) at Bangalore, Long. 77° 75′ (or 5ʰ 10ᵐ 20ˢ) E and Lat. 13° N.

The Local Mean Time of birth will be 7ʰ 10ᵐ 20ˢ p.m.

The *Ephemeris* is calculated for 5.30 p.m. (IST) or 12 noon (GMT).

This means the positions of planets are correct for 5ʰ 10ᵐ 20ˢ (LMT) Bangalore or 4ʰ 51ᵐ 16ˢ (LMT) Bombay, or 5ʰ 53ᵐ 24ˢ (LMT) Calcutta or 5ʰ 21ᵐ 17ˢ p.m. (LMT) Madras or 5ʰ 16ᵐ 48ˢ p.m. (LMT) Nagpur or 12ʰ 58ᵐ p.m. (LMT) Berlin and so on.

The positions required are for 7ʰ 10ᵐ 20ˢ p.m. (LMT) Bangalore on 8-8-1992 :

Position of the Sun :

From Ephemeris :   15th August   140° 58′
                          3rd August   131° 23′

	°	′	″
Motion in 10 days :		9	35
Motion in 1 day :	0	57	30
Motion in 1 hour :	0	2	24
Ephemeris position on the 3rd August			
(5-30 p.m. IST)	131	23	00
For 5 days from 3rd August to 8th August:	4	47	30
Position on 8th August :	136	10	30
Add motion in 2 hours :	0	4	48
This is the Sayana or Western position :	136	15	18
Deducting the year's Ayanamsa :	22	18	01
The Hindu or Nirayana position :	113	57	17
= Cancer	23	57	17

Position of the Moon:

		°	′	″
From Ephemeris:	9th August	274	00	
	7th August	249	26	
Motion in 2 days:		24	34	
Motion in 1 day:		12	17	
Motion in 1 hour:		0	30	43
Moon's position on 7th Agust :		249	26	
Add 1 day's motion :		12	17	

Moon's position on 8th August
(at 5–30 p.m. IST)   261   43

Since the birth time is at 7h 10m 20s p.m.
LMT (or 7–30 p.m., IST) and the
Ephemeris is given for 5h 10m 20s
p.m., LMT or 5–30 p.m., IST) add
to the above:

	°	′	″
Motion for 2 hours :	1	1	26
Moon's position at birth :	262	44	26

This is the Sayana or Western position.
Deduct the year's Ayanamsa to get the
Nirayana or the Hindu position.

	°	′	″
Sayana position :	262	44	26
Less Ayanamsa :	22	18	1
The Moon's Nirayana position	240	26	25
= Sagittarius	0	26	

Nakshatra

Reference to the Table of Nakshatras (Table IV) reveals that upto 253° 20′ (*i.e.*, Sagittarius 13° 20′), the constellation Moola prevails.

		°	′
In this example the Moon is in Sagittarius		0	26
	=	8s	26
	=	240	26
	=		14426′
Dividing the Moon's position			14426′
in minutes by 800	=		

$$= \frac{14426'}{800}$$

= Quotient 18
Remainder 26′

The ruling star is the 19th, *i.e.*, Moola. 26′ have been covered in this star and the balance to be covered is (800−26′) = 774′ = A.

Corresponding to this balance A, the period of the planet (*i.e.*, the lord of the ruling star, *viz.*, Ketu) remaining at the time of birth can be ascertained thus (See Table IV) :

$$\frac{A \times \text{Dasa Duration of lord of the ruling Star}}{800}$$

In this case the lord of the ruling star being Ketu and his Dasa period being 7 years, the period remaining at the time of the epoch will be $\frac{774 \times 7}{800}$ = 6 years, 9 months and 8 days.

Reference to Table V gives the ruling Dasa and the balance on the basis of the Moon's position. The Moon here is in Sagittarius 0° 26″. For this, Table IV gives the balance of Ketu Dasa 6 years, 9 months and 8 days.

Tithi (Lunar Day)

To know the *tithi* ruling on 8–8–1992 at the epoch time : First we deduct the longitude of the Sun (113° 57′ or 6827′) from that of the Moon (240° 26′ or 14426′). The remainder is 126° 29′ (7589′). It is less than 180° and hence it is the bright half (Sukla Paksha). Dividing the balance, *viz.*, 126° 29′ by 12, the quotient is 10 and remainder 6° 29′. The lunar day is the 11th day of the bright half (Sukla Ekadasi), 6° 29′ or 389′ of its portion having been traversed, 5° 31′ or 331 of arc is yet to be traversed. If the remainder 5° 31′ is multiplied by 24 and divided by the difference of the daily motions of the Sun and the Moon, we get the number of hours (from the time of the birth or epoch) still covering the tithi in question.

The daily motion of the Moon on the day of epoch is		12° 17′
The daily motion of the Sun is		0 56′
	Difference :	11° 19′
	=	679′.

Multiplying 5° 31′ (331′) by 24 and dividing the product by 679 we get $\frac{331 \times 24}{679}$ = 11h 41m 24s.

which added to the time of epoch gives (7h 30m p.m. + 11h 41m 24s) 7h 11m 24s a.m. (IST) on 9th August which will be the ending moment of the 11th lunar day.

Yoga

In our example the sum of the Sun's and the Moon's longitudes is 354° 23'. According to Table V Vaidhruti Yoga commences at 346° 40' and extends till 360°. Since the combined longitude of the Sun and the Moon is 354° 23', the Yoga at the epoch time is Vaidruti.

Position of Mars :

August 13th	71° 47'
August 3rd	65° 12'
Motion in 10 days	6° 35'
Motion in 1 day	0° 39' 30"
Motion in 1 hour	0° 1' 39"
Position on 3rd August	65° 12' 00"
For 5 days from 3rd to 8th August	3° 17' 30"
Position on 8th August	68° 29' 30"
Add motion in 2 hours	0° 3' 18"
Sayana position at epoch	68° 32' 48"
Deduct Ayanamsa for the year	22° 18' 01"
	46° 14' 47"
' = Taurus	16° 14' 47"
	16° 14' 47"

Position of *Mercury :

	August 3rd	130° 18'
	August 8th	127° 08'
(R) Motion in 5 days		3° 10'
(R) Motion in 1 day		0° 38'
(R) Motion in 1 hour		0° 1' 35"

---

* Mercury's position is given for every 5 days. The birth is on 8th August and the position of Mercury is given in the Ephemeris for this date ; hence it can be taken as it is. The motion for 2 hours is to be deducted as Mercury is retrograde.

Position on 8th August	127° 48′ 00″
Deduct (R) Motion for 2 hours	0° 03′ 10″
Sayana position	127° 04′ 50″
Less Ayanamsa :	22° 18′ 01″
Nirayana Position	104° 46′ 49″
− Cancer	14° 46′ 49″

Position of Jupiter :

August 13th	167° 37′ 00″
August 3rd	165° 28′ 00″
Motion in 10 days	1° 59′ 00″
Motion in 1 day	0° 11′ 54″
Motion in 1 hour	0° 0′ 5″
Position on 3rd August	165° 38′ 00″
For 5 days from 3rd to 8th August	0° 59′ 30″
Position on 8th August	166° 37′ 30″
Add Motion for 2 hours	0° 0′ 10″
Sayana position at epoch	166° 37′ 40″
Less Ayanamsa	22° 18′ 01″
Nirayana position	144° 19′ 39″
− Leo	24° 19′ 39″

Position of Venus :

August 13th	157° 40′
August 3rd	145° 22′
Motion in 10 days	12° 18′
Motion in day	1° 13′ 48″
Motion in 1 hour	− 0° 3′ 4″.5
Position on 3rd August	145° 22′ 00″
For 5 days from 3rd to 8th August	6° 09′ 00″
Position on 8th August	151° 03′ 00″
Add Motion for 2 hours	0° 06′ 09″
Sayana position at epoch	151° 37′ 09″
Less Ayanamsa	22° 18′ 01″
Nirayana Position	129° 19′ 08″
= Leo	9° 19′ 8″

Position of *Saturn :

	August 3rd	315° 25′
	August 13th	314° 40′

(R) Motion in 10 days	0° 45′
(R) Motion in 1 day	0° 4′ 30″
(R) Motion for 1 hour	0° 0′ 11″
Position on 3rd August	315° 25′ 00″
Deduct (R) Motion for 5 days from 3rd to 8th August	0° 22′ 30″
Position on 8th August	315° 2′ 30″
Deduct Motion for 2 hours	0° 0′ 22″
Sayana position at epoch	315° 2′ 8″
Less Ayanamsa	22° 18′ 1″
Nirayana position	282° 44′ 7″
Capricorn	22° 44′ 7″

Position of **Rahu :

	August 3rd	268° 23′ 00″
	August 13th	267° 52′ 00″

(R) Motion in 10 days	0° 35′ 00″
(R) Motion in 1 day	0° 3′ 30″
(R) Motion in hour	0° 0′ 8″.75
Position of Rahu on 3rd August	268° 23′ 00″
Deduct Motion for 5 days	0 17′ 30″
Position of Rahu on 8th August	268° 5′ 30″
Deduct Motion for 2 hours	0° 0′ 17″.5
Sayana position at epoch	268° 5′ 12″.5
Less Ayanamsa	22° 18′ 1″
Nirayana position	245° 47′ 11″.5
= Sagittarius	5° 47′ 11″.5

Position of Uranus :

Position on 1–8–1992	285° 04′ 00″
Position on 1–9–1992	284° 14′ 00″
(R) Motion in 30 days	0° 50′ 00″
(R) Motion in 1 day	0° 1′ 4″

---

* Saturn is retrograde and hence his motion is negative.
** Rahu's motion is always backward. Add 180° to Rahu's position to get Ketu's position.

Position of Uranus on 1-8-1992	285° 04'	00"
Deduct (R) Motion for 8 days	0° 13'	20"
Position on 8th August	284° 51'	40"
Deduct (R) Motion for 2 hours	0° 0'	8"
Sayana position of Uranus	284° 51'	32"
Less Ayanamsa	22° 18'	1"
Nirayana position	262° 33'	31"
= Sagittarius	22° 31'	31"

Position of Neptune :

Position on 1-8-1992	286° 58'	00"
Position on 1-9-1992	286° 22'	00"
(R) Motion in 30 days	0° 36'	00"
(R) Motion in 1 day	0° 1'	12"
(R) Motion in 1 hour	0° 0'	3"
Position on 1-8-1982	286° 58'	00"
Deduct for 8 days	0° 9'	54'
Position on 8th August	286° 48'	6"
Deduct Motion for 2 hours	0° 0'	6"
Sayana position at epoch	286° 48'	0"
Deduct Ayanamsa	22° 18'	01"
Nirayana position	246° 29'	59"
= Sagittarius	6° 29'	59"

Position of Pluto :

Position on 1-9-1992	230° 27'	00"
Position on 1-8-1992	230° 09'	00"
Motion in 30 days	0° 18'	00"
Motion in 1 day	0° 0'	36"
Motion in 1 hour	0° 0'	1".5
Position of Pluto on 1-8-1992	230° 09'	00"
Add Motion for 8 days	0° 04'	48"
Sayana position on 8th August	230° 13'	48"
Deduct Ayanamsa	22° 18'	01"
Nirayana Position	207° 55'	47"
= Libra	27° 55'	47"

THE SIDEREAL TIME

The required Sidereal Time = Y + D ± I ± K ± C.

In the example chart, the time given is 7–30 p.m. I.S.T. equivalent to $7^h 10^m 20^s$ L.M.T. on 8-8-1992 A.D.

The Sidereal Time of the epoch will be

$$
\begin{array}{rrrr}
Y = & 18^h & 40^m & 41^s \\
D = & 14 & 23 & 26 \\
I = & 7 & 10 & 8^0 \\
K = & 0 & 1 & 10 \\
\hline
& 40 & 15 & 37 \\
\end{array}
$$

Expunging multiples of 24 from this, we get the Sidereal Time as $16^h 15^m 37^s$ or $16^h 16^m$. When the Sidereal Time is known, the longitudes of the ascendant and other houses can be easily ascertained with the aid of any standard. *Tables of Houses or preferably from our own book *The Nirayana Tables of Houses* for 0° 60° N. Lat.

For the Sidereal Time of the epoch, *vi.*, 16^h 15^m 37^s the ascendant and the other houses are as follows :

		°	′
Ascendant	Aquarius	7	14
2nd house	Pisces	9	30
3rd house	Aries	11	46
4th house	Taurus	14	02
5th house	Gemini	11	46
6th house	Cancer	9	30
7th house	Leo	7	14
8th house	Virgo	9	30
9th house	Libra	11	06
10th house	Scorpio	14	02
11th house	Sagittarius	11	46
12th house	Capricorn	9	30

---

* Most Tables of Houses are given on the basis of Sayana (or Tropical). Therefore from the longitudes of the ascendant, etc.. obtained from such a Table of Houses, the Ayanamsa for the year in question should be deducted. *Nirayana Tables of Houses*, published by Raman Publications, gives the correct Hindu or sidereal longitudes of the ascendant, etc.

The Rasi Kundali (zodiacal diagram) in respect of the epoch, *viz.*, 8-8-1992 at 7-30 p.m. (I.S.T.) will be

		Mars 16°14′47″	Ketu 5°47′11″
Ascdt. 7° 14′	RASI		Sun 22°47′17″ Merc. 14°46′49″
Saturn 22° 4′ 7″			Jupiter 24°19′13″ Venus 9° 18′ 8″
Moon 0° 26′ Neptune 6° 29′ 50″ Rahu 5°47′ 11″ Uranus 22°33′31″	Pluto 27°55′47″		

Retrogression Tables of Planets

Planet Year	Venus ♀	Mars ♂	Jupiter ♃	Saturn ♄	Neptune ♆	Uranus ♅	Pluto P
1890	13 Nov R 24 Dec D	24 April R 5 July D	2 June R 29 Sep D	29 April D 29 Dec R	13 Feb D 13 Sep R	2 Feb R 4 July D	11 Feb D 6 Sep R
1891			10 July R 4 Nov D	13 May D	16 Feb D 16 Sep R	4 Feb R 9 July D	13 Feb D 8 Sep R
1892	18 June R 31 July D	6 July R 3 Sep D	14 Aug R 10 Dec D	10 Jan R 27 May D	17 Feb D 13 Sep R	10 Feb R 10 July D	13 Feb D 8 Sep R
1893			21 Sep R	25 Jan R 10 June D	17 Feb D 16 Sep R	15 Feb R 15 July D	14 Feb D 9 Sep R
1894	27 Jan R 10 Mar D	16 Sep R 22 Nov D	17 Jan D 26 Oct R	6 Feb R 23 June D	20 Feb D 22 Sep R	19 Feb R 21 July D	15 Feb D 10 Sep R
1895	30 Aug R 11 Oct D		21 Feb D· 27 Nov R	15 Feb R 6 July D	22 Feb D 22 Sep R	24 Feb R 25 July D	16 Feb D 11 Sep R
1896		2 Nov R	25 Mar D 27 Dec R	28 Feb R 17 July D	26 Feb D 25 Sep R	2 Mar R 1 Aug D	17 Feb D 12 Sep R
1897	8 April R 21 May D	17 Jan D	27 April D	13 Mar R 29 July D	27 Feb D 26 Sep R	2 Mar R 5 Aug D	18 Feb D 13 Sep R
1898	12 Nov R 23 Dec D	11 Dec R	25 Jan R 29 May D	22 Mar R 11 Aug D	1 Mar D 29 Sep R	10 Mar R 9 Aug D	19 Feb D 14 Sep R
1899		28 Feb D	26 Feb R 28 June D	4 April R 23 Aug D	6 Mar D 2 Oct R	14 Mar R 13 Aug D	21 Feb D 16 Sep R
1900	17 June R 30 July D		29 Mar R 30 July D	15 April R 4 Sep D	6 Mar D 2 Oct R	18 Mar R 19 Aug D	22 Feb D 17 Sep R
1901		14 Jan R 5 April D	2 May R 31 Aug D	26 April R 15 Sep D	8 Mar D 5 Oct R	23 Mar R 23 Aug D	23 Feb D 18 Sep R
1902	25 Jan R 8 Mar D		7 June R 5 Oct D	9 May R 27 Sep D	11 Mar D 9 Oct R	28 Mar R 28 Aug D	24 Feb D 19 Sep R
1903	28 Aug R 10 Oct D	19 Feb R 10 May D	15 July R 10 Nov D	21 May R 9 Oct D	14 Mar D 12 Oct R	2 April R 2 Sep D	26 Feb D 21 Sep R
1904			21 Aug R 16 Dec D	2 June R 20 Oct D	15 Mar D 12 Oct R	5 April R 5 Sep D	26 Feb D 21 Sep R
1905	7 April R 19 May D	4 April R 18 June D	26 Sep R	14 June R 1 Nov D	17 Mar D 15 Oct R	9 April R 10 Sep D	27 Feb D 22 Sep R

Planet Year	Venus ♀	Mars ♂	Jupiter ♃	Saturn ♄	Neptune ♆	Uranus ♅	Pluto P
1906	21 Nov R		22 Jan D	27 June R	20 Mar D	14 April R	1 Mar D
	10 Dec D		30 Oct R	13 Nov D	17 Oct R	15 Sep D	24 Sep R
1907		6 June R	26 Feb D	10 July R	22 Mar D	18 April R	2 Mar D
		10 Aug D	2 Dec R	26 Nov D	2 Nov R	19 Sep D	25 Sep R
1908	15 June R		31 Mar D	23 July R	24 Mar D	22 April R	2 Mar D
	28 July D		31 Dec R	7 Dec D	21 Oct R	23 Sep D	25 Sep R
1909		24 Aug R	2 May D	6 Aug R	26 Mar D	26 April R	4 Mar D
		24 Oct D		20 Dec D	24 Oct R	28 Sep D	27 Sep R
1910	5 Mar D		2 Feb R	20 Aug R	29 Mar D	2 May R	5 Mar D
	23 Jan R		3 June D		26 Oct R	3 Oct D	28 Sep R
1911	25 Aug R	19 Oct R	2 Mar R	3 Jan D	31 Mar D	5 May R	6 Mar D
	7 Oct D	30 Dec D	3 July D	3 Sep R	28 Oct R	6 Oct D	29 Sep R
1912			2 April R	16 Jan D	2 April D	8 May R	7 Mar D
			3 Aug D	17 Sep R	30 Oct R	10 Oct D	30 Sep R
1913	4 April R	27 Nov R	6 May R	29 Jan D	4 April D	13 May R	8 Mar D
	16 May D		4 Sep D	2 Oct R	2 Nov R	14 Oct D	1 Oct R
1914	8 Nov R	13 Feb D	12 June R	12 Feb D	7 April R	18 May R	9 Mar D
	18 Dec D		10 Oct D	16 Oct R	4 Nov R	19 Oct D	2 Oct R
1915			20 July R	27 Feb D	10 April D	21 May R	11 Mar D
			15 Nov D	30 Oct R	6 Nov R	23 Oct D	4 Oct R
1916	12 June R	1 Jan R	25 Aug R	12 Mar D	10 April D	25 May R	11 Mar D
	25 July D	22 Mar D	21 Dec D	12 Nov R	7 Nov R	26 Oct D	4 Oct R
1917			2 Oct R	26 Mar D	13 April D	29 May R	11 Mar D
				26 Nov R	10 Nov R	30 Oct D	6 Oct R
1918	21 Jan R	4 Feb R	27 Jan D	9 April D	15 April D	2 June R	14 Mar D
	3 Mar D	26 April D	4 Nov R	10 Dec R	12 Nov R	4 Nov D	7 Oct R
1919	23 Aug R		3 Mar D	24 April D	18 April D	7 June R	14 Mar D
	4 Oct D		5 Dec R	23 Dec R	15 Nov R	8 Nov D	7 Oct R
1920		15 Mar R	4 April D	7 May D	19 April D	10 June R	15 Mar D
		2 June D			16 Nov R	11 Nov D	8 Oct R
1921	2 April R		4 Jan R	4 Jan R	22 April D	14 June R	17 Mar D
	14 May D		6 May D	21 May D	19 Nov R	15 Nov D	10 Oct R
1922	5 Nov R	8 May R	3 Feb R	17 Jan R	24 April D	19 June R	19 Mar D
	16 Dec D	17 July D	6 June D	3 June D	21 Nov R	20 Nov D	12 Oct R
1923			6 Mar R	30 Jan R	27 April D	23 June R	20 Mar D
			7 July D	17 June D	24 Nov R	24 Nov D	13 Oct R
1924	10 June R	24 July R	6 April R	11 Feb R	28 April D	26 June R	21 Mar D
	23 July D	22 Sep D	7 Aug D	29 June D	25 Nov R	27 Nov D	14 Oct R

Planet Year	Venus ♀	Mars ♂	Jupiter ♃	Saturn ♄	Neptune ♆	Uranus ♅	Pluto P
1925			11 May R 9 Sep D	22 Feb R 12 July D	9 May D 27 Nov R	2 July R 2 Dec D	22 Mar D 15 Oct R
1926	18 Jan R 28 Feb D	29 Sep R 7 Dec D	16 June R 14 Oct D	6 Mar R 24 July D	3 May D 30 Nov R	5 July R 6 Dec D	24 Mar D 17 Oct R
1927	20 Aug R 3 Oct D		25 July R 20 Nov D	18 Mar D 6 Aug D	6 May D 2 Dec R	9 July R 10 Dec D	25 Mar D 18 Oct R
1928		12 Nov R	30 Aug R 26 Dec D	29 Mar R 17 Aug D	7 May D 4 Dec R	13 July R 13 Dec D	26 Mar R 19 Oct D
1929	30 Mar R 12 May D	27 Jan D	5 Oct R	10 April R 29 Aug D	10 May D 6 Dec R	17 July R 17 Dec D	27 Mar R 20 Oct D
1930	2 Nov R 13 Dec D	19 Dec R	31 Jan D 8 Nov R	22 April R 10 Sep D	12 May D 9 Dec R	22 July R 21 Dec D	29 Mar D 22 Oct R
1931		9 Mar D	7 Mar D 10 Dec R	4 May R 22 Sep D	15 May D 11 Dec R	26 July R 26 Dec D	31 Mar D 24 Oct R
1932	8 June R 21 July D		9 April D	15 May R 3 Oct D	17 May D 13 Dec R	29 July R 29 Dec D	31 Mar D 24 Oct R
1933		21 Jan R 12 April D	8 Jun R 10 May D	27 May R 15 Oct D	20 May D 18 Dec R	4 Aug R	2 April D 26 Oct R
1934	15 Jan R 26 Feb D		7 Feb R 11 June D	9 June R 27 Oct D	21 May D 18 Dec R	3 Jan D 7 Aug R	4 April D 28 Oct R
1935	18 Aug R 30 Sep D	27 Feb R 18 May D	10 Mar R 12 July D	22 June R 8 Nov D	26 May D 21 Dec R	7 Jan D 12 Aug R	5 April D 29 Oct R
1936			11 April R 12 Aug D	4 July R 19 Nov D	25 May D 21 Dec R	11 Jan D 16 Aug R	7 April D 31 Oct R
1937	28 Mar R 9 May D	15 April R 27 June D	16 May R 14 Sep D	17 July R 2 Dec D	29 May D 24 Dec R	14 Jan D 19 Aug R	9 April D 2 Nov R
1938	31 Oct R 11 Dec D		22 June R 19 Oct D	31 July R 15 Dec D	30 May D 26 Dec R	18 Jan D 24 Aug R	11 April D 4 Nov R
1939		23 June R 24 Aug D	30 July R 25 Nov D	14 Aug R 29 Dec D	2 June D 28 Dec R	22 Jan D 29 Aug R	13 April D 5 Nov R
1940	5 June R 19 July D		5 Sep R	28 Aug R	3 June D 30 Dec R	27 Jan D 2 Sep R	14 April D 6 Nov R
1941		7 Sep R 10 Nov D	2 Jan D 10 Oct R	9 Jan D 12 Sep R	6 Jun D	30 Jan D 6 Sep R	15 April D 8 Nov R
1942	13 Jan R 23 Feb D		5 Feb D 13 Nov R	23 Jan D 25 Sep R	2 Jan R 8 June D	4 Feb D 10 Sep R	16 April D 8 Nov R
1943	16 Aug R 27 Sep D	28 Oct R	12 Mar D 14 Dec R	8 Feb D 10 Oct R	5 Jan R 11 June D	8 Feb D 15 Sep R	17 April D 10 Nov R

Planet Year	Venus ♀	Mars ♂	Jupiter ♃	Saturn ♄	Neptune ♆	Uranus ♅	Pluto P
1944		10 Jan D	13 April D 23 Oct R	21 Feb D	7 Jan R 13 June D	13 Feb D 19 Sep R	18 April D 11 Nov R
1945	25 Mar R 7 May D	5 Dec R	12 Jan R 15 May D	6 Mar D 7 Nov R	8 Jan R 15 June D	16 Feb D 23 Sep R	20 April D 12 Nov R
1946	28 Oct R 8 Dec D	22 Feb D	11 Feb D 20 June D	20 Mar D 21 Nov R	10 Jan R 17 June D	20 Feb D 28 Sep R	22 April R 14 Nov D
1947			14 Mar R 16 July D	4 April D 4 Dec R	13 Jan R 20 June D	25 Feb D 3 Oct R	23 April D 16 Nov R
1948	3 June R 16 July D	9 Jan R 30 Mar D	15 April R 16 Aug D	17 April D 17 Dec R	15 Jan R 21 June D	1 Mar D 6 Oct R	24 April D 17 Nov R
1949			21 May R 20 Sep D	2 May D 30 Dec R	17 Jan R 24 June D	5 Mar D 11 Oct R	26 April D 19 Nov R
1950	11 Jan R 22 Feb D	13 Feb R 5 May D	28 June R 26 Oct D	15 May D	19 Jan R 27 June D	10 Mar D 16 Oct R	28 April D 21 Nov R
1951	14 Aug R 26 Sep D		4 Aug R 30 Nov D	12 Jan R 29 May D	21 Jan R 28 June D	15 Mar D 22 Oct R	20 April D 23 Nov R
1952		26 Mar R 11 June D	10 Sep R	27 Jan R 12 June D	23 Jan R 1 July D	18 Mar D 26 Oct R	1 May D 24 Nov R
1953	24 Mar R 5 May D		6 Jan D 15 Oct R	8 Feb R 25 June D	25 Jan R 3 July D	24 May D 30 Oct R	2 May D 26 Nov R
1954	27 Oct R 7 Dec D	23 May R 29 July D	11 Feb D 18 Nov R	17 Feb R 8 July D	27 Jan R 5 July D	29 Mar D 4 Nov R	4 May D 28 Nov R
1955			16 Mar R 18 Dec R	28 Feb R 19 July D	29 Jan R 7 July D	2 April D 9 Nov R	6 May D 30 Nov R
1956	2 June R 15 July D	10 Aug R 9 Oct D	18 April D	15 Mar R 31 July D	31 Jan R 9 July D	6 April D 13 Nov R	7 May D 1 Dec R
1957			17 Jan R 20 May D	24 Mar R 13 Aug D	2 Feb R 11 July D	11 April D 18 Nov R	9 May D 3 Dec R
1958	9 Jan R 20 Feb D	11 Oct R 21 Dec D	17 Feb R 20 June D	6 April R 25 Aug D	4 Feb R 13 July D	17 April D 24 Nov R	11 May D 5 Dec R
1959	12 Aug R 24 Sep D		18 Mar R 21 July D	17 April R 6 Sep D	6 Feb R 15 July D	21 April D 28 Nov R	13 May D 7 Dec R
1960		21 Nov R	21 April R 21 Aug D	28 April R 17 Dec D	8 Feb R 17 July D	26 April D 4 Dec R	15 May D 9 Dec R
1961	22 Mar R 3 May D	6 Feb D	26 May R 24 Sep D	11 May R 29 Sep D	10 Feb R 19 July D	4 May D 8 Dec R	17 May D 11 Dec R
1962	25 Oct R 5 Dec D	27 Dec R	4 July R 31 Oct D	23 May R 11 Oct D	12 Feb R 21 July D	9 May D 14 Dec R	19 May D 13 Dec R

Planet Year	Venus ♀	Mars ♂	Jupiter ♃	Saturn ♄	Neptune ♆	Uranus ♅	Pluto P
1963		15 Mar D	9 Aug R 5 Dec D	4 June D 22 Oct D	14 Feb R 23 July D	9 May D 17 Dec R	22 May D 16 Dec R
1964	31 May R 13 July D		16 Sep R	14 June R 3 Nov D	16 Feb R 25 July D	14 May D 21 Dec R	23 May D 17 Dec R
1965		30 Jan R 20 April D	11 Jan D 20 Oct R	29 June R 15 Nov D	18 Feb R 27 July D	20 May D 26 Dec R	25 May D 19 Dec R
1966	7 Jan R 18 Feb D		16 Feb D 22 Nov R	12 July R 28 Nov D	20 Feb R 29 July D	25 May D	28 May D 22 Dec R
1967	10 Aug R 22 Sep D	8 Mar R 25 May D	21 Mar D 23 Dec R	25 July R 9 Dec D	21 Feb R 28 July D	1 Jan R 30 May D	30 May D 24 Dec R
1968			22 April D	8 Aug R 22 Dec D	22 Feb R 29 July D	5 Jan R 3 June D	2 June D 26 Dec R
1969	20 Mar R 1 May D	27 April R 8 July D	21 Jan R 25 May D	22 Aug R	24 Feb R 30 July D	10 Jan R 9 June D	5 June D 29 Dec R
1970	23 Oct R 3 Dec D		20 Feb R 25 June D	6 Jan D 5 Sep R	25 Feb R 1 Aug D	16 Jan R 14 June D	7 June D 31 Dec R
1971		9 July R 6 Sep D	23 Mar R 25 July D	18 Jan D 19 Sep R	27 Feb R 3 Aug D	20 Jan R 20 June D	3 Jan R 10 June D
1972	29 May R 11 July D		26 April R 26 Aug D	31 Jan D 5 Oct R	1 Mar R 5 Aug D	25 Jan R 22 June D	4 Jan R 11 June D
1973	29 Sep R 25 Nov D		1 June R 29 Sep D	14 Feb D 18 Oct R	3 Mar R 7 Aug D	28 Jan R 29 June D	7 Jan R 14 June D
1974	5 Jan R 16 Feb D		10 July R 4 Nov D	1 Mar D 1 Nov R	5 Mar R 9 Aug D	3 Feb R 6 July D	10 Jan R 17 June D
1975	8 Aug R 20 Sep D	5 Nov R 10 Dec D	14 Aug R 10 Dec D	14 Mar D 14 Nov R	8 Mar R 13 Aug D	6 Feb R 11 July D	12 Jan R 19 June D
1976		20 Jan D	21 Sep R	28 Mar D 28 Nov R	11 Mar R 15 Aug D	12 Feb R 12 July D	14 Jan R 21 June D
1977	18 Mar R 29 April D	14 Dec R	17 Jan D 26 Oct R	11 April D 12 Dec R	13 Mar R 17 Aug D	17 Feb R 17 July D	17 Jan R 24 June D
1978	21 Oct R 1 Dec D	3 Mar D	21 Feb D 27 Nov R	26 April D 25 Dec R	15 Mar R 20 Aug D	21 Feb R 23 July D	20 Jan R 27 June D
1979			26 Mar D 27 Dec R	9 May D	18 Mar R 23 Aug D	26 Feb R 27 July D	22 Jan R 29 June D
1980	27 May R 9 July D	17 Jan R 8 April D	27 April D	6 Jan R 23 May D	21 Mar R 25 Aug D	3 Mar R 3 Aug D	24 Jan R 1 July D

Planet Year	Venus ♀	Mars ♂	Jupiter ♃	Saturn ♄	Neptune ♆	Uranus ♅	Pluto P
1981			26 Jan R 29 May D	19 Jan R 6 June D	30 Mar R 6 Sep D	6 Mar R 7 Aug D	28 Jan R 4 July D
1982	2 Jan R 12 Feb D	22 Feb R 13 May D	26 Feb R 29 June D	2 Feb R 20 June D	2 April R 9 Sep D	12 Mar R 11 Aug D	2 Feb R 7 July D
1983	5 Aug R 17 Sep D		29 Mar R 30 July D	14 Feb R 3 July D	3 April R 11 Sep D	16 Mar R 16 Aug D	3 Feb R 10 July D
1984		7 April R 21 June D	2 May R 31 Aug D	26 Feb R 15 July D	5 April R 13 Sep D	20 Mar R 19 Aug D	6 Feb R 11 July D
1985	15 Mar R 26 April D		6 June R 4 Oct D	9 Mar R 27 July D	7 April R 15 Sep D	25 Mar R 25 Aug D	8 Feb R 15 July D
1986	17 Oct R 27 Nov D	10 June R 13 Aug D	14 July R 10 Nov D	21 Mar R 9 Aug D	9 April R 16 Sep D	30 Mar R 29 Aug D	11 Feb R 17 July D
1987			21 Aug R 17 Dec D	2 April R 21 Aug D	11 April R 20 Sep D	3 April R 3 Sep D	14 Feb R 20 July D
1988	24 May R 6 July D	28 Aug R 29 Oct D	26 Sep R	12 April R 2 Sep D	14 April R 21 Sep D	7 April R 7 Sep D	16 Feb R 23 July D
1989	30 Dec R		21 Jan D 30 Oct R	25 April R 13 Sep D	16 April R 23 Sep D	11 April R 11 Sep D	18 Feb R 26 July D
1990	9 Feb D	22 Oct R	26 Feb D 2 Dec R	6 May R 25 Sep D	18 April R 27 Sep D	15 April R 17 Sep D	20 Feb R 28 July D
1991	2 Aug R 14 Sep D	3 Jan D	2 April D	18 May R 6 Oct D	21 April R 28 Sep D	20 April R 22 Sep D	24 Feb R 31 July D
1992		30 Nov R	2 Jan R 2 May D	30 May R 18 Oct D	22 April R 2 Oct D	24 April R 25 Sep D	26 Feb R 2 Aug D
1993	12 Mar R 24 April D	16 Feb D	30 Jan R 2 June D	12 June R 30 Oct D	24 April R 2 Oct D	29 April R 30 Sep D	2 Mar R 4 Aug D
1994	14 Oct R 25 Nov D		2 Mar R 3 July D	25 June R 11 Nov D	28 April R 5 Oct D	2 May R 30 Oct D	3 Mar R 8 Aug D
1995		4 Jan R 26 Mar D	3 April R 4 Aug R	7 July R 24 Nov D	30 April R 6 Oct D	8 May R 9 Oct D	6 Mar R 10 Aug D
1996	21 May R 3 July D		6 May R 5 Sep D	20 July R 5 Dec D	3 May R 9 Oct D	11 May R 12 Oct D	8 Mar R 11 Aug D
1997	28 Dec R	7 Feb R 29 April D	11 June R 9 Oct D	3 Aug R 18 Dec D	3 May R 11 Oct D	15 May R 16 Oct D	11 Mar R 16 Aug D
1998	7 Feb D		19 July R 15 Nov D	17 Aug R 31 Dec D	7 May R 15 Oct D	19 May R 20 Oct D	13 Mar R 16 Aug D
1999	31 July R 12 Sep D	20 Mar R 5 June D	26 Aug R 22 Dec D	2 Sep R	9 May R 16 Oct D	24 May R 26 Oct D	16 Mar R 21 Aug D

Retrogression Tables of Mercury

1890	1891	1892	1893	1894	1895	1896
21 Jan R	5 Jan R	9 Jan D	23 Mar R	6 Mar R	17 Feb R	2 Feb R
10 Feb D	25 Jan D	10 April R	15 April D	28 Mar D	11 Mar D	22 Feb D
18 May R	30 April R	4 May D	26 July R	7 July R	19 June R	30 May R
11 June D	22 May D	11 Aug R	19 Aug D	31 July D	13 July D	23 June D
17 Sep R	30 Aug R	3 Dec R	16 Nov R	31 Oct R	15 Oct R	27 Sep R
8 Oct D	23 Sep D	23 Dec D	6 Dec D	20 Nov D	4 Nov D	18 Oct D
	20 Dec R					

1897	1898	1899	1900	1901	1902	1903
14 Jan R	18 Jan D	1 Jan D	16 Mar R	27 Feb R	10 Feb R	25 Jan R
4 Feb D	21 April R	3 April R	8 April D	21 Mar D	4 Mar D	15 Feb D
10 May R	15 May D	26 April D	19 July R	2 July R	12 June R	23 May R
3 June D	24 Aug R	6 Aug R	12 Aug D	25 July D	6 July D	16 June D
10 Sep R	26 Sep D	29 Aug D	10 Nov R	25 Oct R	8 Oct R	21 Sep R
2 Oct D	13 Dec R	27 Nov R	30 Nov D	14 Nov D	29 Oct D	13 Oct D
29 Dec R		17 Dec D				

1904	1905	1906	1907	1908	1909	1910
9 Jan R	12 Jan D	27 Mar R	9 Mar R	21 Feb R	3 Feb R	18 Jan R
29 Jan D	14 April R	19 April D	1 April D	14 Mar D	24 Feb D	8 Feb D
3 May R	8 May D	30 July R	12 July R	22 June R	3 June R	15 May R
26 May D	17 Aug R	23 Aug D	5 Aug D	16 July D	27 June D	8 June D
3 Sep R	9 Sep D	21 Nov R	4 Nov R	18 Oct R	2 Oct R	14 Sep R
25 Sep D	7 Dec R	10 Dec D	24 Nov D	7 Nov D	22 Oct D	6 Oct D
23 Dec R	27 Dec D					

1911	1912	1913	1914	1915	1916	1917
2 Jan R	5 Jan D	19 Mar R	2 Mar R	13 Feb R	27 Jan R	10 Jan R
22 Jan D	6 April R	11 April D	24 Mar D	6 Mar D	18 Feb D	31 Jan D
25 April R	29 April D	22 July R	4 July R	14 June R	25 May R	6 May R
19 May D	9 Aug R	14 Aug D	27 July D	8 July D	18 June D	30 May D
27 Aug R	2 Sep D	13 Nov R	28 Oct R	10 Oct R	23 Sep R	6 Sep R
19 Sep D	29 Nov R	3 Dec D	17 Nov D	31 Oct D	14 Oct D	28 Sep D
16 Dec R	19 Dec D					25 Dec R

1918	1919	1920	1921	1922	1923	1924
14 Jan D	29 Mar R	11 Mar R	22 Feb R	5 Feb R	20 Jan R	4 Jan R
17 April R	22 April D	3 April D	16 Mar D	27 Feb D	10 Feb D	24 Jan D
10 May D	2 Aug R	14 July R	25 June R	6 June R	18 May R	27 April R
19 Aug R	25 Aug D	7 Aug D	19 July D	30 June D	10 June D	21 May D
12 Sep D	23 Nov R	6 Nov R	20 Oct R	3 Oct R	16 Sep R	29 Aug R
9 Dec R	13 Dec D	26 Nov D	9 Nov D	24 Oct D	8 Oct D	21 Sep D
29 Dec D						18 Dec R

1925	1926	1927	1928	1929	1930	1931
7 Jan D	22 Mar R	4 Mar R	16 Feb R	29 Jan R	13 Jan R	17 Jan D
8 April R	14 April D	27 Mar D	9 Mar D	20 Feb D	3 Feb D	20 April R
3 May D	25 July R	6 July R	17 June R	28 May R	9 May R	14 May D
12 Aug R	18 Aug D	31 July D	11 July D	21 June D	3 June D	22 Aug R
4 Sep D	16 Nov R	30 Oct R	13 Oct R	26 Sep R	9 Sep R	14 Sep D
2 Dec R	5 Dec D	19 Nov D	2 Nov D	17 Oct D	2 Oct D	12 Dec R
22 Dec D					28 Dec R	

1932	1933	1934	1935	1936	1937	1938
2 Jan D	14 Mar R	25 Feb R	8 Feb R	23 Jan R	6 Jan R	10 Jan D
31 Mar R	6 April D	19 Mar D	2 Mar D	13 Feb D	26 Jan D	12 April R
24 April D	17 July R	28 June R	9 June R	20 May R	2 May R	6 May D
4 Aug R	10 Aug D	22 July D	3 July D	13 June D	24 May D	15 Aug R
27 Aug D	8 Nov R	23 Oct R	6 Oct R	18 Sep R	2 Sep R	7 Sep D
25 Nov R	28 Nov D	12 Nov D	27 Oct D	10 Oct D	24 Sep D	5 Dec R
14 Dec D					21 Dec R	24 Dec D

1939	1940	1941	1942	1943	1944	1945
25 Mar R	6 Mar R	17 Feb R	2 Feb R	16 Jan R	20 Jan D	3 Jan D
17 April D	29 Mar D	12 Mar D	23 Feb D	6 Feb D	22 April R	4 April R
28 July R	9 July R	20 June R	2 June R	13 May R	16 May D	27 April D
21 Aug D	2 Aug D	14 July D	25 June D	5 June D	24 Aug R	7 Aug R
19 Nov R	2 Nov R	15 Oct R	29 Sep R	12 Sep R	16 Sep D	30 Aug D
8 Dec D	21 Nov D	5 Nov D	20 Oct D	4 Oct D	14 Dec R	27 Nov R
				31 Dec R		17 Dec D

1946	1947	1948	1949	1950	1951	1952
17 Mar R	28 Feb R	11 Feb R	25 Jan R	9 Jan R	14 Jan D	28 Mar R
9 April D	22 Mar D	4 Mar D	15 Feb D	30 Jan D	15 April R	20 April D
20 July R	2 July R	11 June R	24 May R	4 May R	8 May D	31 July R
13 Aug D	26 July D	6 July D	16 June D	28 May D	17 Aug R	24 Aug D
11 Nov R	26 Oct R	8 Oct R	22 Sep R	4 Sep R	10 Sep D	21 Nov R
2 Dec D	15 Nov D	29 Oct D	13 Oct D	27 Sep D	7 Dec R	11 Dec D
				24 Dec R	26 Dec D	

1953	1954	1955	1956	1957	1958	1959
10 Mar R	21 Feb R	5 Feb R	18 Jan R	2 Jan R	6 Jan D	20 Mar R
1 April D	15 Mar D	26 Feb D	8 Feb D	23 Jan D	8 April R	12 April D
13 July R	24 June R	4 June R	16 May R	26 April R	30 April D	23 July R
6 Aug D	18 July D	28 June D	8 June D	20 May D	11 Aug R	16 Aug D
5 Nov R	1 Oct R	10 Oct R	14 Sep R	28 Aug R	3 Sep D	14 Nov R
25 Nov D	9 Nov D	22 Oct D	6 Oct D	20 Sep D	1 Dec R	4 Dec D
				17 Dec R	21 Dec D	

1960	1961	1962	1963	1964	1965	1966
3 Mar R	14 Feb R	29 Jan R	12 Jan R	15 Jan D	31 Mar R	13 Mar R
25 Mar D	8 Mar D	19 Feb D	1 Feb D	18 April R	23 April D	5 April D
5 July R	16 June R	28 May R	6 May-R	12 May D	3 Aug R	15 July R
29 July D	10 July D	21 June D	30 May D	21 Aug R	27 Aug D	8 Aug D
29 Oct R	12 Oct R	25 Sep R	6 Sep R	12 Sep D	24 Nov R	8 Nov R
18 Nov D	1 Nov D	16 Oct D	28 Sep D	10 Dec R	14 Dec D	28 Nov D
			26 Dec R	30 Dec D		

1967	1968	1969	1970	1971	1972	1973
24 Feb R	7 Feb R	21 Jan R	5 Jan R	9 Jan D	23 Mar R	6 Mar R
17 Mar D	28 Feb D	10 Feb D	25 Jan D	10 April R	15 April D	28 Mar D
26 June R	8 June R	18 May R	30 April R	4 May D	26 July R	7 July R
20 July D	30 June D	11 June D	22 May D	11 Aug R	19 Aug D	31 July D
20 Oct R	4 Oct R	17 Sep R	30 Aug R	5 Sep D	16 Nov R	31 Oct R
11 Nov D	25 Oct D	8 Oct D	23 Sep D	3 Dec R	6 Dec D	20 Nov D
			20 Dec R	23 Dec D		

1974	1975	1976	1977	1978	1979	1980
17 Feb R	1 Feb R	14 Jan R	18 Jan D	2 Jan D	16 Mar R	27 Feb R
11 Mar D	22 Feb D	4 Feb D	21 April R	3 April R	8 April D	21 Mar D
19 June R	30 May R	10 May R	15 May D	26 April D	19 July R	1 July R
13 July D	23 June D	3 June D	24 Aug R	6 Aug R	12 Aug D	25 July D
15 Oct R	27 Sep R	10 Sep R	16 Sep D	29 Aug D	10 Nov R	25 Oct R
4 Nov D	18 Oct D	2 Oct D	13 Dec R	27 Nov R	30 Nov D	14 Nov D
		29 Dec R		17 Dec D		

1981	1982	1983	1984	1985	1986	1987
10 Feb R	24 Jan R	8 Jan R	12 Jan D	26 Mar R	8 Mar R	20 Feb R
3 Mar D	14 Feb D	29 Jan D	13 April R	18 April D	31 Mar D	15 Mar D
11 June R	22 May R	3 May R	7 May D	29 July R	11 July R	22 June R
5 July D	15 June R	27 May D	16 Aug R	22 Aug D	4 Aug D	16 July D
7 Oct R	20 Sep R	3 Sep R	8 Sep D	20 Nov R	3 Nov R	18 Oct R
28 Oct D	12 Sep D	26 Sep D	6 Dec R	9 Dec D	23 Nov D	7 Nov D
		23 Dec R	26 Dec D			

1988	1989	1990	1991	1992	1993	1994
3 Feb R	17 Jan R	2 Jan R	5 Jan R	18 Mar R	2 Mar R	12 Feb R
25 Feb D	7 Feb D	21 Jan D	6 April R	10 April D	24 Mar D	6 Mar D
2 June R	14 May R	24 April R	29 April D	21 July R	3 July R	14 June R
26 June D	6 June D	18 May D	9 Aug R	14 Aug D	27 July D	8 July D
30 Sep R	13 Sep R	27 Aug R	2 Sep D	12 Nov R	27 Oct R	10 Oct R
21 Oct D	5 Oct D	19 Sep D	30 Nov R	2 Dec D	16 Nov D	31 Oct D
		16 Dec R	13 Dec D			

1995	1996	1997	1998	1999	2000
27 Jan R	11 Jan R	14 Jan D	29 Mar R	11 Mar R	22 Feb R
17 Feb D	31 Jan D	16 April R	21 April D	3 April D	16 Mar D
25 May R	5 May R	10 May D	2 Aug R	14 July R	25 June R
18 June D	29 May D	19 Aug R	25 Aug D	7 Aug D	19 July D
23 Sep R	5 Sep R	11 Sep D	22 Nov R	6 Nov R	20 Oct R
15 Oct D	25 Dec R	9 Dec R	12 Dec D	26 Nov D	9 Nov D
	25 Dec R	28 Dec D			

RAMAN'S

One Hundred and Ten-Year Ephemeris
of
PLANETARY POSITIONS

(1891 to 2000 A.D.)

Longitudes of Planets

1891		Sun	Mars	Merc.	Merc.	Jupiter	Venus	Saturn	Rahu
Jan.	5	284 55	344 33	300 25R	297 16	315 29	247 2	167 7R	72 58
	15	295 6	352 1	291 0	285 55	317 45	252 34	166 52	72 26
	25	305 17	359 26	284 23D	286 3	328 5	260 6	166 27	71 55
Feb.	4	315 26	6 49	289 52	295 2	322 28	268 59	165 57	71 23
	14	325 33	14 9	301 6	307 48	324 52	278 47	165 12	70 52
	24	335 38	21 25	315 1	322 42	327 16	289 13	164 27	70 20
March	6	345 39	28 38	330 50	339 25	329 38	300 4	163 32	69 48
	16	355 38	35 46	348 30	358 4	331 58	311 15	162 52	69 16
	26	5 33	42 51	8 5	18 19	334 14	322 39	162 7	68 45
April	5	15 25	49 51	28 17	37 16	336 25	334 13	161 29	68 13
	15	25 14	56 47	44 35	49 49	338 29	345 54	160 57	67 41
	25	34 59	63 40	52 43	53 15R	340 25	357 41	160 35	67 9
May	5	44 41	70 28	51 43	48 56	342 11	9 33	160 22	66 37
	15	54 21	77 12	46 6	44 23	343 46	21 28	160 20D	65 59
	25	63 57	83 54	44 23D	46 15	345 9	33 25	160 28	65 34
June	4	73 32	90 32	49 49	54 55	346 17	45 25	160 46	65 2
	14	83 6	97 7	61 23	69 8	347 9	57 28	161 14	64 30
	24	92 38	103 40	78 6	88 7	347 44	69 32	161 51	63 58
July	4	102 10	110 10	98 49	109 37	348 00	81 40	162 36	63 27
	14	111 43	116 38	120 2	129 47	347 57R	93 50	163 28	62 55
	24	121 15	123 4	138 49	147 7	347 34	106 2	164 27	62 23
Aug.	3	130 49	129 29	154 42	161 31	346 53	118 17	165 31	61 51
	13	140 25	135 53	167 31	172 31	345 56	130 35	166 39	61 19
	23	151 51	142 15	176 16	178 21	344 46	142 56	167 50	60 48
Sep.	2	159 42	148 37	178 14R	175 34	343 29	155 19	169 4	60 16
	12	169 25	154 58	170 50	166 11	342 10	167 45	170 19	59 44
	22	179 10	161 19	164 16	166 21D	340 54	180 12	171 34	59 13
Oct.	2	188 59	167 40	171 51	179 24	339 49	192 40	172 48	58 41
	12	198 52	174 00	187 51	196 29	338 57	205 10	174 00	58 9
	22	208 48	180 21	205 2	213 23	338 23	217 39	175 8	57 37
Nov.	1	218 48	186 41	221 31	229 29	338 9D	230 10	176 13	57 6
	11	228 50	193 2	237 17	244 58	338 15	242 40	177 11	56 34
	21	238 55	199 22	252 31	259 57	338 41	255 10	178 4	56 2
Dec.	1	249 3	205 43	267 10	273 56	339 27	267 48	178 48	55 30
	11	259 12	212 3	279 47	283 44	340 30	280 10	179 24	54 58
	21	269 23	212 23	284 13R	280 7	341 49	292 39	179 49	54 26
	31	279 34	224 42	273 31	269 1	343 23	305 6	180 5	53 55

Ayanamsa: 20° 53′ 17″

Longitude of the Moon

1891		Sun.	Tues.	Thurs.	Sat.	Mon.	Wed.	Fri.
Jan.	1			169 41	193 43	218 41	245 9	273 22
	11	302 59	333 1	2 17	30 8	56 34	81 53	106 28
	25	130 35	154 24	178 8	202 9			
Feb.	1	214 25	239 50	266 56	295 57	326 21	356 48	25 58
	15	53 17	78 58	103 32	127 32	151 19	175 6	199 3
March	1	223 29	248 50	275 38	304 16	334 26	4 59	34 31
	15	62 10	88 0	112 32	136 25	160 8	184 1	208 16
	29	233 2	258 37					
April	1						271 50	299 18
	5	328 14	358 10	28 1	56 39	83 32	108 49	133 1
	19	156 47	180 38	204 56	229 53	225 37	282 14	
May	1							309 48
	3	338 20	7 27	36 30	64 90	91 27	116 48	141 6
	17	164 55	188 60	213 22	238 49	265 17	292 41	320 45
	31	349 11						
June	1					3 26	31 47	59 35
	7	86 28	112 15	136 58	160 58	184 46	208 58	234 9
	21	260 39	288 26	317 6	345 57	14 24		
July	1						42 8	69 6
	5	95 15	120 34	145 4	169 0	192 44	216 54	242 6
	19	268 53	297 19	326 51	356 26	25 10	52 40	79 3
Aug.	1				91 53	117 1	141 31	165 50
	9	189 11	213 00	237 30	263 22	291 6	320 36	350 57
	23	20 49	49 15	76 4	101 37	126 18		
Sep.	1	---	138 25	162 22	186 5	209 47	233 52	258 53
	13	285 27	313 57	344 5	14 41	44 21	72 17	98 23
	27	123 22	147 30					
Oct.	1			171 17	194 59	218 51	243 8	268 16
	11	294 42	322 48	352 28	22 48	52 35	80 48	107 14
	25	132 13	156 17	179 59	203 46			
Nov.	1	215 46	240 12	265 26	291 22	318 34	346 58	16 20
	15	45 54	74 46	102 11	128 2	152 55	176 25	200 8
	29	224 16						
Dec.	1		249 10	275 1	301 46	329 18	357 28	26 2
	13	54 39	82 48	109 57	135 48	160 26	184 17	208 00
	27	232 14	257 31	284 6				

Áyanamsa : 20° 53' 17"

Longitudes of Planets

1892		Sun	Mars	Merc.	Merc.	Jupit.	Venus	Saturn	Rahu
Jan.	5	284 40	227 52	269 1R	268 32D	344 15	311 20	180 8	53 39
	15	294 51	234 09	271 10D	275 43	346 8	323 44	180 7R	53 7
	25	305 2	240 26	281 29	287 53	348 8	336 3	179 56	52 35
Feb.	4	315 11	296 40	294 51	302 12	350 15	348 21	179 34	52 3
	14	325 18	252 51	309 56	318 1	352 30	0 30	179 13	51 32
	24	335 23	259 00	326 31	335 24	354 52	12 34	178 23	51 00
March	6	346 25	265 41	346 38	356 24	357 28	25 40	177 36	50 25
	16	356 23	271 40	6 17	15 44	359 53	37 21	176 49	49 53
	26	6 18	277 34	23 58	30 8	2 19	48 49	176 2	49 22
April	5	16 10	283 18	33 42	34 26R	4 43	60 00	175 17	48 50
	15	25 58	288 53	32 41	29 27	7 5	70 48	174 36	48 18
	25	35 43	294 14	26 14	24 18	9 27	81 7	174 3	47 46
May	5	45 25	299 18	24 17D	26 10	11 42	90 48	173 40	47 15
	15	55 4	304 00	29 44	34 42	13 50	99 35	173 24	46 43
	25	64 41	308 14	40 54	48 13	15 53	107 7	173 19	46 11
June	4	74 16	311 51	56 35	65 57	17 47	112 49D	173 25	45 39
	14	83 49	314 40	76 16	87 7	19 31	115 52	173 40	45 8
	24	93 22	316 32	98 1	108 27	21 03	115 23R	174 5	44 35
July	4	102 54	317 14	118 10	127 4	22 23	111 7	174 39	44 4
	14	112 26	316 42R	135 7	142 20	23 27	105 2	175 21	43 32
	24	121 59	314 58	148 40	153 59	24 15	100 35	176 11	43 00
Aug.	3	131 33	312 27	158 3	160 35	24 43	99 49D	177 6	42 28
	13	141 8	309 54	161 9R	159 27	24 56R	102 37	178 10	41 57
	23	150 46	307 55	155 42	151 14	24 47	108 10	179 16	41 25
Sep.	2	160 26	307 5D	148 15	148 28D	24 18	115 34	180 26	40 53
	12	170 9	307 36	152 17	158 58	23 32	124 17	181 38	40 21
	22	179 55	309 22	167 19	176 18	22 29	133 55	182 52	39 49
Oct.	2	189 45	312 16	185 20	194 9	21 16	144 14	184 7	39 18
	12	199 37	316 5	202 41	210 55	19 55	155 5	185 19	38 46
	22	209 34	320 35	218 53	226 38	18 35	166 19	186 31	38 14
Nov.	1	219 33	325 41	234 10	241 30	17 20	177 52	187 50	37 42
	11	229 36	331 11	248 35	255 18	16 19	189 41	188 44	37 11
	21	239 41	337 3	261 21	266 11	15 33	201 40	189 44	36 33
Dec.	1	249 49	343 8	268 39R	267 26	15 6	213 47	190 36	36 7
	11	259 58	349 24	261 40	255 18	14 59D	226 2	191 22	35 36
	21	270 9	355 49	252 28D	253 44	15 13	238 22	191 58	35 3
	31	280 21	2 19	257 38	263 8	15 48	250 44	192 25	34 32

Ayanamsa : 20° 54' 8"

Longitude of the Moon

1892		Sun.	Tue.	Thur.	Sat.	Mon.	Wed.	Fri.
Jan.	1							297 50
	3	325 54	354 18	22 36	50 34	78 5	105 0	131 2
	17	156 4	180 13	203 53	227 44	252 28	278 41	306 32
	31	335 32						
Feb.	1					350 12	19 14	47 28
	7	74 46	101 16	127 2	152 4	176 22	200 7	233 41
	21	247 52	273 13	300 20	329 16	359 15		
March	1		14 15	43 36	71 37	98 18	123 55	148 45
	13	172 59	196 47	220 23	244 12	268 48	294 49	322 42
	27	352 19	22 45	52 41				
April	1							67 9
	3	94 48	120 55	145 50	169 59	192 44	217 22	241 10
	17	265 29	290 46	317 30	345 55	15 45	46 3	75 38
May	1	103 40	129 58	154 52	178 52	202 30	226 12	250 17
	15	275 1	300 38	327 24	355 26	24 38	54 24	83 47
	29	111 55	138 24					
June	1						151 3	175 26
	5	199 10	222 50	246 56	271 49	297 36	324 17	351 48
	19	20 4	48 55	77 53	106 17	133 27	159 7	
July	1							183 32
	3	207 16	231 00	255 21	280 44	307 16	334 42	2 41
	17	30 54	59 12	87 21	114 59	141 40	167 7	191 28
	31	215 10						
Aug.	1					227 00	251 2	276 6
	7	302 36	330 25	359 00	27 41	56 00	83 47	110 58
	21	137 25	162 57	187 31	211 21	234 57	258 57	
Sep.	1			271 20	297 13	324 48	353 46	23 18
	11	52 27	80 41	107 51	134 3	159 23	183 56	207 51
	25	231 25	255 6	279 31				
Oct.	1				305 17	332 50	2 5	32 13
	9	62 5	90 48	118 1	143 52	168 41	192 48	216 30
	23	240 4	263 50	288 16	313 52	341 6		
Nov.	1		355 23	25 6	55 32	85 28	113 55	140 35
	13	165 43	189 51	213 30	237 5	260 54	285 14	310 21
	27	336 34	4 12					
Dec.	1			33 20	63 27	93 29	122 17	149 14
	11	174 27	198 31	222 5	245 45	269 53	294 43	310 18
	25	346 43	14 7	42 34	71 55			

Ayanamsa: 20° 54' 8"

Longitudes of Planets

1893		Sun	Mars	Merc.	Merc.	Jupit.	Venus	Saturn	Rahu
Jan.	5	285 27	5 36	263 8	269 29	16 12	256 57	192 35	34 16
	15	295 38	12 12	276 22	283 37	17 14	269 23	192 46	33 45
	25	305 43	18 49	291 8	298 56	18 33	281 51	192 47R	33 13
Feb.	4	315 57	25 28	307 2	315 27	20 5	294 17	192 37	32 41
	14	326 4	32 6	324 14	333 20	21 50	306 47	192 17	32 09
	24	336 9	38 44	342 46	352 14	23 45	319 15	191 48	31 37
March.	6	346 10	45 21	1 15	8 54	25 48	331 40	191 11	31 6
	16	356 9	51 57	14 15	16 28	27 58	344 7	190 29	30 34
	26	6 4	58 31	15 26R	12 4R	30 13	356 32	189 42	30 2
April	5	15 55	65 3	8 5	5 17	32 33	8 56	188 57R	29 30
	15	25 44	71 34	4 31D	5 52	34 56	21 20	188 11	28 59
	25	35 29	78 2	9 0	13 35	37 19	33 41	187 31	28 26
May	5	45 11	84 30	19 24	26 13	39 42	46 0	186 55	27 55
	15	54 50	90 55	33 56	42 32	42 5	58 21	185 29	27 26
	25	64 27	97 19	52 0	62 20	44 25	70 38	186 10	26 51
June	4	74 2	103 42	73 13	84 10	46 42	82 56	186 2	26 19
	14	83 35	110 5	94 40	104 24	48 55	95 11	186 3D	25 48
	24	93 8	116 26	113 16	121 7	51 1	107 26	186 14	25 16
July	4	102 40	122 45	128 0	133 51	53 0	119 40	186 36	24 44
	14	112 12	129 5	138 29	141 40	54 50	131 55	187 6	24 12
	24	121 45	135 26	143 5	142 3R	56 31	144 7	187 46	23 41
Aug.	3	131 19	141 46	139 48R	135 58	58 0	156 18	188 32	23 9
	13	140 54	148 6	132 28	131 3	59 15	168 28	189 25	22 37
	23	150 32	154 28	132 42D	137 23	60 15	180 35	190 26	22 5
Sep.	2	160 12	160 51	144 42	153 31	60 59	192 40	191 30	21 34
	12	169 55	167 14	162 57	172 22	61 23	204 41	192 39	21 2
	22	179 41	173 39	181 20	190 14	61 27R	216 38	193 49	20 30
Oct.	2	189 30	180 3	198 37	206 39	61 10	228 33	195 3	19 59
	12	199 23	186 34	214 22	221 48	60 37	240 20	196 15	19 27
	22	209 19	193 4	228 55	235 40	59 45	252 1	197 28	18 56
Nov.	1	219 19	199 36	241 58	247 23	58 37	263 36	198 41	18 23
	11	229 21	206 10	251 24	252 56R	57 18	274 58	199 50	17 51
	21	239 27	212 46	250 35R	244 33	55 58	286 2	200 54	17 20
Dec.	1	249 34	219 26	238 37	236 43D	54 39	296 47	201 54	16 48
	11	259 44	226 8	238 54D	243 38	53 28	306 56	202 47	16 16
	21	269 55	232 51	249 43	256 29	52 29	316 19	203 35	15 44
	31	280 6	239 36	263 40		51 49	324 35	204 12	15 12

Ayanamsa: 20° 54' 58"

Longitude of the Moon

1893		Sun.	Tue.	Thur.	Sat.	Mon.	Wed.	Fri.
Jan.	1	86 43	115 57	143 52	170 4	194 44	218 30	242 67
	15	266 9	291 5	316 57	343 39	10 58	38 50	67 11
	29	95 51	124 16					
Feb.	1						138 9	164 57
	5	190 17	214 29	238 7	261 56	286 36	312 28	339 31
	19	7 25	35 39	63 56	92 2	119 48		
March	1						146 56	173 5
	5	198 8	222 16	245 56	269 47	294 27	320 29	348 2
	19	16 44	45 52	74 44	102 52	130 6	156 24	181 49
April	1				194 13	218 27	242 13	265 54
	9	290 3	315 16	342 3	10 30	40 9	70 2	99 11
	23	127 0	153 25	178 41	203 8			
May	1					227 3	250 44	274 28
	7	298 29	323 57	350 21	18 39	48 27	78 51	108 34
	21	136 43	163 6	188 5	212 11	235 54	259 34	
June	1			271 28	295 14	320 18	346 2	13 10
	11	41 57	72 1	102 22	131 40	159 8	184 48	209 10
	25	232 54	256 33	280 29				
July	1				304 56	330 1	355 55	22 56
	9	51 17	80 50	110 48	139 59	167 31	193 15	217 39
	23	241 23	265 7	289 18	314 12	339 50		
Aug.	1		352 56	19 43	47 22	75 55	105 5	134 6
	13	162 8	188 37	213 37	237 39	261 22	285 25	310 15
	27	336 4	2 49	30 17				
Sep.	1							44 14
	3	72 27	100 54	129 15	157 1	183 43	209 11	233 35
	17	257 24	281 14	305 42	331 16	358 9	26 8	54 46
Oct.	1	83 27	111 47	139 28	166 20	192 18	217 20	241 35
	15	265 21	289 9	313 32	339 6	6 14	34 53	64 27
	29	93 56	122 33					
Nov.	1						136 24	163 9
	5	188 51	213 43	237 58	261 40	285 30	309 27	334 11
	19	0 19	28 14	57 52	88 16	118 9	146 31	
Dec.	1							173 9
	3	198 25	222 49	246 46	270 30	294 15	318 15	342 54
	17	8 45	36 19	65 45	97 23	126 46	155 37	182 29
	31	207 42						

Ayanamsa : 20° 54′ 58″

Longitudes of Planets

1894		Sun.	Mars.	Merc.	Merc.	Jupit.	Venus	Saturn	Rahu
Jan.	5	285 12	243 1	271 4	278 41	51 37R	328 5	204 29	14 56
	15	295 23	249 52	286 30	294 30	51 25	333 25	204 53	14 24
	25	305 34	256 44	302 49	311 21	51 36D	335 43	205 7	13 53
Feb.	4	315 43	263 38	320 12	329 12	52 6	334 9R	205 11	13 21
	14	325 50	270 34	338 16	346 44	52 55	328 52	205 3R	12 49
	24	335 54	277 34	353 49	358 13	54 0	323 0	204 46	12 18
March	6	345 56	284 30	359 0R	356 17R	55 22	320 0R	204 19	11 46
	16	355 54	291 35	351 44	347 44	56 56	320 57D	203 45	11 14
	26	5 49	298 39	345 49	346 10D	58 42	325 13	203 4	10 42
April	5	15 41	305 42	348 51D	352 59	60 36	331 48	202 20	10 11
	15	25 30	312 47	358 20	4 42	62 38	339 55	201 34	9 39
	25	35 14	319 50	11 53	19 51	64 46	349 5	200 47	9 7
May	5	44 57	326 53	28 39	38 10	66 58	358 59	200 5	8 35
	15	54 36	333 50	48 25	59 15	69 16	9 25	199 28	8 4
	25	64 13	340 47	70 10	80 40	71 34	20 11	199 0	7 31
June	4	73 48	347 37	90 23	99 3	73 52	31 16	193 37	7 0
	14	83 22	354 16	106 36	113 0	76 12	42 32	198 26	6 28
	24	92 54	0 45	118 9	121 50	78 30	53 58	198 25D	5 57
July	4	102 26	7 0	123 52	124 1R	80 45	65 33	198 32	5 24
	14	111 59	12 57	122 15R	119 9	82 57	77 17	198 53	4 53
	24	121 31	18 28	115 47	113 46	85 3	89 3	199 19	4 21
Aug.	3	131 5	23 29	114 1	117 0D	87 4	101 0	199 53	3 49
	13	140 41	27 50	122 35D	130 24	88 57	112 59	200 38	3 17
	23	150 18	31 20	139 36	149 21	90 42	125 7	201 30	2 46
Sep.	2	159 58	33 48	159 15	168 40	92 15	137 20	202 27	2 14
	12	169 41	34 58	177 39	186 10	93 36	149 36	203 30	1 42
	22	179 27	34 45R	194 16	201 57	94 42	161 56	204 37	1 10
Oct.	2	189 17	33 7	207 15	216 12	95 33	174 20	205 47	0 39
	12	199 9	30 18	222 37	228 25	96 6	186 48	206 58	0 7
	22	209 5	27 1	233 12	236 22	96 21	199 18	208 11	359 35
Nov.	1	219 5	24 2	236 54R	233 43R	96 14R	213 50	209 23	359 3
	11	229 7	22 1	227 27	222 9	95 48	224 24	210 34	358 32
	21	239 12	21 21	221 12D	224 18D	95 3	236 58	211 42	358 0
Dec.	1	249 20	21 58D	229 47	236 25	94 3	249 32	212 48	357 28
	11	259 29	23 47	243 36	251 4	92 49	262 7	213 48	356 56
	21	269 40	26 33	258 40	266 21	91 30	274 41	214 43	356 26
	31	279 51	30 5	274 12	—	90 9	287 16	215 32	355 52

Ayanamsa: 20° 55' 48"

Longitude of the Moon

1894		Sun.	Tue.	Thur.	Sat.	Mon.	Wed	Fri.
Jan.	1					219 53	243 48	267 29
	7	291 17	315 20	339 15	5 6	31 33	59 36	89 13
	21	119 37	149 26	177 35	203 49	228 33	252 27	
Feb.	1			264 17	288 2	312 10	336 51	2 11
	11	28 20	55 31	83 54	113 15	114 48	171 32	198 44
	25	224 19	248 42					
March	1			272 36	296 19	320 39	345 48	11 49
	11	38 41	66 19	94 34	123 13	151 47	179 43	206 32
	25	232 4	256 32	280 24	304 15			
April	1	316 22	341 17	7 23	34 39	62 49	91 22	119 50
	15	147 53	175 17	201 52	227 33	252 20	276 24	300 11
	29	324 14						
May	1		349 11	15 33	43 27	72 31	101 54	130 44
	13	158 32	185 17	211 7	236 13	260 40	284 38	308 22
	27	332 33	357 14	23 53				
June	1							37 27
	3	66 29	96 34	126 27	155 8	182 17	208 8	233 4
	17	257 25	281 22	305 7	328 55	353 14	18 40	45 48
July	1	74 51	105 14	135 35	164 42	192 0	217 45	242 25
	15	266 29	290 16	314 2	337 58	2 25	27 51	54 49
	29	83 33	113 41					
Aug.	1						128 56	158 56
	5	187 25	214 5	239 14	263 27	287 14	311 1	335 2
	19	359 31	24 44	51 1	78 39	107 39	137 30	167 9
Sep	1				181 34	209 14	235 14	259 56
	9	283 52	307 37	331 39	356 16	21 41	47 59	75 12
	23	103 20	132 10	161 2	189 45			
Oct.	1					217 11	243 13	267 59
	7	291 56	315 41	339 51	4 51	30 58	58 7	86 1
	21	114 17	142 38	170 47	198 27	225 19	251 6	
Nov.	1			263 35	287 52	311 37	335 28	0 5
	11	26 0	53 24	81 56	110 52	139 29	167 24	194 35
	25	221 3	246 47	271 42				
Dec.	1				295 51	319 32	343 17	7 48
	9	33 46	61 34	90 52	120 43	149 59	178 1	204 50
	23	230 41	255 47	280 15	304 12	327 49		

Ayanamsa : 20° 55′ 48″

Longitudes of Planets

1895	Sun	Mars	Merc.	Merc.	Jupit.	Venus	Saturn	Rahu
Jan. 5	284 57	32 3	282 10	290 16	89 29R	293 32	215 53	355 37
15	295 8	36 25	298 36	307 7	88 17	306 8	216 28	355 5
25	305 19	41 10	315 46	324 57	87 21	318 39	216 54	354 33
Feb. 4	315 28	46 13	332 16	338 41	86 40	331 10	217 10	354 1
14	325 35	51 31	342 7	341 29R	86 20	343 38	217 15	353 30
24	335 39	57 1	337 17R	332 7	86 19D	356 5	217 12R	352 56
March 6	345 41	62 38	328 38	327 51D	86 37	8 29	216 56	352 26
16	355 40	68 21	329 30D	333 2	87 13	20 47	216 32	351 54
26	5 35	74 10	337 55	343 50	88 7	33 2	215 59	351 23
April 5	16 27	80 3	350 34	358 1	89 17	45 13	215 21	350 51
15	25 15	86 0	6 10	14 58	90 41	57 18	214 36	350 19
25	35 0	91 59	24 28	34 36	92 17	69 13	213 52	349 47
May 5	44 43	98 1	45 17	56 8	94 2	81 3	213 6	349 16
15	54 22	104 3	66 33	76 7	95 56	92 45	212 24	348 43
25	63 59	110 7	84 30	91 34	97 56	104 18	211 46	348 12
June 4	73 34	116 13	97 17	101 25	100 1	115 33	211 15	347 40
14	83 8	122 21	103 54	104 30R	102 10	126 36	210 52	347 8
24	92 41	128 31	103 19	100 44	104 22	161 4	270 53	346 36
July 4	102 13	134 41	97 46	95 39	106 38	147 33	210 34D	346 5
14	111 45	140 53	95 20D	97 16	108 52	157 15	210 39	345 33
24	121 18	147 7	101 28	107 51	111 5	166 4	270 53	345 1
Aug. 3	130 51	153 23	116 6	125 41	113 18	173 48	211 17	344 29
13	140 27	159 41	135 53	145 58	115 27	179 48	211 50	343 53
23	150 4	166 3	155 42	164 54	117 34	183 23	212 32	343 26
Sep. 2	159 44	172 25	173 32	181 43	119 31	183 37R	213 20	342 54
12	169 27	178 53	189 25	196 36	121 26	180 1	214 16	342 22
22	179 13	185 23	203 16	209 24	123 12	174 6	215 16	341 51
Oct. 2	189 2	191 57	214 37	218 41R	124 48	169 15	216 22	341 19
12	198 55	198 32	220 57R	220 26	126 10	168 2D	217 30	340 47
22	208 51	205 12	216 27	210 18	127 19	170 34	218 40	340 15
Nov. 1	218 50	211 57	205 53	205 57D	128 13	176 3	219 52	339 44
11	228 52	218 44	209 52D	216 1	128 50	183 33	221 4	339 12
21	238 58	225 35	223 11	230 48	129 7	192 28	222 16	338 40
Dec. 1	249 5	232 32	238 34	246 21	129 6R	202 20	223 26	338 3
11	259 14	239 33	254 8	261 37	128 45	212 54	224 29	337 37
21	269 25	246 35	269 52	277 52	128 4	223 57	225 31	337 5
31	279 37	253 43	285 58	–	127 8	235 22	226 27	336 33

Ayanamsa : 20° 56′ 39″

Longitude of the Moon

1895		Sun.	Tue.	Thur.	Sat.	Mon.	Wed.	Fri.
Jan.	1		339 37	3 35	28 35	55 18	83 59	114 8
		144 31	173 51	201 34	227 45	252 40	277 10	301 4
		324 43	348 22	12 25				
Feb.	1							24 44
	3	50 22	77 44	106 56	137 20	167 40	196 44	224 2
	17	249 42	274 12	298 4	321 42	345 25	9 3	
March	1							34 14
	3	59 58	87 5	115 42	145 30	175 33	204 46	232 23
	17	258 17	282 51	306 39	330 16	354 10	18 40	43 59
	31	70 12						
April	1					83 41	111 23	140 2
	7	169 16	198 25	226 41	253 30	278 49	302 59	326 38
	21	350 26	14 56	40 25	66 56	94 18		
May	1						122 14	150 32
	5	178 59	207 17	234 56	261 28	286 42	310 53	334 34
	19	358 25	23 8	49 7	76 26	104 38	133 9	161 30
June	1				175 32	203 18	230 30	256 57
	9	282 25	306 53	330 40	354 20	18 34	44 3	71 9
	23	99 42	128 57	158 2	186 22			
July	1					213 47	240 20	266 5
	7	291 0	315 11	338 52	2 30	26 43	52 11	79 23
	21	108 16	138 10	167 55	196 41	224 7	250 19	
Aug.	1			263 1	287 58	311 56	335 38	359 13
	11	23 6	47 51	74 0	101 57	131 30	161 49	191 42
	25	220 14	247 7	272 33	296 59			
Sep.	1	308 57	332 38	356 14	20 6	44 31	69 56	96 44
	15	125 8	154 54	185 10	214 46	242 48	269 3	293 51
	29	317 46						
Oct.	1		341 21	5 5	29 16	54 7	79 50	106 34
	13	134 31	163 38	193 23	222 51	251 0	277 25	302 17
	27	326 9	349 44	13 38				
Nov.	1							25 50
	3	50 53	76 47	103 29	130 53	159 0	187 45	216 44
	17	245 9	272 19	297 55	322 15	345 54	9 33	34 5
Dec.	1	59 58	86 19	113 49	141 44	169 51	198 2	226 7
	15	253 42	280 20	305 43	330 0	353 40	17 24	41 55
	29	67 44	95 01					

Ayanamsa: 20° 56′ 39″

Longitudes of Planets

1896		Sun	Mars	Merc.	Merc.	Jupit.	Venus	Saturn	Rahu
Jan.	5	284 42	257 18	294 8	302 24	126 34R	241 10	226 53	336 17
	15	294 54	264 31	310 28	317 48	125 20	252 54	227 37	335 45
	25	305 4	271 49	323 30	325 54	124 0	264 48	228 12	335 13
Feb.	4	315 13	279 10	323 58R	318 40R	122 43	276 51	228 40	334 41
	14	325 21	286 35	313 24	310 45	121 30	288 56	228 59	334 10
	24	335 25	294 1	311 80	313 48D	120 27	301 4	229 7	333 38
March	5	345 27	301 30	318 8	323 36	119 41	313 17	229 4R	333 6
	15	355 26	309 6	329 55	336 56	119 14	325 31	228 51	332 35
	25	5 21	316 39	344 33	352 45	119 5	337 45	228 29	332 2
April	4	15 15	324 14	1 32	10 54	119 16D	349 59	227 59	331 31
	14	25 2	331 50	20 53	31 24	119 44	2 15	227 22	330 59
	24	34 47	339 28	42 2	52 19	120 30	14 30	226 40	330 27
May	4	44 29	347 2	61 41	69 39	121 33	26 46	225 55	329 55
	14	54 8	354 35	76 1	80 42	122 50	39 1	225 11	329 24
	24	63 46	2 7	83 35	84 29	124 16	51 15	224 27	328 52
June	3	73 20	9 32	83 34R	81 15R	125 56	63 30	223 50	328 20
	13	82 54	16 53	78 31	76 27	127 40	75 46	223 17	327 48
	23	92 27	24 9	75 57D	77 23D	129 34	88 1	228 51	337 17
July	3	101 59	31 15	80 48	86 6	131 35	100 19	222 34	326 45
	13	111 31	38 13	93 13	101 51	133 38	112 36	222 27	326 13
	23	121 4	44 58	111 43	122 11	135 46	124 58	222 29D	325 41
Aug.	2	130 37	51 32	132 34	142 33	137 53	137 15	222 42	325 10
	12	140 13	57 50	151 58	160 46	140 5	149 34	223 4	324 38
	22	149 50	63 47	168 57	176 36	142 18	161 57	223 35	324 6
Sep.	1	159 30	69 25	183 40	190 3	144 26	174 17	224 13	323 34
	11	169 13	74 36	195 46	200 25	146 35	186 40	224 59	323 3
	21	178 59	79 13	203 42	204 59	143 39	199 1	225 53	322 31
Oct.	1	188 48	83 10	203 25R	198 50R	150 37	211 22	226 52	321 59
	11	198 40	86 22	193 4	189 44	152 29	223 43	227 54	321 27
	21	208 36	88 28	190 45D	195 29D	154 12	236 3	229 3	320 56
	31	218 35	89 24	202 16	—	155 48	248 20	230 13	320 24
Nov.	10	228 38	88 55R	218 0	226 2	157 12	260 36	231 23	319 52
	20	238 43	87 1	234 2	241 57	158 21	272 52	232 36	319 20
	30	248 50	83 52	249 49	—	159 16	285 4	233 46	318 49
Dec.	10	259 0	80 2	265 30	273 23	159 52	297 11	234 64	318 17
	20	269 10	76 21	281 17	289 6	160 11	309 16	236 1	317 45
	30	279 22	73 30	296 38	—	160 11R	321 10	237 4	317 13

Avanamsa : 20° 57′ 29″

Longitude of the Moon

1896		Sun.	Tue.	Thur.	Sat.	Mon.	Wed	Fri.
Jan.	1						109 6	137 46
	5	166 32	194 54	222 40	249 46	276 4	301 28	325 58
	19	349 47	13 22	37 22	62 24	89 1	117 18	146 44
Feb.	1				161 36	191 1	219 29	246 44
	9	272 50	288 0	322 24	346 16	9 53	33 37	57 59
	23	83 34	110 50	139 50	169 59			
March	1	185 9	214 54	243 12	269 50	295 5	319 23	343 10
	15	6 47	30 30	54 37	79 32	105 40	133 26	162 51
	29	193 16	223 27					
April	1						238 3	265 53
	5	291 51	316 25	340 13	3 47	27 32	51 42	76 29
	19	102 5	128 50	156 59	186 29	216 39	246 16	
May	1							274 17
	3	300 25	325 2	348 48	12 25	36 21	60 55	86 12
	17	112 15	139 9	167 3	195 57	225 24	254 30	282 20
	31	308 29						
June	1					320 59	345 9	8 50
	7	32 41	57 12	82 38	108 59	136 5	163 48	192 3
	21	220 40	249 13	277 3	303 38	328 53		
July	1						353 4	16 48
	5	40 44	65 26	91 18	118 19	146 14	174 38	203 5
	19	231 20	259 5	286 2	311 59	336 55	1 1	24 45
Aug.	1				36 39	60 55	86 16	113 3
	9	141 13	170 18	199 34	228 10	255 53	282 33	308 16
	23	333 8	357 19	21 6	44 50	69 3		
Sep.	1		81 30	107 38	135 7	164 20	194 22	224 5
	13	252 35	279 33	305 13	329 55	354 2	17 50	41 33
	27	65 29	90 3					
Oct.	1			115 49	143 14	172 28	202 55	233 12
	11	262 10	289 15	314 43	339 6	2 57	26 40	50 29
	25	74 35	99 16	124 34	151 59			
Nov.	1	166 11	195 48	226 19	256 20	284 42	311 5	335 56
	15	359 53	23 31	47 21	71 37	96 22	121 46	148 6
	29	175 43						
Dec.	1		204 42	234 35	264 17	292 40	319 15	344 14
	13	8 15	31 57	55 54	80 27	105 44	131 47	158 35
	27	186 14	214 42	243 42				

Ayanamsa : 20° 57′ 29″

Longitudes of Planets

1897		Sun.	Mars.	Merc.	Merc.	Jupit.	Venus	Saturn	Rahu
Jan.	5	285 29	72 23R	304 36	308 55	160 1R	328 14	237 36	316 54
	15	295 40	71 36	309 29R	305 28R	159 31	339 54	238 28	316 23
	25	305 50	72 7D	299 15	294 54	158 44	351 14	239 13	315 51
Feb.	4	315 0	73 42	293 57D	295 54D	157 41	2 13	239 51	315 19
	14	326 7	76 13	299 48	305 2	156 27	12 45	240 20	314 48
	24	336 11	79 28	311 7	—	155 8	22 33	240 38	314 16
March	6	346 13	83 16	325 8	332 57	153 51	31 25	240 46	313 44
	16	356 11	87 31	341 16	350 4	152 39	38 52	240 44R	313 12
	26	6 6	92 6	359 26	9 19	151 38	44 20	240 33	312 41
April	5	15 58	97 0	19 36	30 1	150 52	46 53	240 12	312 9
	15	25 46	102 5	39 54	48 37	150 24	45 39R	239 43	311 37
	25	35 31	107 21	55 40	60 48	150 12	40 44	239 7	311 5
May	5	45 13	112 45	63 47	64 36R	150 20D	34 40	238 26	310 33
	15	54 52	118 19	63 28R	60 57	150 45	30 55	237 42	310 1
	25	64 29	124 2	58 12	56 17	151 28	31 2D	236 58	309 29
June	4	74 4	129 46	56 1D	57 35	152 26	34 35	236 15	308 57
	14	83 37	135 36	60 57	65 56	153 38	40 37	235 34	308 26
	24	93 10	141 30	72 27	80 23	155 1	48 18	235 1	307 54
July	4	102 42	147 31	89 35	99 50	156 35	57 8	234 35	307 32
	14	112 14	153 34	110 31	121 8	158 20	66 45	234 17	306 51
	24	121 47	159 43	131 51	140 40	160 9	76 58	234 8	306 19
Aug.	3	131 21	165 56	149 25	157 32	162 5	87 37	234 9D	305 47
	13	140 56	172 13	164 54	171 37	164 8	98 38	234 21	305 15
	23	150 34	178 36	177 33	182 33	166 13	109 55	234 40	304 43
Sep.	2	160 14	185 2	186 15	188 16	168 22	121 24	235 10	304 12
	12	169 57	191 34	187 55R	184 50R	170 31	133 8	235 47	303 40
	22	179 43	198 10	179 42	175 3	172 41	145 0	236 35	303 8
Oct.	2	189 33	204 50	173 42D	176 32D	174 49	157 4	237 27	302 36
	12	199 26	211 36	182 32	190 10	176 55	170 26	238 23	302 5
	22	209 22	218 27	198 26	206 53	178 58	181 30	239 77	301 33
Nov.	1	219 21	225 22	215 12	223 22	180 57	193 53	240 34	301 1
	11	229 24	232 25	231 21	239 15	182 48	206 19	241 42	300 29
	21	239 29	239 31	247 2	254 46	184 31	218 49	242 52	299 58
Dec.	1	249 37	246 42	262 23	269 57	186 3	231 20	244 4	299 26
	11	259 46	253 57	277 20	284 10	187 24	243 53	245 15	298 54
	21	269 57	261 19	289 56	293 26	188 31	256 26	256 26	298 22
	31	280 9	268 44	292 58R	....	189 24	269 0	269 0	297 50

Ayanamsa: 20° 38′ 19″

Longitude of the Moon

1897		Sun.	Tue.	Thur.	Sat.	Mon.	Wed.	Fri.
Jan.	1							258 12
	3	286 46	313 54	339 39	4 11	28 2	51 51	76 12
	17	101 29	127 49	155 7	183 4	211 23	239 44	267 51
	31	295 21						
Feb.	1					308 46	334 49	359 47
	7	23 56	47 42	71 41	96 30	122 36	150 8	178 46
	21	207 49	236 35	264 33	291 33			
March	1					317 51	343 14	7 54
	7	31 57	55 41	79 36	104 18	130 23	158 13	187 35
	21	217 33	246 59	275 7	301 51	327 26	352 15	
April	1			4 26	28 30	52 16	76 1	100 10
	11	125 20	152 8	180 50	211 3	241 32	270 55	298 33
	25	324 32	349 22	13 31				
May	1				37 22	61 6	84 55	109 10
	9	134 17	160 52	189 18	219 22	249 58	279 42	307 38
	23	333 45	358 32	22 32	46 16	70 3		
June	1		82 1	106 16	131 10	157 3	184 22	213 15
	13	243 15	273 17	302 12	329 22	354 54	19 16	43 4
	27	66 50	90 56					
July	1			115 36	141 1	167 20	198 44	223 14
	11	252 30	281 48	310 19	337 25	3 1	27 28	51 9
	25	75 9	99 28	124 36	150 43			
Aug.	1	164 19	191 36	219 44	248 16	276 49	304 58	332 14
	15	358 21	23 18	47 23	71 9	95 13	120 9	146 20
	29	173 47	202 7					
Sep.	1						216 27	245 2
	7	273 14	300 50	327 45	353 51	19 3	43 24	67 12
	21	90 59	115 24	141 5	168 24	197 12	226 40	
Oct.	1							255 49
	3	284 1	311 8	337 19	2 46	27 31	51 40	75 23
	17	99 5	123 13	148 59	176 23	205 40	235 52	265 41
	31	295 18						
Nov.	1					308 0	334 22	359 41
	7	24 17	48 23	72 9	95 47	119 42	144 27	170 43
	21	198 54	228 49	259 25	289 16	317 29		
Dec.	1						343 58	9 6
	5	33 24	57 15	80 57	104 43	128 50	153 42	179 49
	19	207 35	237 0	267 19	297 29	325 56	352 45	18 00

Ayanamsa : 20° 58' 19"

Longitudes of Planets

1898		Sun	Mars	Merc.	Merc.	Jupit.	Venus	Saturn	Rahu
Jan.	5	285 14	272 29	288 0R	281 36R	189 43	275 17	248 0	297 35
	15	295 25	280 2	277 59	278 6D	190 10	287 51	248 58	297 6
	25	305 36	287 37	281 0R	285 38	190 17R	300 26	249 51	296 31
Feb.	4	315 45	295 17	291 21	297 48	190 5	312 59	250 38	295 59
	14	325 52	302 59	304 47	312 12	189 36	325 31	251 16	295 27
	24	335 56	310 45	320 3	–	188 48	338 2	251 45	294 56
March	6	345 58	318 32	337 4	346 10	187 48	350 32	252 5	294 24
	16	355 56	326 19	355 47	5 47	186 36	3 0	252 15	293 52
	26	5 52	334 7	15 51	25 25	185 19	15 26	252 15R	293 20
April	5	15 43	341 54	33 42	40 1	184 3	27 48	252 6	292 49
	15	25 32	349 41	43 56	45 18	182 52	40 9	251 46	292 17
	25	35 17	357 26	44 18R	41 38R	181 51	52 27	251 19	291 45
May	5	44 59	5 8	38 31	36 16	181 4	64 42	250 44	291 14
	15	54 38	12 47	35 41D	36 59	180 34	76 54	250 5	290 42
	25	64 15	20 22	40 3	44 38	180 21	89 4	249 21	290 9
June	4	73 50	27 51	50 24	57 44	180 27D	101 10	248 37	289 38
	14	83 24	35 16	66 4	75 30	180 49	113 12	247 54	289 6
	24	92 56	42 34	85 52	96 42	181 29	125 10	247 14	288 35
July	4	102 28	49 45	107 29	117 46	182 24	137 2	246 39	288 3
	14	112 0	56 49	127 20	136 7	183 33	148 50	246 11	287 31
	24	121 33	63 44	144 8	151 23	184 54	160 30	245 51	287 0
Aug.	3	131 7	70 31	157 48	163 16	186 20	172 1	245 41	286 27
	13	140 42	77 7	167 36	170 27	188 8	183 23	245 40D	285 55
	23	150 20	83 33	171 24	169 58R	189 58	194 31	245 49	285 24
Sep.	2	160 0	89 46	166 13R	161 24	191 54	205 23	246 7	284 52
	12	169 43	95 45	157 58	157 56D	193 53	215 54	246 34	284 21
	22	179 29	101 28	161 42D	168 19	196 1	225 56	247 10	283 49
Oct.	2	189 18	106 53	176 30	185 16	198 10	235 18	247 53	283 17
	12	199 11	111 55	194 4	202 41	200 19	243 41	248 45	282 46
	22	209 7	116 32	211 2	219 10	202 30	250 39	249 41	282 13
Nov.	1	219 7	120 35	227 5	234 49	204 39	255 29	250 43	281 41
	11	229 9	124 1	242 24	249 50	206 46	257 13	251 49	281 10
	21	239 13	126 37	257 4	263 58	208 49	255 5R	252 57	280 38
Dec.	1	249 22	128 14	270 15	275 16	210 48	249 43	254 8	280 6
	11	259 31	128 40R	277 51	276 24R	212 39	244 16	255 18	279 35
	21	269 42	127 45	270 42R	264 29	214 28	241 57	256 29	279 3
	31	279 54	125 29	261 41	....	215 55	243 36D	257 38	278 30

Ayanamsa :   20° 59′ 10″

Longitude of the Moon

1898		Sun.	Tue.	Thur.	Sat.	Mon.	Wed	Fri.
Jan.	1				30 12	54 6	77 46	101 35
	9	125 50	150 45	176 32	203 26	231 34	260 47	290 27
	23	319 37	347 28	13 41	38 29	62 24		
Feb.	1		74 13	97 58	122 15	147 21	173 25	200 21
	13	228 1	256 18	284 58	313 37	341 40	8 33	34 4
	27	58 24						
March	1		82 8	105 54	130 22	156 00	182 51	210 40
	13	238 56	267 14	295 20	323 6	350 19	16 40	41 57
	27	66 14	89 57	113 42				
April	1							125 50
	3	150 59	177 40	205 50	234 51	263 51	292 14	319 49
	17	346 37	12 41	37 56	62 23	86 12	109 48	133 48
May	1	158 56	185 45	214 19	244 2	273 48	302 41	330 17
	15	356 43	22 11	46 54	70 59	94 39	118 14	142 15
	29	167 19	194 1					
June	1						208 4	237 26
	5	267 44	297 43	326 26	353 34	19 17	43 58	67 59
	19	91 38	115 14	139 6	163 40	189 26	216 49	
July	1							245 52
	3	276 4	306 16	333 23	2 48	28 33	53 4	76 53
	17	100 28	124 11	148 22	173 16	199 10	226 22	254 56
	31	284 35						
Aug.	1					299 35	329 17	357 44
	7	24 28	49 36	73 39	97 15	120 58	145 14	170 16
	21	196 11	222 58	250 41	279 16	308 27	337 36	
Sep.	1			351 53	19 24	45 20	69 53	93 38
	11	117 17	141 28	166 36	192 47	219 51	247 31	275 35
	25	303 56	332 22	0 25				
Oct.	1				27 29	53 15	77 45	101 30
	9	125 11	149 30	174 59	201 50	229 46	258 11	286 35
	23	314 42	342 25	9 36	35 58	61 18		
Nov.	1		73 35	97 33	121 8	145 1	169 54	196 17
	13	224 17	253 22	282 40	311 26	339 19	6 14	32 16
	27	57 28	81 52					
Dec.	1			105 41	129 16	153 7	177 52	204 8
	11	232 11	261 43	291 49	321 21	349 35	16 23	41 55
	25	66 32	90 32	114 13	137 50			

Ayanamsa : 20° 59' 10"

Longitudes of Planets

1899		Sun	Mars	Merc.	Merc.	Jupit.	Venus	Saturn	Rahu
Jan.	5	284 59	123 53R	262 49	266 34	216 37	245 42	258 11	278 15
	15	295 11	120 7	271 52	278 3	217 52	251 49	259 15	277 43
	25	305 21	116 9	284 48	291 58	218 53	259 45	260 14	277 11
Feb.	4	315 30	112 46	299 30	307 21	219 32	268 54	261 8	276 39
	14	325 37	110 28	315 32	324 6	220 4	278 53	261 55	276 8
	24	335 42	109 28	333 3	342 23	220 12	89 26	262 34	275 36
March	6	345 43	109 44D	352 2	1 43	220 2R	300 24	263 5	275 5
	16	355 42	111 6	10 53	18 39	219 34	311 39	263 27	274 33
	26	5 37	113 24	24 6	26 40	218 48	323 6	263 39	274 1
April	5	15 29	116 24	26 16R	23 32R	217 48	334 43	263 40R	273 29
	15	25 18	120 2	19 53	16 56	216 38	346 27	263 33	272 57
	25	35 1	124 7	15 45	16 36D	215 23	358 15	263 15	272 25
May	5	44 45	128 34	19 17	23 31	214 6	10 8	262 49	271 54
	15	54 25	133 22	29 3	35 40	212 55	22 4	262/16	271 22
	25	64 2	138 23	43 18	51 55	211 54	34 3	261 37	270 50
June	4	73 37	143 38	61 30	71 54	211 6	46 4	260 55	270 18
	14	83 10	149 4	82 49	93 42	210 34	58 7	260 11	269 46
	24	92 43	154 41	104 6	113 43	210 20D	79 12	259 27	269 15
July	4	102 15	160 26	122 28	131 49	210 23	82 20	258 46	268 43
	14	111 47	166 20	137 20	144 24	210 45	94 30	258 11	268 11
	24	121 19	172 20	148 12	151 43	211 22	106 43	257 42	267 40
Aug.	3	130 53	178 29	153 33	153 19R	212 17	118 59	257 20	267 8
	13	140 29	184 44	150 55R	146 54	213 25	137 17	257 8	266 36
	23	150 6	191 6	142 54	140 56	214 46	143 38	257 5D	266 5
Sep.	2	159 46	197 35	142 14D	146 53	216 18	156 2	257 11	265 32
	12	169 29	204 11	154 6	162 47	218 0	168 27	257 28	265 1
	22	179 15	210 52	172 0	181 11	219 51	180 54	257 53	264 29
Oct.	2	189 4	217 41	190 5	198 40	221 49	193 22	258 27	263 57
	12	198 57	224 36	206 55	214 52	223 52	205 52	259 10	263 26
	22	208 53	231 38	222 34	230 2	225 59	218 21	259 59	262 54
Nov.	1	218 52	238 45	237 14	244 8	228 10	230 51	260 55	262 21
	11	228 54	245 59	250 35	256 14	230 22	243 21	261 56	261 50
	21	238 59	253 19	260 23	262 6	232 35	255 51	263 0	261 18
Dec.	1	249 7	260 44	259 42R	253 32R	234 47	268 21	264 9	260 46
	11	259 17	268 15	247 40	245 50	236 56	280 51	265 19	260 15
	21	269 26	275 50	247 57D	252 29	239 2	293 19	266 30	259 43
	31	279 39	283 29	258 22	—	241 3	305 46	267 40	259 11

Ayanamsa: 21° 0′ 0″

Longitude of the Moon

1899		Sun.	Tue.	Thur.	Sat.	Mon.	Wed.	Fri.
Jan.	1	149 44	173 59	199 17	226 6	254 41	284 42	315 8
	15	334 44	12 39	38 49	63 36	87 33	111 10	134 49
	29	158 46	183 17					
Feb.	1						195 49	221 44
	5	249 0	277 50	307 52	338 6	7 16	34 37	60 9
	19	84 23	108 1	131 38	155 39	180 18		
March	1						205 39	231 48
	5	258 56	287 13	316 32	346 13	15 13	42 38	68 18
	19	92 38	116 17	139 59	164 16	189 25	215 26	242 11
April	1				255 49	283 34	311 57	340 45
	9	9 25	37 11	63 32	88 27	112 25	136 5	160 8
	23	185 7	211 15	238 25	266 18			
May	1					294 31	322 50	351 2
	7	18 48	45 45	71 36	96 20	120 16	143 58	168 4
	21	193 9	219 37	247 26	276 10	305 9	333 48	
June	1			347 52	15 23	41 59	67 39	92 26
	11	116 31	140 13	164 1	188 30	214 14	241 34	270 25
	28	300 10	329 47	358 27				
July	1				25 47	51 51	76 53	101 11
	9	125 2	148 42	172 31	196 58	222 33	249 45	278 42
	23	308 52	339 9	8 18	35 45	61 34		
Aug.	1		73 60	98 14	122 2	145 42	169 29	193 40
	13	218 36	244 45	272 33	302 1	332 31	2 42	31 21
	27	58 4	83 9	107 14				
Sep.	1							119 5
	3	142 44	166 34	190 48	215 35	241 11	267 56	296 10
	17	325 48	356 1	25 32	53 22	79 20	103 53	127 40
Oct.	1	151 21	175 23	200 1	225 19	251 22	278 16	306 13
	15	335 10	4 38	33 38	61 18	87 19	111 57	135 48
	29	159 33	183 46					
Nov.	1						196 10	221 39
	5	248 2	275 11	302 57	331 14	359 48	28 11	55 51
	19	82 19	107 31	131 44	155 30	179 26	204 8	
Dec.	1							230 0
	3	257 7	285 11	313 45	342 17	10 26	37 57	64 40
	17	90 30	115 25	139 35	163 20	187 14	211 51	237 47
	31	265 18						

Ayanamsa : 21° 0′ 0″

Longitudes of Planets

1900		Sun	Mars	Merc.	Merc.	Jupit.	Venus	Saturn	Rahu
Jan.	5	284 45	287 20	264 59	272 1	242 0	311 58	268 14	258 55
	15	294 56	295 6	279 22	286 58	243 50	324 21	269 22	258 23
	25	305 6	302 54	294 49	302 56	245 31	336 42	270 27	257 51
Feb.	4	315 16	310 45	311 20	320 3	247 1	348 57	271 26	257 20
	14	325 23	318 37	329 5	338 21	248 19	1 7	272 21	256 54
	24	335 27	326 30	347 37	356 19	249 22	13 8	273 7	256 16
March	6	345 29	334 23	3 29	8 0	250 10	25 0	273 50	255 44
	16	355 28	342 16	9 6R	6 56R	250 49	36 41	274 7	255 13
	26	5 23	350 7	2 51	358 56	250 52	48 7	274 45	254 41
April	5	15 15	357 56	356 46	356 51D	250 45R	59 16	274 59	254 9
	15	25 4	5 41	358 59	2 47	250 20	70 1	275 2R	253 37
	25	34 49	13 23	7 54	14 5	249 38	80 16	274 56	253 5
May	5	44 31	21 2	21 11	29 9	248 41	89 51	274 41	252 34
	15	54 11	28 35	37 56	47 34	247 32	98 31	274 17	252 2
	25	63 48	36 4	57 57	68 51	246 18	105 50	273 45	251 30
June	4	73 22	43 27	79 47	90 13	245 2	111 15	273 7	250 59
	14	82 56	50 45	99 50	108 28	243 49	113 53R	272 25	250 27
	24	92 29	57 56	116 15	122 38	242 46	112 52	271 41	249 55
July	4	102 1	65 3	128 3	132 7	241 55	108 14	270 58	249 24
	14	111 33	72 1	134 36	135 13R	241 20	102 9	270 16	248 50
	24	121 5	78 53	133 49R	130 44	241 3	98 7	289 39	248 20
Aug.	3	130 39	85 38	127 2	124 21	241 4D	97 52D	269 9	247 48
	13	140 15	92 16	124 1D	126 38	241 22	101 5	268 45	247 16
	23	149 52	98 47	132 6	139 52	241 59	106 53	268 31	246 44
Sep.	2	159 32	105 9	149 0	158 37	242 52	114 30	268 26D	246 10
	12	169 15	111 23	168 10	177 22	244 0	123 20	268 31	245 40
	22	179 0	117 28	186 10	194 33	245 21	133 4	268 45	245 9
Oct.	2	188 50	123 22	202 34	210 14	246 54	143 27	269 9	244 37
	12	198 42	129 4	217 34	224 33	248 38	154 20	269 42	244 5
	22	208 38	134 33	231 6	237 4	250 31	165 37	270 23	243 34
Nov.	1	218 37	139 46	242 5	245 28R	252 31	177 12	271 11	243 2
	11	228 39	144 40	246 7R	242 50R	254 37	189 1	272 6	242 30
	21	238 45	149 12	236 26	231 12R	256 48	201 1	273 6	241 68
Dec.	1	248 52	153 17	230 20D	233 21	259 2	213 10	274 10	241 26
	11	259 1	156 47	238 37	245 3	262 26	225 25	275 18	240 55
	21	269 12	159 37	252 4	259 24	263 35	237 45	276 28	240 23
	31	279 23	161 34	266 55	—	265 51	250 0	277 39	239 51

Ayanamsa: 21° 0' 50"

Longitude of the Moon

1900		Sun	Tue.	Thur.	Sat.	Mon.	Wed.	Fri.
Jan.	1					279 37	308 59	338 28
	7	7 14	34 50	61 18	86 48	111 37	135 50	159 41
	21	183 25	207 30	232 32	259 6	287 32	317 28	
Feb.	1			332 40	2 42	31 20	58 18	83 2
	11	108 30	132 36	156 27	180 12	204 6	228 32	254 4
	25	281 15	310 22					
March	1			340 50	11 19	40 28	67 42	93 15
	11	117 40	141 34	165 18	189 8	213 15	237 53	263 37
	25	290 24	319 3	349 5	19 26			
April	1	34 18	62 45	89 19	114 20	138 25	162 9	185 59
	15	210 12	234 57	260 26	286 52	314 31	343 23	13 1
	29	42 27						
May	1		70 44	97 24	122 34	146 44	170 30	194 26
	13	218 56	244 13	270 23	297 25	325 17	353 48	22 37
	27	51 10	78 52	105 19				
June	1							118 3
	3	142 41	166 38	190 27	214 44	239 57	266 20	293 48
	17	322 2	350 32	18 56	46 54	74 13	100 39	126 7
July	1	150 39	174 34	198 22	222 39	248 3	274 54	303 12
	15	332 19	1 26	29 51	57 18	83 15	109 36	134 35
	29	158 54	182 43					
Aug.	1						194 34	218 27
	5	243 9	269 19	297 17	326 46	356 48	26 11	54 13
	19	80 52	106 27	131 17	155 33	179 24	203 4	226 54
Sep.	1				239 4	264 18	291 15	320 9
	9	350 27	20 52	50 5	77 36	103 32	128 23	152 34
	23	176 23	200 5	223 51	248 4			
Oct.	1					273 15	299 58	328 33
	7	358 40	29 12	58 48	86 38	112 44	137 37	161 31
	21	185 14	208 58	233 0	257 33	282 57	309 35	
Nov.	1			323 27	352 19	22 13	52 9	81 1
	11	108 12	133 46	158 8	181 54	205 37	229 43	254 27
	25	279 59	306 26	333 50				
Dec.	1				2 11	31 13	60 20	88 49
	9	116 0	141 42	166 11	189 58	210 43	238 0	263 14
	23	289 33	316 50	344 44	12 57	41 15		

Ayanamsa: 21° 0′ 50″

Longitudes of Planets

1901	Sun	Mars	Merc.	Merc.	Jupit.	Venus	Saturn	Rahu
Jan. 5	284 30	162 11	274 36	282 27	266 58	256 21	278 14	239 36
15	294 41	162 31	290 29	298 43	269 10	268 47	279 24	239 4
25	304 52	161 34	307 12	315 55	271 18	281 15	280 33	238 32
Feb. 4	315 1	159 19	324 48	333 36	273 20	293 43	281 37	238 0
14	325 8	155 59	341 46	348 15	275 15	306 11	282 38	237 28
24	335 13	152 4	351 46	351 23R	277 1	318 39	283 34	336 56
March 6	345 15	148 18	357 39R	342 45	278 37	331 6	284 23	236 24
16	355 13	145 20	339 12	338 8D	280 0	343 3	285 4	235 53
26	5 9	143 33	339 27	342 39	281 10	355 58	285 38	235 20
April 5	15 39	143 4D	347 19	353 3	282 4	8 22	286 3	234 50
15	24 49	143 48	359 42	7 8	282 41	20 45	286 18	234 18
25	34 35	145 33	15 7	24 10	283 1	33 7	286 24	233 46
May 5	44 17	148 10	33 47	44 6	283 1R	45 7	286 19R	233 15
15	53 56	151 29	54 54	65 46	282 43	57 46	286 6	232 42
25	63 34	155 22	76 11	85 42	282 7	70 5	285 43	232 10
June 4	73 9	159 42	94 6	101 18	281 16	82 21	285 13	231 39
14	82 42	164 26	107 15	111 48	280 11	94 37	284 36	231 6
24	92 15	169 29	114 48	115 59	278 58	106 53	283 55	230 35
July 4	101 47	174 49	115 16R	112 55R	277 41	119 7	283 11	230 4
14	111 19	180 23	109 43	106 59	276 26	131 20	282 28	229 32
24	120 52	186 10	105 57	107 16D	275 19	143 33	281 45	229 0
Aug. 3	130 25	192 9	111 8	117 24	274 23	155 43	281 7	
13	140 31	198 19	125 38	135 9	273 42	167 52	280 35	227 56
23	149 38	204 39	145 9	155 3	273 19	179 58	280 10	227 25
Sep. 2	159 18	211 9	164 33	173 33	273 14D	192 2	279 54	226 50
12	169 0	219 47	182 4	190 8	273 28	204 3	279 47	226 21
22	178 46	224 34	197 46	204 59	274 1	216 0	279 50D	225 50
Oct. 2	187 36	231 30	211 44	217 55	274 52	227 52	280 3	225 15
12	198 28	238 33	223 22	227 41	275 58	239 39	280 25	224 45
22	208 27	245 44	230 9	229 46R	277 19	251 19	280 57	224 14
Nov. 1	218 22	253 2	225 43	219 22R	278 53	262 50	251 37	223 42
11	228 25	260 27	214 57	215 4D	280 38	274 9	252 24	223 11
21	238 30	267 58	218 56	224 54	282 33	285 11	253 18	222 39
Dec. 1	248 37	275 34	231 52	239 17	284 35	295 49	275 34	222 7
11	258 47	283 15	246 52	254 34	286 45	305 54	285 22	221 36
21	268 57	291 1	262 20	270 10	288 59	315 9	286 29	221 3
31	279 9	198 50	278 7	—	291 17	323 11	287 39	220 31

Ayanamsa: 21° 1' 41"

Longitude of the Moon

1901		Sun.	Tue.	Thurs.	Sat.	Mon.	Wed.	Fri.
Jan.	1		55 23	83 20	110 36	136 48	161 49	185 45
	13	209 34	233 32	258 25	284 42	312 13	340 58	9 43
	27	38 3	65 47	92 54				
Feb.	1							106 13
	3	132 17	157 60	181 52	205 37	229 17	253 34	279 11
	17	306 35	335 28	5 7	34 25	62 41	89 49	
March	1							115 29
	3	141 23	166 5	190 10	213 50	237 29	261 43	287 12
	17	314 30	343 38	13 50	43 51	72 39	99 55	125 51
	31	150 47						
April	1					162 59	186 59	210 41
	7	234 19	258 16	283 2	309 14	337 13	6 51	37 16
	21	67 12	95 41	122 28	147 47	172 6		
May	1						195 52	219 30
	7	243 16	267 30	292 31	318 43	346 23	15 30	45 32
	19	75 25	104 9	131 11	156 35	180 51	204 32	228 12
June	1				240 8	264 28	289 34	315 33
	9	342 34	10 39	39 40	69 6	98 10	126 2	152 19
	23	177 8	201 2	224 40	248 39			
July	1					273 24	299 9	325 50
	7	353 17	21 18	49 46	78 25	106 46	134 13	160 20
	21	185 7	209 1	232 40	256 47	281 55	308 18	
Aug.	1			321 57	349 51	18 18	46 26	74 33
	11	102 20	129 31	155 46	180 55	205 5	228 43	252 31
	25	277 10	303 14	330 50	359 34			
Sep.	1	14 6	43 3	71 25	99 1	125 50	151 51	177 0
	15	201 18	225 1	248 36	272 42	297 58	324 55	353 35
	29	23 17						
Oct.	1		58 1	81 53	109 30	135 54	161 17	185 52
	13	209 51	233 27	257 3	281 7	306 16	331 1	1 35
	27	31 33	61 53	91 23				
Nov.	1							105 35
	3	132 43	158 21	182 54	206 48	230 24	254 2	277 50
	17	302 35	328 9	355 35	24 30	54 40	85 0	114 17
Dec.	1	141 47	167 29	191 53	215 35	239 9	262 57	286 15
	15	312 14	338 5	5 5	33 23	62 54	92 53	122 13
	29	149 58	175 53					

Ayanamsa: 21° 1′ 41″

Longitudes of Planets

1902		Sun	Mars	Merc.	Merc.	Jupit.	Venus	Saturn	Rahu
Jan.	5	284 14	302 45	286 12	294 27	292 27	326 33	288 14	220 15
	15	294 26	310 38	302 50	311 19	294 47	331 34	289 25	219 45
	25	304 37	318 32	319 36	327 12	297 8	333 21R	290 36	219 12
Feb.	4	314 46	326 27	332 52	335 27	299 28	331 8	291 44	218 41
	14	324 53	334 27	333 40R	328 39	301 46	325 38	292 50	218 9
	24	334 58	342 15	323 31	320 47	303 59	320 1	293 51	217 7
March	6	345 0	350 6	320 52D	323 16	306 8	317 33	294 48	217 5
	16	354 59	357 55	327 20	332 38	308 9	319 2D	295 38	216 33
	26	4 54	5 41	338 51	345 49	310 2	323 41	296 21	216 2
April	5	14 46	13 22	353 26	1 42	311 46	330 32	294 57	215 30
	15	24 35	21 0	10 35	20 8	313 18	338 50	297 23	214 58
	25	34 20	28 33	30 18	40 56	314 38	348 8	297 40	214 26
May	5	44 3	36 1	51 41	61 59	315 43	358 9	297 48	213 55
	15	53 43	43 23	71 18	79 20	316 31	8 38	297 46R	213 23
	25	63 20	50 41	85 57	91 1	317 3	19 29	297 34	212 51
June	4	72 55	57 53	94 26	96 2	317 15	30 33	297 14	212 19
	14	82 29	65 0	95 45R	93 49R	317 9R	41 51	296 44	211 53
	24	92 1	72 1	91 0	88 26	316 44	53 19	296 9	211 15
July	4	101 33	78 57	87 13	87 56D	316 1	64 56	295 29	210 44
	14	111 5	85 47	90 49	95 49	315 3	76 38	294 45	210 12
	24	120 38	92 32	102 46	111 25	313 53	88 28	294 1	209 40
Aug.	3	130 12	99 12	121 14	131 34	312 36	100 24	293 18	209 8
	13	139 47	105 47	141 47	151 33	311 18	112 25	292 38	208 37
	23	149 24	112 16	160 45	169 24	310 5	124 32	292 5	208 5
Sep.	2	159 4	118 40	177 31	183 38	300 1	136 45	291 39	207 30
	12	168 47	124 58	192 10	198 39	308 12	149 1	291 20	207 1
	22	178 32	131 11	204 27	210 56	307 39	161 22	291 12	206 30
Oct.	2	188 21	137 18	212 51	214 22	307 26	173 47	291 13D	205 55
	12	198 13	143 17	212 58	208 18	307 31D	186 14	291 22	205 26
	22	208 9	149 10	202 19	198 52	307 57	198 44	291 44	204 55
Nov.	1	218 8	154 54	198 58D	204 37	308 41	211 16	292 14	204 22
	11	228 10	160 29	211 14	218 43	309 43	223 49	292 53	203 51
	21	238 14	165 53	226 31	234 23	311 10	236 23	293 40	203 19
Dec.	1	248 22	171 3	242 16	250 7	312 33	248 57	294 34	202 47
	11	258 32	176 0	257 58	265 51	314 10	261 32	295 32	202 16
	21	268 42	180 37	273 47	281 48	316 11	274 6	296 36	201 44
	31	278 53	184 50	289 52	—	318 13	286 42	297 43	201 12

Ayanamsa: 21° 2′ 31″

Longitude of the Moon

1902		Sun.	Tue.	Thur.	Sat.	Mon.	Wed.	Fri.
Jan.	1						188 15	212 13
Jan.	5	235 47	259 32	283 56	309 8	335 7	1 51	29 22
	19	57 43	86 45	115 51	144 8	170 56	196 8	220 12
Feb.	1				232 0	255 40	279 53	305 7
	9	331 25	358 34	26 16	54 18	82 34	110 52	138 46
	23	165 45	191 29	216 0				
March	1				239 47	263 29	287 47	313 15
	9	340 5	8 3	36 37	65 13	93 29	121 12	148 14
	23	174 24	199 36	223 56	274 41	271 24		
April	1		283 26	308 14	334 27	2 16	31 20	60 52
	13	89 58	118 7	145 6	171 1	196 2	220 20	244 9
	27	267 49	291 45					
May	1			316 29	342 34	10 21	39 42	69 52
	11	99 41	128 13	155 10	180 41	205 13	229 9	252 50
	25	276 33	300 36	325 21	351 16			
June	1	4 48	33 11	63 4	93 31	123 15	151 18	177 30
	15	202 17	226 13	249 52	273 36	297 40	322 16	347 39
	29	14 11						
July	1		42 12	71 41	101 56	131 43	159 57	186 16
	13	211 3	234 56	258 35	282 28	306 52	331 55	357 41
	27	24 21	52 7	81 3				
Aug.	1							95 50
	3	125 28	154 18	181 31	207 4	231 21	255 5	278 54
	17	303 17	328 29	354 31	21 18	48 48	76 59	105 43
	31	134 31						
Sep.	1					148 43	176 16	202 25
	7	227 13	251 13	274 58	299 7	324 10	350 21	17 33
	21	45 29	73 48	102 12	130 22	158 0		
Oct.	1						184 46	210 28
	5	235 8	259 5	282 50	306 58	332 5	358 35	26 29
	19	55 21	84 29	113 10	141 23	167 53	193 50	218 56
Nov.	1				231 12	255 17	279 1	302 49
	9	327 16	352 56	20 16	49 16	79 14	109 2	137 42
	23	164 53	190 44	215 38	239 55			
Dec.	1					263 48	287 31	311 19
	7	335 39	1 4	28 9	57 7	87 30	118 1	147 16
	21	174 40	200 22	224 55	248 52	272 37	296 22	

Ayanamsa: 21° 2' 31"

Longitudes of Planets

1903		Sun	Mars	Merc.	Merc.	Jupit.	Venus	Saturn	Rahu
Jan.	5	284 00	186 47	297 55	305 42	319 19	292 58	298 18	200 56
	15	294 11	190 16	312 38	317 37	321 32	305 32	299 29	200 24'
	25	304 21	193 7	319 5R	316 4R	323 50	318 4	300 40	199 52
Feb.	4	314 31	195 8	310 8	305 16	326 12	330 35	301 51	199 21
	14	324 38	196 11	303 30	304 41D	328 36	343 4	303 00	198 49
	24	334 43	196 4R	308 2	—	331 00	355 30	304 7	198 17
March	6	344 45	194 41	318 37	325 10	333 24	7 53	305 9	197 45
	16	354 44	192 4	332 21	340 5	335 46	20 12	306 7	197 14
	26	4 39	188 32	348 22	357 13	338 5	32 27	306 59	196 42
April	5	14 32	184 40	6 37	16 35	340 19	44 37	307 44	196 10
	15	24 34	181 13	27 1	37 33	342 28	56 40	308 21	195 38
	25	34 6	178 45	47 40	56 41	344 29	68 37	308 49	195 6
May	5	43 49	177 33R	64 13	70 1	346 22	80 26	309 9	194 35
	15	53 28	177 39D	73 57	75 52	348 4	92 6	309 18	193 57
	25	63 6	178 55	75 49	74 3R	349 35	103 36	309 18R	193 31
June	4	72 41	181 12	71 23R	68 53	350 53	114 52	309 8	192 59
	14	82 14	184 19	67 36	68 5	351 55	125 52	308 50	192 28
	24	91 47	188 7	70 29D	74 43D	352 41	136 31	308 22	191 56
July	4	101 19	192 30	80 41	88 14	353 9	146 42	307 48	191 24
	14	110 51	197 20	97 13	107 17	353 18	156 17	307 9	190 51
	24	120 24	202 34	117 52	128 21	353 8R	165 00	306 25	190 20
Aug.	3	129 58	208 9	138 22	147 47	352 38	172 30	305 41	—
	13	139 33	214 2	156 31	164 38	351 51	178 14	304 57	189 17
	23	149 10	220 11	172 9	179 3	350 49	181 24	304 17D	188 51
Sep.	2	158 49	226 34	185 14	190 34	349 35	181 11R	303 42R	188 14
	12	168 32	233 10	194 48	197 28	348 16D	177 18	303 14	187 41
	22	178 18	239 57	197 56R	195 32R	346 58R	171 19	302 54	187 10
Oct.	2	188 7	246 55	190 31	185 12	345 45	166 44	302 43	186 38
	12	197 59	254 2	182 54	184 57D	344 44	165 52	302 42	186 6
	22	207 55	261 19	190 21	197 35	343 59	168 53D	302 51D	185 35
Nov.	1	217 53	268 43	205 35	213 46	343 30R	174 40	303 11	185 3
	11	227 55	276 13	221 55	229 59	343 25D	182 23	303 39	184 30
	21	238 00	283 50	237 59	245 49	343 39	191 27	304 17	183 59
Dec.	1	248 8	291 32	253 38	261 26	344 13	201 25	305 2	183 27
	11	258 17	299 18	269 11	276 58	345 6	212 3	305 55	182 56
	21	268 27	307 6	284 35	291 48	346 16	223 9	306 54	182 24
	31	278 38	314 57	298 5	—	347 41	234 35	307 57	181 52

Ayanamsa : 21° 3' 21"

Longitude of the Moon

1903		Sun.	Tues.	Thur.	Sat.	Mon.	Wed.	Fri.
Jan.	1			308 18	332 27	357 14	23 11	50 48
	11	80 13	110 47	141 6	169 52	196 38	221 45	245 51
	25	269 33	293 18	317 21	341 51			
Feb.	1	354 18	19 50	46 29	74 33	104 00	134 5	163 34
	15	191 29	217 36	242 17	266 10	289 53	313 55	338 32
March	1	3 53	30 00	56 60	84 56	113 43	142 52	171 38
	15	199 51	225 23	250 12	274 12	297 58	322 6	347 3
	29	13 00	39 57					
April	1						53 44	81 45
	5	110 8	138 33	166 40	194 4	220 27	245 45	270 6
	19	293 56	317 50	342 24	8 8	35 14	63 31	
May	1							92 24
	3	121 10	149 21	176 43	203 16	228 59	253 55	278 8
	17	301 57	325 48	350 19	16 7	43 34	72 34	102 19
	31	131 44						
June	1					146 2	173 41	200 6
	7	225 36	250 23	274 37	298 29	322 17	346 15	11 14
	21	37 47	66 14	96 12	126 33	155 58		
July	1						183 47	210 2
	5	235 7	259 31	283 29	307 15	331 00	355 6	20 3
	19	46 27	74 43	104 39	135 13	165 1	193 7	219 27
Aug.	1				232 4	256 35	280 32	304 17
	9	328 6	352 11	16 52	42 32	69 40	96 26	128 27
	23	158 37	187 44	215 8	240 52	265 23		
Sep.	1		277 22	301 7	324 57	349 9	13 56	39 30
	13	66 6	93 52	122 45	152 16	181 32	209 42	236 19
	27	261 29	285 39					
Oct.	1			309 25	333 19	357 50	23 12	49 31
	11	76 43	104 38	133 4	161 43	190 7	217 44	244 11
	25	269 23	293 34	317 19	341 15			
Nov.	1	353 29	18 46	45 20	73 1	101 22	129 50	158 2
	15	185 48	212 59	239 25	264 54	289 27	313 27	336 59
	29	1 11						
Dec.	1		26 36	53 37	82 9	111 28	140 36	168 52
	13	196 11	220 37	248 20	273 19	297 37	321 22	344 59
	27	9 4	34 22	61 26				

Longitudes of Planets

1904		Sun.	Mars.	Merc.	Merc.	Jupit.	Venus	Saturn	Rahu
Jan.	5	283 45	318 52	302 16	302 41R	348 29	240 24	308 30	181 36
	15	293 56	326 44	299 38R	292 10	350 14	252 11	309 39	200 24
	25	304 7	334 35	297 52	287 9D	352 9	264 7	310 50	199 52
Feb.	4	314 16	342 25	289 21	293 30	354 26	276 9	312 2	199 21
	14	324 23	350 14	298 52	305 4	356 24	288 18	313 13	198 48
	24	334 28	357 59	311 54	319 13	358 41	300 27	314 24	198 17
March	6	345 30	6 26	328 38	336 59	1 17	313 53	315 38	197 45
	16	355 29	14 3	345 50	355 10	3 41	326 7	316 41	197 14
	26	5 25	21 36	5 1	15 13	6 6	338 22	317 40	196 48
April	5	15 16	29 4	25 27	35 6	8 31	350 38	318 32	196 10
	15	25 5	36 28	43 26	49 55	10 55	2 54	319 18	195 38
	25	34 51	43 46	54 14	56 15	13 16	15 9	319 57	195 6
May	5	44 33	50 59	56 00R	53 57R	15 34	27 24	320 27	194 41
	15	54 12	58 8	51 3	48 33	17 47	39 40	320 47	194 3
	25	63 49	65 11	47 24	48 3D	19 54	51 55	320 58	193 31
June	4	73 24	72 9	50 32	54 40	21 53	64 10	321 00R	192 59
	14	82 58	79 3	60 18	67 18	23 43	76 26	320 51	192 28
	24	92 31	85 52	75 34	85 3	25 23	88 42	320 34	191 56
July	4	102 2	92 37	95 26	106 14	26 51	100 59	320 8	191 24
	14	111 35	99 18	116 52	126 58	28 5	113 17	319 34	190 52
	24	121 7	105 54	136 22	145 3	29 4	125 36	318 55	190 20
Aug.	3	130 41	112 27	153 00	160 15	29 45	139 10	318 12	189 49
	13	140 16	118 57	166 45	172 22	30 8	150 16	317 27	189 17
	23	149 54	125 23	176 55	180 4	30 12R	162 37	316 43	188 45
Sep.	2	159 33	131 46	181 20	178 59R	29 55	174 58	316 2	188 14
	12	169 16	138 5	176 28R	171 21	29 19	187 19	315 25	187 41
	22	179 2	144 21	167 32	168 21D	28 26	199 40	314 56	187 10
Oct.	2	188 51	150 35	171 1	177 34	27 26	212 00	314 35	186 35
	12	198 44	156 44	185 35	194 7	26 1	224 20	314 23	186 6
	22	208 40	162 50	202 41	211 16	24 49	236 38	314 21D	185 35
Nov.	1	218 39	168 53	219 19	227 21	23 22	248 56	314 30	185 3
	11	228 41	174 51	235 13	242 59	22 12	261 12	314 48	184 31
	21	238 46	180 43	250 37	258 10	21 15	273 26	315 16	183 59
Dec.	1	248 53	186 31	265 33	272 40	20 36	285 37	315 54	183 27
	11	259 31	192 11	279 10	284 24	20 16	297 44	316 39	182 56
	21	269 14	197 44	287 3	285 31R	20 18D	309 45	317 32	182 24
	31	279 25	203 8	279 47R	....	20 40	321 39	318 30	181 52

Ayanamsa: 21° 4′ 12″

Longitude of the Moon

1904	Sun.	Tue.	Thur.	Sat.	Mon.	Wed.	Fri.
Jan. 1							75 42
3	105 21	135 31	164 58	193 1	219 41	245 14	270 2
17	294 15	318 3	341 39	5 25	29 55	55 50	83 39
31	113 17						
Feb. 1					128 31	159 00	188 25
7	216 8	242 14	267 7	291 16	315 1	338 39	2 25
21	26 39	51 50	78 25	106 44	136 33		
March 1		151 45	181 57	210 57	238 12	263 47	288 11
13	311 57	335 34	359 24	23 44	48 49	74 52	102 9
27	130 42	160 13	189 56				
April 1							204 34
3	232 49	259 25	284 30	308 32	332 9	355 57	20 22
17	45 39	71 51	98 55	126 47	155 17	184 11	212 55
May 1	240 48	267 21	292 29	316 34	340 13	4 7	28 15
15	54 44	81 45	109 34	137 45	166 1	194 12	222 4
29	249 16	275 25					
June 1						288 3	312 31
5	336 17	359 59	24 21	49 58	77 3	105 21	134 11
19	162 50	190 57	218 26	245 15	271 15	296 22	
July 1							320 36
3	344 18	7 59	32 21	58 3	85 28	114 23	143 59
17	173 16	201 37	228 52	255 6	280 28	305 4	329 2
31	352 39						
Aug. 1					4 26	28 22	53 17
7	79 46	108 3	137 47	167 57	197 25	225 30	252 7
21	277 30	302 00	325 55	349 33	13 11	37 13	
Sep. 1			49 32	75 5	102 13	131 5	161 12
11	191 29	220 46	248 24	274 22	299 2	322 57	346 33
25	10 14	34 17	58 58				
Oct. 1				84 37	111 31	129 53	169 30
9	199 37	229 5	257 00	283 7	307 46	331 34	355 9
23	19 1	43 29	68 42	94 44	121 41		
Nov. 1		135 31	163 58	193 13	222 38	251 15	278 19
13	303 44	327 55	351 32	15 17	39 44	65 10	91 31
27	118 37	146 15					
Dec. 1			174 22	202 51	231 23	259 22	286 9
11	311 31	335 43	359 22	23 10	47 48	73 40	100 48
25	128 46	157 5	185 20	213 23			

Ayanamsa: 21° 4' 12"

Longitudes of Planets

1905		Sun	Mars	Merc.	Merc.	Jupit.	Venus	Saturn	Rahu
Jan.	5	284 31	205 45	273 39R	270 56R	20 58	327 32	319 2	162 14
	15	294 42	210 51	271 57D	275 29	21 49	339 8	320 8	161 42
	25	304 53	215 41	280 35	286 36	22 58	350 27	321 17	161 10
Feb.	4	315 -2	220 13	293 16	300 24	24 31	1 24	322 28	160 38
	14	325 9	224 22	307 55	315 49	25 58	11 49	323 48	160 6
	24	335 14	228 1	324 6	332 48	27 47	21 31	324 53	159 35
March	6	345 16	231 5	341 56	351 29	29 45	30 31	326 3	159 3
	16	355 15	233 24	1 23	11 15	31 51	37 29	327 12	158 31
	26	5 10	234 47	20 31	28 21	34 3	42 36	328 17	157 00
April	5	15 2	235 4R	33 59	36 58R	36 19	44 42R	329 17	157 28
	15	24 51	234 6	37 15R	35 13	38 39	42 56	330 12	156 56
	25	34 36	231 55	31 57	28 56	41 1	37 40	331 0	156 24
May	5	44 18	228 44R	27 20	27 37D	43 24	31 43	331 40	155 52
	15	53 58	225 7	29 47	33 36	45 47	28 29	332 12	155 20
	25	63 35	221 49	38 48	45 12	48 8	29 7D	332 36	154 49
June	4	73 10	219 27	52 45	61 22	50 27	33 5	332 50	154 17
	14	82 44	218 23	71 0	81 28	52 41	39 22	332 54R	153 45
	24	92 16	218 40D	92 23	103 11	54 50	47 14	332 48	153 13
July	4	101 48	220 12	113 25	122 55	56 54	56 11	332 33R	152 41
	14	111 21	222 50	131 35	139 27	58 50	65 54	332 8	152 10
	24	120 53	226 22	146 28	152 36	60 36	76 11	331 37	151 38
Aug.	3	130 27	230 38	157 42	161 30	62 12	86 53	330 58	151 6
	13	140 2	235 33	163 42	163 51R	63 35	97 55	330 15	150 34
	23	149 40	240 56	161 40R	157 33	64 44	109 13	329 30	150 3
Sep.	2	159 20	246 46	153 7R	150 40	65 37	120 46	328 46R	149 28
	12	169 2	252 58	151 43D	156 17	66 13	132 30	328 3	148 59
	22	178 48	259 27	163 27	171 59	66 ??	144 23	327 25	148 27
Oct.	2	188 37	266 11	180 57	189 54	66 26R	156 17	326 54	147 53
	12	198 29	273 9	198 36	207 00	66 2	168 37	326 30R	147 24
	22	208 25	280 17	215 9	223 3	65 20	180 54	326 16	146 52
Nov.	1	218 24	287 35	230 45	238 15	64 20	193 16	326 12D	146 20
	11	228 26	295 00	245 33	252 36	63 8	205 42	326 19	145 48
	21	238 31	302 30	259 15	265 8	61 49	218 12	326 35	145 17
Dec.	1	248 39	310 4	269 33R	271 17	60 27R	230 43	327 2	144 45
	11	258 48	317 42	268 47	262 32R	59 10	243 17	327 38	144 13
	21	268 59	325 21	256 46	255 1	58 4	255 51	328 22	143 41
	31	279 10	333 00	256 58D	...	57 13	268 25	329 14	143 10

Ayanamsa: 21° 5' 02''

Longitude of the Moon

1905		Sun.	Tue.	Thurs.	Sat.	Mon.	Wed.	Fri.
Jan.	1	227 17	254 43	281 22	306 59	331 33	355 21	18 58
	15	43 5	68 22	95 12	123 29	152 35	181 43	210 15
	29	237 54	264 38					
Feb.	1						277 40	303 4
	5	327 40	351 36	15 12	38 58	63 30	89 24	117 2
	19	146 14	176 13	205 56	234 31	261 39		
March	1						287 27	312 16
	5	336 24	0 7	23 44	47 34	72 4	97 46	125 5
	19	154 9	184 25	214 44	243 54	271 18	297 00	321 30
April	1				333 27	357 7	20 44	44 35
	9	68 55	94 1	120 17	148 5	177 27	207 48	237 53
	23	266 32	293 15	318 18	342 17			
May	1					5 53	29 34	53 42
	7	78 26	103 53	130 15	157 47	186 36	216 21	246 6
	21	274 42	301 32	326 40	350 42	14 20	38 10	
June	1			50 18	75 10	100 49	127 15	154 26
	11	182 26	211 13	240 19	268 58	296 23	322 15	346 48
	25	10 36	34 21	58 40				
July	1				83 55	110 13	137 23	165 12
	9	193 24	221 49	250 8	277 54	304 40	330 13	354 41
	23	18 31	42 18	66 42	92 11	118 59		
Aug.	1		132 51	161 14	190 00	218 38	246 44	274 5
	13	300 33	326 4	350 42	14 41	38 24	62 23	87 14
	27	113 28	141 18	170 25				
Sep.	1							185 14
	3	214 46	243 30	271 1	297 19	322 37	347 19	11 10
	17	34 54	58 41	82 57	108 17	135 12	163 54	193 57
Oct.	1	224 13	253 30	281 7	307 8	331 58	356 7	19 55
	15	43 39	67 30	91 49	117 1	143 38	172 3	202 6
	29	232 43	262 28					
Nov.	1						276 41	303 39
	5	328 56	353 9	16 55	40 38	64 34	88 32	113 45
	19	139 34	166 44	195 31	225 35	255 50	284 55	
Dec.	1							312 8
	3	337 34	1 48	25 31	49 17	73 28	98 12	123 35
	17	149 44	176 52	205 10	234 27	263 59	292 44	319 58
	31	345 33						

Ayanamsa: 21° 5' 02"

Longitudes of Planets

1906		Sun	Mars	Merc.	Merc.	Jupit.	Venus	Saturn	Rahu
Jan.	5	284 16	336 50	261 20	267 2	56 54R	274 42	329 43	142 54
	15	294 27	344 28	273 28	280 25	56 31	287 17	330 44	142 22
	25	304 38	352 4	287 43	295 19	56 29D	299 51	331 49	141 50
Feb.	4	314 47	359 38	303 12	311 24	56 47	312 24	332 59	141 18
	14	324 54	7 9	319 56	328 50	57 25	324 56	334 10	140 47
	24	334 59	14 36	338 6	—	58 21	337 28	335 23	140 14
March	6	345 1	21 59	357 6	5 55	59 32	349 57	336 36	139 43
	16	355 0	29 17	13 9	17 48	60 58	2 25	337 48	139 11
	26	4 55	36 31	19 19R	17 47R	62 36	14 51	338 58	138 40
April	5	14 47	43 41	14 14	10 27	64 25	27 14	340 4	138 8
	15	24 36	50 46	8 2	7 40D	66 22	39 35	341 6	137 36
	25	34 22	57 47	9 22D	12 46	68 26	51 53	342 3	137 4
May	5	44 4	64 43	17 36	23 34	70 35	64 8	342 53	136 33
	15	53 43	71 35	30 33	38 29	72 49	76 20	343 37	136 1
	25	63 21	78 23	47 19	57 3	75 6	88 29	344 12	135 29
June	4	72 56	85 7	67 32	78 29	77 24	100 34	344 38	134 57
	14	82 30	91 48	89 22	99 40	79 43	112 36	344 55	134 25
	24	92 2	98 25	109 11	117 47	82 1	124 33	345 2	133 53
July	4	101 34	105 00	125 26	132 6	84 7	136 25	344 59R	133 22
	14	111 6	111 31	137 44	142 6	86 30	148 11	344 46	132 50
	24	120 39	118 1	145 00	146 4	88 40	159 50	344 25	132 18
Aug.	3	131 10	125 6	145 2R	142 2	90 43	171 20	343 54	131 46
	13	139 48	130 53	138 2	134 46	92 41	182 40	343 17	131 15
	23	149 26	137 16	133 53D	136 11D	94 31	196 43	342 35	130 49
Sep.	2	159 5	143 38	141 35	149 17	96 9	204 35	341 50R	130 8
	12	168 48	149 59	158 18	167 43	97 37	213 69	341 5	129 39
	22	178 34	156 19	177 1	186 00	98 52	224 57	340 21	129 7
Oct.	2	188 23	162 37	194 37	202 52	99 51	234 11	339 41R	128 33
	12	198 15	168 55	210 49	218 28	100 34	242 23	339 7	127 59
	22	208 11	175 12	225 50	232 54	100 59	249 4	338 41	127 32
Nov.	1	218 10	181 27	239 36	245 45	101 3R	253 30	338 25	127 00
	11	228 12	187 42	250 58	254 34	100 48	254 40R	338 18	126 29
	21	238 17	193 56	255 18R	251 56R	100 14	251 57	338 23D	125 57
Dec.	1	248 24	200 8	245 24	240 15	99 22	246 19	338 37	125 25
	11	258 33	206 19	239 27D	242 21	98 15	241 10	339 2	125 00
	21	268 44	212 27	247 27	253 41	96 58	239 28D	339 36	124 22
	31	278 55	218 34	260 32	—	95 37	241 39	340 19	123 50

Ayanamsa: 21° 5′ 52″

Longitude of the Moon

1906		Sun.	Tue.	Thur.	Sat.	Mon.	Wed.	Fri.
Jan.	1					357 51	21 50	45 33
	7	69 37	94 23	120 2	146 32	173 47	201 41	230 6
	21	258 44	287 3	314 28	340 38	5 34	29 38	
Feb.	1			41 31	65 22	89 49	115 20	142 5
	11	169 54	198 21	226 55	255 11	282 54	309 52	335 59
	25	1 10	25 32					
March	1			49 22	73 11	97 34	123 8	150 16
	11	178 52	208 17	231 36	266 1	293 18	319 32	344 55
	25	9 37	33 46	57 33	81 20			
April	1	93 22	118 19	144 23	172 27	202 8	232 25	262 0
	15	290 6	316 37	341 56	6 28	30 32	54 20	78 4
	29	102 2						
May	1		126 44	152 46	180 41	210 24	241 1	271 7
	13	299 35	326 12	351 23	15 40	39 31	63 15	87 4
	27	111 12	136 1	162 00				
June	1							175 35
	3	204 7	234 8	264 35	294 7	321 57	347 55	12 33
	17	36 30	60 13	84 4	108 18	133 6	158 46	185 35
July	1	213 47	243 11	273 3	302 17	330 5	356 13	21 00
	15	44 58	68 43	92 43	117 19	142 43	169 00	196 12
	29	224 18	253 5					
Aug.	1					267 36		296 25
	5	324 32	351 19	16 45	41 7	64 56	88 49	113 18
	19	138 47	165 22	192 56	221 7	249 32	277 52	305 49
Sep.	1				319 34	346 24	12 12	36 57
	9	60 57	84 42	108 50	133 59	160 32	188 29	217 19
	23	246 16	274 40	302 18	329 9			
Oct.	1					355 14	20 33	45 9
	7	68 59	92 40	116 42	141 49	168 34	197 6	226 47
	21	256 31	285 18	312 47	339 7	4 34	29 21	
Nov.	1			41 31	65 30	89 10	112 53	137 16
	11	162 59	190 36	220 4	250 30	280 32	309 7	336 3
	25	1 38	26 19	50 26				
Dec.	1				74 13	97 53	121 42	146 6
	9	171 41	198 58	228 7	258 31	288 53	317 58	345 15
	23	10 55	35 26	59 19	83 0	106 46		

Ayanamsa: 21° 5' 52″

Longitudes of Planets

1907		Sun	Mars	Merc.	Merc.	Jupit.	Venus	Saturn	Rahu
Jan.	5	284 1	221 36	267 45	275 12	94 57R	243 58	340 44	123 34
	15	294 12	227 38	282 52	290 44	93 41	250 24	341 38	123 2
	25	304 23	233 36	298 51	307 13	92 36	258 33	342 39	122 30
Feb.	4	314 32	239 29	315 52	324 48	91 45	267 51	343 44	121 59
	14	324 40	245 17	333 56	342 58	91 13	277 57	344 54	121 27
	24	334 45	250 57	351 18	357 51	91 00	288 35	346 6	120 55
March	6	344 46	256 28	1 28	1 26R	91 7D	299 36	347 19	120 23
	16	354 45	261 49	358 13R	353 41R	91 34D	310 54	348 33	119 51
	26	4 41	266 56	350 5	348 41D	92 18	322 23	349 46	119 20
April	5	14 33	271 46	349 37D	353 15	93 19	334 1	350 57	118 48
	15	24 22	276 15	356 52	3 39	94 34	345 47	352 5	118 10
	25	34 8	280 16	8 57	16 19	96 2	357 37	353 10	117 44
May	5	43 50	283 42	24 29	33 26	97 41	9 30	354 9	117 13
	15	53 30	286 25	43 11	53 28	99 30	21 27	355 2	116 41
	25	63 7	288 12	64 32	75 25	101 26	33 27	355 48	116 9
June	4	72 42	288 55R	85 45	95 11	103 28	45 28	356 26	115 37
	14	82 16	288 21	103 36	110 54	105 35	57 32	356 55	115 6
	24	91 49	286 38	117 5	121 57	107 45	69 38	357 16	114 34
July	4	101 21	284 1	125 23	127 6	109 58	81 46	357 26	114 2
	14	110 53	281 6	126 53R	124 48R	112 12	93 56	357 27R	113 30
	24	120 26	278 1	121 28	118 23	114 26	106 9	357 17	112 58
Aug.	3	129 59	277 12	116 28R	117 14D	116 39	118 25	356 58	112 26
	13	139 35	277 7D	120 47	126 56	118 50	130 44	356 30	111 55
	23	149 12	278 24	135 8	136 57	120 58	143 5	355 54	111 23
Sep.	2	158 51	280 54	154 22	164 1	123 00	155 28	355 13	110 49
	12	168 34	284 26	173 17	182 7	124 57	167 53	354 28	110 19
	22	178 19	288 48	190 30	198 28	126 46	180 20	353 42	109 48
Oct.	2	188 8	293 49	206 5	213 18	128 26	192 48	352 56	109 13
	12	198 25	299 22	220 8	226 28	129 55	205 17	352 15	108 44
	22	207 56	305 19	232 5	236 37	131 12	217 46	351 59	108 13
Nov.	1	217 55	311 35	239 19R	239 2R	132 14	230 16	351 10	107 41
	11	227 57	318 5	234 53	228 23	133 00	242 46	350 51	107 9
	21	238 2	324 46	224 1	224 11D	133 28	255 16	350 42	106 37
Dec.	1	248 9	331 35	227 58D	233 44	133 37R	267 45	350 43D	106 5
	11	258 18	338 30	240 30	247 44	133 26	280 14	350 56	105 34
	21	268 29	345 29	255 11	262 48	132 56	292 47	351 18	105 2
	31	278 40	352 29	270 32	–	132 8	305 9	351 51	104 30

Ayanamsa: 21° 6′ 43″

Longitude of the Moon

1907	Sun.	Tue.	Thur.	Sat.	Mon.	Wed.	Fri.
Jan. 1		118 46	143 8	168 57	194 36	222 25	251 40
13	281 43	311 29	339 57	6 42	31 53	56 1	79 41
27	103 26	127 38	152 32				
Feb. 1							165 18
3	191 29	218 39	246 48	275 44	304 58	333 45	1 20
17	27 24	52 6	75 38	99 38	123 44	148 41	
March 1							174 43
3	201 44	229 27	257 35	285 56	314 15	342 12	9 18
17	35 13	59 55	83 48	107 28	131 38	156 33	183 33
31	211 77						
April 1					225 42	254 20	280 44
7	310 40	338 4	4 49	30 45	55 44	79 51	107 30
21	127 18	151 58	178 7	205 57	235 4		
May 1						264 32	293 27
5	321 23	348 19	14 23	39 40	64 13	88 7	111 42
19	135 28	160 6	186 12	214 10	243 42	273 49	303 23
June 1				317 41	345 14	11 27	36 38
9	61 3	84 57	108 32	132 11	156 20	181 35	208 26
23	237 7	267 10	297 30	326 58			
July 1					354 50	21 5	46 2
7	70 8	93 48	117 24	141 13	165 36	190 56	217 38
21	245 55	275 35	305 49	335 29	3 40	30 4	
Aug. 1			42 41	67 3	90 46	114 21	138 14
11	162 41	187 56	214 7	241 27	269 57	299 24	329 4
25	357 58	25 23	51 5	75 28			
Sep. 1	87 22	110 57	134 48	159 21	184 47	211 6	238 13
15	266 2	294 29	323 22	352 6	19 58	46 24	71 24
29	95 22						
Oct. 1		118 59	142 57	167 51	193 55	221 4	248 52
13	276 59	305 10	333 19	1 11	28 21	54 24	79 15
27	103 11	126 47	150 47				
Nov. 1							163 9
3	188 55	216 9	244 33	273 22	302 00	330 5	357 32
17	24 15	50 9	75 8	99 17	122 55	146 36	170 59
Dec. 1	196 44	224 11	253 9	282 50	312 15	340 42	7 57
15	34 5	59 17	83 44	107 37	131 13	154 56	179 15
29	204 48	232 2					

Ayanamsa: 21° 6′ 43″

Longitudes of Planets

1908		Sun.	Mars.	Merc.	Merc.	Jupit.	Venus	Saturn	Rahu
Jan.	5	283 46	356 00	278·24	286 25	131 38R	311 21	352 11	104 14
	15	293 57	3 2	294 37	303 1	130 38	323 45	352 56	103 42
	25	304 8	10 3	311 38	320 20	129 11	336 4	353 50	103 11
Feb.	4	314 17	17 3	328 53	336 38	127 51	348 19	354 50	102 39
	14	324 25	24 1	342 29	345 2	126 35	0 28	355 55	102 13
	24	334 30	30 57	343 29R	338 53R	125 27	12 29	357 4	101 35
March	6	345 34	38 31	333 11	330 48D	124 28	25 30	358 23	101 00
	16	355 31	45 21	331 5D	331 5	123 53	37 9	359 37	100 29
	26	5 26	52 8	337 39	337 39	123 35	48 32	0 52	99 57
April	5	15 18	58 53	349 15	356 18	123 37	59 36	2 6	99 25
	15	25 7	65 34	4 3	12 30	123 58	70 15	3 19	98 53
	25	34 52	72 13	21 37	31 27	124 36	80 23	4 28	98 22
May	5	44 34	78 49	41 53	52 44	125 30	89 47	5 34	97 50
	15	54 14	85 33	63 28	73 34	126 39	98 11	6 35	97 18
	25	63 51	90 54	82 37	90 27	128 1	105 7	7 30	96 46
June	4	73 26	98 23	96 59	102 7	129 34	109 59	8 19	96 15
	14	82 59	104 50	105 10	107 29R	131 16	111 51R	9 00	95 43
	24	92 32	111 6	107 26R	105 37	133 7	109 56	9 32	95 10
July	4	102 4	117 40	102 44	99 52	135 4	104 40	9 55	94 39
	14	111 36	124 3	98 16	98 44D	137 6	98 46	10 8	94 8
	24	121 9	130 75	101 32D	106 41	139 12	95 33	10 11R	93 35
Aug.	3	130 43	136 47	113 55	122 51	141 21	96 11	10 4	93 3
	13	140 18	143 9	132 44	142 54	143 32	100 5	9 47	92 32
	23	149 55	149 31	152 49	162 16	145 43	106 25	9 21	92 00
Sep.	2	159 35	155 53	171 10	179 35	147 53	114 16	8 46	91 26
	12	169 18	162 15	187 30	194 58	150 1	123 20	8 6	90 57
	22	179 4	168 38	201 57	208 25	152 7	133 14	7 21	90 25
Oct.	2	188 53	175 2	214 11	219 3	154 8	143 44	6 34	89 50
	12	198 45	181 27	222 29R	223 41R	156 3	154 42	5 48	89 21
	22	208 41	187 54	221 42	216 22	157 50	166 3	5 5	88 50
Nov.	1	218 41	194 21	210 25	207 51	159 29	177 40	4 27	88 18
	11	228 43	200 50	209 49D	214 53	160 56	189 31	3 56	87 52
	21	238 48	207 20	221 32	228 54	162 11	201 33	3 35	87 14
Dec.	1	248 55	213 52	236 32	244 17	163 12	213 44	3 24D	86 43
	11	259 5	220 25	252 3	261 26	163 57	226 00	3 24	86 11
	21	269 15	227 00	267 44	275 41	164 23	238 21	3 34	85 30
	31	279 27	233 36	283 45	....	164 31R	250 45	3 55	85 7

Ayanamsa: 21° 7' 33"

1908		Sun.	Tues.	Thur.	Sat.	Mon.	Wed.	Fri.
Jan.	1						246 20	276 1
	5	306 20	336 4	4 23	31 3	56 20	80 40	104 29
	19	128 6	151 48	175 54	200 46	226 52	254 34	283 55
Feb.	1				299 2	329 29	359 6	26 59
	9	53 2	77 39	101 27	125 2	148 47	172 57	197 44
	23	223 20	250 1	278 3	307 25			
March	1	322 25	352 26	21 24	48 35	73 59	98 8	121 44
	15	145 26	169 40	194 38	220 21	246 51	274 10	302 26
	29	331 30	0 48					
April	1						15 15	43 9
	5	69 26	94 12	118 3	141 42	165 48	190 46	216 44
	19	243 35	271 41	299 2	327 23	355 54	24 5	
May	1							51 21
	3	77 19	102 2	125 56	149 38	173 49	199 1	225 30
	17	253 7	281 26	309 28	338 22	6 20	33 40	60 7
	31	85 33						
June	1					97 53	122 00	145 42
	7	169 35	194 14	220 11	247 40	276 26	305 47	334 55
	21	3 14	30 29	56 40	81 55	106 23		
July	1						130 18	153 58
	5	177 50	202 25	228 17	255 49	284 57	315 00	344 52
	19	13 33	40 42	66 26	91 9	115 14	138 58	162 39
Aug.	1				174 33	198 44	223 47	250 15
	9	278 27	308 17	338 49	8 42	36 56	63 20	88 16
	23	112 19	136 1	159 42	183 37	207 59		
Sep.	1		220 25	246 4	273 5	301 47	331 52	2 18
	13	31 41	59 12	84 52	109 14	132 58	156 39	180 37
	27	205 6	230 10					
Oct.	1			256 1	282 57	311 12	340 39	10 34
	11	39 46	67 21	93 9	117 35	141 21	165 6	189 18
	25	214 13	239 54	266 30	293 32			
Nov.	1	307 27	335 53	4 53	33 45	61 43	88 14	113 21
	15	137 27	161 11	185 11	209 58	235 48	262 38	290 27
	29	318 25						
Dec.	1		3	15 3	42 56	70 3	96 7	121 6
	13	145 13	16 59	192 58	217 47	243 53	271 24	300 00
	27	329 1	357 46	25 46				

Ayanamsa: 21° 7' 33"

Longitudes of Planets

1909		Sun	Mars	Merc.	Merc.	Jupit.	Venus	Saturn	Rahu
Jan.	5	284 33	236 55	291 56	300 13	164 28R	256 58	4 10D	84 51
	15	294 44	243 33	308 29	316 23	164 7	269 25	4 46	84 19
	25	304 55	250 13	323 14	327 42	163 28	281 53	5 31	83 48
Feb.	4	315 4	256 53	328 17R	324 35	162 32	294 22	6 23	83 16
	14	325 11	263 35	318 53	314 36	161 24	306 50	7 23	82 44
	24	335 16	270 17	313 17D	—	160 8	319 19	8 28	82 13
March	6	345 17	276 59	318 7	322 56	158 50	331 46	9 37	81 41
	16	355 16	283 42	328 46	335 23	157 35	344 13	10 50	81 9
	26	5 12	290 25	342 40	350 33	156 28	356 38	12 4	80 43
April	5	15 4	297 6	359 2	8 6	155 34	9 3	13 20	80 5
	15	24 52	303 46	17 48	28 5	154 56	21 26	14 35	79 33
	25	34 38	310 23	38 48	49 19	154 35R	33 48	15 49	79 2
May	5	44 20	316 56	59 15	68 1	154 33D	46 8	17 00	78 30
	15	54 00	323 24	75 21	81 5	154 49	58 27	18 8	77 58
	25	63 37	329 43	85 7	87 18R	155 23	70 45	19 12	77 27
June	4	73 12	335 52	87 34R	86 5	156 12	83 2	20 10	76 55
	14	82 45	341 47	83 28	80 49	157 17	95 18	21 2	76 23
	24	92 18	347 23	79 12D	79 20D	158 34	107 33	21 46	75 51
July	4	101 50	352 34	81 29	85 38	160 2	119 47	22 22	75 19
	14	111 22	357 13	91 41	99 29	161 41	132 00	22 49	74 48
	24	120 55	1 9	108 44	118 55	163 27	144 12	23 7	74 16
Aug.	3	130 29	4 12	129 22	138 35	165 21	156 21	23 14R	73 44
	13	140 4	6 9	149 16	158 22	167 20	168 29	23 10	73 12
	23	149 42	6 48R	166 51	174 47	169 24	180 35	22 57	72 38
Sep.	2	159 21	6 3	182 9	188 57	171 31	192 38	22 34	72 6
	12	169 4	4 3	195 5	200 23	173 10	204 37	22 2	71 37
	22	178 50	1 16	204 35	207 8	175 50	216 32	21 3	71 5
Oct.	2	188 38	358 29	207 18R	204 22	177 59	228 23	20 39	70 31
	12	198 31	356 23	198 51	193 40D	180 7	240 8	19 52	70 2
	22	208 27	355 28	192 11D	195 2	182 12	251 46	19 4	69 30
Nov.	1	218 26	355 53D	200 49	208 5	184 12	263 13	18 19	68 58
	11	228 28	357 31	215 55	223 54	186 7	274 28	17 39	68 26
	21	238 33	0 12	231 53	239 49	187 54	285 25	17 6	67 54
Dec.	1	248 40	3 48	247 42	255 33	189 32	295 55	16 41	67 23
	11	258 50	7 53	263 24	271 18	190 59	305 49	16 27	66 51
	21	269 1	12 33	279 13	287 9	192 14	314 48	16 23D	66 19
	31	279 12	17 36	294 57	—	193 14	322 27	16 30	65 48

Ayanamsa: 21° 8' 23"

Longitude of the Moon

1909		Sun.	Tue.	Thurs.	Sat.	Mon.	Wed.	Fri.
Jan.	1							39 26
	3	66 6	91 55	116 56	141 15	165 5	188 51	213 4
	17	238 22	265 16	293 52	323 39	353 31	22 24	49 52
	31	76 00						
Feb.	1					88 41	113 28	137 44
	7	161 38	185 22	209 15	233 48	259 37	287 14	316 42
	21	347 14	17 24	46 4	72 54			
March	1					98 16	122 41	146 38
	7	170 25	194 12	218 13	242 49	268 29	295 47	324 55
	21	355 21	25 46	54 49	81 57	107 23	131 42	
April	1			143 39	167 23	191 11	215 17	239 52
	11	265 11	291 36	319 30	348 57	18 57	48 37	76 49
	25	103 14	128 10	152 13				
May	1				175 57	199 52	224 17	249 29
	9	275 14	302 2	329 52	358 40	27 56	56 55	84 48
	23	111 13	136 15	160 22	184 9	208 10		
June	1		220 25	245 35	271 44	298 50	326 41	355 3
	13	23 35	51 55	79 36	106 17	131 49	156 19	180 12
	27	204 3	228 28					
July	1			253 56	280 44	308 44	337 24	6 7
	11	34 24	62 00	88 50	114 52	140 1	164 22	188 12
	25	211 59	236 22	261 57	289 10			
Aug.	1	303 23	232 40	2 14	31 9	58 56	85 35	111 20
	15	136 22	160 46	184 39	208 20	232 15	257 3	283 24
	29	311 39	341 29					
Sep.	1						356 39	26 40
	5	55 25	82 35	108 24	133 18	157 36	181 29	205 10
	19	228 54	253 8	278 31	305 36	334 38	5 3	
Oct.	1							35 31
	3	64 43	92 8	117 56	142 36	166 38	190 22	214 5
	17	237 59	262 24	287 47	314 39	343 14	13 14	43 36
	31	73 3						
Nov.	1					87 10	114 00	139 17
	7	163 30	187 15	210 58	234 58	259 30	284 47	311 3
	21	338 33	7 17	36 51	66 25	95 00		
Dec.	1						122 3	147 30
	5	171 49	195 33	219 19	243 35	268 40	294 40	321 34
	19	349 13	17 31	46 12	74 55	102 53	129 47	155 19

Ayanamsa: 21° 8′ 23″

Longitudes of Planets

1910		Sun	Mars	Merc.	Merc.	Jupit.	Venus	Saturn	Rahu
Jan.	5	284 18	20 15	302 17	308 26	193 39	325 35	16 38	65 32
	15	294 30	25 43	312 12R	311 30R	194 14	329 54	17 2	65 00
	25	304 40	31 24	306 9	300 37	194 31R	330 46R	17 35	64 28
Feb.	4	314 49	37 13	297 1	296 49D	194 29	327 35	18 18	63 56
	14	324 56	43 9	297 15	303 27	194 6	321 42	19 9	63 25
	24	335 46	49 10	308 51	—	193 31	316 38	20 7	62 47
March	6	343 3	55 14	321 58	329 24	192 37	315 10	21 11	62 21
	16	355 2	61 21	337 20	345 47	191 30	317 32	22 20	61 49
	26	4 57	67 30	354 46	4 18	190 16	322 48	23 32	61 18
April	5	14 49	73 41	14 21	24 45	188 59	330 4	24 47	60 42
	15	24 38	79 52	35 7	44 48	187 37	339 36	26 10	60 14
	25	34 24	86 4	53 10	59 49	186 28	348 12	27 19	59 42
May	5	44 6	92 16	64 32	67 10R	185 43	358 20	28 34	59 10
	15	53 46	98 28	67 40R	66 18	185 4	8 55	29 48	58 38
	25	63 23	104 41	63 42	61 1	184 42	19 50	30 58	58 7
June	4	72 59	110 54	59 20D	59 19D	184 37D	31 00	32 4	57 35
	14	82 32	117 7	61 9	64 47	184 51	42 21	33 6	—
	24	92 4	123 21	70 4	76 52	185 22	53 51	34 1	57 3
July	4	101 36	129 35	85 7	94 38	186 9	65 28	34 49	56 00
	14	111 9	135 50	105 2	115 44	187 11	77 13	35 29	55 28
	24	120 41	142 7	126 11	136 5	188 26	89 4	36 00	54 56
Aug.	3	130 15	148 24	145 19	153 53	189 53	101 1	36 22	54 54
	13	139 50	154 44	161 47	169 2	191 30	113 3	36 33	53 53
	23	149 28	161 4	175 35	181 20	193 16	125 11	36 35R	53 12
Sep.	2	159 7	167 27	186 5	189 30	195 9	137 23	36 25	52 49
	12	168 50	173 52	191 5R	190 10R	197 8	149 41	36 5	52 17
	22	178 36	180 20	186 28	181 5	199 12	162 2	35 37	51 46
Oct.	2	188 25	186 50	176 57D	176 37D	201 19	174 27	35 00	51 14
	12	198 17	193 23	180 20	186 48	203 28	186 55	34 17	52 48
	22	208 12	199 58	194 36	202 54	205 39	199 25	33 30	52 46
Nov.	1	218 12	206 37	211 15	219 29	207 49	211 57	32 42	51 17
	11	228 14	213 20	227 35	235 32	209 58	224 30	31 55	49 7
	21	238 18	220 5	243 24	251 10	212 3	237 4	31 12	48 35
Dec.	1	248 26	226 54	258 54	266 34	214 5	249 39	30 36	48 3
	11	258 35	233 46	274 8	281 28	216 00	262 14	30 8	47 29
	21	268 46	240 42	288 12	293 36	217 48	274 48	29 49	47 00
	31	278 57	247 41	296 17	—	219 27	287 22	29 42	46 28

Ayanamsa : 21° 9' 14"

Longitude of the Moon

1910		Sun.	Tue.	Thur.	Sat.	Mon.	Wed.	Fri.
Jan.	1				167 37	191 36	215 17	239 19
	9	264 17	290 27	317 51	345 58	14 19	42 32	70 27
	23	97 56	124 45	150 36	175 25	199 23		
Feb.	1		211 13	234 57	259 24	285 13	312 38	341 21
	13	10 32	39 20	67 19	94 27	120 50	146 29	171 23
	27	195 32						
March	1		219 13	242 54	267 17	293 4	320 40	349 56
	13	19 54	49 26	77 45	104 45	130 39	155 43	180 7
	27	204 2	227 39	251 21				
April	1							263 25
	3	288 20	314 50	343 15	13 11	43 33	73 7	101 9
	17	127 36	152 48	177 8	200 59	224 36	248 19	272 27
May	1	297 27	323 49	351 52	21 28	51 47	81 38	110 4
	15	136 45	161 55	186 6	209 47	233 25	257 21	281 52
	29	307 12	333 39					
June	1						347 22	15 47
	5	45 16	75 6	104 17	132 00	158 2	182 40	206 30
	19	230 7	254 4	278 42	304 11	330 34	357 51	
July	1							25 58
	3	54 47	83 53	112 34	140 7	166 9	190 49	214 38
	17	238 18	262 27	287 32	313 43	340 52	8 40	36 48
	31	65 7						
Aug.	1					79 18	107 28	135 00
	7	161 26	186 35	210 43	234 21	258 14	283 1	309 8
	21	336 35	4 57	33 33	61 56	89 52	117 17	
Sep.	1			130 45	157 4	182 24	206 46	230 30
	11	254 8	278 22	303 53	331 3	359 42	29 6	58 19
	25	86 44	114 10	140 39				
Oct.	1				166 14	191 1	215 6	238 43
	9	262 19	286 30	311 55	339 2	7 55	37 54	67 52
	23	96 52	124 26	150 35	175 39	199 57		
Nov.	1		211 53	235 32	259 7	283 00	307 40	333 39
	13	1 22	30 46	61 9	91 19	120 9	147 13	172 40
	27	197 00	220 44					
Dec.	1			244 18	268 2	292 11	317 2	342 55
	11	10 12	39 2	69 3	99 16	128 28	155 53	181 28
	25	205 44	229 22	252 57	276 56			

Ayanamsa: 21° 9′ 14″

Longitudes of Planets

1911		Sun	Mars	Merc.	Merc.	Jupit.	Venus	Saturn	Rahu
Jan.	5	284 3	251 12	294 42R	288 59R	220 13	293 39	29 42	46 12
	15	294 14	258 17	283 00D	280 17D	221 34	306 13	29 52	45 41
	25	304 25	265 25	261 8	284 28	222 43	318 45	30 12	45 8
Feb.	4	314 34	272 36	289 22	295 15	223 36	331 16	30 43	44 36
	14	324 41	279 51	301 49	308 53	224 12	343 44	31 23	44 5
	24	334 46	287 8	316 25	324 22	224 31R	356 10	32 12	43 33
March	6	344 48	294 29	332 46	341 37	224 31	8 33	33 8	43 1
	16	354 47	301 51	350 56	0 43	224 12	20 51	34 11	42 29
	26	4 43	309 16	10 49	20 53	223 35	33 15	35 18	41 58
April	5	14 35	316 42	30 14	38 6	222 42	45 14	36 30	41 26
	15	24 24	324 9	43 56	47 24R	221 37	57 16	37 45	40 55
	25	34 10	331 37	48 19R	47 2	220 24R	69 12	39 1	40 22
May	5	43 52	339 3	44 15	41 16	219 8	80 59	40 18	39 51
	15	53 32	346 28	39 15D	38 58D	217 54	92 37	41 35	39 19
	25	63 9	353 51	40 33	43 51	216 47	104 4	42 50	38 47
June	4	72 45	1 10	48 41	54 51	215 51	115 17	44 2	38 15
	14	82 18	8 23	62 16	70 52	215 10	126 13	45 11	37 44
	24	91 51	15 30	80 34	91 6	214 46R	136 46	46 15	37 12
July	4	101 23	22 27	101 58	112 36	214 44D	146 49	47 14	36 40
	14	110 55	29 14	122 41	132 1	214 52	156 13	48 6	36 8
	24	120 28	35 47	140 36	148 26	215 21	164 41	48 50	35 37
Aug.	3	130 1	42 3	155 29	161 43	216 7	171 49	49 26	35 6
	13	139 36	48 00	166 59	171 30	217 8	177 1	49 52	34 33
	23	149 14	53 32	173 35R	173 53R	218 23	179 25R	50 8	34 1
Sep.	2	158 53	58 33	172 7	167 56	219 49	178 10	50 14R	33 30
	12	168 36	62 57	163 6	160 15D	221 27	173 21	50 9	32 57
	22	178 21	66 34	161 7D	165 39	223 14	167 24	49 53	32 26
Oct.	2	188 10	69 13	172 45	181 6	225 8	163 46	49 28	31 54
	12	198 2	70 43	189 51	198 32	227 9	164 00D	48 54	31 23
	22	207 58	70 50R	207 3	215 19	229 15	167 45	48 13	30 50
Nov.	1	217 57	69 29	228 22	231 14	231 24	174 3	47 26	30 19
	11	227 59	66 47	238 56	246 30	233 36	182 7	46 38	29 47
	21	238 4	63 13	253 55	261 8	235 49	191 25	45 50	29 16
Dec.	1	248 11	59 32	267 59	274 5	238 2	201 34	45 5	28 43
	11	258 20	56 33	278 42R	280 29R	240 14	212 19	44 25	28 12
	21	268 31	54 45	277 53	271 35	242 22	223 30	43 54	27 40
	31	278 43	54 20D	265 57	–	244 26	235 1	43 32	27 8

Ayanamsa : 21° 10' 4"

Longitude of the Moon

1911		Sun.	Tues.	Thur.	Sat.	Mon.	Wed.	Fri.
Jan.	1	289 9	314 7	339 50	6 27	34 6	62 53	92 27
	15	121 56	150 17	176 55	201 54	225 49	249 23	273 17
	29	297 56	323 31					
Feb.	1						336 38	3 25
	5	30 49	58 48	87 20	116 6	144 26	171 37	197 20
	19	221 45	245 28	269 12	293 35	319 6		
March	1						345 49	13 26
	5	41 33	69 48	97 59	125 57	153 21	179 50	205 12
	19	229 32	253 17	277 2	301 27	327 7	354 16	22 39
April	1				37 7	66 9	94 49	122 44
	9	149 48	175 57	201 13	225 39	249 31	273 11	297 11
	23	322 7	348 30	16 32	45 55			
May	1					75 46	105 6	133 14
	7	159 59	185 33	210 13	234 17	258 1	281 42	305 44
	21	330 36	356 48	24 42	54 13	84 34	114 30	
	31	85 33						
June	1			128 59	156 37	182 35	207 18	231 18
	11	254 59	278 41	302 40	327 11	352 37	19 24	47 56
	25	77 44	108 11	137 49				
July	1				165 42	191 44	216 20	240 11
	9	263 49	287 39	311 55	336 46	2 25	29 7	57 11
	23	86 35	116 38	146 9	174 7	200 15		
Aug.	1		212 43	236 52	260 33	284 21	308 41	333 42
	13	359 27	25 58	53 22	81 45	110 54	140 9	168 33
	27	195 27	220 47	244 59				
Sep.	1							256 52
	3	280 37	304 49	329 51	355 51	22 43	50 15	78 19
	17	106 45	135 15	163 18	190 23	216 12	240 50	264 45
Oct.	1	288 31	312 46	338 2	4 33	32 14	60 39	82 18
	15	117 43	145 36	172 45	199 1	224 21	248 48	272 40
	29	296 24	320 36					
Nov.	1						333 3	358 59
	5	26 31	55 25	84 59	114 14	142 31	169 34	195 33
	19	220 40	245 6	269 3	292 46	316 36	341 5	
Dec.	1							6 49
	3	34 18	63 33	93 52	123 56	152 40	179 41	205 16
	17	229 52	253 56	277 43	301 27	325 20	349 45	15 15
	31	42 23						

Ayanamsa: 21° 10' 4"

6

Longitudes of Planets

1912		Sun.	Mars.	Merc.	Merc.	Jupit.	Venus	Saturn	Rahu
Jan.	5	283 48	54 36	264 12D	266 3	245 26	240 51	43 24R	26 52
	15	294 00	56 00	270 12	275 42	247 21	252 41	43 18R	26 21
	25	304 11	56 23	262 00	286 51	249 7	264 30	43 24D	25 49
Feb.	4	314 20	61 33	296 6	303 42	250 44	276 43	43 40	25 17
	14	324 27	65 19	311 39	319 57	252 9	288 52	44 7	24 45
	24	334 32	69 33	328 27	337 44	253 20	301 3	44 44	24 14
March	5	344 34	74 9	347 13	356 58	254 17	313 17	45 30	23 42
	15	354 33	79 3	6 38	15 35	254 57	325 31	46 24	23 10
	25	4 29	84 10	22 53	27 45	255 19	337 47	47 25	22 38
April	4	14 21	89 29	29 43	28 50R	255 23R	350 3	48 31	22 6
	14	24 10	94 56	25 54R	22 20	255 8	2 19	49 42	21 35
	24	33 56	100 30	19 42	18 53D	254 35	14 35	50 56	21 3
May	4	43 38	106 10	20 3	23 1	253 46	26 51	52 13	20 31
	14	53 18	111 55	27 29	33 13	252 43	39 6	53 30	19 59
	24	62 55	117 45	40 2	47 54	251 32R	51 22	54 47	19 28
June	3	72 31	123 39	56 44	56 44	250 16	63 37	56 4	18 55
	13	82 4	129 36	77 8	88 6	249 1	75 53	57 18	18 24
	23	91 37	135 36	98 53	109 4	247 52	88 10	58 29	17 52
July	3	101 9	141 40	118 27	126 59	246 54R	100 27	59 36	17 21
	13	110 41	147 47	134 39	141 25	246 10	112 45	60 38	16 49
	23	120 14	153 57	147 12	151 51	245 42R	125 3	61 34	16 17
Aug.	2	129 47	160 11	155 5	156 23R	245 33R	137 23	62 22	15 45
	12	139 22	166 28	155 53R	153 2	245 42D	149 43	63 2	15 13
	22	149 00	172 49	148 48	144 59	246 9	162 4	63 34	14 41
Sep.	1	158 39	179 14	143 37	145 41D	246 53	174 75	63 55	14 10
	11	168 22	185 42	151 1	158 41	247 53	186 45	64 5	13 38
	21	178 7	192 15	167 32	176 42	249 8	199 6	64 6R	13 7
Oct.	1	187 56	198 52	185 46	194 33	250 35	211 26	63 54	12 34
	11	197 48	205 33	203 00	211 9	252 14	223 45	63 33	12 3
	21	207 43	212 19	219 2	226 40	254 2	236 3	63 2	11 31
	31	217 42	219 9	234 5	241 16	255 59	248 20	62 23	10 59
Nov.	10	227 44	226 4	248 7	254 27	258 3	260 35	61 38	10 27
	20	237 49	223 4	259 54	263 41R	260 12	272 48	60 50	9 56
	30	247 56	240 8	264 29R	260 59	262 25	284 58	60 1	9 24
Dec.	10	258 6	247 13	254 34	249 21D	264 41	297 5	59 14	8 52
	20	268 16	254 33	248 38D	251 22	266 56	309 5	58 32	8 20
	30	278 25	261 50	248 15	...	269 15	320 57	57 57	7 49

Áyanamsa: **21° 10′ 54″**

Longitude of the Moon

1912		Sun.	Tue.	Thurs.	Sat.	Mon.	Wed.	Fri.
Jan.	1					56 41	86 34	117 17
	7	147 20	175 39	202 2	226 56	250 59	274 43	298 27
	21	322 24	346 44	11 44	37 50	65 30	94 51	
Feb.	1			109 59	140 24	169 52	197 31	223 18
	11	247 45	271 33	295 16	319 15	343 44	8 50	34 42
	25	61 35	89 43	118 57				
March	1							133 48
	3	163 19	191 44	218 31	243 45	267 55	291 40	315 34
	17	340 4	5 21	31 31	58 31	86 17	114 41	143 26
	31	172 00						
April	1					186 1	213 12	239 4
	7	263 46	287 44	311 32	335 47	0 57	27 17	54 44
	21	82 57	111 29	139 52	167 50	195 8		
May	1						221 35	247 5
	5	271 40	295 38	319 26	343 40	8 56	35 40	63 52
	19	93 1	122 15	150 47	178 19	204 53	230 36	255 36
June	1				267 50	291 55	315 40	339 33
	9	4 10	30 8	57 53	87 16	117 21	146 54	175 8
	23	201 55	227 32	252 21	276 38			
July	1					300 31	324 14	348 7
	7	12 39	38 31	66 12	95 43	126 13	156 17	184 52
	21	211 43	237 8	261 37	285 37	309 24	333 9	
Aug.	1			345 6	9 21	34 29	61 4	89 26
	11	119 23	149 52	179 32	207 33	233 42	258 33	282 37
	25	306 23	330 10	354 15	18 50			
Sep.	1	31 25	57 22	84 40	113 25	143 13	173 5	201 57
	15	229 10	254 47	279 13	303 2	326 49	300 56	15 42
	29	41 15						
Oct.	1		67 43	95 8	123 29	152 30	181 34	209 58
	13	237 6	262 47	287 18	311 8	334 56	359 4	24 29
	27	50 48	78 5	106 2				
Nov.	1							120 9
	3	148 29	176 46	204 41	231 52	258 00	283 00	307 6
	17	330 48	354 46	19 40	45 56	73 37	102 14	131 3
Dec.	1	159 28	187 12	214 6	240 39	266 16	291 1	315 1
	15	338 39	2 32	27 22	53 47	82 00	111 29	141 11
	29	170 6	197 48					

Ayanamsa : 21° 10' 54"

RAMAN'S EPHEMERIS

Longitudes of Planets

1913		Sun	Mars	Merc.	Merc.	Jupit.	Venus	Saturn	Rahu
Jan.	5	284 35	266 15	263 36	270 24	270 37	328 00	57 40R	7 29
	15	294 46	273 41	277 34	285 1	272 51	339 33	57 20	6 57
	25	304 57	281 10	292 44	300 42	275 1	350 47	57 10	6 26
Feb.	4	315 6	288 43	308 58	317 33	277 7	1 37	57 13D	5 54
	14	325 13	296 19	326 27	335 40	279 6	11 55	57 26	5 23
	24	335 18	303 58	345 3	354 13	280 57	21 26	57 50	4 51
March	6	345 20	311 39	2 23	8 33	282 38	29 50	58 24	4 19
	16	355 19	319 23	11 40R	11 23	284 7	36 41	59 8	3 47
	26	5 14	327 7	8 17	4 7	285 24	41 12	60 00	3 15
April	5	15 6	334 51	0 49	359 33	286 26	42 27R	60 59	2 43
	15	24 55	342 35	0 28D	3 16	287 12	39 45	62 4	2 9
	25	34 40	350 19	7 36	13 9	287 40	33 59	63 14	1 40
May	5	44 22	358 00	19 42	27 11	287 50	28 26R	64 27	1 8
	15	54 2	5 38	35 29	44 41	287 41R	26 4	35 43	0 37
	25	63 39	13 13	54 41	65 23	287 14	27 36D	67 1	0 5
June	4	73 14	20 44	76 22	87 7	286 30	32 11	68 19	359 33
	14	82 48	28 9	97 12	106 22	285 31	38 54	69 36	359 01
	24	92 20	35 28	114 33	121 44	284 21	47 4	70 52	358 29
July	4	101 52	42 40	127 50	132 45	283 5	56 14	72 5R	357 57
	14	111 25	49 44	136 16	138 4R	281 49	66 6	73 14	357 26
	24	120 57	56 39	137 55R	135 46	280 37	76 29	74 18	356 54
Aug.	3	130 31	63 24	132 12	128 37	279 35	87 16	75 16	356 23
	13	140 6	69 57	126 41	127 29D	278 46	98 22	76 8	355 51
	23	149 44	76 55	131 21	137 55	278 14	109 43	76 52	355 19
Sep.	2	159 24	82 23	146 23	155 47	278 1	121 18	77 27	354 47
	12	169 6	88 12	165 22	174 43	278 6D	133 3	77 52	354 15
	22	178 52	93 40	183 41	192 15	278 31	144 59	78 6	353 44
Oct.	2	188 41	98 45	200 27	208 17	279 13	157 3	78 10R	353 12
	12	198 33	103 21	215 49	223 1	280 12	169 15	78 3	352 40
	22	208 29	107 21	229 51	236 13	281 27	181 82	77 45	352 8
Nov.	1	218 28	110 39	241 52	246 20	282 55	193 55	77 17	351 36
	11	228 30	113 3	248 43	247 45R	284 36	206 22	76 41	351 4
	21	238 35	114 22	242 44	236 13	286 27	218 52	75 57	350 33
Dec.	1	248 43	114 25	232 47	233 49D	288 26	231 23	75 9	350 1
	11	258 52	113 4	237 58	243 48	290 33	243 57	74 20	349 29
	21	269 2	110 23	250 29	257 37	292 46	256 31	73 32	348 51
	31	279 14	106 43	265 1	–	295 8	269 5	72 48	348 26

Ayanamsa: 21° 11' 45"

Longitude of the Moon

1913	Sun.	Tue.	Thur.	Sat.	Mon.	Wed.	Fri.
Jan. 1						211 13	237 19
5	262 39	287 20	311 25	335 5	358 2	22 52	48 16
19	75 30	104 38	134 57	165 6	193 59	221 16	247 10
Feb. 1				259 42	284 14	308 15	331 57
9	355 33	19 27	44 7	70 10	98 3	127 40	158 11
23	188 16	216 52	243 43				
March 1				269 2	293 21	317 7	340 45
9	4 30	28 41	53 36	79 40	107 11	136 13	166 14
23	196 13	225 4	252 14	277 44	302 3		
April 1		313 56	337 32	1 19	25 36	50 39	76 35
13	103 30	131 29	160 24	189 47	218 51	246 50	273 15
27	298 12	322 10					
May 1			345 48	9 43	34 24	60 6	86 46
11	114 13	142 14	170 38	199 11	227 29	254 57	281 11
25	306 7	330 6	353 45	17 47			
June 1	30 7	55 45	82 42	110 38	139 2	167 24	195 30
15	223 13	250 22	276 39	301 53	336 9	349 50	13 35
29	38 6						
July 1		63 59	91 28	120 12	149 13	178 13	206 18
13	233 32	259 57	285 33	310 19	334 21	357 59	21 42
27	46 12	72 6	99 47				
Aug. 1							114 14
3	143 56	173 44	202 43	230 27	256 56	282 24	307 2
17	331 3	354 42	18 19	42 21	67 25	94 3	122 29
31	152 21						
Sep. 1					167 31	197 35	226 26
7	253 41	279 26	304 5	328 2	351 41	15 19	39 15
21	63 52	89 35	116 48	145 39	175 42		
Oct. 1						205 57	235 12
5	262 45	288 34	313 4	336 50	0 25	24 13	48 32
19	63 31	99 25	126 26	154 44	184 10	214 2	243 18
Nov. 1				257 23	284 14	309 25	333 27
9	357 2	20 48	45 11	70 24	96 26	123 13	150 46
23	179 6	208 3	237 4	265 18			
Dec. 1					292 7	317 21	341 26
7	5 2	28 53	53 35	79 22	106 12	133 45	161 40
21	189 47	218 2	246 8	273 37	299 59	325 6	

Ayanamsa: 21° 11' 45"

Longitudes of Planets

1914		Sun	Mars	Merc.	Merc.	Jupit.	Venus	Saturn	Rahu
Jan.	5	284 20	104 43R	272 35	280 20	296 12	275 22	72 28R	348 10
	15	294 31	100 55	288 16	296 25	298 33	287 57	71 54	347 38
	25	304 42	97 55	304 48	313 26	300 55	300 31	71 30	347 6
Feb.	4	314 51	96 8	322 18	331 15	303 16	314 20	71 16	346 34
	14	324 58	95 41D	339 55	347 32	305 35	325 37	71 13D	346 3
	24	335 3	96 27	352 54R	—R	307 51	338 8	71 27	345 31
March	6	345 5	98 16	352 53	348 25	310 2	350 38	71 41	344 59
	16	355 4	100 54	343 54	341 21D	312 8	3 5	72 12	344 27
	26	4 59	104 13	341 17D	343 24	314 6	15 31	72 51	343 56
April	5	14 52	108 4	347 13	352 19	315 55	27 54	73 40	343 21
	15	24 40	112 19	358 26	5 25	317 33	40 14	74 36	342 52
	25	34 26	116 56	13 10	21 39	319 00	52 32	75 38	342 20
May	5	44 8	121 48	30 53	40 51	320 13	64 47	76 46	341 49
	15	53 48	126 55	51 27	62 32	321 10	76 58	77 58	341 17
	25	63 25	132 13	73 6	88 8	321 51	89 7	79 13	340 45
June	4	73 25	137 41	92 10	100 4	322 13	101 12	80 30	340 13
	14	82 34	143 17	106 46	112 12	322 17R	113 12	81 49	339 42
	24	92 7	149 1	116 12	118 34R	322 1	125 8	83 6	339 10
July	4	101 39	154 52	119 4R	117 40	321 27	136 59	84 23	338 38
	14	111 11	160 40	114 49	111 34	320 37	148 44	85 38	338 6
	24	120 44	166 53	109 18D	109 4D	319 32	160 20	86 49	337 28
Aug.	3	130 17	173 3	111 23	116 16	318 18	171 48	87 57	337 3
	13	139 52	179 19	123 27	132 20	317 1	183 4	88 58	336 31
	23	149 30	185 40	142 8	152 5	315 44	194 6	89 54	335 59
Sep.	2	159 10	192 8	161 46	170 59	314 34	204 5	90 42	335 28
	12	168 52	198 41	179 44	188 1	313 37	215 9	91 21	334 55
	22	178 38	203 20	195 52	203 19	312 55	224 55	91 51	334 24
Oct.	2	188 27	212 14	210 21	216 54	312 32	233 55	92 11	333 52
	12	198 19	218 55	222 50	227 54	312 28D	241 47	92 20R	333 20
	22	208 15	225 52	231 34R	232 59R	312 44	247 58	92 17	332 48
Nov.	1	218 14	232 54	231 2	225 32	313 15	251 41	92 4	332 17
	11	228 16	240 2	219 28	216 59D	314 13	251 54R	91 40	331 45
	21	238 21	247 16	218 57D	223 53	315 23	248 16	91 7	331 7
Dec.	1	248 28	254 36	230 20	237 29	316 48	243 23	90 26	330 41
	11	258 37	262 00	244 57	252 34	318 27	237 54	89 40	330 10
	21	268 48	269 30	260 16	268 4	320 17	237 12D	88 51	329 38
	31	278 59	277 5	265 57	—	322 16	240 15	88 2	329 6

Ayanamsa: 21° 12′ 35″

Longitude of the Moon

1914		Sun.	Tue.	Thur.	Sat.	Mon.	Wed.	Fri.
Jan.	1			337 15	1 1	24 40	48 56	74 23
	11	101 16	129 20	158 00	186 37	214 50	242 29	269 28
	25	295 38	320 50	345 10	8 53			
Feb.	1	20 41	44 31	69 16	95 27	123 19	152 28	182 5
	15	211 15	239 24	266 22	292 16	317 16	341 34	5 21
March	1	28 58	52 48	77 27	103 26	131 10	160 32	190 47
	15	220 43	249 23	276 24	301 58	326 29	350 23	14 2
	29	37 42	61 40					
April	1						73 53	99 4
	5	125 37	153 52	183 40	214 10	244 3	272 18	298 40
	19	323 31	347 28	11 3	34 44	58 45	83 19	
May	1							108 40
	3	135 6	162 56	192 14	222 25	252 18	280 45	307 18
	17	332 12	356 7	19 43	43 31	67 53	92 56	118 43
	31	145 21						
June	1					159 3	187 15	216 28
	7	246 1	274 56	302 21	328 4	352 28	16 11	39 56
	21	64 15	90 25	115 28	142 17	169 48		
July	1						197 56	226 34
	5	255 17	283 27	310 25	335 59	0 23	24 10	48 0
	19	72 28	96 00	124 42	152 20	180 33	208 58	237 19
Aug.	1				251 22	279 1	305 49	331 33
	9	356 16	20 14	43 58	68 4	92 7	119 31	147 20
	23	176 11	205 29	234 17	262 4	290 2		
Sep.	1		302 19	327 41	352 25	16 31	40 15	64 3
	13	88 29	114 6	141 20	170 12	200 5	229 54	255 41
	27	285 1	311 56					
Oct.	1			336 55	1 12	25 5	48 47	72 37
	11	96 50	122 24	149 24	173 16	208 31	236 58	266 17
	25	295 47	321 35	346 11	10 9			
Nov.	1	22 2	45 46	69 37	93 48	118 38	144 35	172 8
	15	201 27	231 55	262 12	291 1	317 51	343 00	7 6
	29	30 40						
Dec.	1		54 35	78 40	168 12	128 22	154 24	181 40
	13	210 23	240 13	270 9	296 56	326 00	351 19	15 31
	27	39 14	61 4	87 25				

Ayanamsa: 21° 12' 35"

Longitudes of Planets

1915		Sun	Mars	Merc.	Merc.	Jupit.	Venus	Saturn	Rahu
Jan.	5	284 5	280 53	293 59	292 10	323 19	242 53	87 38R	328 50
	15	294 16	288 34	300 32	309 2	325 30	249 49	86 54	328 18
	25	304 27	296 18	317 32	325 41	327 46	258 18	86 17	327 47
Feb.	4	314 36	304 5	332 40	337 12	330 7	267 50	85 48	327 15
	14	324 44	311 54	337 51R	334 27	332 30	278 5	85 30	326 43
	24	334 49	319 45	329 4	—	334 54	288 00	85 22	326 12
March	6	344 50	327 37	323 16	324 23D	337 19	299 56	85 26	325 39
	16	354 50	335 28	327 31	332 7	339 42	311 18	85 41	325 8
	26	4 42	343 19	337 48	344 20	342 3	322 51	86 7	324 36
April	5	14 37	351 9	357 35	359 30	344 20	334 31	86 42	324 5
	15	24 26	358 57	8 3	17 15	346 32	346 19	87 27	323 32
	25	34 12	6 41	27 7	37 34	348 37	358 10	88 19	323 1
May	5	43 55	14 22	48 21	58 59	350 35	10 5	89 19	322 29
	15	53 34	21 59	68 54	77 41	352 23	22 3	90 24	321 51
	25	63 12	29 32	85 8	91 9	354 00	34 3	91 34	321 25
June	4	72 47	36 59	95 38	98 24	355 25	46 6	92 48	320 53
	14	82 21	44 20	99 20R	98 25R	356 36	58 10	94 4	320 22
	24	91 53	51 36	96 3	93 8	357 31	70 16	95 22	319 50
July	4	101 25	58 45	90 54D	90 17D	358 9	82 23	96 40	339 18
	14	110 57	65 47	91 47	95 29	358 28	94 36	97 57	318 47
	24	120 30	72 42	101 18	109 2	358 28R	106 49	99 13	318 15
Aug.	3	130 3	79 39	118 16	128 23	358 9	119 5	100 26	317 37
	13	139 39	86 9	138 40	148 39	357 30	131 24	101 36	317 11
	23	149 16	92 40	158 8	167 3	356 35	143 45	102 41	316 40
Sep.	2	158 55	99 1	175 25	183 17	355 27	156 8	103 39	316 5
	12	168 38	105 12	190 38	197 28	354 10	168 34	104 31	315 36
	22	178 24	111 12	203 42	209 10	352 50	181 1	105 14	315 14
Oct.	2	188 12	116 59	213 35	216 23	351 34	193 29	105 49	314 33
	12	198 5	122 32	216 47R	213 54	350 26	205 57	106 14	314 1
	22	208 7	127 48	208 11	202 49D	349 32	218 27	106 27	313 29
Nov.	1	217 59	132 43	201 21	204 13	348 55	230 56	106 30R	312 57
	11	228 1	137 14	209 53	216 55	348 38	243 26	106 22	312 25
	21	238 6	141 16	224 32	232 20	348 41D	255 55	106 2	311 54
Dec.	1	248 13	144 42	240 11	248 1	349 5	268 24	105 33	311 22
	11	258 22	147 23	255 51	263 43	349 49	280 53	104 55	310 50
	21	268 33	149 9	271 38	279 38	350 50	293 21	104 11	310 19
	31	278 44	149 49	287 44	—	352 8	305 47	103 23	309 46

Ayanamsa: 21° 13' 25"

Longitude of the Moon

1915		Sun.	Tue.	Thurs.	Sat.	Mon.	Wed.	Fri.
Jan.	1							99 50
	3	125 15	151 24	178 21	206 12	234 54	264 12	292 48
	17	320 26	346 35	11 23	35 21	59 6	83 15	108 15
	31	134 16						
Feb.	1					147 39	175 3	203 3
	7	231 23	259 45	287 49	315 12	341 35	6 51	31 11
	21	55 00	78 53	103 26	129 10			
March	1					156 18	184 38	213 34
	7	242 24	270 35	297 56	324 26	350 6	14 59	39 11
	21	62 59	86 48	111 16	136 58	164 22	133·21	
April	1			208 15	238 6	267 10	294·55	321 21
	11	346 47	11 30	35 41	59 32	83 15	107 15	132 7
	25	158 30	186 47	216 43				
May	1				247 12	276 53	304 54	331 14
	9	356 20	20 39	44 35	68 19	92 5	116 10	141 1
	23	167 14	195 16	225 3	255 41	285 41		
June	1		300 6	327 30	353 13	17 44	41 39	65 23
	13	89 11	113 17	137 56	163 32	190 29	219 4	248 58
	27	279 80	308 26					
July	1			336 1	1 53	26 28	50 22	74 6
	11	98 4	122 31	147 40	173 42	200 48	229 4	258 16
	25	287 45	316 35	344 5	10 3			
Aug.	1	22 31	46 45	70 31	94 25	118 54	144 13	170 30
	15	197 42	225 38	254 6	282 45	311 8	338 45	5 13
	29	30 27	54 42					
Sep.	1						66 37	90 24
	5	114 38	139 50	166 18	193 57	222 19	250 53	279 11
	19	307 00	334 11	0 35	26 4	50 38	74 32	
Oct.	1							98 15
	3	122 27	147 47	174 41	203 7	232 26	261 39	290 3
	17	317 25	343 53	9 34	34 33	58 52	82 40	106 19
	31	130 25						
Nov.	1					142 51	168 53	196 50
	7	226 25	256 36	286 7	314 14	340 55	6 29	31 17
	21	55 32	79 22	103 00	126 47	151 16		
Dec.	1						177 7	204 51
	5	234 26	264 59	295 6	323 43	350 35	16 1	40 36
	19	64 27	88 9	111 52	135 50	160 26	186 12	213 34

Ayanamsa: 21° 13′ 25″

Longitudes of Planets

1916		Sun	Mars.	Merc.	Merc.	Jupit.	Venus	Saturn	Rahu
Jan.	5	283 49	149 41R	295 52	303 55	352 52	312 00	102 58R	309 31
	15	294 1	148 44	311 25	317 47	354 31	324 22	102 9	308 58
	25	304 12	145 50	321 26R	320 53R	356 21	336 41	101 23	308 27
Feb.	4	314 21	142 16	316 13	310 25	358 21	348 55	100 42	307 55
	14	324 29	138 18	306 49	306 23D	0 29	1 3	100 10	307 24
	24	334 34	134 46	308 33D	312 32	2 43	13 2	99 47	306 52
March	5	344 35	131 59	317 45	323 53	5 2	24 51	99 35	306 20
	15	354 35	130 34	330 43	338 8	7 25	36 28	99 34D	305 42
	25	4 31	130 25D	346 8	354 41	9 49	47 50	99 43	305 16
April	4	14 23	131 26	3 49	13 32	12 14	58 51	100 4	304 44
	14	24 12	133 26	23 47	34 21	14 39	69 28	100 35	304 00
	24	33 58	136 13	44 48	54 30	17 2	79 31	101 16	303 41
May	4	43 41	139 40	62 55	69 45	19 22	88 49	102 5	303 9
	14	53 20	143 38	74 50	78 2	21 38	97 3	103 1	302 38
	24	62 58	148 1	79 16R	78 34R	23 48	103 47	104 3	302 06
June	3	72 33	152 45	76 24	73 39	25 52	108 18	105 11	301 34
	13	82 7	157 48	71 28D	70 49D	27 48	109 42R	106 23	301 2
	23	91 39	163 5	71 53	74 57	29 35	107 16	107 37	300 31
July	3	101 11	168 35	79 52	86 29	31 10	101 43	108 54	299 58
	13	110 43	174 18	94 41	104 13	32 33	96 1	110 12	299 27
	23	120·16	180 10	114 34	125 8	33 41	93 17	111 30	298 55
Aug.	2	129 50	186 13	135 24	145 6	34 34	94 24D	112 46	298 23
	12	139 25	192 25	154 10	162 36	35 8	91 39	114 1	297 51
	22	149 2	198 45	170 27	177 41	35 24	105 11	115 12	297 20
Sep.	1	158 42	205 14	184 17	190 9	35 19R	113 16	116 19	296 48
	11	168 24	211 51	195 6	198 46	34 55	122 27	117 20	296 16
	21	178 10	218 35	200 37R	199 57R	34 12	132 25	118 15	295 44
Oct.	1	187 58	225 28	196 16	190 39	33 13	142 59	119 3	295 13
	11	197 50	232 27	186 15D	185 52D	32 1	153 59	119 41	294 41
	21	207 46	239 34	189 35	195 56	30 41	165 21	120 10	294 9
	31	217 45	246 47	203 83	—	29 20	177 1	120 29	293 37
Nov.	10	227 47	254 7	219 45	227 50	28 4	188 53	120 35R	293 5
	20	237 51	261 33	235 49	243 43	26 59	200 56	120 32	292 34
	30	247 59	269 5	251 34	—	26 9	213 7	120 17	292 2
Dec.	10	258 8.	276 42	267 12	275 1	25 37	225 23	119 52	291 30
	20	268 18	284 34	282 46	290 20	25 25	237 45	119 18	290 58
	30	278 30	292 10	297 18	—	25 35D	250 9	118 36	290 21

Ayanamsa: 21° 14′ 16″

Longitude of the Moon

1916		Sun.	Tues.	Thur.	Sat.	Mon.	Wed.	Fri.
Jan.	1				227 54	257 42	288 6	317 50
	9	345 59	12 22	37 18	61 70	85 1	108 45	132 50
	23	217 30	183 00	209 35	237 26	266 29		
Feb.	1		281 18	311 00	339 57	7 25	33 14	57 45
	13	81 32	105 12	129 17	154 7	179 52	206 32	233 59
	27	262 9	290 49					
March	1						305 14	333 53
	5	1 44	28 19	53 30	77 38	101 18	125 11	149 53
	19	175 46	202 50	230 43	258 59	287 13	315 19	343 4
April	1				356 43	23 24	48 59	73 20
	9	97 18	120 59	145 16	170 46	197 50	226 13	255 12
	23	284 00	312 9	339 35	6 17			
May	1					32 14	57 20	81 37
	7	105 19	128 58	153 13	178 45	206 3	234 58	264 43
	21	294 14	322 44	350 1	16 14	41 33	66 8	
June	1			78 11	101 57	125 31	149 22	174 8
	11	200 26	228 35	258 18	288 35	318 14	346 30	13 13
	25	38 39	63 10	87 5				
July	1				110 42	134 18	158 17	183 7
	9	209 17	237 10	266 39	296 59	326 59	355 39	23 35
	23	37 57	72 15	95 57	119 32	143 20		
Aug.	1		155 24	180 3	205 39	232 31	260 48	290 49
	13	320 22	349 51	17 53	44 9	68 55	92 47	116 21
	27	140 10	154 35	189 46				
Sep.	1							202 41
	3	229 12	256 39	285 5	314 16	343 35	12 11	30 20
	17	64 52	89 8	112 46	136 30	160 53	186 14	212 35
Oct.	1	239 44	267 26	295 35	324 3	352 32	20 29	47 18
	15	72 44	97 00	120 30	144 26	169 00	194 49	221 55
	29	249 55	278 16					
Nov.	1						292 26	320 37
	5	348 30	15 56	42 36	68 16	92 52	116 41	140 17
	19	184 22	189 36	216 24	244 40	273 49	302 57	
Dec.	1							331 28
	3	359 6	25 51	51 44	76 46	101 2	124 46	148 22
	17	172 23	197 29	224 12	252 41	282 25	312 24	341 36
	31	9 27						

Ayanamsa: 21° 14' 16"

Longitudes of Planets

1917		Sun	Mars	Merc.	Merc.	Jupit.	Venus	Saturn	Rahu
Jan.	5	284 37	296 51	303 42R	305 40R	25 51	257 37	118 8R	290 8
	15	294 48	304 41	303 3	297 1	26 32	270 4	117 20	289 36
	25	304 59	312 34	291 39	289 39	27 32	282 33	116 30	289 4
Feb.	4	315 8	320 28	290 53D	294 22D	28 48	295 2	115 43	288 32
	14	325 15	328 23	299 18	305 12	30 18	307 30	115 1	288 00
	24	335 20	336 17	311 48	—	32 00	319 59	114 26	287 29
March	6	345 21	344 10	326 35	334 42	33 53	332 27	114 1	286 57
	16	355 20	352 1	343 17	352 24	35 55	344 53	113 44	286 25
	26	5 16	359 50	2 1	12 6	38 4	357 19	113 35D	285 54
April	5	15 8	7 35	22 25	32 30	40 18	9 44	113 45	285 22
	15	24 56	15 6	41 39	49 15	42 36	22 7	114 2	284 50
	25	34 42	22 54	54 52	58 19	44 56	34 29	114 29	284 18
May	5	44 24	30 26	59 30R	58 34R	47 19	46 49	115 6	283 46
	15	54 4	37 54	56 8	53 16	49 41	59 8	115 52	283 14
	25	63 41	45 16	51 10	50 38D	52 3	71 26	116 45	282 42
June	4	73 16	52 33	51 56	55 1	54 22	83 43	117 45	282 11
	14	82 50	59 45	59 43	65 54	56 38	95 59	118 50	281 39
	24	92 23	66 50	73 26	82 15	58 50	108 13	120 00	281 7
July	4	101 55	73 50	92 12	102 50	60 57	120 27	121 13	280 36
	14	111 27	80 44	113 36	128 59	62 56	132 40	122 29	280 4
	24	120 59	87 32	133 44	142 47	64 47	144 51	123 46	279 32
Aug.	3	130 33	94 15	151 7	158 45	66 28	157 00	125 3	279 00
	13	140 8	100 51	165 41	171 50	67 57	169 17	126 20	278 29
	23	149 46	107 21	177 4	181 7	69 13	181 12	127 35	277 57
Sep.	2	159 25	113 45	183 35	183 55R	70 14	193 14	128 47	277 25
	12	169 8	120 2	181 38R	177 1	70 59	205 11	129 56	276 54
	22	178 54	126 13	172 1	169 32	71 25	217 5	130 59	276 21
Oct.	2	188 43	132 15	171 6D	176 14D	71 31R	228 54	131 56	275 50
	12	198 35	138 10	183 33	191 49	71 17	240 37	132 41	275 18
	22	208 31	143 55	200 21	208 48	70 43	252 12	133 27	274 46
Nov.	1	218 30	149 29	217 5	225 12	69 52	263 36	133 59	274 15
	11	228 32	154 51	233 8	240 57	68 46	274 46	134 20	273 43
	21	238 37	159 59	248 40	256 18	67 29	285 36	134 31	273 11
Dec.	1	248 44	164 49	263 49	271 9	66 7	295 59	134 31R	272 39
	11	258 54	169 18	278 7	284 14	64 48	305 41	134 19	272 7
	21	269 5	173 22	288 33	289 53R	63 35	314 23	133 57	271 35
	31	279 16	176 54	285 55R	—	62 37	321 37	133 25	271 4

Ayanamsa: 21° 15′ 6″

Longitude of the Moon

1917	Sun.	Tue.	Thur.	Sat.	Mon.	Wed.	Fri.
Jan. 1					22 51	48 41	73 32
7	97 42	121 27	145 3	168 52	193 19	218 58	246 14
21	275 16	305 31	335 49	5 1	32 27	58 13	
Feb. 1			70 36	94 43	118 24	142 1	165 51
11	190 10	215 15	241 28	269 10	298 25	328 40	358 46
25	27 30	54 20					
March 1			79 28	103 29	127 4	150 45	174 53
11	199 39	225 8	251 29	278 54	307 32	337 8	6 49
25	35 30	62 28	87 43	111 48			
April 1	123 37	147 15	171 20	196 13	221 57	248 27	275 39
15	303 34	332 9	1 6	29 42	57 11	83 9	107 46
29	131 35						
May 1		155 18	179 33	204 47	231 9	258 26	286 20
13	314 33	342 53	11 5	38 47	65 33	91 8	115 38
27	139 28	163 13	187 31				
June 1							200 4
3	226 10	253 37	282 6	310 59	339 42	7 50	35 10
17	61 36	87 6	111 44	135 41	159 22	183 18	208 5
July 1	234 13	261 59	291 5	320 49	350 11	18 28	45 28
15	71 16	96 9	120 21	144 9	167 49	191 45	216 26
29	242 25	270 7					
Aug. 1						284 37	314 35
5	344 55	14 22	42 11	68 20	93 14	117 21	141 6
19	164 47	188 38	212 56	238 8	264 41	292 59	322 53
Sep. 1				338 10	8 34	37 38	64 46
9	90 10	114 26	138 9	161 50	185 44	210 2	234 57
23	260 46	287 54	316 35	346 34			
Oct. 1					16 47	45 57	73 17
7	98 48	123 4	146 47	170 31	194 40	219 24	244 49
21	270 59	298 6	326 22	355 36	25 8	53 55	
Nov. 1			67 47	94 12	119 8	143 7	166 50
11	190 52	215 38	241 18	267 48	295 2	322 54	351 18
25	19 56	48 17	75 45				
Dec. 1				101 57	126 53	150 56	174 41
9	198 46	223 43	249 51	277 10	305 19	333 51	22 18
23	30 19	57 43	84 19	109 58	134 43		

Ayanamsa: 21° 15' 6"

Longitudes of Planets

1918		Sun	Mars	Merc.	Merc.	Jupit.	Venus	Saturn	Rahu
Jan.	5	284 22	178 26	279 24R	274 33	62 13R	324 28	133 6R	290 48
	15	294 33	180 56	273 34D	275 48	61 41	328 3R	132 24	270 26
	25	304 44	182 32	280 4	285 35	61 28D	327 57	131 37	269 44
Feb.	4	314 53	183 4R	291 53	298 44	61 36	323 53	130 48	269 12
	14	325 00	182 21	306 2	313 44	62 4	317 51	130 00	268 41
	24	335 5	180 21	321 49	330 19	62 51	313 30	129 15	268 9
March	6	345 7	177 13	339 15	348 37	63 55	313 2D	128 38	267 37
	16	355 6	173 24	358 24	8 24	65 13	316 13	128 8	267 5
	26	5 1	169 36	18 9	26 54	66 45	322 3	127 47	266 33
April	5	14 53	166 39	33 51	38 26	68 28	329 43	127 38D	266 2
	15	24 42	164 31	40 21R	39 43R	70 21	338 36	127 39	265 30
	25	34 28	163 51	37 8	33 52	72 21	348 17	127 51	264 58
May	5	44 10	164 25D	31 18	30 23	74 27	358 31	128 13	264 27
	15	53 50	166 5	31 23D	34 10	76 38	9 15	128 45	263 55
	25	63 27	168 39	38 30	44 11	78 53	20 14	129 26	263 23
June	4	73 2	171 58	51 3	59 3	81 10	31 27	130 16	262 57
	14	82 36	175 54	68 8	78 12	83 28	42 50	131 12	262 19
	24	92 9	180 20	88 56	99 51	85 46	54 23	132 14	261 48
July	4	101 41	185 11	110 24	120 17	88 3	66 2	163 22	261 16
	14	111 13	190 23	129 23	137 41	90 17	77 49	134 33	260 43
	24	120 46	195 55	145 11	151 50	92 28	89 41	135 47	260 12
Aug.	3	130 19	201 42	157 34	162 11	94 34	101 38	137 3	259 40
	13	139 55	207 44	165 25	166 52R	96 35	113 42	138 20	259 9
	23	149 32	213 59	166 4R	162 57	98 27	125 50	139 36	258 37
Sep.	2	159 12	220 26	158 22	154 25D	100 11	138 3	140 52	258 6
	12	168 54	227 4	153 19	155 57	101 44	150 21	142 5	257 27
	22	178 40	233 52	161 49	169 41	103 5	162 43	143 14	257 2
Oct.	2	188 29	240 50	178 27	187 23	104 12	175 8	144 19	256 30
	12	198 21	247 57	196 10	204 42	105 2	187 36	145 18	255 58
	22	208 17	255 12	212 57	220 58	105 35	200 6	146 11	255 26
Nov.	1	218 16	262 34	228 46	236 23	105 49	212 38	146 55	254 55
	11	228 18	270 4	243 50	251 4	105 43	225 12	147 31	254 23
	21	238 22	277 39	258 00	264 35	105 18R	237 46	147 56	253 51
Dec.	1	248 29	285 20	269 50	273 18D	104 33	250 20	148 11	253 20
	11	258 39	293 5	273 19R	268 50	103 23	262 55	148 15R	252 48
	21	268 49	300 53	262 9	258 00	102 20	275 29	148 8	252 16
	31	279 1	308 44	258 2	—	101 00	288 3	147 49	251 44

Ayanamsa : 21° 15′ 56″

Longitude of the Moon

1918		Sun.	Tues.	Thur.	Sat.	Mon.	Wed.	Fri.
Jan.	1		146 48	170 38	194 26	218 49	244 23	271 29
	13	300 3	329 27	358 45	27 13	54 31	80 46	106 9
	27	130 51	155 00	178 48				
Feb.	1							190 39
	3	214 36	239 20	265 30	293 28	323 6	353 24	23 5
	17	51 16	77 50	103 8	127 40	151 43	175 32	
March	1							199 17
	3	223 16	247 55	273 50	301 33	231 8	1 45	31 58
	17	60 36	87 20	112 32	136 48	160 39	184 24	208 16
	31	237 27						
April	1					244 44	270 00	296 36
	7	324 53	354 44	25 10	54 50	82 47	108 53	133 36
	21	157 33	181 17	205 10	229 27	254 19		
May	1						279 58	306 41
	5	334 41	3 54	33 40	62 56	90 50	117 5	141 56
	19	165 56	189 42	213 43	238 21	263 48	290 7	317 18
June	1				331 14	359 38	28 30	57 16
	9	85 18	112 7	137 36	162 1	185 52	209 45	234 13
	23	259 41	286 17	313 54	342 9			
July	1					10 38	38 59	66 53
	7	94 5	120 21	145 36	169 57	193 47	217 39	242 11
	21	267 55	295 8	323 38	352 44	21 38	49 47	
Aug.	1			63 32	90 21	116 22	141 36	166 7
	11	190 2	213 44	237 46	262 48	289 26	317 51	347 33
	25	17 25	46 24	74 2	100 24			
Sep.	1	113 12	138 15	162 42	186 39	210 20	234 4	258 25
	15	284 4	311 33	340 56	11 23	41 32	70 16	97 18
	29	122 5						
Oct.	1		147 35	171 41	195 28	219 8	242 57	267 21
	13	292 52	320 5	349 10	19 34	49 59	79 9	106 29
	27	132 11	156 43	180 37				
Nov.	1							192 28
	3	216 10	240 4	264 25	289 32	315 48	343 35	12 50
	17	42 55	72 43	101 13	127 58	153 10	177 19	201 1
Dec.	1	224 6	248 58	273 50	299 32	326 9	353 47	22 23
	15	51 34	80 42	108 57	135 48	161 10	185 24	209 6
	29	232 55	257 23					

Ayanamsa: 21° 15′ 56″

Longitudes of Planets

1919		Sun	Mars.	Merc.	Merc.	Jupit.	Venus	Saturn	Rahu
Jan.	5	284 7	312 41	261 11	266 10	100 19R	294 20	147 36R	251 28
	15	294 18	320 34	272 12	278 51	99 1	306 53	147 4	250 56
	25	304 29	328 27	285 56	293 22	97 50	319 25	146 24	250 25
Feb.	4	314 38	336 20	301 6	309 8	96 52	331 56	145 38	249 53
	14	324 45	344 12	317 31	326 15	96 11	344 24	144 50	249 21
	24	334 50	352 1	335 22	—	95 49	356 49	144 2	248 49
March	6	344 52	359 47	354 26	3 46	95 47D	9 12	143 16	248 17
	16	354 51	7 30	12 3	18 17	96 4	21 30	142 36	247 46
	26	4 47	15 9	21 40R	21 55R	96 40	33 43	142 3	247 14
April	5	14 39	22 44	19 28	15 42	97 33	45 50	141 39	246 42
	15	24 28	30 11	12 22	10 44D	98 41	57 52	141 25	246 10
	25	34 13	37 38	11 16D	13 43	100 3	69 46	141 21D	245 39
May	5	43 56	44 58	17 31	22 47	101 37	81 32	141 28	245 7
	15	53 36	52 13	29 10	36 33	103 21	93 8	141 46	244 35
	25	63 13	59 22	44 52	54 7	105 12	104 32	142 14	244 3
June	4	72 49	66 26	64 14	75 00	107 11	115 41	142 50	243 32
	14	82 27	73 26	85 59	96 38	109 16	126 32	143 36	243 00
	24	91 55	80 20	106 35	115 40	111 24	136 59	144 28	242 28
July	4	101 27	87 9	123 51	131 6	113 35	146 55	145 27	241 56
	14	110 59	93 54	137 21	142 31	115 49	156 7	146 32	241 25
	24	120 32	100 34	146 21	148 35R	118 2	164 18	147 41	240 53
Aug.	3	130 6	107 10	148 51R	146 59	120 16	171 3	148 53	240 21
	13	139 41	113 42	143 22	139 20	122 27	175 39	150 7	239 49
	23	150 16	120 10	136 48D	137 11D	124 36	177 14R	151 23	239 18
Sep.	2	158 51	126 33	140 52	147 33	126 41	175 3	152 39	238 46
	12	168 40	132 53	155 46	165 00	128 40	169 39	153 55	238 14
	22	178 26	139 8	174 20	183 27	130 32	163 58	155 8	237 42
Oct.	2	188 14	145 19	192 14	200 39	132 16	161 12D	156 19	237 11
	12	198 6	157 26	208 44	216 32	133 50	162 20	157 25	236 39
	22	208 2	157 28	224 3	231 91	135 12	166 46	158 26	236 7
Nov.	1	218 1	163 24	238 16	244 48	136 21	173 32	159 20	235 35
	11	228 3	169 14	250 39	255 20	137 14	181 56	160 7	235 3
	21	238 8	174 58	257 53R	256 55R	137 50	191 27	160 46	234 31
Dec.	1	248 15	180 33	251 45	245 13	128 7R	201 45	161 15	234 00
	11	258 24	185 59	241 53	242 54D	138 5	212 36	161 33	233 28
	21	268 35	191 14	246 54D	252 32	137 43	223 53	161 41R	232 56
	31	278 46	196 16	259 3	—	137 3	235 27	161 37	232 25

Ayanamsa: 21° 16' 47"

Longitude of the Moon

1919		Sun	Tue.	Thur.	Sat.	Mon.	Wed.	Fri.
Jan.	1						269 59	295 59
	5	322 57	350 39	18 47	47 7	75 25	103 21	130 27
	19	156 24	181 9	205 4	228 45	252 52	278 4	304 41
Feb.	1				318 30	346 50	15 31	43 56
	9	71 50	99 11	125 54	151 51	176 53	201 3	224 44
	23	248 30	273 4	299 6				
March	1				326 52	356 1	25 34	54 34
	9	82 32	109 26	135 28	160 45	185 20	209 18	232 55
	23	256 39	281 9	307 6	334 54	4 24		
April	1		19 30	49 35	78 40	106 7	132 32	157 43
	13	182 9	206 6	229 44	253 24	297 30	302 36	329 16
	27	357 45	27 43					
May	1			58 7	87 42	115 42	142 3	167 4
	11	191 14	214 57	238 34	262 24	286 46	312 2	338 36
	25	6 42	36 12	66 21	96 3			
June	1	110 24	137 50	163 35	188 4	211 50	235 27	259 20
	15	283 48	309 3	335 15	2 32	30 55	60 11	89 43
	29	118 35						
July	1		146 4	171 55	196 26	220 11	243 51	267 59
	13	292 57	318 52	345 41	13 13	4 22	69 59	98 43
	27	126 59	154 10	179 57				
Aug.	1							192 20
	3	216 23	240 1	263 57	288 47	314 50	342 1	9 58
	17	38 12	66 26	94 32	122 18	149 22	175 25	200 18
	31	224 16						
Sep.	1					236 5	259 47	284 11
	7	309 52	337 5	5 31	34 28	63 13	91 22	118 48
	21	145 30	171 22	196 20	220 29	244 7		
Oct.	1						267 46	292 7
	5	317 48	345 13	14 12	43 57	73 26	101 56	129 13
	19	155 23	180 36	205 3	228 56	252 30	276 10	300 27
Nov.	1				313 1	339 21	7 30	37 12
	9	67 32	97 18	125 38	152 20	177 40	202 2	225 50
	23	249 26	273 5	297 8	321 59			
Dec.	1					348 4	15 47	45 8
	7	75 29	105 41	134 31	161 31	49	210 59	234 37
	21	258 12	282 5	306 30	331 38	43	25 6	

Ayanamsa: 21° 16' 47

7

Longitudes of Planets

1920		Sun	Mars	Merc.	Merc.	Jupit.	Venus	Saturn	Rahu
Jan.	5	283 52	198 41	266 2	273 20	136 36R	241 19	161 31R	232 9
	15	294 2	203 17	280 52	288 38	135 32	253 11	161 12	231 37
	25	304 14	207 30	296 37	304 52	134 18	265 11	160 42	231 5
Feb.	4	314 23	211 16	313 24	322 14	132 59	277 17	160 5	230 33
	14	324 31	214 28	331 20	340 32	131 40	289 26	159 22	230 2
	24	334 36	216 57	349 25	357 8	130 28	301 39	158 35	229 30
March	5	344 38	218 33	2 34	4 41R	129 38	313 53	157 47	228 58
	15	354 37	219 6R	3 13R	359 16	128 42	326 9	157 00	228 26
	25	4 33	218 25	354 58	352 13	128 15	338 25	156 18	227 54
April	4	14 25	216 28	351 46D	353 59	128 6D	350 42	155 43R	227 23
	14	24 14	213 26	356 59	1 50	128 16	2 58	155 15	226 51
	24	34 00	209 45	9 6	14 40	128 45	15 15	154 57	226 19
May	4	43 42	206 9	22 23	30 54	129 30	27 31	154 49D	225 47
	14	53 22	203 17	40 14	50 20	130 31	39 47	154 52	225 16
	24	62 59	201 37	61 4	72 2	131 46	52 2	155 5	224 44
June	3	72 34	201 17D	82 43	92 39	133 12	64 18	155 28	224 13
	13	82 8	202 14	101 38	109 34	134 49	76 34	156 1	223 40
	23	91 41	204 18	116 25	122 6	136 35	88 50	156 42	223 19
July	3	101 13	207 19	126 28	129 18	138 28	101 8	157 31	222 38
	13	110 45	211 7	130 18R	129 21R	140 27	113 25	158 27	222 5
	23	120 18	215 33	126 38	123 5	142 31	125 44	159 28	221 33
Aug.	2	129 51	220 31	120 10D	119 17D	144 38	138 4	160 34	221 2
	12	139 26	225 57	121 9	125 50	146 48	150 24	161 45	220 29
	22	149 4	231 45	132 58	141 48	148 59	162 44	162 58	219 58
Sep.	1	158 43	237 53	151 26	161 10	151 9	175 5	164 12	219 26
	11	168 26	244 13	170 37	179 38	153 19	187 25	165 28	218 54
	21	178 11	250 58	188 13	196 23	155 26	199 45	166 43	218 22
Oct.	1	188 00	257 51	204 11	211 38	157 29	212 5	167 56	217 51
	11	197 52	264 55	218 42	225 21	159 27	224 23	169 7	217 19
	21	207 48	272 9	231 28	236 43R	151 19	236 41	170 14	216 47
	31	217 46	279 31	240 37R	—	153 2	248 57	171 16	216 15
Nov.	10	227 48	287 1	240 16	234 37	164 36	261 11	172 13	215 44
	20	237 53	294 36	228 29	226 5	165 57	273 23	173 2	215 12
	30	248 00	302 16	228 3	—	167 6	285 32	173 43	214 40
Dec.	10	258 9	309 58	239 5	246 2	167 59	297 37	174 14	214 8
	20	268 20	317 43	253 21	260 51	168 35	309 36	174 36	213 37
	30	278 31	325 29	268 30	—	168 53	321 25	174 47	213 5

Ayanamsa : 21° 17' 37"

Longitude of the Moon

1920	Sun.	Tue.	Thur.	Sat.	Mon.	Wed.	Fri.
Jan. 1			39 13	68 32	98 34	128 14	156 26
11	182 46	207 31	231 18	254 52	278 44	303 17	328 37
25	354 43	21 35	49 19	77 56			
Feb. 1	92 30	121 46	150 24	177 28	203 12	227 29	251 8
15	274 52	299 18	324 45	351 13	18 26	46 10	74 16
29	102 37						
March 1					116 49	144 59	172 19
7	198 24	223 12	247 7	270 47	294 53	320 1	346 28
21	14 7	42 29	71 2	99 23	127 19	154 37	
Apri1 1			167 58	193 58	218 58	243 8	266 50
11	290 39	315 12	341 2	8 27	37 12	66 36	95 48
25	124 11	151 28	177 42				
May 1				202 58	227 29	251 25	275 6
9	298 55	323 25	349 9	16 31	45 32	75 34	105 30
23	134 21	161 39	187 30	212 16	236 21		
June 1		248 15	271 56	295 42	319 52	344 52	11 11
13	39 11	68 48	99 15	129 13	157 40	184 16	209 20
27	233 26	257 8					
July 1			280 49	304 46	329 10	354 18	20 31
11	48 12	77 26	107 40	137 43	166 22	193 6	218 11
25	242 13	265 52	289 40	313 53			
Aug. 1	326 13	351 22	17 17	44 12	72 19	101 35	131 21
15	160 31	188 11	214 6	238 37	262 25	286 10	310 22
29	335 18	1 4					
Sep. 1						14 13	14 6
5	68 44	97 7	126 1	154 49	182 45	209 18	234 25
19	258 33	282 17	306 17	331 4	356 55	23 49	
Oct. 1							51 30
3	79 41	108 3	136 20	164 13	191 19	217 21	242 18
17	266 23	290 8	314 7	338 57	5 4	32 36	61 13
31	90 15						
Nov. 1					104 43	133 10	160 47
7	187 29	213 16	238 14	262 30	286 18	310 3	334 16
21	359 35	26 29	55 6	84 52	114 45		
Dec. 1						143 42	171 14
5	197 24	222 33	247 00	271 00	294 45	318 29	342 37
19	7 43	34 22	62 54	93 3	123 37	153 14	181 4

Ayanamsa: 21° 17′ 37″

Longitudes of Planets

1921		Sun	Mars	Merc.	Merc.	Jupit.	Venus	Saturn	Rahu
Jan.	5	284 39	330 9	277 52	285 50	168 55R	328 26	174 48R	212 46
	15	294 50	337 55	294 00	302 23	168 42	339 55	174 41	212 14
	25	305 9	345 38	310 58	319 43	168 10	351 5	174 24	211 42
Feb.	4	315 9	353 20	328 26	336 38	167 21	1 49	173 57	211 10
	14	325 17	0 59	343 21	347 15	166 18	11 57	173 22	210 39
	24	335 21	8 34	347 14R	—	165 5	21 15	172 40	210 7
March	6	345 23	16 5	338 21	334 43	163 47	29 21	171 54	209 35
	16	355 22	23 32	333 28D	334 42D	162 30	35 44	171 7	209 3
	26	5 17	30 55	337 52	342 29	161 19	39 35	170 20	208 32
April	5	15 9	38 12	348 12	354 48	160 26	39 57R	169 37	208 00
	15	24 58	45 25	2 9	10 13	159 34	36 22	169 00	207 28
	25	34 44	52 33	18 59	28 27	159 6	30 18	168 31	206 56
May	5	44 26	59 36	38 36	49 18	158 56	25 19	168 10	206 24
	15	54 6	66 35	60 11	70 42	159 4D	23 55D	168 00	205 52
	25	63 43	73 29	80 21	88 53	159 30	26 14	167 59D	205 21
June	4	73 18	80 19	96 11	102 11	160 12	31 24	168 9	204 49
	14	82 52	87 5	106 45	109 42	161 10	38 31	168 29	204 18
	24	92 24	93 47	110 50R	110 6	162 22	46 58	168 59	203 45
July	4	101 56	100 25	107 46	104 41R	163 45	56 19	169 37	203 14
	14	111 28	107 1	102 6D	101 9D	165 19	66 19	170 23	202 42
	24	120 4	113 33	102 28	106 13	167 2	76 49	171 16	202 10
Aug.	3	130 35	120 2	112 17	120 20	168 53	87 40	172 15	201 38
	13	140 10	126 29	129 46	139 49	170 50	98 50	173 20	201 7
	23	149 47	132 53	149 52	159 31	172 52	110 14	174 28	200 35
Sep.	2	159 27	139 16	168 41	177 20	174 58	121 50	175 40	200 3
	12	169 10	145 36	185 30	193 12	177 6	133 38	176 53	199 31
	22	178 56	151 54	200 27	207 14	179 15	145 35	178 8	198 59
Oct.	2	188 45	158 11	213 27	218 55	181 25	157 41	179 22	198 28
	12	198 37	164 26	223 17	225 55R	183 34	159 53	180 35	197 56
	22	208 33	170 38	225 52R	222 17	185 40	182 12	181 46	197 24
Nov.	1	218 32	176 49	216 7	211 51D	187 42	194 34	182 53	196 53
	11	228 34	182 58	210 47D	214 18	189 40	207 2	183 56	196 21
	21	238 39	189 4	220 4	217 10	191 30	219 32	184 53	195 49
Dec.	1	248 46	195 8	234 38	242 17	193 12	232 4	185 43	195 17
	11	258 56	201 8	250 1	257 48	194 44	244 38	186 25	194 45
	21	269 6	207 4	265 37	273 32	196 5	257 12	186 58	194 13
	31	278 18	212 56	281 33	—	197 11	269 46	187 21	193 42

Ayanamsa: 21° 18′ 27″

Longitude of the Moon

1921		Sun.	Tue.	Thurs.	Sat.	Mon.	Wed.	Fri.
Jan.	1				194 17	219 39	242 2	267 56
	9	291 41	315 27	339 28	4 1	29 38	56 50	85 53
	23	116 19	146 50	176 2	203 16	228 44		
Feb.	1		240 59	264 56	288 38	312 26	336 32	1 7
	13	26 22	52 41	80 26	109 39	139 45	169 33	197 55
	27	224 47						
March	1		249 25	273 26	297 9	321 3	345 28	10 33
	13	36 24	63 7	90 49	119 28	148 42	177 43	205 43
	27	232 15	257 21	281 30				
April	1							293 23
	3	317 12	341 29	6 38	32 46	59 51	87 40	115 58
	17	144 27	172 46	200 28	227 12	252 47	277 21	301 16
May	1	325 6	349 27	14 50	41 34	69 31	98 13	127 00
	15	155 21	182 58	209 48	235 49	260 59	285 23	309 16
	29	333 4	357 22					
June	1						9 55	36 7
	5	64 00	93 13	122 53	151 58	179 54	206 38	232 23
	19	257 24	281 48	305 45	329 28	353 23	18 6	
July	1							44 15
	3	72 16	101 57	132 16	161 56	190 5	216 40	242 2
	17	266 36	290 41	314 30	338 13	2 10	26 51	52 52
	31	50 43						
Aug.	1					95 21	125 37	156 6
	7	185 28	213 2	238 57	263 41	287 45	311 32	335 17
	21	359 15	23 42	49 4	75 49	104 15	134 7	
Sep.	1			149 18	179 20	208 2	234 57	260 18
	11	284 36	308 24	332 9	356 12	20 47	46 4	72 21
	25	99 49	128 30	158 1				
Oct.	1				187 31	216 3	243 5	268 35
	9	292 56	316 43	340 32	4 50	29 56	55 56	82 50
	23	110 32	138 52	167 33	196 10	224 7		
Nov.	1		237 42	263 51	288 46	312 47	336 30	0 34
	13	25 33	51 45	79 6	107 15	135 40	163 56	191 51
	27	219 17	246 1					
Dec.	1			271 50	296 37	320 36	344 16	8 17
	11	33 20	59 56	88 5	117 12	146 22	174 50	202 23
	25	229 5	255 2	280 17	304 47			

Ayanamsa : 21° 18′ 27″

Longitudes of Planets

1922		Sun	Mars	Merc.	Merc.	Jupit.	Venus	Saturn	Rahu
Jan.	5	284 24	215 50	289 43	298 00	197 39	276 4	187 29	193 26
	15	294 35	221 33	306 21	314 35	198 22	288 38	187 36R	192 54
	25	304 45	227 9	322 11	228 13	198 47	301 12	187 33	192 23
Feb.	4	314 55	232 36	331 9	329 49R	198 54R	313 46	187 18	191 51
	14	325 2	237 52	324 51R	319 29	198 41	326 18	186 54	191 19
	24	335 6	242 55	316 26D	—	198 10	338 49	186 22	190 47
March	6	345 9	247 41	318 38	322 40	197 23	351 19	185 42	190 15
	16	355 7	252 8	327 55	334 5	196 21	3 46	184 58	189 43
	26	5 3	256 8	340 59	348 32	195 10	16 12	184 11	189 12
April	5	14 55	259 36	356 42	5 28	193 53	28 35	183 25	188 40
	15	24 44	262 23	14 51	24 52	192 37	40 55	182 41	188 8
	25	34 29	264 19	35 23	46 7	191 27	53 12	182 2	187 37
May	5	44 12	265 14R	56 29	65 57	190 26	65 27	181 30	187 4
	15	53 51	264 57	74 7	80 49	189 40	77 38	181 7	186 33
	25	63 29	263 25	85 55	89 19	189 10	89 45	180 53	186 1
June	4	73 4	260 49	90 49R	90 26R	188 58D	101 49	180 49D	185 29
	14	82 37	252 37	88 27	85 40	189 4	113 49	180 55	184 58
	24	92 10	254 30	83 14	82 8D	189 28	125 44	181 11	184 21
July	4	101 42	252 12	82 58D	85 51	190 8	137 33	181 37	183 54
	14	111 14	251 9D	90 46	97 34	191 4	149 16	182 11	183 22
	24	120 47	251 29	106 3	115 47	192 13	160 50	182 54	182 50
Aug.	3	130 21	253 9	124 9	136 29	193 35	172 15	183 44	182 15
	13	139 56	255 57	146 26	155 48	195 8	183 28	184 41	181 47
	23	149 33	259 43	164 36	172 49	196 50	194 25	185 43	181 15
Sep.	2	159 13	264 15	180 29	187 36	198 40	205 3	186 49	180 44
	12	168 55	269 26	194 8	199 58	200 37	215 14	187 59	180 12
	22	178 41	275 7	204 53	208 29	202 39	224 50	189 11	179 40
Oct.	2	188 30	281 12	210 10R	209 4R	204 45	233 34	190 25	179 8
	12	198 22	287 38	204 47	198 54	206 54	241 4	191 38	178 36
	22	208 18	294 18	195 00D	195 32D	209 4	246 43R	192 51	178 4
Nov.	1	218 17	301 12	199 53	206 25	211 15	249 39R	194 2	177 33
	11	228 19	308 15	213 56	221 49	213 25	248 53	195 10	177 1
	21	238 24	315 24	229 46	237 42	215 32	244 25	196 13	176 29
Dec.	1	248 31	322 40	245 35	253 27	217 35	238 53	197 11	175 58
	11	258 41	229 58	261 18	269 11	219 34	234 52D	198 3	175 26
	21	268 51	337 19	277 8	285 7	221 25	235 10	198 47	174 54
	31	279 3	344 40	293 4	—	223 8	239 00	199 22	174 22

Ayanamsa: 21° 19′ 18″

Longitude of the Moon

1922		Sun.	Tue.	Thur.	Sat.	Mon.	Wed.	Fri.
Jan.	1	316 47	340 27	4 7	28 27	54 10	81 44	111 2
	15	141 7	170 46	199 9	226 7	251 58	276 59	301 22
	29	325 17	348 54					
Feb.	1						0 42	24 35
	5	49 24	75 47	104 7	134 6	164 37	194 20	222 27
	19	248 55	274 5	298 24	322 14	345 52		
March	1						9 33	33 37
	5	58 30	84 43	112 39	142 12	172 35	202 34	231 8
	19	257 54	283 8	307 20	331 1	354 39	18 33	43 00
April	1				55 31	81 17	108 15	136 32
	9	165 57	195 47	225 2	252 54	279 4	303 49	327 40
	23	351 17	15 11	39 45	65 12			
May	1					91 34	118 48	146 51
	7	175 33	204 34	233 14	260 52	287 3	311 51	335 45
	21	359 24	23 28	48 27	74 35	101 44	129 35	
June	1			143 39	171 54	200 11	228 16	255 46
	11	282 16	307 33	331 47	355 28	19 17	43 55	69 53
	25	97 17	125 41	154 25				
July	1				182 54	210 52	238 16	264 58
	9	290 50	315 44	339 49	3 27	27 15	51 47	78 4
	23	105 53	135 1	164 31	193 32	221 34		
Aug.	1		235 11	261 42	287 20	312 9	336 17	359 37
	13	23 34	47 42	72 59	99 57	128 42	158 38	188 39
	27	217 44	245 24	271 40				
Sep.	1							284 22
	3	309 4	333 8	356 49	20 24	44 17	68 56	94 52
	17	122 29	151 47	182 4	212 11	241 4	268 13	293 47
Oct.	1	318 13	342 00	5 36	29 20	53 29	78 21	104 15
	15	131 32	160 19	190 13	220 20	249 30	276 56	302 36
	29	326 57	350 38					
Nov.	1						2 25	26 10
	5	50 26	75 24	101 10	127 49	155 30	184 14	213 43
	19	243 6	271 25	298 4	323 6	347 3	10 38	
Dec.	1							34 32
	3	59 11	84 47	111 16	138 26	166 9	194 23	223 00
	17	251 35	279 23	305 52	330 54	354 53	18 30	42 27
	31	67 22						

Ayanamsa: 21° 19′ 18″

Longitudes of Planets

1923		Sun	Mars	Merc.	Merc.	Jupit.	Venus	Saturn	Rahu
Jan.	5	284 8	348 20	300 47	307 46	223 56	241 57	199 35	174 6
	15	294 20	355 40	313 2R	315 00R	225 24	249 19	199 56	173 34
	25	304 31	2 59	312 34	306 33	226 38	258 7	200 6R	173 3
Feb.	4	314 40	10 15	301 19	299 13D	227 38	267 52	200 5	172 31
	14	324 47	17 29	300 14D	303 28	228 22	278 16	199 54	171 59
	24	334 52	24 39	308 12	—	228 48	289 7	199 32	171 27
March	6	344 54	31 46	320 29	327 36	228 56R	300 18	199 2	170 56
	16	354 53	38 49	335 16	343 27	228 45	311 44	198 25	170 24
	26	4 49	45 48	352 10	1 26	228 16	323 19	197 42	169 52
April	5	14 41	52 43	11 15	21 32	227 31	335 2	196 56	169 20
	15	24 30	59 35	32 1	42 11	226 31	346 51	196 10	168 48
	25	34 16	66 23	51 22	59 3	225 21	358 44	195 26	168 17
May	5	43 58	73 8	64 56	68 52	224 5	10 40	194 46	167 45
	15	53 38	79 49	70 44	70 33R	222 9	22 40	194 12	167 13
	25	63 15	86 27	68 41	65 57	221 39	34 41	193 46	166 42
June	4	72 50	93 3	63 30	62 20	220 38	46 44	193 29	166 10
	14	82 24	99 35	62 56D	65 25	219 50	58 49	193 22D	165 39
	24	91 57	106 6	68 41	75 34	219 18	70 56	193 24	165 5
July	4	101 29	112 34	82 59	91 49	219 4D	83 5	193 37	164 34
	14	111 1	119 00	101 47	112 23	219 8	95 16	193 59	164 3
	24	120 33	125 26	122 59	133 10	219 30	107 30	194 30	163 31
Aug.	3	130 7	131 49	142 44	151 38	220 9	121 00	195 10	162 59
	13	139 42	138 12	159 52	167 29	221 3	132 5	195 57	162 27
	23	149 19	144 25	174 26	180 40	222 12	144 27	191 51	161 56
Sep.	2	158 59	150 56	186 3	190 19	223 34	150 50	197 51	161 24
	12	168 41	157 18	193 5	193 43R	225 7	169 15	198 56	160 52
	22	178 27	163 40	191 36	186 53	226 5D	181 42	200 4	160 20
Oct.	2	188 15	170 1	181 33	178 50	228 42	194 10	201 15	159 49
	12	198 8	176 23	180 23D	185 30	230 40	206 38	202 27	159 17
	22	208 8	162 46	192 40	200 42	232 44	219 8	203 40	158 45
Nov.	1	218 2	189 9	208 59	217 15	234 53	231 37	204 53	158 13
	11	228 4	195 32	225 23	233 24	237 4	244 6	206 4	157 41
	21	238 9	201 56	241 18	249 7	239 17	256 35	207 12	157 9
Dec.	1	248 16	208 21	256 53	264 36	241 31	269 14	208 16	156 38
	11	258 26	214 46	272 17	279 50	243 43	287 33	209 14	156 6
	21	268 36	221 11	287 1	293 21	245 54	294 00	210 7	155 34
	31	278 48	227 37	297 48	—	248 00	306 25	210 52	155 3

Ayanamsa: 21° 20' 8"

Longitude of the Moon

1923	Sun.	Tue.	Thur.	Sat.	Mon.	Wed.	Fri.
Jan. 1					80 17	107 3	134 46
7	162 57	191 11	219 19	247 11	274 33	301 2	326 25
21	350 46	14 28	38 9	62 31	88 10	115 21	
Feb. 1			129 28	158 22	187 28	216 8	244 1
11	271 2	297 10	322 25	346 52	10 42	34 18	58 13
25	83 4	109 23					
March 1			137 26	166 53	196 51	226 16	254 27
11	281 14	306 48	331 27	355 29	19 11	42 49	66 46
25	91 32	117 37	145 26	174 54			
April 1	190 3	220 27	249 56	277 44	303 49	328 34	352 32
15	16 10	39 49	63 44	88 12	113 34	140 13	168 29
29	198 15						
May 1		228 41	258 29	286 37	312 50	337 32	1 22
13	24 57	48 44	72 58	97 49	123 26	150 3	177 57
27	207 10	237 7	266 43				
June 1							281 1
3	308 17	333 46	358 00	21 39	45 24	69 40	94 40
17	120 26	146 25	174 20	202 36	231 36	260 47	289 15
July 1	316 18	341 47	6 4	29 48	53 38	78 9	103 38
15	130 5	157 21	185 12	213 28	241 57	270 16	297 55
29	324 26	349 42					
Aug. 1						1 56	25 52
5	49 37	73 48	98 59	125 26	153 5	181 31	210 13
19	238 42	266 39	293 52	320 10	345 30	9 59	33 51
Sep. 1				45 43	69 35	94 11	120 3
9	147 29	176 18	205 49	235 8	263 32	290 43	316 47
23	341 55	6 22	30 19	54 1			
Oct. 1					77 52	102 21	128 4
7	155 28	184 35	214 48	244 52	273 41	300 50	326 30
21	351 9	15 13	39 00	62 44	86 39	111 7	
Nov. 1			123 42	149 56	177 57	207 42	238 20
11	268 24	296 47	323 14	348 11	12 15	35 59	59 44
25	83 43	108 6	133 8				
Dec. 1				159 13	186 49	216 4	246 23
9	276 29	305 8	331 50	356 53	20 56	44 37	68 27
23	92 43	117 33	143 3	169 22	196 48		

Ayanamsa: 21° 20′ 8″

Longitudes of Planets

1924		Sun	Mars	Merc.	Merc.	Jupit.	Venus	Saturn	Rahu
Jan.	5	283 53	230 49	298 46R	295 6R	249 2	312 38	211 11	154 47
	15	294 5	237 15	288 42	283 57	251 00	324 59	211 43	154 15
	25	304 6	243 40	282 53D°	284 55D	252 50	337 17	212 6	153 43
Feb.	4	314 25	250 5	288 58	294 18	254 31	349 30	212 18	153 11
	14	324 32	256 28	300 39	307 16	256 2	1 36	212 20R	152 40
	24	334 37	263 51	314 33	322 16	257 20	13 34	212 11	152 8
March	5	344 39	269 11	330 26	339 4	258 23	25 21	211 52	151 36
	15	354 39	275 29	348 10	357 45	259 11	36 55	211 24	151 4
	25	4 34	281 44	7 45	17 56	259 42	48 13	210 49	150 33
April	4	14 27	287 54	27 48	36 37	259 54R	59 10	210 8	150 1
	14	24 16	293 58	43 41	48 33	259 47	69 40	209 23	149 9
	24	34 1	299 54	51 3R	51 8R	259 23	79 34	208 33	148 57
May	4	43 44	305 41	49 15	46 18	258 40	88 40	207 53	148 25
	14	53 24	311 14	43 35	42 9D	257 44	96 37	207 12	147 54
	24	63 1	316 41	42 32D	44 45	256 36	102 54	206 37	147 22
June	3	72 36	321 25	48 37	53 58	255 21	106 47	206 8	146 50
	13	82 10	325 49	60 38	68 33	254 5	107 21R	205 49	146 18
	23	91 43	329 36	77 39	87 47	252 53	104 2	205 39	145 47
July	3	101 15	332 35	98 31	109 20	251 49	98 7	205 38D	145 15
	13	110 47	334 32	119 43	129 25	250 58	92 54	205 48	144 43
	23	120 19	335 18R	138 24	146 37	250 23	91 4D	206 7	144 11
Aug.	2	129 53	334 46	154 7	160 50	250 5	92 59	206 35	143 40
	12	139 28	333 3	166 41	171 31	250 6D	97 51	207 12	143 8
	22	149 5	330 34	175 2	176 49R	250 25	104 46	207 56	142 36
Sep.	1	158 45	328 00	176 20R	173 20	251 2	113 9	208 48	142 4
	11	168 27	326 6	168 31	164 11D	251 55	122 31	209 46	141 32
	21	178 12	325 20D	162 45D	165 19	253 4	132 37	210 48	141 00
Oct.	1	188 1	325 53	171 8	178 53	254 26	143 18	211 55	140 29
	11	197 53	327 41	187 26	196 7	256 00	154 23	213 5	139 57
	21	207 49	330 34	204 42	213 3	257 45	165 49	214 16	139 25
	31	217 48	334 18	221 12	—	259 38	177 30	215 29	138 54
Nov.	10	227 50	338 44	236 56	244 35	261 40	189 25	216 41	138 22
	20	237 54	343 41	252 7	259 29	263 47	201 29	217 51	137 50
	30	248 1	349 3	266 37	273 16	265 59	213 42	219 00	137 18
Dec.	10	258 11	354 43	278 54	282 30R	268 14	225 59	220 4	136 46
	20	268 21	0 37	282 28R	277 53	270 31	238 22	221 3	136 15
	30	278 33	6 42	281 17	—	273 3	252 2	222 2	135 43

Ayanamsa : 21° 20' 58"

Longitude of the Moon

1924		Sun	Tue.	Thur.	Sat.	Mon.	Wed.	Fri.
Jan.	1		210 58	240 7	269 47	298 52	326 32	352 31
	13	17 7	40 59	64 44	88 56	113 52	139 40	166 16
	27	193 38	221 40	250 14				
Feb.	1							264 35
	3	293 8	320 53	347 26	12 41	36 55	60 42	84 39
	17	109 19	135 6	162 4	190 00	218 27	246 57	275 7
March	1				289 1	316 16	342 41	8 9
	9	32 44	56 40	80 27	104 38	129 52	156 34	184 47
	23	214 1	243 21	271 59	299 34	326 5		
April	1		339 1	4 17	28 53	52 57	76 42	100 32
	13	125 4	150 55	178 32	207 53	238 4	267 51	296 16
	27	323 9	348 45					
May	1			13 30	37 43	61 35	85 18	109 9
	11	133 37	159 18	186 47	216 9	246 40	276 58	305 49
	25	332 50	358 19	22 47	46 44			
June	1	58 37	82 21	106 12	130 26	155 29	181 53	210 2
	15	239 49	270 20	300 11	328 23	354 45	19 40	43 44
	29	67 29						
July	1		91 16	115 20	139 56	165 18	191 48	219 42
	13	248 56	278 51	308 24	336 36	3 7	28 10	52 16
	27	76 1	99 54	124 18				
Aug.	1							136 46
	3	162 18	188 44	216 8	244 28	273 26	302 29	330 53
	17	358 3	23 49	48 23	72 16	96 4	120 21	145 32
	31	171 47						
Sep.	1					185 18	212 58	241 11
	7	269 36	297 55	325 50	352 59	19 6	44 8	68 17
	21	92 1	116 00	140 50	167 4	194 36		
Oct.	1						223 12	252 5
	5	280 36	308 26	335 31	1 53	27 28	52 14	76 16
	19	99 57	123 51	148 38	174 58	203 4	232 31	262 51
Nov.	1				276 53	305 18	332 27	358 35
	9	23 55	48 36	72 43	96 25	120 5	144 14	169 34
	23	106 43	225 48	256 6	286 17			
Dec.	1					315 13	342 31	8 24
	7	33 18	57 34	81 26	105 6	128 49	153 1	178 14
	21	205 5	233 50	264 4	294 34	324 1	351 44	

Ayanamsa: 21° 20′ 58″

Longitudes of Planets

1925		Sun	Mars.	Merc.	Merc.	Jupit.	Venus	Saturn	Rahu
Jan.	5	284 40	10 25	266 55R	267 36	274 11	258 15	222 25	135 24
	15	294 51	16 41	271 00	276 3	276 27	270 43	223 7	134 52
	25	305 2	23 1	282 4	288 42	278 40	283 12	223 39	134 20
Feb.	4	315 11	29 25	295 48	303 17	280 48	295 41	224 3	133 48
	14	325 18	35 50	311 7	319 18	282 50	308 10	224 16	133 17
	24	335 23	42 16	327 53	336 53	284 45	320 29	224 19R	132 45
March	6	345 25	48 48	346 17	356 1	286 31	333 6	224 11	132 13
	16	355 23	55 10	5 50	15 11	288 6	345 33	223 54	131 41
	26	5 19	61 36	26 11	29 2	289 30	357 59	223 27	131 10
April	5	15 11	68 1	32 10R	32 26R	290 39	10 24	222 53	130 38
	15	25 00	74 25	30 17	26 52	291 33	22 47	222 13	130 6
	25	34 45	80 49	23 45	22 8	292 10	35 9	221 29.	129 34
May	5	44 28	87 11	22 27D	24 40	292 29	47 29	220 44	129 3
	15	54 7	93 32	28 31	33 43	292 29R	59 48	220 00	128 30
	25	63 45	99 52	40 7	47 34	292 10	72 6	219 8	127 59
June	4	73 20	106 12	56 4	65 34	291 34	84 23	218 42	127 27
	14	82 53	112 31	75 55	86 48	290 41	96 38	218 13	126 56
	24	92 26	118 49	97 41	108 5	289 36	108 53	217 52	126 24
July	4	101 58	125 8	117 44	126 33	288 23	121 6	217 40	125 52
	14	111 30	131 36	134 32	141 38	287 6	133 18	217 38D	125 20
	24	121 3	137 45	147 50	152 58	285 51	145 29	217 45	124 48
Aug.	3	130 36	144 4	156 49	159 3R	284 43	157 38	218 3	124 16
	13	140 12	150 24	159 17R	157 15	283 43	169 44	218 29	123 45
	23	149 49	156 45	153 20	149 1	283 8	181 48	219 4	123 13
Sep.	2	159 29	163 8	146 27D	147 10	282 45	193 48	219 47	122 41
	12	169 11	169 31	151 24	158 20	282 42D	205 44	220 37	122 9
	22	178 57	175 57	166 50	175 54	282 58	217 37	221 34	121 38
Oct.	2	188 46	182 25	184 59	193 49	283 32	229 24	222 35	121 6
	12	198 38	188 54	202 20	210 34	284 24	241 4	223 41	120 34
	22	208 34	195 26	218 31	226 15	285 32	252 36	224 50	120 2
Nov.	1	218 33	202 1	233 45	241 2	286 55	263 56	226 1	119 31
	11	228 35	208 37	248 3	254 39	288 30	275 1	227 12	118 59
	21	238 40	215 17	260 33	265 7	290 17	285 45	228 24	118 27
Dec.	1	248 47	222 00	267 12R	265 17R	292 13	295 59	229 34	117 55
	11	258 57	228 45	259 22	253 14	294 18	305 28	230 42	117 24
	21	269 7	235 33	250 55D	252 34D	296 28	313 52	231 46	116 51
	31	279 19	242 24	256 48	—	298 44	320 39	232 46	116 20

Ayanamsa: 21° 21′ 49″

Longitude of the Moon

1925		Sun.	Tue.	Thurs.	Sat.	Mon.	Wed.	Fri.
Jan.	1			4 56	30 15	54 34	78 23	102 4
	11	125 52	150 3	174 56	200 55	228 22	257 20	287 20
	25	317 20	346 12	13 22	38 54			
Feb.	1	51 10	75 8	98 46	122 35	146 54	171 57	197 51
	15	224 44	252 39	281 29	310 47	339 50	7 48	34 16
March	1	59 16	83 17	106 56	130 51	155 32	181 14	207 57
	15	235 26	263 28	291 48	320 14	348 25	15 51	42 6
	29	67 6	91 8					
April	1						102 58	126 42
	5	151 5	176 40	203 37	231 39	260 10	288 37	316 41
	19	344 18	11 19	37 34	62 49	87 8	110 51	
May	1							134 33
	3	158 57	184 43	212 8	240 56	270 18	299 19	327 28
	17	354 41	21 2	46 34	71 20	95 24	119 2	142 42
	31	167 4						
June	1					179 44	206 40	234 46
	7	264 31	294 30	323 41	351 33	18 5	43 32	68 9
	21	92 11	115 49	139 25	163 23	188 20		
July	1						214 48	243 5
	5	272 54	303 16	332 58	1 13	27 48	53 2	77 19
	19	101 4	124 39	148 22	172 33	197 36	223 56	251 53
Aug.	1				266 27	296 25	326 39	355 59
	9	23 41	49 39	74 15	98 4	121 38	145 23	169 39
	23	194 37	220 31	247 32	275 48	305 8		
Sep.	1		320 2	349 41	18 18	45 15	70 33	94 40
	13	118 17	142 00	166 20	191 29	217 31	244 22	271 58
	27	300 18	329 12					
Oct.	1			358 9	26 22	53 13	78 33	102 41
	11	126 19	150 8	174 45	200 30	227 19	254 54	282 53
	25	311 2	339 16	7 20	34 48			
Nov.	1	48 10	73 57	98 32	122 20	145 58	170 11	195 35
	15	222 26	250 31	279 12	307 51	336 3	3 42	30 41
	29	56 53						
Dec.	1		62 8	106 30	130 14	153 51	178 00	203 23
	13	230 23	259 00	288 31	318 1	346 41	14 14	40 39
	27	66 7	90 47	114 50				

Ayanamsa: 21° 21' 49"

Longitudes of Planets

1926	Sun	Mars	Merc.	Merc.	Jupit.	Venus	Saturn	Rahu
Jan. 5	284 25	245 50	262 27	268 55	299 53	323 11	233 13	116 4
15	294 36	252 45	275 51	283 9	302 13	325 57R	234 4	115 32
25	304 47	259 43	290 42	298 32	304 35	324 52	234 46	115 1
Feb. 4	314 56	266 44	306 40	315 5	306 57	320 2	235 20	114 29
14	325 3	273 47	323 50	332 58	309 17	314 5	235 45	113 57
24	335 8	280 53	342 21	351 46	311 15	310 37D	236 00	113 25
March 6	345 10	288 1	0 39	8 5	313 49	311 6	236 5R	112 53
16	355 9	295 12	13 2	14 45R	315 58	315 3	235 59	112 22
26	5 5	302 23	13 15R	9 34	318 00	321 25	235 44	111 50
April 5	14 57	309 37	5 37	3 4	319 54	329 26	235 20	111 18
15	24 46	316 51	2 40D	4 21	321 38	338 33	234 47	110 46
25	34 31	324 5	7 47	12 35	323 10	348 24	234 9	110 15
May 5	44 14	331 18	18 33	25 29	324 30	358 48	233 26	109 43
15	53 54	338 29	33 19	42 2	325 36	9 35	232 41	109 11
25	63 31	345 37	51 37	61 59	326 25	20 38	231 57	108 39
June 4	73 6	352 41	72 52	83 49	326 57	31 54	231 15	108 8
14	82 40	359 38	94 17	103 57	327 10R	43 20	230 38	107 36
24	92 12	6 26	112 40	120 26	327 4	54 54	230 7	107 4
July 4	101 44	13 3	127 11	132 51	326 39	66 36	229 44	106 32
14	111 17	19 26	137 15	140 9	325 56	78 23	229 30	106 1
24	120 49	25 29	141 15R	140 17R	324 58	90 16	229 25D	105 28
Aug. 3	130 23	31 10	137 26	133 35	323 48	102 15	229 31	104 51
13	139 58	36 21	130 23D	129 25D	322 31	114 19	229 44	104 25
23	149 55	40 54	131 29	136 25	321 13	126 28	230 9	103 54
Sep. 2	159 15	44 42	144 6	153 3	319 59	138 42	230 41	103 22
12	168 58	47 30	162 33	172 00	318 55	151 00	231 22	102 50
22	178 43	49 8	181 8	189 53	318 5	168 22	232 10	102 18
Oct. 2	188 32	49 23R	198 15	206 15	317 33	175 48	233 5	101 46
12	198 24	48 9	213 57	221 20	317 19D	188 16	234 5	101 14
22	208 20	45 36	228 24	235 5	317 26	200 47	235 10	100 43
Nov. 1	218 19	42 14	241 14	246 29	317 52	213 19	236 18	100 11
11	228 21	38 50	250 14R	251 20R	318 37	225 52	237 28	99 39
21	238 25	36 11	248 31	242 15	319 40	238 26	238 39	99 7
Dec. 1	248 33	34 44	236 39	235 16D	320 59	251 00	239 50	98 36
11	258 42	34 39D	237 52	242 15	322 32	263 35	241 00	98 4
21	268 52	35 50	249 5	255 57	324 17	246 9	242 8	97 32
31	279 4	38 3	263 11	—	326 12	288 43	243 13	97 00

Ayanamsa: 21° 22' 39″

Longitude of the Moon

1926	Sun	Tue.	Thur.	Sat.	Mon.	Wed.	Fri.
Jan. 1							126 41
3	150 17	174 5	198 40	224 37	252 20	281 41	311 56
17	341 52	10 32	37 35	63 11	87 44	111 40	135 19
31	158 59						
Feb. 1					170 54	195 8	220 16
7	246 45	274 55	304 39	335 7	5 1	33 21	59 48
21	84 43	108 41	132 17	155 57			
March 1					179 58	204 33	229 53
7	256 15	283 59	313 6	343 10	13 4	41 37	68 18
21	93 18	117 15	140 50	164 37	188 59	214 5	
April 1			226 55	253 8	280 13	308 17	337 17
11	6 43	35 38	63 9	89 00	113 28	137 12	160 55
25	185 11	210 22	236 30				
May 1				263 26	290 59	319 3	347 32
9	16 6	44 13	71 14	96 53	121 20	145 7	168 53
23	193 18	218 48	245 32	273 16	301 36		
June 1		315 50	344 16	12 24	40 00	66 46	92 30
13	117 14	141 12	164 54	188 56	213 54	240 14	268 3
27	296 57	326 13					
July 1			355 7	23 10	50 10	76 10	101 15
11	125 36	149 27	173 7	197 7	222 00	248 18	276 17
25	305 43	335 46	5 19	33 35			
Aug. 1	47 8	73 11	98 9	122 24	146 13	169 54	193 42
15	218 3	243 26	270 21	299 4	329 13	359 41	29 10
29	56 52	82 48					
Sep. 1						95 15	119 19
5	143 16	166 56	190 46	214 57	239 49	265 45	293 14
19	322 25	352 47	23 5	52 1	79 00	104 15	
Oct 1							128 23
3	152 4	175 47	199 51	224 24	249 35	275 38	302 53
17	331 32	1 18	31 13	60 6	87 12	112 35	136 47
31	160 29						
Nov. 1					172 21	196 24	221 5
7	246 30	272 40	299 36	327 25	356 5	25 13	54 1
21	81 42	107 53	132 41	156 38	180 23		
Dec. 1						204 32	229 32
5	255 34	282 33	310 15	338 24	6 46	35 3	62 52
19	89 49	115 39	140 25	164 25	188 10	212 18	237 24

Ayanamsa: 21° 22′ 39″

Longitudes of Planets

1927		Sun	Mars	Merc.	Merc.	Jupit.	Venus	Saturn	Rahu
Jan.	5	284 10	39 29	270 39	278 17	327 13	295 00	243 43	96 44
	15	294 21	42 55	286 7	294 10	329 21	307 33	244 41	96 12
	25	304 31	46 56	302 26	310 59	331 35	320 5	245 32	95 41
Feb.	4	314 41	51 23	319 47	328 46	333 54	332 35	246 15	95 9
	14	324 48	56 12	337 44	346 6	336 16	345 3	246 50	94 37
	24	334 54	61 17	352 55	356 54	338 41	357 28	247 17	94 5
March	6	344 55	66 34	357 9R	353 59	341 5	9 50	247 33	93 33
	16	354 54	72 2	349 16	345 28	343 83	22 7	247 40R	93 2
	26	4 50	77 38	343 55D	344 47	345 52	34 20	247 36	92 30
April	5	14 43	83 19	347 37	351 58	348 11	46 26	247 23	91 58
	15	24 31	89 6	357 30	3 59	350 26	58 27	247 1	91 26
	25	34 17	94 56	11 17	19 22	352 35	70 19	246 30	90 55
May	5	44 00	100 50	28 12	37 47	354 26	82 4	245 53	90 23
	15	53 39	106 47	48 6	58 55	356 29	93 37	245 11	89 51
	25	63 17	112 47	69 50	80 17	358 19	104 58	244 27	80 20
June	4	72 52	118 48	89 53	98 26	359 44	116 4	243 43	88 48
	14	82 26	124 52	105 50	112 3	1 2	126 50	243 00	88 16
	24	91 58	130 58	116 57	120 23	2 6	137 10	242 22	87 44
July	4	101 31	137 7	122 4R	121 52	2 53	146 57	241 50	87 13
	14	111 3	143 7	119 49	116 36	3 21	155 56	241 25	86 41
	24	120 35	149 30	118 29	111 50D	3 31R	163 50	241 9	86 9
Aug.	3	130 9	155 45	112 32	115 55	3 21	170 8	241 2D	85 37
	13	139 44	162 3	121 50	129 51	2 52	174 6	241 4	85 5
	23	149 21	168 24	139 12	149 6	2 5	174 49R	241 17	84 35
Sep.	2	159 1	174 48	158 54	168 20	1 3	171 44	241 38	84 2
	12	168 43	181 15	177 18	185 48	359 50	165 56	242 9	83 30
	22	178 29	187 45	193 52	201 32	358 30	160 42	242 48	82 58
Oct.	2	188 18	194 19	208 48	215 39	357 11	158 52D	243 35	82 27
	12	198 10	200 57	221 59	227 37	355 58	160 51	244 28	81 55
	22	208 5	207 38	232 12	235 4	354 56	165 54	245 27	81 23
Nov.	1	218 4	214 24	235 10R	231 31	354 11	173 6	246 30	80 51
	11	228 6	221 14	225 10	220 18	353 44	181 47	247 37	80 20
	21	238 11	228 8	219 54D	223 22	353 37D	191 30	248 47	79 48
Dec.	1	248 18	235 7	229 4	235 50	353 51	201 56	249 58	79 16
	11	258 27	242 10	243 7	250 37	354 25	212 54	251 9	78 44
	21	268 38	249 17	258 16	265 59	355 18	224 15	252 19	68 12
	31	278 49	256 28	273 50	—	356 28	235 53	253 27	67 41

Áyanamsa: 21° 23′ 29″

Longitude of the Moon

1927		Sun.	Tue.	Thur.	Sat.	Mon.	Wed.	Fri.
Jan.	1				250 26	277 34	305 52	334 46
	9	3 35	31 47	59 9	85 40	111 21	136 14	160 26
	23	184 14	208 3	232 29	258 9	285 29		
Feb.	1		299 47	329 18	359 11	28 19	56 7	82 34
	13	107 00	132 41	156 53	180 44	204 28	228 28	253 17
	27	279 32						
March	1		307 40	337 31	8 3	37 52	66 00	92 25
	13	117 31	141 49	165 44	189 30	213 18	237 24	262 12
	27	288 16	316 5	345 42				
April	1							0 57
	3	31 31	60 57	88 30	114 17	138 50	162 45	186 29
	17	210 20	234 30	259 11	284 42	311 30	339 51	9 34
May	1	39 44	69 6	96 51	122 49	147 28	171 22	195 7
	15	219 7	243 38	268 50	294 52	321 54	350 1	19 4
	29	48 27	77 17					
June	1						91 15	118 2
	5	143 23	167 40	191 28	215 23	239 52	265 13	291 32
	19	318 46	346 43	15 10	43 45	72 4	99 37	
July	1							126 3
	3	151 19	175 37	199 26	223 22	248 00	273 47	300 51
	17	328 59	357 38	26 13	54 21	81 50	108 34	134 27
	31	159 25						
Aug.	1					171 36	195 32	219 17
	7	243 27	268 42	295 30	323 53	353 15	22 38	51 13
	21	78 41	105 9	130 46	155 41	179 59	203 48	
Sep.	1			215 37	239 25	263 57	289 54	317 42
	11	347 13	17 28	47 9	75 26	102 12	127 46	152 32
	25	176 45	200 35	224 14				
Oct.	1				248 2	272 29	298 16	325 54
	9	355 25	25 59	56 12	84 55	111 51	137 18	161 47
	23	185 43	209 26	233 9	257 7	281 42		
Nov.	1		294 23	320 50	349 3	18 50	49 17	79 4
	13	107 15	133 38	158 35	182 38	206 20	230 50	254 9
	27	278 48	304 15					
Dec.	1			330 47	358 37	27 40	57 25	86 53
	11	115 9	141 47	166 54	191 00	214 40	238 30	262 55
	25	288 10	314 20	341 22	9 10			

Ayanamsa: 21° 23′ 29″

Longitudes of Planets

1928		Sun	Mars	Merc.	Merc.	Jupit.	Venus	Saturn	Rahu
Jan.	5	283 55	260 5	281 47	289 53	357 9	241 46	254 00	77 25
	15	294 6	267 23	298 13	306 42	358 41	253 41	255 3	76 53
	25	304 17	274 44	315 18	323 46	0 26	255 43	266 00	76 21
Feb.	4	314 26	282 9	331 35	337 42	2 22	277 50	256 52	75 49
	14	324 34	289 38	340 40	339 29R	4 26	290 1	257 37	75 19
	24	334 39	297 10	334 55R	329 46	6 37	302 14	258 13	74 46
March	5	344 41	304 44	326 37	326 13D	8 54	314 30	258 41	74 14
	15	354 40	312 20	328 13D	331 59	11 15	326 46	258 59	73 42
	25	4 36	319 59	337 3	343 6	13 38	339 3	259 7R	73 11
April	4	14 28	327 38	349 57	357 29	16 3	351 20	259 6	72 39
	14	24 17	335 18	5 42	14 34	18 28	3 37	258 54	72 7
	24	34 3	342 57	24 6	34 17	20 51	15 54	258 34	71 35
May	4	43 46	350 35	44 58	55 46	23 13	28 10	258 5	71 3
	14	53 25	358 11	66 9	75 35	25 31	40 26	257 29	70 32
	24	63 3	5 45	83 48	90 41	27 44	52 42	256 48	70 00
June	3	72 38	13 14	96 7	100 00	29 52	64 58	256 5	69 28
	13	82 12	20 38	102 7	102 23R	31 52	77 14	255 21	68 56
	23	91 45	27 56	100 52R	98 9	33 43	89 31	254 38	68 25
July	3	101 17	35 6	95 17	93 30	35 25	101 48	253 58	67 52
	13	110 49	42 8	93 35D	95 55	36 54	114 6	253 25	67 21
	23	120 21	49 00	100 29	107 9	38 10	126 25	252 58	66 49
Aug.	2	129 55	55 40	115 36	125 18	39 10	138 44	252 40	66 18
	12	139 30	62 7	135 31	145 40	39 54	151 4	252 31	65 46
	22	149 7	68 19	155 23	164 33	40 19	163 24	252 31D	65 14
Sep.	1	158 47	74 11	173 11	181 18	40 25R	175 45	252 42	64 42
	11	168 29	79 42	188 56	196 4	40 11	188 4	253 1	64 10
	21	178 15	84 46	202 40	208 38	39 37	200 24	253 30	63 38
Oct.	1	188 3	89 19	213 44	217 34	38 45	212 43	254 18	63 7
	11	197 55	93 12	219 30	218 33R	37 39	225 1	254 53	62 35
	21	207 51	96 17	214 13R	208 4	36 22	237 17	255 45	62 3
	31	217 49	98 22	204 8	204 42	35 1	249 33	256 32	61 32
Nov.	10	227 51	99 16	209 00	215 22	33 41	261 46	257 45	61 00
	20	237 56	98 48R	222 40	230 20	32 30	273 57	258 51	60 28
	30	248 3	96 53	238 8	—	31 32	286 5	260 00	59 57
Dec.	10	258 12	93 45	253 46	261 37	30 50	298 8	261 11	59 34
	20	268 23	89 53	269 31	277 29	30 29	310 5	262 22	58 53
	30	278 34	86 7	285 34	—	30 28D	321 52	263 32	58 21

Ayanamsa : 21° 24' 20"

Longitude of the Moon

1928	Sun.	Tue.	Thur.	Sat.	Mon.	Wed.	Fri.
Jan. 1	23 19	51 59	80 47	109 7	136 24	162 18	186 56
15	210 46	234 28	258 41	283 54	310 22	337 53	6 00
29	34 18	62 28					
Feb. 1						76 28	104 10
5	131 16	157 26	212 32	236 41	230 21	254 13	278 58
19	305 9	332 54	1 44	30 47	59 20	87 7	
March 1			100 42	127 21	153 17	178 25	202 46
11	226 32	250 10	274 19	299 43	326 52	355 45	25 35
25	55 13	83 48	111 7	137 18			
April 1	150 3	175 00	199 18	223 7	246 43	270 32	295 10
15	321 17	349 15	18 53	49 14	79 2	107 25	134 13
29	169 42						
May 1		184 15	208 12	231 52	255 31	279 29	304 13
13	330 14	357 55	27 14	57 31	87 34	116 27	143 26
27	168 55	193 18	217 4				
June 1							228 52
3	257 32	276 33	301 13	326 47	353 33	21 41	51 2
17	80 57	110 25	138 32	164 57	189 52	213 49	237 26
July 1	261 14	285 39	310 51	336 57	3 58	31 53	60 37
15	89 48	118 45	146 41	173 6	198 2	222 00	245 38
29	269 36	294 34					
Aug. 1						307 12	333 35
5	0 50	28 39	56 50	85 14	113 35	141 25	168 13
19	193 42	218 2	241 44	265 29	290 00	315 45	342 51
Sep. 1				356 49	25 11	53 40	81 55
9	109 46	137 7	163 44	189 23	214 00	237 51	216 26
23	285 29	310 39	337 24	5 41			
Oct. 1					34 54	64 8	92 44
7	120 24	147 8	173 1	198 3	222 19	246 1	269 35
21	293 34	318 38	345 20	13 49	43 35	73 36	
Nov. 1			88 22	116 58	144 8	170 1	194 53
11	219 3	242 47	266 21	290 6	314 31	340 9	7 26
25	36 29	66 44	97 4				
Dec. 1				126 16	153 44	179 33	204 6
9	227 57	251 33	275 12	299 12	323 48	349 23	16 18
23	44 47	74 38	104 59	134 33	162 25		

Ayanamsa: 21° 24′ 20″

Longitudes of Planets

1929		Sun	Mars	Merc.	Merc.	Jupit.	Venus	Saturn	Rahu
Jan.	5	284 41	84 12R	295 22	303 31	30 38	328 51	264 13	58 2
	15	294 53	81 56	311 23	318 20	31 9	340 17	265 20	57 30
	25	305 3	81 1D	323 9R	324 14R	32 00	351 22	266 23	57 8
Feb.	4	315 12	81 23	320 54	315 7	33 8	1 58	267 20	56 26
	14	325 20	82 52	310 29	308 54	34 32	11 57	268 12	55 55
	24	335 24	85 16	310 9D	313 29	36 8	21 1	268 57	55 23
March	6	345 26	88 24	318 16	324 4	37 56	28 47	269 34	54 51
	16	355 25	92 7	330 38	337 51	39 53	34 39	270 2	54 19
	26	5 21	96 17	345 39	354 1	41 58	37 47R	270 21	53 48
April	5	15 31	100 49	2 58	12 30	44 9	37 13	270 30R	53 16
	15	25 2	105 38	22 38	33 10	46 25	32 49	270 29	52 44
	25	34 47	110 41	43 25	53 48	48 44	26 40	270 19	52 12
May	5	44 29	115 55	62 43	70 11	51 6	22 24	269 59	51 42
	15	54 9	121 19	75 59	80 1	53 28	21 56D	269 31	51 9
	25	63 47	126 51	82 7	82 17R	55 50	25 1	268 56	50 37
June	4	73 21	132 30	80 42	78 5	58 10	30 43	268 16	50 5
	14	82 55	138 16	75 30	74 00	60 28	38 13	267 33	49 34
	24	92 28	144 7	74 15D	76 29	62 41	46 54	266 49	49 1
July	4	102 00	150 3	80 37	86 35	64 50	56 26	266 6	48 30
	14	111 32	156 5	94 12	103 18	66 53	66 34	265 26	47 58
	24	121 5	162 12	113 26	123 57	68 48	77 9	264 52	47 76
Aug.	3	130 38	168 24	134 19	144 11	70 34	88 5	264 24	46 54
	13	140 14	174 40	153 25	162 3	72 9	99 17	264 5	46 23
	23	149 51	181 1	170 5	177 32	73 32	110 44	263 55	45 51
Sep.	2	159 31	187 28	184 23	190 31	74 40	122 23	263 53D	45 19
	12	169 14	193 59	195 55	200 9	75 33	134 12	264 4	44 47
	22	178 59	200 36	202 48R	203 11R	76 8	146 11	264 23	44 16
Oct.	2	188 48	207 18	200 37	195 22	76 24R	158 17	264 51	43 44
	12	198 41	214 5	190 3	188 2D	76 19	170 31	265 28	43 12
	22	208 36	220 57	190 25	195 59	75 55	182 50	266 12	42 40
Nov.	1	218 35	227 55	203 13	211 7	75 12	195 14	267 3	42 9
	11	228 37	234 59	219 12	227 16	74 12	207 42	268 1	41 37
	21	238 42	242 7	235 15	243 10	72 59	220 12	269 3	41 5
Dec.	1	248 50	249 21	251 1	258 51	71 39	232 44	270 9	40 33
	11	258 59	256 40	266 42	274 33	70 18	245 18	271 18	40 2
	21	269 9	264 4	282 23	290 6	69 2	257 52	272 29	39 30
	31	279 21	271 33	297 25	–	67 56	270 27	273 40	38 58

Ayanamsa: 21° 25' 10″

Longitude of the Moon

1929		Sun.	Tue.	Thurs.	Sat.	Mon.	Wed.	Fri.
Jan.	1		175 37	200 48	224 51	248 25	272 4	296 9
	13	320 53	346 21	12 40	40 3	68 37	98 8	127 49
	27	156 35	183 40	209 00				
Feb.	1							221 10
	3	244 55	268 31	292 33	317 24	343 8	9 39	36 50
	17	64 40	93 8	120 00	150 36	178 11	204 17	
March	1							228 59
	3	252 49	276 28	300 39	325 50	352 11	19 32	47 28
	17	75 39	103 53	132 00	159 41	186 30	212 11	236 46
	31	260 37						
April	1					272 27	296 19	321 1
	7	347 2	14 29	43 00	71 56	100 41	128 48	156 8
	21	182 35	208 8	232 49	256 49	280 29		
May	1						304 22	329 1
	5	355 2	22 40	51 44	81 30	110 57	139 22	166 27
	19	192 20	217 14	241 28	265 17	288 57	312 52	337 29
June	1				350 13	16 52	45 15	75 5
	9	105 24	135 00	163 1	189 20	214 20	238 29	262 14
	23	285 55	309 47	334 7	359 16			
July	1					25 43	53 48	83 28
	7	113 55	143 51	172 10	198 35	223 27	247 26	271 5
	21	294 51	318 58	343 36	8 58	35 22	63 8	
Aug.	1			77 34	107 19	137 25	166 38	194 7
	11	219 46	244 8	267 52	291 35	315 45	340 32	6 1
	25	32 16	59 24	87 34	116 40			
Sep.	1	131 23	160 36	188 43	215 12	240 11	264 12	287 55
	15	311 57	336 44	2 27	29 1	56 18	84 12	112 35
	29	141 10						
Oct.	1		169 29	196 56	223 6	248 2	272 4	295 49
	13	319 54	344 52	11 2	38 23	66 34	95 7	123 35
	27	151 39	179 4	205 39				
Nov.	1							218 35
	3	243 43	268 2	291 50	315 37	330 1	5 36	32 43
	17	61 17	90 41	120 1	148 32	175 54	202 10	227 32
Dec.	1	252 11	276 16	300 1	323 46	348 2	13 25	40 27
	15	69 19	99 26	129 38	158 42	186 6	212 1	236 51
	29	261 3	284 55					

Ayanamsa : 21° 25′ 10″

Longitudes of Planets

1930		Sun	Mars.	Merc.	Merc.	Jupit.	Venus	Saturn	Rahu
Jan.	5	284 27	275 19	303 40	307 39	67 28R	286 44	274 45	38 42
	15	294 38	282 54	307 40R	303 12	66 47	289 19	275 24	38 10
	25	304 48	290 33	296 59	292 59	66 25	301 53	276 31	37 39
Feb.	4	314 58	298 16	292 28D	294 45	66 23D	314 26	277 35	37 7
	14	325 5	306 00	298 53	304 15	66 41	326 59	278 33	36 35
	24	335 10	313 48	310 27	317 17	67 19	339 30	279 26	36 3
March	6	345 12	321 36	324 39	332 30	68 15	351 59	280 2	35 31
	16	355 11	329 26	340 51	349 42	69 26	4 27	280 50	35 00
	26	5 6	337 5	359 5	8 58	70 51	16 52	281 20	34 28
April	5	14 59	345 4	19 5	29 35	72 29	29 15	281 40	33 56
	15	24 47	352 51	39 22	47 54	74 16	41 34	281 51	33 24
	25	34 33	0 36	54 42	59 29	76 12	53 51	281 52R	32 53
May	5	44 15	8 19	62 5	62 30R	78 15	66 5	281 43	32 21
	15	53 55	15 57	60 58R	58 17	80 24	78 16	281 25	31 49
	25	63 32	23 52	55 36	53 59D	82 37	90 23	280 59	31 17
June	4	73 8	31 2	54 4	56 1	84 52	102 26	280 26	30 45
	14	82 41	38 25	59 42	64 58	87 9	114 25	279 46	30 14
	24	92 14	45 44	71 42	79 49	89 4	126 19	279 4	29 42
July	4	101 46	52 55	89 10	99 29	91 44	138 7	278 20	29 10
	14	111 18	59 59	110 13	120 19	93 59	149 47	277 36	28 39
	24	120 51	66 55	130 54	130 18	96 12	161 19	276 56	28 7
Aug.	3	130 25	73 43	149 00	157 1	98 20	172 41	276 20	27 35
	13	140 00	80 22	164 21	170 57	100 23	183 50	275 51	27 3
	23	149 37	86 51	176 45	181 33	102 19	194 43	275 30	26 32
Sep.	2	159 17	93 9	185 2	186 43	104 7	205 15	275 18	26 00
	12	168 59	99 14	186 1R	182 36	105 45	215 17	275 16D	25 28
	22	178 45	105 6	177 25	173 6	107 11	224 41	275 23	24 56
Oct.	2	188 34	110 42	172 18D	175 35	108 25	233 9	275 40	24 24
	12	198 26	115 59	181 50	189 39	109 23	240 14	276 7	23 52
	22	208 22	120 54	192 1	206 29	110 4	245 17	276 42	23 21
Nov.	1	218 21	125 22	214 49	222 19	110 27	247 23R	277 26	22 49
	11	228 23	129 19	231 00	238 52	110 30R	245 37	278 10	22 17
	21	238 28	132 25	246 39	254 20	110 13	240 30	279 13	21 45
Dec.	1	248 35	135 2	261 57	269 27	109 37	234 51	280 14	21 14
	11	258 44	136 29	276 43	283 27	108 43	232 06D	281 20	20 42
	21	268 55	136 45R	288 59	292 5	107 35	233 21	282 29	20 10
	31	279 6	135 41	291 4R	—	106 18	237 55	283 39	19 38

Ayanamsa: 21° 26' 00''

Longitude of the Moon

1930		Sun	Tue.	Thur.	Sat.	Mon.	Wed.	Fri.
Jan.	1						296 48	320 32
	5	344 29	9 7	34 59	62 38	92 9	122 48	153 8
	19	181 54	208 42	233 54	258 8	281 56	305 39	329 31
Feb.	1				341 33	5 58	31 10	57 39
	9	85 48	115 34	146 3	175 53	203 59	230 10	254 54
	23	278 48	302 30	326 23				
March	1				350 41	15 32	41 8	67 44
	9	95 34	124 39	154 24	183 47	211 50	238 12	263 6
	23	287 6	310 50	334 51	359 29	24 55		
April	1			37 58	64 41	92 13	120 30	149 17	178 3
	13	206 8	233 3	258 37	283 5	306 57	330 48	355 14
	27	20 39	47 13					
May	1			74 48	103 4	131 33	159 54	187 47
	11	214 58	241 16	266 34	290 59	314 51	338 42	3 9
	25	28 46	55 51	84 18	113 28			
June	1	128 2	156 44	184 32	211 22	237 22	262 36	287 8
	15	311 7	334 51	358 51	23 46	50 12	78 25	108 3
	29	138 1						
July	1		167 12	195 00	221 28	246 54	271 37	295 49
	13	319 39	343 22	7 20	32 10	58 29	86 43	116 38
	27	147 7	176 49	204 53				
Aug.	1							218 16
	3	243 59	268 42	292 49	316 38	340 22	4 14	28 38
	17	54 5	81 8	110 2	140 18	170 43	199 58	227 25
	31	253 12						
Sep.	1					265 37	289 50	313 38
	7	337 23	1 20	25 43	50 51	77 5	104 47	133 56
	21	163 57	193 42	222 11	248 58	274 13		
Oct.	1						298 26	322 11
	5	346 00	10 14	35 7	60 49	87 27	115 6	143 42
	19	172 52	201 56	230 7	256 55	282 17	306 33	330 18
Nov.	1				342 11	6 18	31 15	57 15
	9	84 14	111 57	140 8	168 31	196 48	224 40	251 42
	23	277 35	302 20	326 17	349 59			
Dec.	1					14 7	39 19	65 55
	7	93 49	122 28	151 9	179 22	206 59	233 58	260 15
	21	285 42	310 17	334 9	357 47	21 50	47 2	

Ayanamsa: 21° 26' 00"

Longitudes of Planets

1931		Sun	Mars.	Merc.	Merc.	Jupit.	Venus	Saturn	Rahu
Jan.	5	284 12	134 38R	286 1R	279 27R	105 38R	241 8	284 15	19 24
	15	294 23	131 39	276 15R	276 47D	104 17	248 54	285 27	18 52
	25	304 34	127 49	280 00	284 49	103 3	257 59	286 36	18 21
Feb.	4	314 43	123 53	290 41	297 13	102 00	267 55	287 43	17 49
	14	324 50	120 33	304 16	311 45	101 9	278 27	288 47	17 17
	24	334 55	118 22	319 37	327 55	100 39	289 25	289 48	16 45
March	6	344 57	117 27	336·38	345 48	100 27	300 44	290 40	16 13
	16	354 57	117 48D	355 26	5 24	100 34D	312 10	291 25	15 42
	26	4 53	119 14	15 25	24 51	101 00	323 48	292 7	15 10
April	5	14 45	121 35	32 54	38 54	101 47	335 33	292 39	14 37
	15	24 34	124 39	42 26	43 22R	102 47	347 24	293 1	14 6
	25	34 19	128 18	41 57R	39 8R	104 00	359 18	293 13	13 35
May	5	44 1	132 25	36 00R	33 57R	105 30	11 16	293 16R	13 3
	15	53 41	136 54	33 44D	35 23	107 10	23 16	293 10	12 31
	25	63 20	141 43	38 41	43 36	108 57	35 17	292 54	11 59
June	4	72 54	146 47	49 44	57 5	110 53	47 21	292 27	11 27
	14	82 29	152 5	65 34	75 6	112 54	59 26	291 56	10 55
	24	92 02	157 34	85 32	96 24	115 00	71 34	291 21	10 24
July	4	101 33	163 14	107 10	117 25	117 10	83 44	290 39R	9 51
	14	111 4	169 3	126 55	135 38	119 22	95 56	289 52	9 20
	24	120 37	175 1	143 34	150 42	121 35	108 10	289 10	8 48
Aug.	3	130 11	181 6	157 00	162 19	123 49	120 27	288 27	8 17
	13	139 47	187 20	166 26	169 00	126 1	132 46	287 52	7 45
	23	149 24	193 42	169 37R	167 50R	128 11	145 8	287 21	7 13
Sep.	2	169 4	200 11	163 56R	159 12R	130 18	157 31	286 57R	6 41
	12	168 46	206 46	156 11R	156 40D	132 19	169 57	286 44	6 9
	22	178 31	213 27	160 49	167 42	134 14	182 24	286 39	5 37
Oct.	2	188 20	220 17	176 2	184 53	136 2	194 51	286 44D	5 5
	12	198 12	227 13	193 42	202 19	137 41	207 19	286 59	4 34
	22	208 8	234 16	210 42	218 49	139 8	219 48	287 24	4 1
Nov.	1	218 6	241 26	226 43	234 26	140 23	232 17	287 59	3 30
	11	228 8	248 41	241 59	249 22	141 22	244 46	288 41	3 00
	21	238 13	256 4	256 32	263 20	142 6	257 15	289 30	2 25
Dec.	1	248 20	263 30	269 27	274 13	142 31	269 44	290 27	1 55
	11	258 29	271 2	276 22	274 23R	142 38R	282 12	291 28	1 24
	21	268 39	278 40	268 24R	262 23R	142 26	294 38	292 33	0 52
	31	278 51	286 22	260 7R	261 40D	141 54	307 3	293 40	0 19

Ayanamsa: 21° 26′ 51″

Longitude of the Moon

1931	Sun.	Tue.	Thur.	Sat.	Mon.	Wed.	Fri.
Jan. 1			60 14	88 00	117 12	146 52	175 58
11	203 56	230 48	256 46	281 59	306 33	330 32	354 9
25	17 51	42 16	68 6	95 51			
Feb. 1	110 26	140 32	170 47	199 59	227 38	253 51	278 59
15	303 24	327 20	350 59	14 37	38 38	63 36	90 7
March 1	118 31	148 30	179 2	208 46	236 53	263 17	288 19
15	312 28	336 11	359 48	23 37	47 55	73 4	99 29
29	127 27	156 52				171 55	202 3
April 1					333 3	356 39	20 30
5	231 16	258 51	284 43	309 15			
19	44 55	70 7	96 14	123 25	151 42	180 52	
May 1							210 21
3	239 16	266 53	292 54	317 31	341 20	4 58	29 2
17	53 55	79 48	106 37	134 10	162 18	190 49	219 27
31	247 41				261 28	288 4	313 18
June 1							
7	337 27	1 7	24 59	49 42	75 38	102 48	130 48
21	159 8	187 25	215 29	243 11	270 14		
July 1						296 19	321 19
5	345 23	9 1	32 55	57 45	84 2	111 51	140 41
19	169 44	198 20	226 11	253 6	279 34	305 1	329 37
Aug. 1				341 38	5 19	28 58	53 13
9	78 46	106 1	134 54	164 40	194 15	222 52	250 15
23	276 28	301 45	326 15	350 10	13 47		
Sep. 1		25 34	49 27	74 13	100 27	128 29	158 6
13	188 23	218 9	246 34	273 23	298 49	323 16	347 7
27	10 44	34 24					
Oct. 1			58 27	83 17	109 21	137 1	166 18
11	196 33	226 40	255 31	282 34	307 58	332 13	355 54
25	19 30	43 23	67 48	92 57			
Nov. 1	105 53	132 35	160 35	189 50	219 47	249 21	277 32
15	303 55	328 43	352 34	16 8	40 1	64 34	89 55
29	116 4				228 25	257 25	285 24
Dec. 1		142 59	170 43	199 17	228 25	257 25	285 24
13	311 49	336 42	0 35	24 11	48 12	73 7	99 8
27	126 5	153 39	181 35				

Ayanamsa: 21° 26′ 51″

Longitudes of Planets

1932		Sun	Mars	Merc.	Merc.	Jupit.	Venus	Saturn	Rahu
Jan.	5	283 56	290 24	261 40	265 42	141 30R	313 15	294 17	0 5
	15	294 8	298 02	271 9	277 27	140 32	325 35	295 28	359 32
	25	304 19	305 52	283 57	291 31	139 22	337 53	296 40	359 1
Feb.	4	314 28	313 44	299 4	306 57	138 4	350 4	297 50	358 29
	14	324 36	321 38	314 55	323 43	136 44	2 10	298 57	357 57
	24	334 41	329 31	332 40	342 00	135 30	14 6	300 3	357 25
March	5	344 43	337 25	351 37	1 15	134 23	25 51	331 00	356 54
	15	354 42	345 18	10 15	17 47	133 31	37 22	301 58	356 22
	25	4 38	353 09	22 52	25 28	132 55	48 5	302 47	355 50
April	4	14 31	0 57	24 7R	21 3R	132 37	59 28	303 29	355 18
	14	24 20	8 41	17 21R	14 37R	132 39D	69 50	304 02	354 46
	24	34 6	16 23	13 44D	14 57	133 00	79 37	304 25	354 14
May	4	43 48	24 00	17 57	22 27	133 37	88 27	304 40	353 43
	14	53 29	31 32	28 10	34 56	134 31	96 4	304 45	353 11
	24	63 6	39 00	42 43	51 27	135 40	101 54	304 41R	352 39
June	3	72 41	46 21	61 6	71 34	137 00	105 5	304 27R	352 7
	13	82 15	53 38	82 30	93 22	138 33	104 46R	304 3	351 36
	23	91 47	60 48	103 43	113 16	140 14	100 39R	303 33	351 4
July	3	101 20	67 52	121 56	129 32	142 3	94 35R	302 56	350 32
	13	110 52	74 50	136 33	142 24	144 00	89 59	302 15	350 1
	23	120 25	81 42	147 4	150 19	146 1	89 00D	301 31	349 29
Aug.	2	129 58	88 27	151 50	151 16R	148 6	91 45	300 46	348 54
	12	130 33	95 5	148 34R	143 41R	150 15	97 9	300 5	348 25
	22	149 10	101 37	140 47	139 16D	152 25	104 27	299 26	347 54
Sep.	1	158 50	108 00	141 3R	146 4	154 36	113 5	298 54	347 22
	11	168 12	114 17	153 32	162 21	156 46	122 39	298 29	346 50
	21	178 17	120 25	171 37	180 50	158 54	132 53	298 13	346 18
Oct.	1	188 6	126 5	189 44	198 23	160 59	143 5	298 7	345 46
	11	198 58	132 12	206 33	214 29	163 00	154 48	298 10D	345 15
	21	208 53	137 48	222 9	229 36	164 55	166 17	298 24	344 43
	31	217 52	143 12	236 44	243 34	166 41	178 1	298 48	344 11
Nov.	10	227 54	148 20	249 53	255 22	168 19	189 58	299 20	343 39
	20	237 58	153 9	259 19	260 31R	169 46	202 3	300 2	343 8
	30	248 5	157 35	257 36R	251 15R	171 00	214 17	300 50	342 36
Dec.	10	258 14	161 33	245 45R	244 25D	172 00	226 16	301 45	342 4
	20	268 25	164 58	246 55	251 43	172 43	238 59	302 46	341 32
	30	278 36	167 40	257 45	264 27	173 8	251 16	303 53	341 00

Ayanamsa : 21° 27′ 41″

Longitude of the Moon

1932	Sun.	Tue.	Thur.	Sat.	Mon.	Wed.	Fri.
Jan. 1							195 39
3	223 55	252 11	279 58	306 43	332 10	356 28	20 8
17	43 53	68 24	94 11	121 21	149 32	178 8	206 38
31	234 43						
Feb. 1					248 35	275 49	302 17
7	327 47	352 21	16 12	39 49	63 50	88 54	115 31
21	143 43	173 00	202 30	231 23	259 14		
March 1		272 44	298 56	324 12	348 41	12 36	36 14
13	59 59	84 23	110 00	137 19	166 19	196 25	226 28
27	255 27	282 51	308 45				
April 1							321 15
3	345 37	9 27	33 5	56 47	80 54	105 48	132 00
17	159 52	189 22	219 50	249 57	278 37	305 13	330 33
May 1	354 40	18 19	41 57	65 51	90 13	115 19	141 26
15	168 57	198 00	228 8	258 15	287 7	314 5	339 19
29	3 24	27 1					
June 1						38 50	62 45
5	87 14	112 24	138 19	165 10	193 9	222 14	251 54
19	281 8	308 59	335 4	359 43	23 32	47 13	
July 1							71 21
3	96 15	122 1	148 34	175 51	203 49	232 25	261 16
17	289 44	317 5	343 1	7 39	31 32	55 17	79 33
31	104 47						
Aug. 1					117 50	144 43	172 26
7	200 39	229 3	257 21	285 15	312 22	338 27	3 26
21	27 33	51 18	75 15	100 1	126 4	153 31	
Sep 1			167 42	196 36	225 38	254 11	281 54
11	308 40	334 30	359 29	23 44	47 33	71 17	95 31
25	120 48	147 37	176 7				
Oct. 1				205 48	235 40	264 42	292 21
9	318 38	343 50	8 18	32 17	56 2	79 47	103 57
23	129 4	155 40	184 6	214 7	244 38		
Nov. 1		259 39	288 29	315 29	340 55	5 20	29 14
13	52 58	76 45	100 48	125 24	151 1	178 10	207 7
27	237 28	267 57					
Dec. 1			297 12	324 29	349 59	14 17	38 3
11	61 46	85 44	110 6	135 2	160 46	187 42	216 7
25	245 49	275 55	305 8	332 38			

Ayanamsa: 21° 27' 41"

Longitudes of Planets

1933		Sun	Mars	Merc.	Merc.	Jupit.	Venus	Saturn	Rahu
Jan.	5	284 43	168 52	265 50	273 1	173 15	258 53	304 33	340 42
	15	294 54	170 6	280 27	288 8	173 11R	271 23	305 43	340 10
	25	305 5	170 10R	296 3	304 14	172 47	283 51	306 54	339 38
Feb.	4	315 14	168 55	312 42	321 28	172 6R	296 21	308 6	339 6
	14	325 22	166 25	330 2	339 48	171 8	308 50	309 16	338 35
	24	335 26	162 56	348 55	357 12	170 00	321 19	310 26	337 59
March	6	345 29	159 00R	3 36	7 3	168 43	337 47	311 28	337 31
	16	355 27	155 21	6 56R	3 50R	167 24	346 14	312 32	336 58
	26	5 23	152 37	359 30	356 2R	166 10	358 40	313 29	336 26
April	5	15 16	151 7R	354 40	355 32D	165 5	11 5	314 17	335 56
	15	25 4	150 55D	358 20	2 39	164 13	22 58	315 00	335 24
	25	34 50	151 54	8 10	14 42	163 38	35 50	315 35	334 52
May	5	44 33	153 53	22 5	29 50	163 20	48 9	315 59	334 20
	15	54 12	156 41	38 53	48 45	163 19D	60 29	316 16	333 48
	25	63 49	160 9	59 18	70 15	163 38	72 46	316 23	333 16
June	4	73 25	164 11	81 35	91 48	164 13	85 2	316 20R	332 45
	14	82 58	168 38	101 8	109 26	165 4	97 18	316 7	332 13
	24	92 31	173 30	116 42	122 53	166 8	109 31	315 46	331 42
July	4	102 3	178 42	127 48	131 19	167 28	121 45	315 17R	331 10
	14	111 35	184 8	133 8	133 00R	168 57	133 57	314 40	331 35
	24	121 8	189 53	130 57	127 32	170 36	146 7	313 57	330 6
Aug.	3	130 42	195 47	124 6	122 11	172 24	158 14	313 15	329 34
	13	140 17	201 55	122 53	126 35	174 18	170 19	312 31	329 2
	23	149 54	208 13	132 49	141 7	176 17	182 24	311 47	328 37
Sep.	2	159 34	214 42	150 32	160 13	178 21	194 22	311 7	327 55
	12	169 16	221 20	169 43	178 51	180 28	206 18	310 36	327 27
	22	180 2	228 8	187 32	195 49	182 37	218 9	310 10	326 55
Oct.	2	189 51	235 4	203 45	211 19	184 48	229 54	309 52	326 21
	12	198 43	242 9	218 31	225 22	187 00	241 32	309 44	325 52
	22	208 38	249 22	231 43	237 23	189 6	253 00	309 46D	325 20
Nov.	1	218 37	256 40	241 54	244 31	191 9	264 17	309 58	324 48
	11	228 39	264 7	243 59R	239 29R	193 9	275 18	310 21	324 17
	21	238 44	271 39	232 57	228 43	195 00	285 54	310 53	323 45
Dec.	1	248 51	279 18	229 29	233 23	196 43	295 57	311 33	323 13
	11	259 00	287 1	239 10	245 53	198 25	305 12	312 21	322 41
	21	269 11	294 48	253 3	260 28	199 50	313 12	313 16	322 9
	31	279 22	302 38	268 3	275 46	201 3	319 31	314 17	321 37

Ayanamsa: 21° 28′ 31″

Longitude of the Moon

1933		Sun.	Tue.	Thurs.	Sat.	Mon.	Wed.	Fri.
Jan.	1	345 41	10 39	34 39	58 21	82 17	106 45	131 55
	15	157 48	184 29	212 6	240 39	269 49	298 50	326 52
	29	353 25	18 31				30 40	54 31
Feb.	1							
	5	78 20	102 39	127 50	154 2	181 9	208 58	237 13
	19	265 38	293 54	321 34	348 17	13 52		
March	1						38 26	62 20
	5	86 8	110 28	135 51	162 36	190 36	219 21	248 12
	19	276 34	304 11	330 57	356 54	22 2	46 25	70 17
April	1				82 9	106 5	130 49	156 56
	9	184 45	214 00	243 48	273 4	301 7	327 53	353 35
	23	18 31	42 52	66 48	90 31			
May	1					114 24	139 00	165 00
	7	192 50	222 26	252 53	282 47	311 10	337 52	3 15
	21	27 46	51 48	75 35	99 18	123 15	147 51	
June	1			160 35	187 16	215 51	246 2	276 37
	11	306 13	334 2	0 5	24 51	48 53	72 38	96 23
	25	120 22	144 48	170 6				
July	1				196 42	214 57	254 41	284 59
	9	314 35	342 36	8 49	33 39	57 39	81 23	105 14
	23	129 31	154 25	180 49	206 56	234 57		
Aug.	1		249 23	278 50	308 19	336 55	4 2	29 37
	13	54 2	77 52	101 40	125 56	151 00	176 58	203 52
	27	231 35	259 56	288 38				
Sep.	1							302 59
	3	331 19	358 45	24 56	49 53	73 58	97 43	121 46
	17	146 41	172 48	200 6	228 15	256 44	285 6	313 6
Oct.	1	340 32	7 14	33 1	57 49	81 51	105 33	129 34
	15	154 34	181 4	209 8	238 14	267 27	296 1	323 38
	29	350 22	16 19					
Nov.	1						29 1	53 53
	5	78 4	101 47	125 29	149 48	175 26	202 55	232 9
	19	262 15	291 57	320 23	347 23	13 13	38 14	
Dec.	1							62 39
	3	86 36	110 15	133 56	158 11	183 39	210 55	240 7
	17	270 33	300 51	329 51	357 7	22 52	47 33	71 37
	31	95 22						

Ayanamsa: 21° 28′ 31″

Longitudes of Planets

1934		Sun	Mars	Merc.	Merc.	Jupit.	Venus	Saturn	Rahu
Jan.	5	284 28	306 24	275 46	283 39	201 33	321 44	314 53	321 21
	15	294 39	314 26	291 14	300 1	202 23	323 38	316 00	320 50
	25	304 50	322 21	308 32	317 16	202 56	321 33R	317 9	320 18
Feb.	4	314 59	330 16	326 6	334 43	203 11	316 7R	318 22	319 45
	14	325 7	338 10	342 28	348 8	203 7R	310 30	319 34	319 15
	24	335 12	346 02	350 55	349 45R	202 44	308 00	320 46	318 44
March	6	345 14	353 52	344 14R	339 32R	202 3	309 24	321 54	318 11
	16	355 13	2 26	336 45R	336 33D	201 7	314 2	323 2	317 40
	26	5 9	9 23	338 37	342 24	200 00	320 53	324 4	317 8
April	5	15 1	17 2	347 28	353 23	198 44	329 12	325 2	316 36
	15	24 50	24 37	0 29	8 8	197 28	338 33	326 21	316 4
	25	34 35	32 7	16 39	25 40	196 13R	348 33	326 38	315 30
May	5	44 19	39 33	35 25	45 49	195 9	359 4	327 14	315 00
	15	53 59	46 54	56 46	67 33	194 16	9 56	327 42	314 22
	25	63 36	54 9	77 42	86 54	193 40	21 3	328 1	313 56
June	4	73 11	61 18	94 55	101 41	193 20R	32 22	328 10	313 24
	14	82 45	68 22	107 8	111 9	193 18	43 51	328 9R	312 54
	24	92 18	75 21	113 28	113 58R	193 34	55 27	327 59R	312 22
July	4	101 50	82 14	112 32R	109 53R	194 6	67 10	327 40R	311 48
	14	111 12	89 4	106 40R	104 30R	194 56	79 0C	327 12R	311 18
	24	120 55	95 47	104 20D	106 35	196 00	90 53	326 36	310 46
Aug.	3	130 28	102 26	111 18	117 46	197 16	102 52	325 56R	310 15
	13	140 3	109 00	126 59	136 46	198 44	114 57	325 12	309 41
	23	149 11	115 28	146 49	156 36	200 23	126 6	324 27D	309 11
Sep.	2	159 20	121 52	166 3	174 56	202 5	139 21	323 47R	308 36
	12	169 2	128 11	183 20	191 17	204 3	151 40	323 2	308 7
	22	178 48	134 25	198 47	205 50	206 4	164 3	322 28	307 35
Oct.	2	188 36	140 33	212 25	218 22	208 9	176 28	322 00R	307 00
	12	198 29	146 36	223 28	227 13	210 16	188 57	321 41	306 30
	22	208 24	152 32	228 52	227 20R	212 26	201 27	321 31	305 59
Nov.	1	218 23	158 21	222 18	216 36	214 37	214 00	321 31	305 29
	11	228 25	164 2	213 3	214 29D	216 48	226 32	321 42	304 57
	21	238 30	169 34	219 12	225 38	218 56	239 6	322 4D	304 25
Dec.	1	248 36	174 55	232 49	240 20	221 2	251 40	322 35	303 51
	11	258 46	180 3	248 00	255 43	223 6	265 30	323 15	303 20
	21	269 56	184 56	263 21	271 24	224 58	276 49	324 2	302 50
	31	279 8	189 29	279 22	287 28	226,46	289 24	324 57	302 16

Ayanamsa: 21° 29′ 22″

Longitude of the Moon

1934		Sun.	Tue.	Thur.	Sat.	Mon.	Wed.	Fri.
Jan.	1					107 12	139 55	154 59
	7	179 49	205 57	233 48	263 19	293 43	323 44	352 19
	21	19 6	44 20	68 33	92 16	115 56	139 53	
Feb.	1			152 2	176 51	202 33	229 26	257 39
	11	286 59	316 48	346 3	13 56	40 9	64 56	88 50
	25	112 28	136 23					
March	1			160 59	186 26	212 48	240 1	268 1
	11	296 38	325 32	354 9	21 46	48 00	72 53	96 49
	25	120 28	144 31	169 28	195 36			
April	1	209 6	236 44	264 51	293 7	321 18	349 15	16 40
	15	43 9	68 29	92 46	116 28	140 15	164 48	190 41
	29	218 4						
May	1		246 35	275 29	304 5	332 3	359 21	25 58
	13	51 47	76 43	100 49	124 28	148 12	172 45	198 44
	27	226 28	255 39	285 20				
June	1							300 3
	3	328 46	356 20	22 50	48 25	73 14	97 22	121 2
	17	144 38	168 40	193 48	220 36	249 14	279 11	309 21
July	1	338 37	6 26	32 48	57 59	82 20	106 10	129 45
	15	153 25	177 33	202 40	229 18	257 40	287 31	317 53
	29	347 36	15 47					
Aug.	1						29 13	54 55
	5	79 25	103 14	126 49	150 30	174 37	199 27	225 19
	19	252 33	281 15	311 5	341 9	10 21	37 54	63 42
Sep.	1				76 4	100 5	123 40	147 22
	9	171 35	196 31	222 17	248 58	276 41	305 23	334 47
	23	4 6	32 26	59 10	84 18			
Oct.	1					108 19	131 55	155 46
	7	180 21	205 54	232 23	259 36	287 23	315 38	344 13
	21	12 45	40 33	67 4	92 10	116 12	139 49	
Nov.	1			151 41	176 1	201 28	228 13	255 57
	11	284 10	312 26	340 33	8 25	35 46	62 17	87 43
	25	112 6	135 49	159 28				
Dex	1				183 45	209 24	236 34	265 4
	9	294 12	323 19	351 25	18 51	45 26	71 10	96 3
	23	120 11	143 51	167 30	191 44	217 13		

Ayanamsa: 21° 29′ 22″

Longitudes of Planets

1935		Sun	Mars	Merc.	Merc.	Jupit.	Venus	Saturn	Rahu
Jan.	5	284 13	191 37	287 28	295 44	227 36	295 41	325 27	302 1
	15	294 25	195 34	304 6	310 50	229 8	308 13	326 30	301 30
	25	304 35	198 58	320 36	327 42	230 29	320 44	327 34	300 57
Feb.	4	314 45	201 43	332 36	333 50R	231 34	333 14	328 47	300 26
	14	324 52	203 39	330 36R	325 9R	232 28	345 42	330 00	299 55
	24	334 57	204 34	320 36	318 50R	233 00	358 7	331 12	299 23
March	6	345 00	204 22R	320 17D	322 51	233 16	10 28	332 25	298 50
	16	354 59	202 46	327 24	333 2	233 14R	22 45	333 36	298 18
	26	4 54	200 2	339 32	346 43	232 53	34 56	334 40	297 48
April	5	14 47	196 28R	354 12	2 58	232 14R	47 3	335 47	297 17
	15	24 36	192 40R	12 2	21 45	230 20R	59 2	336 47	296 44
	25	34 22	189 21	32 3	42 46	230 13	70 52	337 40	296 12
May	5	44 05	187 5	52 25	63 29	229 00	82 35	338 27	295 40
	15	53 45	186 5R	72 24	79 57	227 44	94 6	339 6	295 9
	25	63 22	186 25D	86 2	90 31	226 34	105 20	339 36	294 36
June	4	72 58	187 54	93 14	94 5	225 24R	116 25	340 00	294 5
	14	82 31	190 23	93 5R	90 43R	224 30R	127 6	340 11	293 33
	24	92 4	193 42	87 53R	85 47R	223 52R	137 20	340 13R	293 1
July	4	101 36	197 41	85 18D	86 51	223 31	146 57R	340 6R	292 29
	14	111 8	202 13	90 33R	96 13	222 26D	155 43	339 48R	292 00
	24	120 41	207 13	103 45	112 52	223 40	163 16	339 22R	291 25
Aug.	3	130 14	212 37	122 56	133 18	224 12	169 6	338 49R	290 55
	13	139 49	218 22	143 28	153 6	225 00	172 23	338 9	290 23
	23	149 26	224 25	162 10	170 40	226 00	172 11R	337 27	289 50
Sep.	2	159 6	230 45	178 38	186 3	227 18	168 45	336 40R	289 17
	12	168 48	237 18	192 57	199 11	228 47	162 15R	335 54	288 48
	22	178 33	244 2	204 41	209 9	230 26	157 38	335 13	288 16
Oct.	2	188 22	251 00	212 4	212 47R	232 14	156 43D	334 37R	287 45
	12	198 14	258 7	210 12R	204 47R	234 11	159 33	334 7R	287 12
	22	207 59	265 23	199 17R	197 16	236 13	165 9	333 45R	286 40
Nov.	1	218 8	272 46	199 38	205 6	238 20	172 45	333 33R	286 8
	11	228 10	280 17	212 8	219 48	240 31	181 42	333 31D	285 42
	21	238 15	287 54	227 41	235 35	242 44	191 36	333 40	285 5
Dec.	1	248 22	295 36	243 28	251 20	244 58	202 10	334 00	284 32
	11	258 31	303 21	259 11	267 04	247 12	213 15	334 28	284 1
	21	268 41	311 9	275 00	283 00	249 23	224 40	335 4	283 30
	31	278 53	318 58	291 3	299 00	251 32	236 21	335 53	282 56

Ayanamsa: 21° 30′ 12″

Longitude of the Moon

1935		Sun	Tue.	Thur.	Sat.	Mon.	Wed.	Fri.
Jan.	1		230 35	258 38	288 6	318 4	347 28	15 39
	13	42 27	68 2	92 44	116 48	140 30	164 7	188 2
	27	212 45	238 47	266 32				
Feb.	1							281 4
	3	311 6	341 30	11 1	38 52	65 00	89 48	113 47
	17	137 26	161 5	185 00	209 27	234 46	261 20	
March	1							289 29
	3	319 8	349 30	19 21	47 36	73 56	98 42	122 34
	17	146 8	169 54	194 9	219 2	244 39	271 14	299 00
	31	328 00						
April	1					342 51	12 42	41 45
	7	69 10	94 47	119 4	142 44	166 26	190 41	215 44
	21	241 35	268 11	295 32	323 39	352 28		
May	1						21 30	49 58
	5	77 6	102 42	127 3	150 46	174 34	199 2	224 31
	19	251 3	278 26	306 21	334 36	2 58	31 11	58 46
June	1				72 11	98 7	122 53	146 50
	9	170 32	194 40	219 47	246 12	273 54	302 26	331 14
	23	359 48	27 46	54 57	81 13			
July	1					106 33	131 00	154 52
	7	178 34	202 41	227 47	254 20	282 27	311 46	341 24
	21	10 25	38 24	65 5	90 40	115 24	139 32	
Aug.	1			151 26	175 6	198 56	223 23	249 2
	11	276 19	305 20	335 30	5 39	34 39	61 59	87 46
	25	112 26	136 28	160 12	183 53			
Sep.	1	195 48	219 56	244 51	271 3	298 57	328 35	359 9
	15	29 17	57 50	84 26	109 28	133 33	157 14	180 57
	29	204 55						
Oct.	1		229 18	254 22	280 28	308 00	337 9	7 23
	13	37 31	66 15	93 4	118 10	142 14	165 54	189 42
	27	213 57	238 48	264 18				
Nov.	1							277 21
	3	304 11	332 11	1 17	30 56	60 5	87 48	113 49
	17	138 26	162 17	186 1	210 12	235 9	260 57	287 34
Dec.	1	314 53	342 53	11 25	40 7	68 23	95 37	121 31
	15	146 12	170 8	193 54	218 9	243 21	269 45	297 14
	29	325 26	353 55					

Ayanamsa: 21° 30' 12"

Longitudes of Planets

1936	Sun	Mars	Merc.	Merc.	Jupit.	Venus	Saturn	Rahu
Jan. 5	283 59	322 53	298 59	306 31	252 35	242 16	336 20	282 42
15	294 10	330 44	312 58	317 00	254 37	254 12	337 18	282 9
25	304 21	338 33	317 00R	312 49R	256 31	266 12	338 21	281 37
Feb. 4	314 31	346 21	306 37R	302 44R	258 17	278 23	339 28	281 5
14	324 38	354 6	302 00D	304 3	259 52	290 37	340 34	280 34
24	334 43	1 47	307 58	313 8	261 17	302 51	341 51	280 2
March 5	344 45	9 26	319 13	325 58	262 27	315 6	343 00	279 31
15	354 44	16 59	333 20	341 15	263 22	327 24	344 18	279 00
25	4 41	24 30	349 40	358 41	264 00	339 41	345 30	278 26
April 4	14 33	31 56	8 12	18 18	264 22	351 59	346 39	277 54
14	24 22	39 16	28 48	39 14	264 25R	4 16	347 43	277 30
24	34 8	46 31	49 3	57 38	264 9R	16 33	348 46	276 52
May 3	42 53	53 00	63 20	68 52	263 38R	27 36	349 36	276 22
13	52 33	60 5	72 25	74 00	262 50R	39 52	350 27	275 50
23	62 11	67 1	73 32R	71 00R	261 48R	51 38	351 10	275 26
June 3	72 44	74 43	69 14R	66 8R	260 32	66 38	351 45	274 45
13	82 17	81 35	65 32D	66 47	259 12R	77 54	352 12	274 12
23	91 50	88 23	69 55	74 48	258 1R	90 31	352 26	273 47
July 3	101 22	95 5	81 19	89 21	256 51R	102 28	352 32	273 10
13	110 54	101 44	98 45	109 4	255 51R	114 47	352 27R	272 37
23	120 27	108 21	119 41	130 6	255 9	127 5	352 13	272 12
Aug. 2	130 00	114 53	139 58	149 11	254 42R	139 25	351 49R	271 34
12	139 35	121 22	157 46	165 43	254 34D	151 44	351 16	271 2
22	149 12	127 47	173 2	179 42	254 45D	164 4	350 37R	270 30
Sep. 1	158 52	134 10	185 35	190 34	255 15	176 24	349 55	270 00
11	168 34	140 30	194 19	196 18	256 2	188 44	349 10	269 27
21	178 19	146 48	195 41R	191 30R	257 4	201 3	348 23	268 55
Oct. 1	188 8	153 2	187 5R	182 30R	258 20	213 21	347 40R	268 22
11	197 59	159 14	181 36D	184 52	259 49	225 38	347 2	267 54
21	207 55	165 23	191 7	198 38	261 30	237 54	346 30	267 20
31	217 53	171 29	206 17	215 1	263 15	250 9	346 6	266 49
Nov. 10	227 55	177 32	223 10	231 13	265 19	262 22	345 52	266 17
20	238 00	183 31	239 10	247 1	267 18	274 32	345 47D	265 45
30	248 7	189 25	254 49	262 35	269 35	286 38	345 53	265 13
Dec. 10	258 16	195 13	270 20	278 2	271 50	298 40	346 10	264 40
20	268 27	200 56	285 31	292 29	274 7	310 35	346 37	264 10
30	278 38	206 30	298 11	301 30	276 25	322 19	347 15	263 37

Ayanamsa : 21° 31′ 2″

Longitude of the Moon

1936		Sun.	Tue.	Thurs.	Sat.	Mon.	Wed.	Fri.
Jan.	1						8 8	36 19
	5	63 57	90 50	116 48	141 49	166 1	189 48	213 42
	19	238 19	264 14	291 42	320 29	349 52	18 57	47 6
Feb.	1				60 46	87 18	112 58	137 53
	9	162 11	186 4	209 48	233 53	258 56	285 33	313 59
	23	343 52	14 4	43 21	71 4			
March	1	84 20	109 57	134 41	158 53	182 46	206 30	230 23
	15	254 48	280 22	307 39	336 54	7 20	37 45	66 46
	29	93 55	119 27					
April	1						131 47	155 56
	5	179 45	203 30	227 24	251 40	276 40	302 54	330 49
	19	0 25	30 53	60 51	89 13	115 43	140 43	
May	1							164 48
	3	188 33	212 21	236 30	261 8	286 31	312 55	340 38
	17	9 40	39 28	69 07	97 19	123 57	149 5	173 14
	31	197 00						
June	1					208 55	233 3	257 49
	7	283 24	309 52	337 15	5 29	34 21	63 18	91 40
	21	118 51	144 39	169 17	193 13	217 2		
July	1						241 18	266 28
	5	292 44	320 2	348 5	16 30	44 56	73 2	100 32
	19	127 7	152 40	177 14	201 9	224 57	249 15	274 39
Aug.	1				287 53	315 25	344 4	13 5
	9	41 45	69 41	96 46	123 4	148 34	173 17	197 21
	23	221 3	244 57	269 41	295 55	323 54		
Sep.	1		338 29	8 17	37 54	66 29	93 45	119 53
	13	145 10	169 48	193 54	217 37	241 17	265 26	290 43
	27	317 45	346 44					
Oct.	1			17 2	47 19	76 24	103 47	129 43
	11	154 36	178 50	202 42	226 22	250 6	274 16	299 28
	25	326 15	354 57	25 10	55 43			
Nov.	1	70 40	99 21	126 13	151 33	175 53	199 42	223 23
	15	247 11	271 21	296 12	322 8	349 32	18 31	48 33
	29	78 35						
Dec.	1		107 29	134 40	160 12	184 32	208 18	231 59
	13	256 1	280 39	306 3	332 23	359 45	28 8	57 18
	27	86 37	115 13	142 29				

Ayanamsa: 21° 31′ 2″

Longitudes of Planets

1937		Sun	Mars	Merc.	Merc.	Jupit.	Venus	Saturn	Rahu
Jan.	5	284 45	209 47	301 30	299 28R	277 48	329 16	347 40	263 19
	15	294 56	215 8	293 39R	287 6R	280 3	340 38	348 31	262 48
	25	305 7	220 17	285 31	286 29D	282 19	351 36	349 28	262 14
Feb.	4	315 16	225 12	289 51	294 44	284 30	2 5	350 30	261 42
	14	325 24	229 47	300 37	307 10	286 37	11 54	351 38	261 12
	24	335 29	234 2	314 16	321 50	288 35	20 44	352 48	260 40
March	6	345 31	237 49	329 52	338 20	290 26	28 7	354 00	260 8
	16	355 30	241 00	347 18	356 46	292 8	33 50	355 16	259 36
	26	5 25	243 28	6 42	16 54	293 37	35 47	356 30	259 5
April	5	15 18	245 2	27 00	36 17	294 54	34 16R	357 43	258 33
	15	25 17	245 32	44 1	49 49	295 55	29 10R	358 54	258 0
	25	34 51	244 47R	53 18	54 56	296 41	23 12R	0 2	257 29
May	5	44 35	242 49	53 22R	50 50R	297 8	19 44	1 5	256 57
	15	54 15	239 49	47 54R	45 49	297 18R	20 10D	2 2	256 25
	25	63 52	236 20	45 19D	46 20	297 10	23 27	2 54	255 54
June	4	73 27	233 5	49 55	54 37	296 42	30 10	3 39	255 22
	14	83 1	230 32	60 46	68 12	295 56	36 58	4 15	254 50
	24	92 33	229 35	76 53	86 40	294 57	46 54	4 41	254 18
July	4	102 6	229 37	97 16	108 5	293 46R	56 36	5 0	253 48
	14	111 38	231 26	118 36	128 32	292 30	66 51	5 7	253 15
	24	121 10	234 6	137 45	146 12	291 14	77 30	5 6R	252 44
Aug.	3	130 44	237 44	153 58	160 59	290 8R	88 00	4 53R	252 12
	13	140 19	242 6	167 12	172 30	289 00	99 46	4 32R	251 40
	23	149 56	247 5	176 33	179 5	288 12	111 15	4 0	251 8
Sep.	2	159 36	252 36	179 34R	177 31R	287 41R	122 56	3 24R	250 35
	12	169 19	258 32	173 4R	168 15	287 30	134 47	2 41R	250 5
	22	179 4	264 50	165 28	166 35D	287 35D	146 47	1 54R	249 32
Oct.	2	188 53	271 25	171 22	178 32	288 1	158 53	1 8R	249 0
	12	198 45	278 15	186 50	195 20	288 45	171 8	0 23R	248 30
	22	208 40	285 17	204 1	212 25	289 47	183 28	359 43R	247 57
Nov.	1	218 39	292 29	220 35	228 36	291 3	195 52	359 11	247 26
	11	228 41	299 48	236 31	244 8	292 32	208 20	358 45	246 54
	21	238 46	307 13	251 43	259 13	294 14	220 52	358 27	246 23
Dec.	1	248 53	314 42	266 29	273 24	296 7	233 24	358 21	245 50
	11	259 2	322 15	279 33	284 5	298 6	245 58	358 25D	245 19
	21	269 13	329 48	285 32R	282 28	300 17	258 33	358 42	244 40
	31	279 24	337 23	276 8R	270 50	302 31	271 9	359 8	244 14

Ayanamsa: 21° 31' 53"

Longitude of the Moon

1937	Sun.	Tue.	Thur.	Sat.	Mon.	Wed.	Fri.
Jan. 1							155 31
3	180 33	204 35	228 15	252 10	276 50	302 30	329 10
17	356 38	24 38	52 58	81 22	109 32	136 58	163 16
31	188 19						
Feb. 1					200 27	224 14	247 57
7	272 17	297 49	324 43	352 46	21 19	49 48	77 51
21	105 24	132 22	158 37	183 55			
March 1					208 19	232 4	255 45
7	280 4	305 42	333 1	1 50	31 17	60 25	88 36
21	115 47	142 5	167 37	192 25	216 33	240 14	
April 1			252 1	275 54	300 43	327 9	355 26
11	25 11	55 18	84 37	112 34	139 8	164 36	189 15
25	213 19	237 1	260 37				
May 1				284 34	309 22	335 39	3 44
9	33 27	63 50	93 40	122 2	148 45	234 4	198 24
23	222 12	245 49	269 33	293 44	318 43		
June 1		331 39	358 38	27 11	57 00	87 11	116 35
13	144 25	170 31	195 15	219 8	242 45	266 31	290 47
27	315 46	341 40					
July 1			8 39	36 48	65 59	95 37	124 48
11	152 41	178 54	203 40	227 32	251 10	275 7	299 50
25	325 27	351 58	19 17	47 16			
Aug. 1	61 30	90 16	119 3	147 12	174 4	199 29	223 43
15	247 23	271 12	295 45	321 28	348 19	16 1	44 7
29	72 20	100 32					
Sep. 1						114 33	142 17
5	169 13	195 00	219 38	243 27	267 6	291 16	316 36
19	343 25	11 32	40 20	69 5	97 22	125 00	
Oct. 1							151 57
3	178 7	203 22	227 43	251 27	275 3	299 10	324 30
17	351 29	20 6	49 41	79 14	107 58	135 32	161 59
31	187 27						
Nov. 1					199 53	224 13	248 00
7	271 33	295 19	319 52	345 48	13 31	42 54	73 10
21	103 8	131 49	158 53	184 31	209 7		
Dec. 1						223 3	256 41
5	280 17	304 11	328 46	354 30	21 49	50 49	81 4
19	111 26	140 40	168 6	193 46	218 9	241 52	265 26

Ayanamsa: 21° 31′ 53″

Longitudes of Planets

1938		Sun	Mars.	Merc.	Merc.	Jupit.	Venus	Saturn	Rahu
Jan.	5	284 30	341 10	270 50R	269 24D	303 40	277 27	359 24	244 00
	15	294 41	348 43	271 23	275 33	306 00	290 1	0 2	243 28
	25	304 52	356 11	281 2	287 19	308 21	302 34	0 54	242 55
Feb.	4	315 1	3 42	294 8	301 27	310 44	315 7	1 49	242 24
	14	325 9	11 7	309 2	317 2	313 5	327 39	2 51	241 52
	24	335 14	18 29	325 26	334 14	315 25	340 10	3 57	241 20
March	6	345 16	25 47	342 57	353 5	317 42	352 39	5 8	240 49
	16	355 15	33 00	2 59	12 42	319 54	5 6	6 22	240 17
	26	5 11	40 10	21 15	28 55	322 00	17 32	7 36	239 44
April	5	15 3	47 15	33 31	35 32	324 00	29 55	8 52	239 14
	15	24 52	54 15	34 49R	32 7R	325 48	42 14	10 6	238 42
	25	34 38	61 12	28 43R	26 6R	327 28	54 1	11 19	238 9
May	5	44 21	68 4	25 11	26 14D	328 54	66 44	12 28	237 39
	15	54 1	74 52	29 4	33 25	330 8	78 54	13 34	237 7
	25	63 38	81 37	39 5	45 54	331 6	91 1	14 34	236 34
June	4	73 13	88 18	53 48	62 46	331 45	103 3	15 26	236 3
	14	82 47	94 56	72 40	83 20	332 9	115 1	16 16	235 31
	24	92 20	101 31	94 17	104 57	332 14	126 53	16 56	235 00
July	4	101 52	108 3	115 0	124 16	331 58R	138 34	17 27	234 27
	14	111 24	114 33	132 41	140 17	331 24	150 18	17 48	233 55
	24	120 59	121 1	147 2	152 49	330 35	161 48	18 1	233 23
Aug.	3	130 30	127 27	157 29	169 45	329 30R	173 7	18 2R	232 51
	13	140 5	133 51	162 16	161 35R	328 16	184 12	17 54R	232 20
	23	149 42	140 15	158 41	154 16	326 58	195 00	17 36	231 48
Sep.	2	159 22	146 36	150 22R	149 2	325 41R	205 24	17 8R	231 10
	12	169 13	152 57	151 17	156 49	324 30R	215 17	16 32R	230 43
	22	178 50	159 18	164 32	173 20	323 32R	224 29	15 50	230 13
Oct.	2	188 38	165 37	182 23	191 19	322 51	232 38	15 5	229 41
	12	198 30	171 57	199 58	208 19	322 29	239 17	14 20	229 8
	22	208 26	178 15	216 24	224 15	322 24D	243 40	13 33	228 37
Nov.	1	218 25	184 34	231 52	239 18	322 42	244 49R	12 49R	228 6
	11	228 26	190 51	246 30	253 24	323 17	242 8R	12 13R	227 34
	21	238 31	197 9	259 48	265 46	324 12	236 32R	11 43	226 56
Dec.	1	248 38	203 26	268 58	269 26R	325 23	231 22	11 24	226 30
	11	258 47	209 43	265 33R	258 56	326 50	229 35D	11 15	226 00
	21	268 58	215 58	255 15	253 48D	328 28	231 45	11 16D	225 28
	31	279 9	222 12	256 43	261 38	330 20	236 59	11 29	224 55

Ayanamsa: 21° 32′ 43″

Longitude of the Moon

1938	Sun.	Tue.	Thurs.	Sat.	Mon.	Wed.	Fri.
Jan. 1				277 16	301 15	325 47	351 5
9	17 26	45 7	74 12	104 14	134 9	162 47	189 34
23	214 38	238 36	262 9	285 54	310 13		
Feb. 1		322 36	348 8	14 21	41 23	69 21	98 15
13	127 37	156 35	184 14	210 12	234 44	258 28	282 7
27	306 20						
March 1		331 29	357 38	24 36	52 8	80 8	108 29
13	136 59	165 5	192 12	217 58	242 30	266 18	290 1
27	314 20	339 46	6 29				
April 1							20 16
3	48 25	76 53	105 17	133 22	160 55	187 42	213 31
17	238 19	262 20	286 1	309 58	334 49	1 3	28 48
May 1	57 43	87 3	116 1	144 7	171 10	197 12	222 19
15	246 42	270 34	294 15	318 12	342 58	9 7	36 57
29	66 17	96 21					
June 1						111 18	140 24
5	168 3	194 14	219 16	243 32	267 22	291 2	314 52
19	339 11	4 29	31 15	59 45	89 43	120 9	
July 1							149 46
3	177 41	203 48	228 34	252 33	276 14	299 57	323 58
17	348 29	13 50	40 24	68 33	98 12	128 35	158 23
31	186 31						
Aug. 1					199 51	225 15	249 28
7	273 10	296 53	320 58	345 35	10 50	36 56	64 8
21	92 38	122 13	152 2	180 55	208 7	233 37	
Sep. 1			245 51	269 45	293 27	317 30	342 12
11	7 41	33 56	60 55	88 44	117 20	146 22	175 7
25	202 47	228 59	253 48				
Oct. 1				277 46	301 31	325 40	350 41
9	16 45	43 47	71 32	99 43	128 5	156 22	184 10
23	211 6	236 54	261 38	285 36	309 21		
Nov. 1		321 20	345 54	11 40	38 49	67 8	96 3
13	124 53	153 7	180 32	207 3	232 42	257 32	281 41
27	305 27	329 15					
Dec. 1			353 42	19 23	46 43	75 40	105 31
11	135 11	163 44	190 53	216 48	241 47	266 10	290 7
25	313 50	337 37	1 56	27 23			

Ayanamsa: 21° 32′ 43″

Longitudes of Planets

1939		Sun	Mars	Merc.	Merc.	Jupit.	Venus	Saturn	Rahu
Jan.	5	284 15	225 18	261 38	267 37	331 19	240 26	11 39	224 39
	15	294 26	231 28	274 18	281 22	333 23	248 36	12 6	224 7
	25	304 37	237 38	288 47	296 27	335 35	257 56	12 46	223 37
Feb.	4	314 46	243 43	304 24	312 40	337 52	268 2	13 32	223 4
	14	324 54	250 14	321 19	330 18	340 13	278 41	14 27	222 33
	24	334 59	255 42	339 35	349 6	342 37	289 45	15 28	222 00
March	6	345 1	261 33	358 25	6 49	345 2	301 5	16 34	221 29
	16	355 1	267 17	13 18	16 57	347 27	312 36	17 45	220 57
	26	4 57	272 52	17 20R	14 59	349 51	324 17	18 57	220 26
April	5	14 49	278 17	10 56R	7 26R	352 11	336 5	20 13	219 55
	15	24 38	283 27	5 44R	6 8D	354 28	347 56	21 29	219 22
	25	34 24	288 19	8 32	12 30	356 40	359 52	22 45	218 50
May	5	44 7	292 48	17 46	24 7	358 47	11 51	23 58	218 19
	15	53 47	296 47	31 25	39 41	0 46	23 52	25 9	217 47
	25	63 24	300 9	48 45	58 43	2 34	35 54	26 18	217 14
June	4	73 00	302 42	68 54	80 22	4 12	47 58	27 21	216 43
	14	82 33	304 17	91 6	101 15	5 38	60 5	28 18	216 12
	24	92 6	304 42R	110 36	118 47	6 49	72 13	29 9	215 40
July	4	101 38	303 50R	126 7	132 26	7 45	83 53	29 53	215 7
	14	111 10	301 53R	137 39	141 3D	8 24	96 36	30 29	214 37
	24	120 43	299 16	143 46	144 5R	8 43	108 50	30 54	213 58,
Aug.	3	130 16	296 38	142 19R	138 52	8 45	121 7	31 10	213 33
	13	139 51	294 41	135 00	132 27	8 25R	133 27	31 16	213 00
	23	149 29	293 56	132 40	136 3	7 47	145 48	31 12R	212 29
Sep.	2	159 8	294 32D	142 16	150 34	6 53R	158 12	30 56R	211 56
	12	168 50	296 26	159 47	169 13	5 44	170 37	30 32	211 25
	22	178 35	299 26	178 30	187 25	4 28	183 3	29 58	210 53
Oct.	2	188 24	303 22	195 57	204 7	3 7	195 29	29 18R	210 20
	12	198 16	308 2	211 48	219 33	1 50R	208 00	28 34	209 50
	22	208 11	313 16	226 49	233 44	0 42	220 28	27 46	209 18
Nov.	1	218 10	318 56	240 00	246 7	359 48R	232 57	26 59R	208 46
	11	228 11	324 57	250 52	253 39	359 10	245 26	26 14	208 15
	21	238 16	331 10	253 10R	248 32R	358 54	257 55	25 35	207 44
Dec.	1	248 23	337 37	242 00R	238 2	358 56D	270 23	25 4	207 12
	11	258 32	344 12	238 35	242 22	359 20	282 51	24 40	206 40
	21	268 43	350 53	247 55	253 26	0 4	295 16	24 28	206 8
	31	278 54	357 37	261 27	268 45	1 4	307 41	24 25	205 35

Áyanamsa: 21° 33' 33"

Longitude of the Moon

1939		Sun.	Tue.	Thur.	Sat.	Mon.	Wed.	Fri.
Jan.	1	40 42	68 48	98 38	129 13	159 7	187 22	213 49
	15	238 54	263 9	287 1	310 45	334 33	358 38	23 23
	29	49 21	77 3					
Feb.	1						91 37	121 51
	5	152 30	182 6	209 48	235 38	260 10	284 2	307 43
	19	331 34	355 44	20 24	45 51	72 31		
March	1						100 41	130 18
	5	160 31	190 3	217 57	244 2	268 42	292 35	316 18
	19	340 17	4 49	30 1	56 00	82 55	110 54	139 50
April	1				154 30	183 44	212 6	239 2
	9	264 28	288 47	312 35	336 28	0 55	26 15	52 34
	23	79 46	107 41	136 4	164 36			
May	1					192 53	220 27	246 58
	7	272 18	296 40	320 30	344 25	8 58	34 40	61 40
	21	89 47	118 28	147 8	175 19	202 48	229 31	
June	1			242 34	268 00	292 37	316 36	340 22
	11	4 30	29 37	56 15	84 29	113 51	143 22	172 7
	25	199 43	226 13	251 50				
July	1				276 44	301 3	324 55	348 38
	9	12 42	37 44	64 23	92 53	122 50	153 2	182 17
	23	209 58	236 11	261 21	285 49	309 51		
Aug.	1		321 45	345 27	9 18	33 44	59 24	86 49
	13	116 8	146 37	176 53	205 45	232 50	258 23	282 54
	27	306 53	330 38					
Sep.	1							6 22
	3	30 37	55 41	82 4	110 9	139 48	170 10	199 58
	17	228 12	254 40	279 40	305 47	327 32	351 19	15 27
Oct.	1	40 7	65 35	92 6	119 54	148 55	178 36	208 1
	15	236 15	262 52	288 1	312 9	335 53	359 46	24 13
	29	49 28	75 38					
Nov.	1						89 3	116 30
	5	144 41	173 22	202 8	230 24	257 36	283 28	308 6
	19	331 59	355 43	19 57	45 11	71 38	99 10	
Dec.	1							127 20
	3	155 41	183 53	211 46	239 8	265 44	291 20	315 55
	17	339 46	3 27	27 40	53 4	80 3	108 27	137 35
	31	166 32						

Ayanamsa: 21° 33′ 33″

Longitudes of Planets

1940		Sun	Mars	Merc.	Merc.	Jupit.	Venus	Saturn	Rahu
Jan.	5	284 00	0 40	268 46	276 17	1 38	313 53	24 28	205 20
	15	294 11	7 49	284 1	291 57	3 8	326 13	24 44	204 49
	25	304 22	14 38	300 7	308 33	4 46	338 29	25 10	204 16
Feb.	4	314 31	21 26	317 15	326 13	6 37	350 39	25 45	203 45
	14	324 39	28 17	335 19	344 9	8 37	2 42	26 28	203 13
	24	334 44	35 1	351 30	357 44	10 44	14 37	27 22	202 41
March	5	344 46	41 46	0 12	359 27R	12 58	26 19	28 22	202 10
	15	354 46	48 29	354 55R	350 25	15 17	37 47	29 27	201 38
	25	4 42	55 10	347 30	346 56D	17 39	48 58	30 36	201 5
April	4	14 34	61 49	348 37	352 5	20 3	59 44	31 48	200 35
	14	24 24	68 25	356 55	2 51	22 28	70 30	33 4	200 3
	24	34 10	74 59	9 40	17 18	24 52	79 35	34 21	199 30
May	4	43 52	81 31	25 44	34 55	27 15	88 15	35 37	198 57
	14	53 33	88 00	44 51	55 27	29 35	95 29	36 53	198 29
	24	63 10	94 27	66 24	77 10	31 51	100 46	38 3	197 54
June	3	72 45	100 53	87 16	96 24	34 7	103 14	39 16	197 22
	13	82 19	107 18	104 27	111 23	36 6	102 00R	40 23	196 48
	23	91 52	113 35	117 6	121 32	38 00	97 10	41 23	196 21
July	3	101 24	120 3	124 12	125 18	39 47	91 7	42 17	195 47
	13	110 56	126 34	124 22	121 45	41 24	87 18	43 5	195 16
	23	120 19	132 45	118 20	115 12	42 47	87 14	43 44	194 44
Aug.	2	130 2	139 6	114 41	116 25	43 56	90 40	44 14	194 12
	12	139 37	145 27	120 54	127 47	44 48	96 33	44 35	193 40
	22	149 14	151 48	136 28	146 7	45 23	104 12	44 45	193 9
Sep.	1	158 54	158 10	155 58	165 36	45 40	113 3	44 45R	192 37
	11	168 36	164 33	174 45	183 27	45 36R	122 47	44 34	192 5
	21	178 21	170 57	191 44	199 36	45 12	133 9	44 14	191 34
Oct.	1	187 59	177 22	207 6	214 6	44 30	144 00	43 44	191 2
	11	198 1	183 48	221 1	226 43	43 30	155 14	43 5	190 30
	21	207 56	190 17	232 14	236 15	42 18	166 46	42 20	189 58
	31	217 55	196 47	238 5	236 35R	40 58	178 33	41 35	189 26
Nov.	10	227 57	203 18	231 23R	225 8	39 47	190 31	40 46	188 55
	20	238 1	209 52	222 6	223 37	38 20	202 38	40 00	188 24
	30	248 9	216 27	228 12	234 23	37 14	214 52	39 18	187 50
Dec.	10	258 18	223 4	241 24	248 45	36 24	227 12	38 43	187 20
	20	268 28	229 44	256 16	263 57	35 52	239 37	38 16	186 49
	30	278 39	236 25	273 17	280 43	35 40	253 3	38 00	186 17

Ayanamsa : 21° 34′ 24″

Longitude of the Moon

1940	Sun.	Tue.	Thur.	Sat.	Mon.	Wed.	Fri.
Jan. 1					180 45	208 31	235 28
7	261 41	287 11	311 54	335 56	359 33	23 19	47 57
21	74 7	102 9	131 43	161 44	191 1	219 00	
Feb. 1			232 30	258 37	283 52	308 27	332 30
11	356 10	19 46	-43 50	69 00	95 54	124 44	154 58
25	185 21	214 38	242 18				
March 1							255 31
3	280 59	305 30	329 27	353 7	16 44	40 39	65 17
17	91 8	118 40	147 55	178 14	208 25	237 22	264 33
31	290 7						
April 1					302 26	326 27	350 5
7	13 44	37 44	62 19	87 48	114 26	142 26	171 42
21	201 35	231 7	259 23	285 57	310 58		
May 1						334 59	358 36
5	22 22	46 43	71 52	97 56	124 55	152 46	181 24
19	210 29	239 24	267 24	293 58	319 4	343 6	6 45
June 1				18 37	42 52	68 6	94 27
9	121 43	149 36	177 48	206 9	234 25	262 12	289 3
23	314 39	339 6	2 51	26 34			
July 1					50 57	76 34	103 35
7	131 42	160 18	188 48	216 55	244 31	271 30	297 40
21	322 51	347 7	10 48	34 31	58 55	84 41	
Aug. 1			98 11	126 23	155 37	184 58	213 41
11	241 26	268 13	294 7	319 12	343 31	7 16	30 51
25	54 48	79 46	106 19	134 40			
Sep. 1	149 25	179 26	209 13	237 54	265 10	291 8	316 5
15	340 19	4 5	27 40	51 25	75 49	101 24	128 37
29	157 35						
Oct. 1		187 45	218 00	247 13	274 46	300 40	325 20
13	349 15	12 52	36 31	60 31	85 8	110 43	137 39
27	166 6	195 52	226 6				
Nov. 1							241 1
3	269 47	296 44	321 59	346 6	9 42	33 22	57 27
17	82 11	107 41	134 3	161 27	189 59	219 25	249 1
Dec. 1	277 44	304 50	330 13	354 21	17 57	41 42	66 7
15	91 26	117 38	144 23	172 5	200 12	228 50	257 35
29	285 44	312 37					

Ayanamsa: 21° 34′ 24

Longitudes of Planets

1941		Sun	Mars	Merc.	Merc.	Jupit.	Venus	Saturn	Rahu
Jan.	5	284 46	240 27	281 13	289 18	35 43	259 31	37 55R	185 58
	15	294 58	247 12	297 34	306 3	36 4	271 59	37 55D	185 25
	25	305 8	253 58	314 40	321 36	36 45	284 30	38 7D	184 53
Feb.	4	315 18	260 47	331 29	338 24	37 46	297 00	38 29	184 21
	14	325 25	267 37	342 41	343 4R	39 00	309 30	39 4	183 50
	24	335 30	274 28	339 33	334 24	40 31	321 58	39 46	183 18
March	6	345 32	281 21	330 20	328 55	42 13	334 27	40 38	182 47
	16	355 31	288 15	330 00D	333 7	44 4	346 54	41 36	182 14
	26	5 27	295 10	327 41	343 22	46 5	359 20	42 41	181 43
April	5	15 19	302 4	349 56	357 12	48 13	11 45	43 50	181 11
	15	25 8	308 58	5 10	13 49	50 25	24 8	45 00	180 40
	25	34 54	315 52	23 8	33 8	52 43	36 30	46 16	180 8
May	5	44 36	322 43	43 43	54 34	55 3	48 50	47 34	179 38
	15	54 16	329 31	65 9	74 57	57 24	61 9	48 51	179 4
	25	63 53	336 13	83 38	91 2	59 45	73 27	50 8	178 33
June	4	73 29	342 49	97 7	101 38	62 20	86 56	51 23	178 1
	14	83 2	349 13	104 33	105 39	64 25	97 58	52 35	177 28
	24	92 35	355 25	104 53R	102 35R	66 40	110 12	53 43	176 56
July	4	102 7	1 18	99 36R	97 8R	68 51	122 24	54 46	176 25
	14	111 39	6 49	96 18D	97 39D	70 57	134 35	55 43	175 53
	24	121 12	11 50	101 18	107 11	73 26	146 45	56 35	175 22
Aug.	3	130 46	16 13	115 1	124 21	74 46	158 52	57 16	174 50
	13	140 21	19 46	134 25	144 6	76 27	170 57	57 50	174 18
	23	149 58	22 19	154 26	163 40	77 56	182 59	58 15	173 47
Sep.	2	159 37	23 36	172 32	180 48	79 12	194 57	58 30	173 14
	12	169 20	23 28R	188 35	195 54	80 12	206 51	58 33R	172 43
	22	179 5	21 57R	202 44	208 58	80 55	218 40	58 26	172 12
Oct.	2	188 54	19 28R	214 27	218 51	81 20	230 22	58 9R	171 40
	12	198 46	16 12R	221 38	221 53R	81 26R	241 57	57 40	171 8
	22	208 42	13 26R	219 43R	212 50R	81 12R	253 22	57 4	170 35
Nov.	1	218 41	11 37	207 38	206 33	80 37R	264 35	56 22	170 00
	11	228 42	11 4D	209 41	215 35	79 45	275 34	55 35	169 32
	21	238 47	11 52	222 25	229 55	78 38	285 58	54 45	169 00
Dec.	1	248 55	13 50	237 39	245 26	77 22R	295 51	54 00R	168 25
	11	259 4	16 43	253 14	261 4	76 00	304 51	53 14	167 54
	21	269 14	20 23	268 57	276 55	74 41	312 32	52 36	167 25
	31	279 26	24 36	284 59	293 10	72 59	318 15	52 7	166 52

Ayanamsa: 21° 35' 14"

1941		Sun	Tue.	Thur.	Sat.	Mon.	Wed.	Fri.
Jan.	1						325 29	350 13
	5	14 2	37 40	61 49	87 00	113 25	140 51	168 51
	19	197 2	225 13	253 14	280 51	307 40	333 23	357 59
Feb.	1				9 57	33 36	57 24	82 3
	9	108 4	135 35	164 12	193 14	222 00	250 5	277 22
	23	303 47	329 19	354 00				
March	1				17 59	41 36	65 24	89 58
	9	115 54	143 32	172 39	202 31	232 5	260 34	237 42
	23	313 34	338 28	2 40	26 27	50 4		
April	1		61 56	86 3	111 6	137 38	165 55	195 44
	13	226 8	255 53	284 5	310 33	335 35	359 43	23 25
	27	47 3	70 52					
May	1			95 09	120 14	146 33	174 28	203 59
	11	234 24	264 28	293 2	319 39	344 39	8 38	32 15
	25	55 56	80 1	104 39	130 00			
June	1	143 2	169 58	198 17	227 51	257 55	287 15	314 57
	15	340 48	5 16	29 00	52 40	76 45	101 31	127 2
	29	153 18						
July	1		180 25	208 29	237 26	266 45	295 33	323 1
	13	348 51	13 22	37 9	60 55	85 13	110 25	136 34
	27	163 33	191 12	219 21				
Aug.	1							233 34
	3	262 7	290 25	317 54	344 8	9 8	33 13	56 57
	17	80 59	105 53	131 59	159 18	187 29	216 5	244 36
	31	272 44						
Sep.	1					286 34	313 38	339 46
	7	4 55	59 14	53 2	76 50	101 12	127 44	153 46
	21	182 15	211 36	240 58	269 34	297 3		
Oct.	1						323 24	348 49
	5	13 28	37 33	61 18	85 4	109 21	134 43	161 41
	19	190 26	220 27	250 37	279 45	307 16	333 16	358 9
Nov.	1				10 19	34 19	58 5	81 50
	9	105 50	130 29	156 21	183 56	213 21	243 55	274 14
	23	303 3	329 55	355 10	19 25			
Dec.	1					43 12	66 56	90 49
	7	115 2	139 50	165 36	192 49	221 44	251 57	282 17
	21	311 22	338 32	3 56	28 9	51 53	75 38	

Longitudes of Planets

1942		Sun	Mars	Merc.	Merc.	Jupit.	Venus	Saturn	Rahu
Jan.	5	284 31	26 55	293 10	301 25	72 57R	320 4	51 56R	166 43
	15	294 43	31 47	309 33	317 10	72 7	321 3R	51 42	166 5
	25	304 53	36 57	323 23	326 46	71 35	318 00	51 38D	165 33
Feb.	4	315 3	42 21	325 53R	321 9R	71 23	312 10	51 46	165 2
	14	325 10	47 57	315 33R	312 10	71 31D	307 6	52 5	164 31
	24	335 15	53 41	311 50	314 2D	71 59	305 33	52 35	163 59
March	6	345 17	59 31	318 00	323 13	72 46	307 52	53 14	163 27
	16	355 16	65 25	329 20	336 11	73 49	313 9	54 2	162 55
	26	5 12	71 23	343 40	351 43	75 7	320 25	54 58	162 24
April	5	15 4	77 24	0 22	9 36	76 38	329 3	56 90	161 52
	15	24 54	83 27	19 28	29 51	78 20	338 35	57 11	161 20
	25	34 39	89 32	40 31	50 56	80 12	348 45	58 20	160 48
May	5	44 22	95 38	60 33	68 52	82 10	359 21	59 35	160 17
	15	54 2	101 46	75 40	81 19	84 15	10 18	60 51	159 45
	25	63 39	107 53	84 9	85 34	86 25	21 28	62 9	159 12
June	4	73 15	114 2	85 6	83 4R	88 39	32 51	63 26	158 40
	14	82 49	120 13	80 17R	78 30R	90 55	44 21	64 39	158 10
	24	92 21	126 23	77 1	77 57D	93 12	56 00	65 57	157 38
July	4	101 53	132 35	80 43	85 44	95 30	67 44	67 7	157 5
	14	111 26	138 49	92 24	100 42	97 44	79 34	68 13	156 34
	24	120 58	145 4	110 18	120 40	99 57	91 30	69 14	156 1
Aug.	3	130 32	151 21	131 8	141 15	102 5	103 20	70 9	155 31
	13	140 7	157 40	150 46	159 43	104 13	115 36	70 55	154 58
	23	149 44	164 1	168 3	175 49	106 12	127 46	71 35	154 26
Sep.	2	159 24	170 24	182 31	189 36	108 3	140 1	72 3	153 53
	12	169 6	176 50	195 27	200 25	109 46	152 20	72 22	153 23
	22	178 51	183 18	204 5	205 55	111 18	164 43	72 30	152 51
Oct.	2	188 40	189 49	205 6R	201 13	112 38	177 9	72 29R	152 20
	12	198 32	196 23	195 27	191 13	113 42	189`38	72 15	151 48
	22	208 27	203 1	191 10	195 8	114 31	202 7	71 52	151 16
Nov.	1	218 26	209 42	201 33	209 6	115 2	214 39	71 20	150 44
	11	229 28	216 26	217 3	225 6	115 14	227 13	70 38	150 13
	21	228 33	223 15	233 6	241 2	115 6R	239 47	69 53	149 40
Dec.	1	248 40	230 8	248 54	256 45	114 39	252 21	69 4R	149 8
	11	258 49	237 8	264 36	272 09	113 53	264 55	68 14	148 37
	21	268 59	244 4	280 23	288 14	112 52	277 29	67 29	148 6
	31	279 10	251 8	295 53	302 53	111 38R	290 4	66 48	147 33

Ayanamsa: 21° 36' 4"

Longitude of the Moon

1942		Sun	Tue.	Thur.	Sat.	Mon.	Wed.	Fri.
Jan.	1			87 38	112 00	136 55	162 32	189 5
	11	216 49	245 48	275 31	304 55	333 1	359 24	24 18
	25	48 17	72 00	96 2	120 43			
Feb.	1	133 22	159 18	186 2	213 31	241 43	270 25	299 8
	15	327 14	354 9	19 43	44 11	68 1	91 52	116 19
March	1	141 45	168 22	196 1	224 18	252 47	281 5	308 55
	15	336 4	2 19	27 36	52 1	75 52	99 41	124 6
	29	149 40	176 44					
April	1						190 56	219 48
	5	249 6	277 54	305 45	332 34	358 30	23 40	48 10
	19	72 8	95 51	119 49	144 38	170 56	199 2	
May	1							228 40
	3	258 47	288 12	316 11	342 42	8 6	32 44	56 53
	17	80 42	104 25	128 22	153 5	179 14	207 15	237 3
	31	267 38						
June	1					282 46	311 58	339 22
	7	5 10	29 52	53 56	77 44	101 27	125 20	149 43
	21	175 3	201 55	230 36	260 46	291 15		
July	1						320 42	348 22
	5	14 18	38 56	62 53	86 37	110 26	134 34	159 17
	19	184 52	211 42	240 1	269 36	299 37	328 55	356 42
Aug.	1				9 56	35 17	59 33	83 20
	9	107 8	131 20	156 13	181 54	208 31	236 8	264 42
	23	293 51	322 54	351 5	17 56	43 21		
Sep.	1		55 37	79 37	103 22	127 28	152 22	178 18
	13	205 15	233 00	261 14	289 40	318 00	345 50	12 50
	27	38 44	63 31					
Oct.	1			87 30	111 14	135 22	160 31	187 1
	11	214 51	243 30	272 15	300 34	328 15	355 14	21 30
	25	46 56	71 32	95 26	119 6			
Nov.	1	131 3	155 33	181 28	209 8	238 17	267 58	297 8
	15	325 11	352 4	18 2	43 15	67 50	91 51	115 30
	29	139 13						
Dec.	1		163 36	189 22	217 3	246 32	276 54	306 47
	13	335 15	2 9	27 46	52 31	76 41	100 30	124 8
	27	147 55	172 18	197 54				

Ayanamsa: 21° 36′ 4″

Longitudes of Planets

1943		Sun	Mars.	Merc.	Merc.	Jupit.	Venus	Saturn	Rahu
Jan.	5	284 16	254 41	302 53	308 22	111 00R	296 21	66 30R	147 17
	15	294 28	261 51	310 48	308 44R	109 38R	308 52	66 2R	146 45
	25	304 38	269 4	303 3R	297 30	108 29R	321 25	65 43R	146 14
Feb.	4	314 48	276 20	295 00	295 47	107 10R	333 54	65 36	145 43
	14	324 55	283 40	298 55	303 36	106 16	346 32	65 39D	145 10
	24	335 00	291 3	309 19	315 48	105 34	358 45	65 54	144 38
March	6	345 3	298 28	322 52	329 57	105 15	11 6	66 19	144 7
	16	355 2	305 57	338 33	347 8	105 11D	23 22	66 55	143 35
	26	4 58	313 28	356 17	5 55	105 30	35 33	67 39	143 3
April	5	14 50	320 30	16 3	26 27	106 6	47 38	68 32	142 31
	15	24 39	328 32	36 40	45 59	107 00	59 36	69 28	142 00
	25	34 25	336 5	53 50	59 50	108 8	71 25	70 38	141 28
May	5	44 8	343 37	63 48	65 36	109 30	83 5	71 48	140 56
	15	53 48	351 7	65 18R	63 17R	111 3	94 34	73 00	140 18
	25	63 25	358 36	60 30R	58 6R	112 46	105 49	74 17	139 51
June	4	73 1	6 0	57 2D	57 46	114 37	116 46	75 35	139 20
	14	82 35	13 19	60 20	64 35	116 35	127 21	76 54	138 49
	24	92 7	20 32	70 47	77 45	118 39	137 28	78 11	138 17
July	4	101 10	27 35	86 26	96 15	120 46	146 54	79 26	137 44
	14	111 12	34 29	106 49	117 32	122 56	155 24	80 38	137 14
	24	120 44	41 12	127 52	137 39	125 9	162 32	81 48	136 42
Aug.	3	130 18	47 41	146 10	155 2	127 21	167 55	82 51	136 9
	13	139 53	53 52	162 45	169 47	129 34	170 27	83 49	135 37
	23	149 30	59 43	176 4	181 30	131 44	169 21R	84 40	135 7
Sep.	2	159 10	65 9	185 49	188 40	133 52	164 40R	85 23	134 32
	12	168 52	70 5	189 26	187 36R	135 56	158 45	85 58	134 4
	22	178 37	74 24	183 9R	177 54	137 54	154 50	86 21	133 30
Oct.	2	188 26	77 56	174 50	175 53D	139 45	154 51D	86 34	133 00
	12	198 18	80 30	180 38	187 11	-141 27	158 23	86 37R	132 28
	22	208 13	81 58	195 46	204 9	143 00	164 38	86 29	131 56
Nov.	1	218 11	82 6R	212 32	220 45	144 19	172 29	86 8	131 24
	11	228 13	80 44	229 49	236 45	145 25	181 40	85 40	130 52
	21	238 18	78 00	244 34	252 19	146 16	192 12	85 2	130 20
Dec.	1	248 25	74 24	260 1	267 37	146 49	202 26	84 18	129 49
	11	258 34	70 39	275 6	282 14	147 3	213 35	83 30	129 17
	21	268 44	67 29	288 36	293 17	146 58R	225 4	82 41	128 46
	31	278 56	65 30	294 46R	291 39	146 33	236 48	81 54	128 12

Ayanamsa: 21° 36' 55"

Longitude of the Moon

1943		Sun.	Tue.	Thur.	Sat.	Mon.	Wed.	Fri.
Jan.	1							211 20
	3	239 40	269 38	300 12	329 58	358 7	24 30	49 32
	17	73 42	97 27	121 7	144 58	169 15	194 21	220 41
	31	248 33						
Feb.	1					263 5	292 58	323 6
	7	352 21	19 57	45 50	70 25	94 14	117 52	141 46
	21	166 12	191 23	217 29	244 36			
March	1					272 48	301 52	331 17
	7	0 11	27 50	53 54	78 35	102 26	126 5	150 9
	21	175 2	200 56	227 47	255 22	283 28	311 54	
April	1			326 10	354 34	22 19	48 56	74 14
	11	98 27	122 8	145 58	170 37	196 31	223 43	251 50
	25	280 17	308 37	336 37				
May	1				4 11	31 8	57 12	82 14
	9	106 22	130 1	153 50	178 33	204 44	232 31	261 28
	23	290 42	319 27	347 21	14 23	40 36		
June	1		53 25	78 25	102 40	126 22	149 58	174 8
	13	199 30	226 37	255 27	285 19	315 5	343 53	11 22
	27	37 37	62 53					
July	1			87 23	111 18	134 54	158 32	182 42
	11	208 00	234 58	263 45	293 49	324 5	353 25	21 11
	25	47 22	72 19	96 27	120 8			
Aug.	1	131 55	155 34	179 34	204 21	230 21	257 56	287 6
	15	317 18	347 25	16 22	43 34	69 6	93 26	117 9
	29	140 43	164 34					
Sep.	1						176 40	201 24
	5	227 00	253 42	281 41	310 53	340 44	10 16	38 30
	19	65 00	89 55	113 49	137 24	161 14	185 43	
Oct.	1							211 2
	3	237 12	264 11	291 57	320 30	349 34	18 31	46 30
	17	72 58	97 56	121 52	145 28	169 27	194 18	220 17
	31	247 15						
Nov.	1					261 00	288 49	316 54
	7	345 10	13 24	41 10	67 57	93 27	117 47	141 28
	21	165 11	189 39	215 24	242 33	270 46		
Dec.	1						299 24	327 53
	5	355 57	23 30	50 23	76 25	101 29	125 40	149 20
	19	173 27	197 27	223 12	250 38	279 30	309 2	338 18

Ayanamsa: 21° 36′ 55″

Longitudes of Planets

1944		Sun	Mars	Merc.	Merc.	Jupit.	Venus	Saturn	Rahu
Jan.	5	284 2	65 2R	291 39R	285 22	146 14R	242 44	81 31R	127 59
	15	294 13	65 2D	280 9	278 41D	145 23	254 43	80 50	127 26
	25	304 24	66 15	280 29	284 28	144 17	266 47	80 19	126 54
Feb.	4	314 33	68 29	289 44	295 53	143 4	278 57	79 55	126 22
	14	324 41	71 29	302 38	309 53	141 44	291 11	79 43	125 51
	24	334 46	75 8	317 32	325 37	140 26	303 26	79 41D	125 13
March	5	344 48	79 15	334 6	343 14	139 16	315 43	79 51	124 47
	15	354 47	83 45	352 30	2 21	138 17	328 00	80 13	124 16
	25	3 44	88 33	12 26	22 21	137 34	340 19	80 44	123 43
April	4	14 36	93 35	31 17	38 32	137 9R	352 37	81 24	123 12
	14	24 25	98 50	43 33	46 6	137 2D	4 54	82 14	122 40
	24	34 11	104 14	46 7R	44 6R	137 14	17 12	83 11	122 8
May	4	43 54	109 44	41 1R	38 14R	137 43	29 29	84 14	121 35
	14	53 34	115 22	36 51R	37 18	138 30	41 46	85 23	121 5
	24	63 11	121 6	39 35	43 31	139 32	54 2	86 35	120 33
June	3	72 47	126 55	48 51	55 29	140 47	66 18	87 50	120 1
	13	82 21	132 47	63 17	72 57	142 15	78 35	89 6	119 29
	23	91 53	138 45	82 14	92 56	143 51	90 51	90 25	118 58
July	3	101 26	144 46	103 48	114 20	145 37	103 9	91 42	118 26
	13	110 57	150 50	124 13	133 20	147 31	115 27	93 00	117 54
	23	120 31	157 00	141 42	149 18	149 29	127 45	94 13	117 23
Aug.	2	130 14	163 12	156 6	162 00	151 32	140 5	95 25	116 50
	12	139 39	169 29	166 52	170 22	153 38	152 24	96 31	116 18
	22	149 16	175 49	172 18	171 59R	155 46	164 44	97 32	115 47
Sep.	1	158 55	182 15	169 11R	164 37R	157 57	177 3	98 25	115 14
	11	168 37	188 44	160 14R	158 32	160 8	189 23	99 12	114 43
	21	178 23	195 17	160 40	166 10	162 16	201 41	99 51	114 12
Oct.	1	188 11	201 56	173 48	182 23	164 23	213 59	100 19	113 37
	11	198 3	208 38	191 11	199 54	166 25	226 15	100 38	113 9
	21	207 58	215 26	208 22	216 35	168 23	238 31	100 46	112 37
	31	217 57	222 19	224 36	232 23	170 12	250 44	100 42R	112 4
Nov.	10	227 58	229 17	240 2	247 34	171 55	268 25	100 27	111 33
	20	238 3	236 20	254 54	261 59	173 26	275 4	100 2	111 2
	30	248 10	243 28	268 36	274 17	174 45	287 10	99 28	110 30
Dec.	10	258 19	250 40	278 8	278 37R	175 51	299 10	98 46	109 56
	20	268 30	257 57	274 36	268 2	176 41	311 3	98 00	109 26
	30	279 42	265 19	263 25	262 57D	177 15	322 44	97 12	108 54

Ayanamsa: 21° 37' 45″

Longitude of the Moon

1944		Sun.	Tue.	Thur.	Sat.	Mon.	Wed.	Fri.
Jan.	1				352 37	20 26	47 9	72 54
	9	97 48	122 1	145 45	169 21	193 19	218 12	244 35
	23	272 45	302 25	332 39	2 17	30 31		
Feb.	1		44 1	69 57	94 45	118 51	142 33	166 11
	13	190 2	214 26	239 51	266 47	295 25	325 28	355 55
	27	25 28	53 17					
March	1						66 30	91 44
	5	115 53	139 32	163 9	187 3	211 26	236 32	262 36
	19	290 00	318 52	348 51	18 57	47 55	75 2	100 23
April	1				112 33	136 21	159 56	183 50
	9	208 21	233 34	259 32	286 21	314 12	343 4	12 34
	23	41 47	69 44	95 58	120 42			
May	1					144 33	168 13	192 18
	7	217 12	243 2	269 42	297 1	324 57	353 24	22 6
	21	50 29	77 52	103 53	128 35	152 29	176 12	
June	1			188 13	212 52	238 39	265 36	293 25
	11	321 44	350 9	18 25	46 15	73 20	99 24	124 24
	25	148 32	172 15	196 9				
July	1				220 51	246 50	274 16	302 53
	9	332 2	1 1	29 16	56 33	82 51	108 13	132 47
	23	156 45	180 26	204 18	228 56	254 52		
Aug.	1		268 27	296 51	326 31	356 28	25 40	53 29
	13	79 52	105 6	129 32	153 28	177 10	230 54	225 4
	27	250 9	276 41	305 00				
Sep.	1							319 48
	3	350 10	20 28	49 28	76 38	102 11	126 37	150 29
	17	174 11	197 56	221 59	246 36	272 14	299 19	328 10
Oct.	1	358 27	28 54	58 14	85 39	111 15	135 35	159 20
	15	183 1	206 57	231 20	256 16	282 2	308 57	337 18
	29	6 56	37 1					
Nov.	1						51 50	80 19
	5	106 57	131 57	155 57	179 38	203 32	228 1	253 11
	19	279 5	305 45	333 19	1 50	31 00	60 3	
Dec.	1							88 8
	3	114 43	139 50	163 57	187 41	211 40	236 24	262 7
	17	288 48	316 15	344 16	12 36	40 59	69 2	96 19
	31	122 30						

Ayanamsa: 21° 37′ 45″

Longitudes of Planets

1945		Sun	Mars	Merc.	Merc.	Jupit.	Venus	Saturn	Rahu
Jan.	5	284 48	269 46	263 17	266 31	177 25	329 39	96 43R	108 35
	15	294 59	277 8	271 30	277 30	177 29R	340 56	95 53	108 3
	25	305 10	284 48	284 08	291 13	177 9R	351 50	95 11	107 31
Feb.	4	315 19	292 24	298 38	306 25	176 38R	2 11	94 35	106 59
	14	325 26	300 4	314 32	322 59	175 47	11 48	94 10R	106 28
	24	335 31	307 46	331 51	341 6	174 43	20 20	93 53	105 56
March	6	345 33	315 31	350 41	0 25	173 29	27 19	93 49D	105 24
	16	355 33	323 16	9 48	17 59	172 12	32 2	93 55	104 53
	26	5 28	331 3	24 4	27 22	170 55	33 34R	94 13	104 21
April	5	15 20	338 50	27 41R	25 27R	169 46	31 6	94 42	103 50
	15	25 10	346 36	21 54R	18 39R	168 47	25 28	95 18	103 17
	25	34 55	354 20	17 00	17 5D	168 5	19 48	96 4	102 45
May	5	44 38	2 - 2	19 35	23 27	167 40	17 15R	97 00	102 14
	15	54 18	9 41	28 39	34 1	167 31D	18 35D	97 59	101 41
	25	63 55	17 17	42 24	50 47	167 42	23 1	99 9	101 10
June	4	73 30	24 47	60 8	70 22	168 9	29 39	100 16	100 38
	14	83 4	32 13	81 11	92 8	168 54	37 47	101 30	100 6
	24	92 37	39 33	102 40	112 30	169 53	46 55	102 46	99 35
July	4	102 9	46 46	121 28	129 33	171 6	56 46	104 5	99 2
	14	111 41	53 55	136 45	143 00	172 31	67 6	105 22	98 31
	24	121 14	60 46	148 11	152 3	174 6	77 52	106 40	98 1
Aug.	3	130 47	67 33	154 26	154 40R	175 50	88 56	107 55	97 28
	13	140 23	74 10	152 47R	149 2	177 41	100 15	109 6	96 56
	23	149 59	80 34	144 51	142 13	179 39	111 46	110 15	96 25
Sep.	2	159 39	86 46	142 40D	146 32	181 41	123 29	111 18	95 52
	12	169 22	92 43	153 13	161 38	183 47	135 21	112 15	95 20
	22	179 7	98 20	170 47	180 00	185 55	147 22	113 5	94 49
Oct.	2	188 56	103 35	189 58	197 37	188 6	159 31	113 47	94 14
	12	198 48	108 35	205 56	213 55	190 15	171 46	114 20	93 46
	22	208 44	113 00	221 33	229 15	192 23	184 7	114 41	93 12
Nov.	1	218 42	116 49	236 31	243 30	194 29	196 31	114 52	92 41
	11	228 43	119 54	250 5	255 58	196 30	209 1	114 53R	92 10
	21	238 49	122 4	260 38	263 3	198 27	221 30	114 42	91 39
Dec.	1	248 56	123 9	261 43R	256 13	200 16	234 4	114 20	91 6
	11	259 6	122 56R	249 52	246 55	201 56	246 38	113 48	91 35
	21	269 16	121 19	248 12D	252 16	203 27	259 12	113 8	91 2
	31	279 27	118 27	257 53	264 20	204 45	271 47	112 23	89 30

Ayanamsa: 21° 38' 35"

Longitude of the Moon

1945		Sun.	Tue.	Thurs.	Sat.	Mon.	Wed.	Fri.
Jan.	1					135 9	159 42	183 36
	7	207 24	231 43	257 6	283 50	311 49	340 33	9 21
	21	37 44	65 22	92 9	118 7	143 15	167 39	
Feb.	1			179 37	203 23	227 18	251 59	278 3
	11	305 48	335 1	4 50	34 10	62 17	89 4	114 46
	25	199 41	164 2					
March	1			187 58	211 43	235 36	260 9	286 1
	11	313 42	343 12	13 39	43 41	72 13	99 1	124 24
	25	148 54	172 55	196 43	220 29			
April	1	232 26	256 38	281 42	308 12	336 34	6 35	37 13
	15	66 59	94 58	121 8	145 56	169 58	193 44	217 32
	29	241 33						
May	1		266 2	291 17	317 44	345 46	15 16	45 30
	13	75 12	103 21	129 43	154 37	178 39	202 24	226 17
	27	250 37	275 34	301 19				
June	1							314 35
	3	341 53	10 17	39 33	69 00	97 36	124 48	150 28
	7	174 57	198 49	222 38	246 55	272 00	298 00	324 56
July	1	352 41	21 1	49 40	78 11	106 3	132 51	158 25
	15	182 55	206 48	230 38	255 3	280 30	307 12	335 2
	29	3 20	32 5					
Aug.	1						46 17	74 18
	5	101 41	128 18	154 1	178 49	202 52	226 36	250 37
	19	275 34	301 58	329 57	359 5	28 27	57 12	84 55
Sep.	1				98 24	124 41	150 12	175 1
	9	199 11	222 56	246 38	270 56	296 30	323 52	353 2
	23	23 10	53 00	81 35	108 41			
Oct.	1					164 32	159 31	183 53
	7	207 49	231 29	255 11	279 25	304 50	332 1	1 9
	21	31 36	61 59	91 4	118 24	144 10	168 51	
Nov.	1			180 56	204 49	228 30	252 14	276 16
	11	301 4	327 9	354 57	24 27	54 54	84 58	113 35
	25	140 23	165 38	189 51				
Dec.	1				213 35	237 17	261 13	285 39
	9	310 49	337 2	4 32	33 22	63 5	92 47	121 27
	23	148 31	173 58	198 15	221 58	245 42		

Ayanamsa: 21° 38′ 35″

Longitudes of Planets

1946		Sun	Mars	Merc.	Merc.	Jupit.	Venus	Saturn	Rahu
Jan.	5	284 33	116 36	264 20	271 17	205 19	278 5	112 00R	89 16
	15	294 44	112 41R	278 35	286 7	206 15	290 39	111 10	88 43
	25	304 55	108 56	293 54	301 57	206 55	303 14	110 22	88 12
Feb.	4	315 4	106 5	310 17	318 55	207 18	315 46	109 37	87 40
	14	325 12	104 27	327 54	337 7	207 21R	328 19	108 58	87 9
	24	335 17	104 8D	346 26	355 20	207 7	340 50	108 28	86 36
March	6	345 19	105 2	2 59	8 13	206 32	353 19	108 8	86 5
	16	355 18	106 56	10 12	8 46R	205 43	5 46	107 58	85 34
	26	5 14	109 39	5 00R	0 52	204 38	18 12	107 59D	85 1
April	5	15 6	113 31	358 12	357 43D	203 27	30 34	108 11	84 30
	15	24 55	116 53	359 23	2 48	202 10	42 53	108 33	83 57
	25	34 41	121 11	7 36	13 33	200 55	55 10	109 7	83 25
May	5	44 24	125 50	20 25	28 11	199 46R	67 22	109 49	82 54
	15	54 4	130 44	36 47	46 12	198 46	79 31	110 38	82 23
	25	63 41	135 52	56 25	67 16	198 4	91 37	111 37	81 50
June	4	73 16	141 12	78 12	88 19	197 36	103 39	112 40	81 18
	14	82 50	146 42	98 38	107 30	197 28	115 36	113 48	80 47
	24	92 23	152 21	115 22	122 12	197 35D	127 27	115 00	80 16
July	4	101 55	158 9	127 54	132 20	198 1	139 11	116 15	79 43
	14	111 27	164 4	135 14	136 21R	198 43	150 48	117 32	79 11
	24	120 00	170 5	135 30	132 43	199 42	162 15	118 49	78 40
Aug.	3	130 33	176 13	129 2	125 55	200 53	173 31	120 7	78 9
	13	140 8	182 28	124 54D	126 47	202 17	184 31	121 22	77 35
	23	149 46	188 50	131 37	138 53	203 51	195 14	122 36	77 4
Sep.	2	159 25	195 18	147 46	157 20	205 34	205 31	123 46	76 32
	12	169 8	201 52	166 55	176 12	207 26	215 16	124 52	76 00
	22	178 53	208 31	185 00	193 34	209 24	224 12	125 51	75 29
Oct.	2	188 42	215 17	201 40	209 24	211 27	232 3	126 44	74 57
	12	198 34	222 10	216 49	223 54	213 34	238 12	127 30	74 26
	22	208 29	229 9	230 34	236 43	215 44	241 52	128 6	73 54
Nov.	1	218 28	236 14	242 00	245 15	217 56	242 7R	128 33	73 22
	11	228 30	243 25	247 23R	245 1R	220 6	238 29	128 48	72 50
	21	238 34	250 41	239 11	233 11	222 17	232 37	128 53R	72 19
Dec.	1	248 42	258 3	231 11	233 24	224 24	228 7	128 47	71 46
	11	258 51	265 31	238 15	244 27	226 28	227 19D	128 29	71 15
	21	269 1	273 3	251 21	258 37	228 28	230 19	128 3	70 43
	31	279 13	280 41	266 15	278 11	230 16	236 9	127 27	70 11

Ayanamsa : 21° 39′ 26″

Longitude of the Moon

1946		Sun	Tue.	Thur.	Sat.	Mon.	Wed.	Fri.
Jan.	1		257 43	282 17	307 42	334 1	1 11	29 10
	13	57 46	86 40	115 17	142 55	169 12	194 7	218 5
	27	241 45	265 46	290 41				
Feb.	1							303 35
	3	330 16	357 53	26 1	54 16	82 25	110 19	137 42
	17	164 12	189 36	213 58	237 42	261 26	285 55	
March	1							314 42
	3	339 2	7 35	36 33	65 13	93 11	120 26	146 59
	17	172 48	197 47	221 58	245 39	269 21	293 47	319 37
	31	347 14						
April	1					1 40	31 17	60 58
	7	89 48	117 24	143 53	169 28	194 17	218 29	242 13
	21	265 49	289 47	314 46	341 22	9 53		
May	1						39 45	70 1
	5	99 26	127 22	153 48	179 2	203 25	227 18	250 46
	19	274 37	298 43	323 44	350 11	18 21	48 3	78 24
June	1				93 26	122 34	150 2	175 51
	9	200 27	234 20	247 57	271 40	295 47	320 36	346 26
	23	13 33	42 6	71 45	101 43			
July	1					130 56	158 36	184 34
	7	209 9	232 57	256 34	280 29	305 2	330 24	356 40
	21	23 52	52 2	81 1	110 19	139 10	166 46	
Aug.	1			179 58	205 13	229 20	252 59	276 49
	11	301 22	326 54	353 27	20 46	48 38	76 54	105 23
	25	133 46	161 29	188 00	213 10			
Sep.	1	225 19	249 6	272 47	297 3	322 28	349 12	17 1
	15	45 21	73 43	101 52	129 41	156 58	183 26	208 52
	29	233 16						
Oct.	1		256 59	280 38	304 55	330 28	357 37	26 10
	13	55 22	84 24	112 43	140 10	166 44	192 28	217 20
	27	241 28	265 6	288 43				
Nov.	1							300 42
	3	325 27	351 44	19 47	49 11	79 18	108 45	136 57
	17	163 45	189 23	214 5	238 9	261 50	285 24	309 16
Dec.	1	133 56	359 57	27 43	57 11	87 34	117 41	146 27
	15	173 27	198 53	223 14	246 59	270 34	294 17	318 22
	29	343 10	9 2					

Ayanamsa: 21° 39′ 26″

Longitudes of Planets

1947		Sun	Mars	Merc.	Merc.	Jupit.	Venus	Saturn	Rahu
Jan.	5	284 18	284 31	273 43	281 32	231 9	239 51	127 4R	69 56
	15	294 30	292 15	289 30	297 37	232 46	248 20	126 19	69 26
	25	304 41	300 1	306 7	314 48	234 11	257 53	125 30	68 51
Feb.	4	314 50	307 50	323 40	332 31	235 24	268 10	124 40	68 20
	14	324 57	315 41	340 56	347 57	236 22	278 56	123 55	67 49
	24	335 2	323 33	352 17	352 52R	237 4	290 5	123 14	67 16
March	6	345 5	331 26	349 49R	344 58	237 28	301 29	122 41	66 45
	16	355 4	339 18	340 57	339 14	237 34R	313 4	122 15	66 14
	26	5 00	347 9	340 1D	342 48	237 21	324 47	122 1	65 42
April	5	14 52	355 00	347 7	352 37	236 49	336 37	121 57D	65 10
	15	24 41	2 45	359 4	6 22	236 2	348 30	122 4	64 38
	25	34 27	10 29	14 17	23 00	235 00	0 27	122 22	64 6
May	5	44 10	18 9	32 26	42 35	233 48	12 26	122 50	63 35
	15	53 50	25 45	53 18	64 13	232 33	24 28	123 28	62 56
	25	63 28	33 15	74 46	84 31	231 18	36 31	124 14	62 31
June	4	73 3	40 40	93 12	100 43	230 8	48 36	125 7	61 58
	14	82 37	48 1	107 00	111 54	229 9	60 43	126 8	61 27
	24	92 9	55 15	115 18	117 00	228 23	72 52	127 13	60 55
July	4	101 41	62 23	116 45R	114 44	227 54R	85 2	128 24	60 23
	14	111 13	69 24	111 39	108 40	227 42	97 15	129 36	59 52
	24	120 46	76 18	107 7	107 49D	227 48D	109 30	130 52	59 20
Aug.	3	130 20	83 5	111 3	116 45	228 12	121 47	132 8	58 48
	13	139 55	89 45	124 3	133 50	228 54	134 7	133 26	58 16
	23	149 32	96 17	143 46	153 43	229 50	146 28	134 43	57 45
Sep.	2	159 11	102 39	163 18	172 26	231 2	158 49	135 57	57 11
	12	168 53	108 53	181 3	189 14	232 26	171 17	137 8	56 42
	22	178 39	114 56	196 57	204 16	234 00	183 44	138 15	56 9
Oct.	2	188 27	120 49	211 9	217 29	235 46	196 11	139 17	55 35
	12	198 19	126 28	223 9	227 47	237 39	208 39	140 14	55 5
	22	208 14	131 53	230 48	231 13R	239 53	221 7	141 2	54 34
Nov.	1	218 13	137 00	229 2R	223 15	241 45	233 37	141 41	54 1
	11	228 15	141 47	216 42	215 41D	243 55	246 5	142 11	53 28
	21	238 20	146 8	218 48	224 22D	246 8	258 33	142 31	52 58
Dec.	1	248 27	150 00	231 9	238 28	248 23	271 2	142 39	52 27
	11	258 36	153 14	246 1	253 42	250 37	283 28	142 38R	51 55
	21	268 46	155 41	261 26	269 16	252 49	295 54	142 24	51 22
	31	278 57	157 12	277 11	285 14	255 00	308 18	142 2	50 51

Ayanamsa: 21° 40' 16"

Longitude of the Moon

1947	Sun.	Tue.	Thur.	Sat.	Mon.	Wed.	Fri.
Jan. 1						22 29	50 37
5	80 15	110 37	140 30	168 50	195 14	220 3	243 55
19	267 28	291 11	315 23	340 15	5 51	32 23	60 5
Feb. 1				74 24	103 49	133 39	162 46
9	190 18	216 2	240 22	264 1	287 40	311 52	336 53
23	2 45	29 22	56 40				
March 1				84 41	113 22	142 20	170 50
9	198 6	223 50	248 15	271 58	295 42	320 5	345 32
23	12 5	39 31	67 27	95 38	123 54		
April 1		138 1	165 56	193 5	219 7	243 58	267 57
13	291 38	315 40	340 41	7 3	34 44	63 20	92 11
27	120 45	148 42					
May 1			175 53	202 11	227 34	252 5	275 59
11	299 40	323 42	348 40	15 6	43 7	72 24	102 5
25	131 15	159 19	186 5	211 44			
June 1	224 3	248 38	272 33	296 14	320 3	344 27	9 58
15	37 5	65 55	95 59	126 10	155 21	182 52	208 48
29	233 33						
July 1		257 36	281 20	305 2	328 58	353 27	18 53
13	45 46	74 20	104 22	134 50	164 24	192 10	218 6
27	242 41	266 32	290 12				
Aug. 1							302 4
3	326 3	350 30	15 37	41 43	69 9	98 5	128 8
17	158 11	187 00	213 57	239 12	263 19	287 00	310 48
31	335 5						
Sep. 1					347 27	12 41	38 39
7	65 30	93 26	122 25	151 56	181 2	208 47	234 51
21	259 31	283 23	307 8	331 19	356 18		
Oct. 1						22 10	48 50
5	76 12	104 12	132 42	161 22	189 36	216 49	242 42
19	267 22	291 17	315 3	339 19	4 33	30 58	58 29
Nov. 1				72 33	100 58	129 27	157 39
9	185 18	212 11	238 7	263 5	287 14	311 00	334 53
23	359 32	25 28	52 57	81 45			
Dec. 1					111 8	140 15	168 27
7	195 32	221 37	246 51	271 24	295 25	319 8	342 58
21	7 27	33 12	60 43	89 58	120 12	150 8	

Ayanamsa: 21° 40′ 16″

Longitudes of Planets

1948		Sun	Mars	Merc.	Merc.	Jupit.	Venus	Saturn	Rahu
Jan.	5	284 3	157 33	285 14	293 27	256 6	314 29	141 44R	50 36
	15	294 15	157 20R	301 49	310 17	258 10	326 48	141 7	50 3
	25	304 26	155 46	318 41	326 31	260 8	339 3	140 24	49 32
Feb.	4	314 35	152 54	332 49	336 15	261 58	351 13	139 37R	49 00
	14	324 43	149 11	335 30R	331 4	263 40	3 15	138 48	48 30
	24	334 48	145 15	325 42R	322 16	265 10	15 8	138 2	47 57
March	5	344 50	141 48R	321 40D	323 34	266 27	26 48	137 18R	47 25
	15	354 49	139 21	327 17	332 19	267 29	38 12	136 42	46 54
	25	4 45	138 12	338 19	345 6	268 16	49 17	136 14	44 21
April	4	14 38	138 19D	352 34	0 41	268 46	59 58	135 55	45 50
	14	24 27	139 34	9 25	18 48	268 57	70 7	135 46	45 18
	24	34 13	141 45	28 49	39 23	268 49	79 30	135 48	44 48
May	4	43 56	144 42	50 10	60 37	268 23	87 52	136 1	44 14
	14	53 36	148 17	70 12	78 33	267 40	94 45	136 25	43 43
	24	63 13	152 21	85 32	91 2	266 42	129 29	136 58	43 11
June	3	72 48	156 51	94 52	96 55	265 33R	101 9	137 40	42 40
	13	82 23	161 42	97 7R	95 34	264 17	99 00R	138 30	42 6
	23	91 55	166 51	92 52	90 6	263 31	93 35	139 27	41 36
July	3	101 27	172 14	88 29	88 41D	261 49R	87 47	140 29	41 4
	13	111 00	177 51	91 00	95 29	260 47	84 47	141 37	40 31
	23	120 32	183 40	102 00	110 15	259 57	85 37	142 48	40 00
Aug.	2	130 6	189 40	119 51	130 6	259 24	89 41	144 00	39 25
	12	139 41	195 50	140 22	150 15	259 8	96 3	145 18	38 56
	22	149 18	202 10	159 36	168 22	259 10D	104 00	146 34	38 24
Sep.	1	158 57	208 38	176 37	184 19	259 31	113 5	147 50	37 52
	11	168 39	215 15	191 31	198 9	260 10	122 57	149 5	37 20
	21	178 24	222 30	204 8	209 16	261 5	133 26	150 16	36 49
Oct.	1	188 13	228 54	213 11	215 16	262 16	144 22	151 26	36 17
	11	198 5	235 55	214 38R	210 42R	263 41	155 40	152 29	35 46
	21	208 00	243 4	204 43	200 22	265 17	167 15	153 27	35 15
	31	217 59	250 19	200 22D	204 18	267 3	179 4	154 15	34 41
Nov.	10	228 00	257 41	210 34	217 53	269 00	191 4	155 1	34 10
	20	238 5	265 9	225 38	233 30	271 3	203 13	155 35	33 39
	30	248 12	272 43	241 22	249 13	273 11	215 29	155 58	33 7
Dec.	10	258 21	280 18	257 4	264 56	275 25	227 49	156 11	32 34
	20	268 31	288 6	272 52	280 51	277 43	240 14	156 12R	32 4
	30	278 43	295 54	288 55	298 37	280 2	252 40	155 57	31 32

Ayanamsa : 21° 41′ 06″

Longitude of the Moon

1948		Sun.	Tue.	Thurs.	Sat.	Mon.	Wed.	Fri.
Jan.	1			164 39	192 26	218 41	243 46	268 9
	11	292 7	315 52	339 37	3 41	28 34	54 51	83 2
	25	112 59	143 41	173 40	201 53			
Feb.	1	215 16	240 49	265 12	289 8	312 51	336 39	0 42
	15	25 14	50 42	77 36	106 15	136 23	166 52	196 19
	29	223 53						
March	1					236 53	261 59	286 3
	7	309 45	333 33	357 41	22 20	47 41	73 58	101 31
	21	130 23	160 9	189 47	218 14	245 1	270 14	
April	1			282 24	306 17	330 2	354 9	18 56
	11	44 30	70 56	98 14	126 21	155 7	184 2	212 26
	25	239 43	265 37	290 20				
May	1				314 17	338 5	2 19	27 26
	9	53 39	80 56	108 59	137 24	165 50	193 55	221 24
	23	248 1	273 36	298 14	322 12	346 00		
June	1		358 1	22 43	48 41	76 7	104 44	133 50
	13	162 28	190 40	217 47	244 4	269 33	294 18	318 24
	27	342 10	6 3					
July	1			30 42	56 44	84 32	113 51	143 46
	11	173 8	201 14	228 1	253 43	278 39	303 00	326 56
	25	350 38	14 29	39 3	64 59			
Aug.	1	78 38	107 24	137 35	167 56	197 11	224 45	250 47
	15	275 43	299 59	323 52	347 36	11 23	35 35	60 43
	29	87 22	115 53					
Sep.	1						130 47	161 16
	5	191 28	220 15	247 13	272 37	297 1	320 53	344 37
	19	8 28	32 40	57 32	83 27	110 47	139 40	
Oct.	1							169 38
	3	199 37	228 30	255 42	281 16	305 40	329 29	353 14
	17	17 18	41 57	67 22	93 42	121 4	149 28	178 37
	31	207 53						
Nov.	1					222 17	250 13	276 39
	7	301 41	325 46	349 29	13 26	38 7	63 47	90 28
	21	117 57	146 00	174 21	202 45	230 51		
Dec.	1						258 13	284 28
	5	309 30	333 36	357 17	21 15	46 8	72 20	99 53
	19	128 19	156 58	185 17	213 4	240 18	266 51	292 36

Ayanamsa: 21° 41' 06"

Longitudes of Planets

1949		Sun	Mars.	Merc.	Merc.	Jupit.	Venus	Saturn	Rahu
Jan.	5	284 50	300 36	298 37	306 25	281 25	260 10	155 50R	31 13
	15	295 1	308 28	313 26	318 32	283 44	272 40	155 25	30 41
	25	305 12	316 21	320 9R	317 15	286 00	285 9	154 50	30 8
Feb.	4	315 21	324 16	311 28	306 30	288 13	297 39	154 8R	29 36
	14	325 29	332 11	304 35	305 39D	290 23	310 9	153 22	29 3
	24	335 34	340 5	308 55	313 38	292 26	322 37	152 38	28 34
March	6	345 36	347 57	319 23	325 55	294 21	335 7	151 46	28 3
	16	355 35	355 47	333 4	340 47	296 8	347 34	151 3	27 30
	26	5 31	3 33	349 3	357 51	297 44	0 1	150 25	26 58
April	5	15 23	11 27	7 15	17 13	299 08	12 25	149 54	26 27
	15	25 12	18 56	27 38	38 10	300 18	24 49	149 32	25 55
	25	34 57	26 32	48 18	57 23	301 12	37 10	149 21	25 22
May	5	44 40	34 2	65 00	70 53	301 49	49 30	149 19D	24 52
	15	54 20	41 27	74 53	76 57	302 8	61 49	149 29	24 20
	25	63 57	48 48	77 00R	75 19R	302 9R	74 7	149 49	23 47
June	4	73 32	56 2	72 39	70 8	301 50	86 23	150 19	23 17
	14	83 6	63 11	68 45	69 8D	301 13	98 38	150 57	22 44
	24	92 39	70 14	71 27	75 35	300 21	110 51	151 43	22 12
July	4	102 11	77 12	81 27	88 57	299 14	123 4	152 38	21 40
	14	111 43	84 3	97 52	107 54	298 00	135 14	153 38	21 9
	24	121 15	90 51	118 28	108 58	296 44	147 23	154 43	20 37
Aug.	3	130 49	97 32	139 00	148 25	295 29	159 00	155 53	20 5
	13	140 24	104 8	157 11	165 20	294 21	171 34	157 5	19 33
	23	150 2	110 38	172 53	179 48	293 25	183 34	158 20	19 2
Sep.	2	159 41	117 2	184 50	191 24	292 47	195 31	159 35	18 29
	12	169 23	123 20	195 51	198 25	292 25	207 23	160 51	17 58
	22	179 9	129 31	199 0R	196 44	292 21	219 10	162 5	17 26
Oct.	2	188 58	135 37	191 49	186 28	292 39	230 50	163 17	16 54
	12	198 50	141 35	183 59	185 51D	293 14	242 23	164 26	16 23
	22	208 45	147 24	191 7	198 17	294 7	253 45	165 31	15 50
Nov.	1	218 44	153 4	206 16	214 26	295 17	264 52	166 30	15 20
	11	228 46	158 34	222 35	230 39	296 42	275 40	167 22	14 48
	21	238 51	163 52	238 37	246 29	298 19	285 56	168 6	14 16
Dec.	1	248 58	168 55	254 18	262 6	300 7	295 43	168 42	13 43
	11	259 7	173 40	269 54	277 40	302 6	304 25	169 7	13 12
	21	269 18	178 4	285 17	292 34	304 11	311 41	169 22	12 41
	31	279 30	181 56	298 54	302 29	306 24	316 48	169 26R	12 8

Ayanamsa: 21° 41' 57"

Longitude of the Moon

1949		Sun.	Tue.	Thur.	Sat.	Mon.	Wed.	Fri.
Jan.	1				305 8	329 31	353 17	16 57
	9	41 14	66 49	94 7	122 59	152 33	181 46	210 00
	23	237 9	263 22	288 51	313 38	337 46		
Feb.	1		349 38	13 13	37 2	61 46	88 5	116 8
	13	146 9	176 25	205 53	233 54	260 27	285 51	310 28
	27	334 32						
March	1		358 14	21 50	45 42	70 23	96 30	124 28
	13	154 10	184 40	214 39	243 10	269 58	295 17	319 38
	27	343 26	7 2	30 45				
April	1							42 44
	3	67 11	92 37	119 26	147 51	177 37	207 50	237 22
	17	265 22	291 36	316 25	340 20	3 56	57 40	51 53
May	1	76 49	102 39	129 33	157 36	186 40	216 14	245 26
	15	273 27	299 50	324 44	348 40	12 17	36 11	60 49
	29	86 03	112 54					
June	1						126 28	154 8
	5	182 24	211 4	239 46	267 54	294 52	320 25	344 47
	19	8 30	32 15	56 42	82 17	109 6	136 51	
July	1							165 3
	3	193 20	221 30	249 24	276 45	303 10	328 27	352 42
	17	16 24	40 10	64 43	90 38	118 3	146 38	175 36
	31	204 16						
Aug.	1					218 22	246 3	273 00
	7	299 10	324 27	348 53	12 40	36 16	60 19	85 31
	21	112 21	140 52	170 27	200 5	228 54	256 34	
Sep.	1			269 57	295 58	321 4	345 27	9 17
	11	32 51	56 36	81 6	106 57	134 34	163 52	194 5
	25	224 2	252 47	279 56				
Oct.	1				305 40	330 21	354 20	18 00
	9	41 36	65 30	90 5	115 48	143 5	172 3	202 12
	23	232 29	261 42	289 10	314 55	339 23		
Nov.	1		351 20	14 57	38 35	62 34	87 6	112 26
	13	138 48	166 29	195 32	225 28	255 18	283 55	310 43
	27	335 51	359 51					
Dec.	1			23 26	47 11	71 30	96 36	122 29
	11	149 9	176 39	205 3	234.11	263 24	291 46	318 37
	25	343 50	7 54	31 30	55 21			

Ayanamsa: 21° 41′ 57″

Longitudes of Planets

1950		Sun	Mars	Merc.	Merc.	Jupit.	Venus	Saturn	Rahu
Jan.	5	284 35	183 48	303 11	303 47R	307 31	318 14	169 25R	11 52
	15	294 46	186 54	299 36	293 30	309 50	318 14R	169 15	11 21
	25	304 57	189 15	289 2	288 10D	312 12	314 16	168 50	10 49
Feb.	4	315 6	190 41	290 17	294 20	314 36	308 17	168 17	10 17
	14	325 14	191 00R	299 39	305 49	316 58	303 54	167 37	9 46
	24	335 19	190 5R	312 37	319 56	319 20	303 23D	166 53	9 14
March	6	345 21	187 52	327 42	335 57	321 39	306 31	166 05	8 42
	16	355 20	184 35	344 41	353 54	323 54	312 22	165 18	8 10
	26	5 16	180 46	3 38	13 47	326 5	320 3	164 34	7 38
April	5	15 8	177 5	24 3	33 54	328 7	328 56	163 54	7 7
	15	24 58	174 9	42 37	49 35	330 1	338 39	163 21	6 35
	25	34 44	172 26	54 27	57 3	331 47	348 58	162 56	6 4
May	5	44 26	172 1D	57 20R	55 43	332 21	359 40	162 41	5 32
	15	54 6	172 50	52 56	50 13	334 42	10 41	162 35D	5 00
	25	63 44	174 43	48 41	48 51	335 49	21 55	162 40	4 28
June	4	73 19	177 30	50 53	54 37	336 39	33 20	162 56	3 55
	14	82 53	181 00	59 53	66 32	337 12	44 53	163 21	3 24
	24	92 25	185 5	74 31	83 44	337 26	56 33	163 56	2 53
July	4	101 57	189 42	93 56	104 40	337 21R	68 19	164 38	2 22
	14	111 30	194 36	115 23	125 38	336 58	80 10	165 29	1 50
	24	121 2	200 3	135 12	144 3	336 16	92 6	166 26	1 17
Aug.	3	130 35	205 45	152 10	159 36	335 19	104 7	167 28	0 47
	13	140 11	211 42	161 17	172 8	334 8	116 14	168 35	0 14
	23	149 48	217 53	176 58	180 30	332 51R	128 25	169 46	359 42
Sep.	2	159 27	224 18	182 18	181 47R	331 33	140 41	170 59	359 8
	12	169 10	230 54	178 39	173 40	330 19	153 00	172 14	358 39
	22	178 55	237 42	169 16	168 2D	329 13	165 23	173 29	358 7
Oct.	2	188 43	244 40	170 53	176 52	328 24	177 50	174 43	357 34
	12	198 36	251 48	184 38	193 5	327 51	190 19	175 56	357 3
	22	208 31	259 03	201 39	210 6	327 36	202 48	177 6	356 31
Nov.	1	218 30	266 25	218 21	226 26	327 42D	215 21	178 11	356 00
	11	228 32	273 56	234 20	242 7	328 8	227 53	179 11	355 27
	21	238 36	281 32	249 47	257 22	328 52	240 28	180 4	354 57
Dec.	1	248 43	289 13	264 48	272 00	329 55	253 2	180 50	354 25
	11	258 52	297 00	278 43	284 20	331 15	265 36	181 28	353 53
	21	269 3	304 48	287 41	287 21R	332 49	278 10	181 56	353 21
	31	279 14	312 39	282 26	277 9	334 34	289 29	182 15	352 48

Ayanamsa: 21° 42′ 47″

Longitude of the Moon

1950		Sun.	Tue.	Thurs.	Sat.	Mon.	Wed.	Fri.
Jan.	1	67 33	92 42	118 55	145 57	173 32	201 31	229 47
	15	258 10	286 14	313 21	339 9	3 42	27 29	51 9
	29	75 25	100 51					
Feb.	1						114 25	141 28
	5	169 43	198 14	226 37	254 37	282 6	308 51	334 40
	19	359 29	23 30	47 7	70 59	95 46		
March	1						121 57	149 46
	5	178 47	208 13	237 15	265 21	292 23	318 24	343 30
	19	7 53	31 43	55 20	79 12	103 52	129 55	157 41
April	1				172 12	202 5	232 12	261 27
	9	289 13	315 28	340 30	4 44	28 32	52 9	75 55
	23	100 11	125 23	152 00	180 21			
May	1					210 14	240 44	270 22
	7	298 40	324 57	349 48	13 45	37 23	61 3	85 2
	21	109 31	134 49	161 17	189 15	218 43	249 2	
June	1			264 8	293 22	320 47	346 22	10 39
	11	34 19	57 59	82 00	106 36	131 53	157 58	185 5
	25	213 25	242 50	272 35				
July	1				301 35	328 59	354 38	18 59
	9	42 42	66 27	90 44	115 49	141 42	168 21	195 45
	23	223 55	252 42	281 38	309 58	337 00		
Aug.	1		349 58	14 53	38 53	62 37	86 42	111 40
	13	137 41	164 44	192 30	220 43	249 7	277 25	305 14
	27	332 11	358 2	22 47				
Sep.	1							34 51
	3	58 38	82 29	107 1	132 43	159 48	188 4	216 59
	17	245 52	274 12	301 42	328 17	353 58	18 48	42 56
Oct.	1	66 42	90 31	114 57	140 36	167 52	196 43	226 29
	15	256 10	284 49	312 4	338 4	3 6	27 28	51 24
	29	75 8	98 56					
Nov.	1						111 1	135 49
	5	162 2	190 2	219 46	250 16	280 11	308 31	335 3
	19	0 11	24 27	48 18	72 3	95 52	119 59	
Dec.	1							144 46
	3	170 43	198 21	227 47	258 21	288 39	317 24	344 10
	17	9 17	33 24	57 8	80 53	104 55	129 21	154 24
	31	180 22						

Ayanamsa: 21° 42′ 47″

Longitudes of Planets

1951		Sun	Mars	Merc.	Merc.	Jupit.	Venus	Saturn	Rahu
Jan.	5	284 20	316 35	275 59R	272 17	335 34	297 1	182 19	352 33
	15	294 31	324 27	272 28	275 31	337 33	309 34	182 21R	352 1
	25	304 42	332 19	280 16	286 7	339 42	322 4	182 12	351 30
Feb.	4	314 51	340 12	292 38	299 39	341 57	334 36	181 52	350 57
	14	324 59	348 2	307 5	314 53	344 17	347 1	181 24	350 26
	24	335 4	355 48	323 5	331 41	346 39	359 25	180 47	349 54
March	6	345 6	3 32	340 42	350 11	349 4	11 46	180 5	349 22
	16	355 6	11 13	0 1	9 57	351 29	24 00	179 19	348 50
	26	5 2	18 49	19 26	27 41	353 54	36 11	178 31	348 18
April	5	14 54	26 20	33 54	37 35	356 17	48 14	177 46	347 47
	15	24 43	33 48	38 30R	37 00	358 37	60 11	177 2	347 15
	25	34 29	41 10	33 55	30 41	0 51	71 58	176 28	346 43
May	5	44 12	48 26	28 42	28 31D	3 1	83 36	176 1	346 12
	15	53 52	55 39	30 15	33 38	5 3	95 2	175 43	345 40
	25	63 30	62 45	38 30	44 40	7 00	106 13	175 34	345 8
June	4	73 5	69 46	51 54	60 15	8 43	117 7	175 35D	344 36
	14	82 39	76 42	69 39	79 57	10 16	127 37	175 45	344 5
	24	92 12	83 33	90 49	101 39	11 35	137 35	176 8	343 33
July	4	101 44	90 21	112 4	121 44	12 40	146 49	176 37	343 00
	14	111 16	97 4	130 36	138 39	13 29	155 3	177 16	342 30
	24	121 48	103 43	145 54	152 15	13 59	161 53	178 3	341 8
Aug.	3	130 22	110 18	157 38	161 46	14 10	166 37	178 58	341 26
	13	139 57	116 49	164 24	165 9R	14 3R	168 20	179 58	340 54
	23	149 34	123 15	163 29	159 45	13 34	166 19R	181 2	340 23
Sep.	2	159 14	129 38	155 11	152 3	12 50	161 1	182 13	339 50
	12	168 56	135 59	152 12	155 58D	11 47	155 15	183 25	339 19
	22	178 41	142 15	162 37	170 54	10 33	152 15	184 37	338 47
Oct.	2	188 30	148 28	179 49	188 47	9 14	153 9D	185 52	338 12
	12	198 21	154 36	197 32	206 1	7 54	157 23	187 6	337 43
	22	208 17	160 40	214 12	222 10	6 41	164 00	188 17	337 11
Nov.	1	218 15	166 41	229 55	237 27	5 41	172 18	189 27	336 39
	11	228 17	172 36	244 50	251 56	4 53	181 4	190 33	336 7
	21	238 22	178 25	258 43	264 50	4 24	191 55	191 35	335 36
Dec.	1	248 29	184 8	269 43	272 14	4 15D	202 43	192 30	335 4
	11	258 38	189 42	271 50R	265 14	4 28	213 58	193 17	334 33
	21	268 48	195 9	258 55	256 5	5 00	225 31	193 57	334 02
	31	279 00	200 24	257 18D	261 10	5 51	237 18	194 27	333 29

Ayanamsa : 21° 43′ 37″

Longitude of the Moon

1951		Sun	Tue.	Thur.	Sat.	Mon.	Wed.	Fri.
Jan.	1					193 50	221 55	251 26
	7	281 37	311 12	339 9	5 15	29 55	53 47	77 30
	21	101 31	126 7	151 22	177 22	204 15	232 7	
Feb.	1			246 26	275 35	304 48	333 12	0 10
	11	25 36	49 55	73 42	97 35	122 4	147 27	173 49
	25	201 3	228 56					
March	1			257 15	285 43	313 57	341 31	8 1
	11	33 21	57 42	81 32	105 25	129 58	155 39	182 41
	25	210 50	239 36	268 19	296 30			
April	1	310 20	337 24	3 38	29 2	53 37	77 36	101 21
	15	125 26	150 28	177 1	205 13	234 38	264 18	293 14
	29	320 55						
May	1		347 25	12 39	37 49	62 5	85 57	109 39
	13	133 40	158 35	185 3	213 25	243 20	273 42	303 11
	27	331 5	357 24	22 32				
June	1							34 49
	3	58 59	82 49	106 32	130 22	154 45	180 16	207 29
	17	236 36	267 3	297 28	326 36	353 53	19 32	44 4
July	1	68 1	91 45	115 31	139 33	164 8	189 42	216 44
	15	245 29	275 33	305 50	335 5	2 35	28 23	52 56
	29	76 49	100 32					
Aug.	1						112 27	136 34
	5	161 14	186 44	213 9	240 53	269 49	299 37	328 52
	19	357 10	23 52	49 6	73 17	97 3	120 55	145 20
Sep.	1				157 50	183 31	210 6	237 34
	9	265 47	294 29	323 15	351 30	18 41	44 34	69 15
	23	93 11	116 57	141 10	166 20			
Oct.	1					192 43	220 12	248 23
	7	276 49	305 6	333 1	0 23	26 57	52 32	77 9
	21	101 2	124 45	148 54	174 18	201 11	229 32	
Nov.	1			244 3	273 14	301 56	329 47	356 45
	11	22 58	48 27	73 10	97 14	120 53	144 40	169 16
	25	195 22	223 19	252 51				
Dec.	1				282 53	312 15	340 16	6 57
	9	32 36	57 30	81 49	105 41	129 18	153 4	177 33
	23	203 27	231 15	260 53	291 24	321 24		

Ayanamsa :21° 43′ 37″

11

Longitudes of Planets

1952		Sun	Mars	Merc.	Merc.	Jupit.	Venus	Saturn	Rahu
Jan.	5	284 5	202 57	261 15	266 36	6 27	243 15	194 39	333 14
	15	294 17	208 22	272 53	279 43	7 44	255 15	194 54	332 41
	25	304 28	212 27	286 56	294 27	9 16	267 22	194 59R	332 9
Feb.	4	314 37	216 43	302 16	310 24	11 1	279 33	194 52	331 37
	14	324 44	220 30	318 52	327 46	12 56	291 47	194 36	331 7
	24	334 50	223 43	336 51	346 20	14 59	304 3	194 12	330 34
March	5	344 52	226 14	355 53	4 57	17 10	316 21	193 35	330 2
	15	354 51	227 53	12 38	18 1	19 26	328 39	192 53	329 31
	25	4 47	228 27	20 18	19 29R	21 46	340 59	192 9	328 58
April	4	14 40	227 50R	16 19R	12 27	24 8	353 17	191 23	328 27
	14	24 30	225 57	9 36	8 42	26 33	5 35	190 37	327 58
	24	34 15	222 58	9 54D	12 54	28 58	17 53	189 55	327 24
May	4	43 58	219 21	17 23	23 4	31 21	30 10	189 18	326 51
	14	53 38	215 50	29 52	37 32	33 42	42 26	188 47	326 21
	24	63 16	213 00	46 9	55 40	36 00	54 42	188 26	325 49
June	3	72 51	211 27	66 0	76 53	38 12	66 59	188 15	325 17
	13	82 25	211 13	87 49	97 48	40 20	79 17	188 12D	324 44
	23	91 58	212 19D	108 00	116 50	42 21	91 33	188 20	324 13
July	3	101 30	214 24	124 43	131 38	44 12	103 51	188 38	323 41
	13	111 2	217 40	137 32	142 15	45 54	116 9	189 5	323 9
	23	120 34	221 36	145 32	147 5	47 24	128 27	189 41	322 38
Aug.	2	130 8	226 10	146 35R	144 00	48 40	140 46	190 26	322 6
	12	139 43	231 18	140 7	136 30	49 41	153 6	191 17	321 34
	22	149 20	236 54	134 55	136 25D	50 26	165 24	192 14	321 00
Sep.	1	158 59	242 51	141 6	148 20	50 51	177 44	193 17	320 29
	11	168 41	249 9	157 8	166 28	50 58R	190 4	194 23	320 00
	21	178 27	255 43	175 50	184 53	50 45	202 22	195 32	319 27
Oct.	1	188 15	262 31	193 35	201 55	50 14	214 38	196 45	318 55
	11	198 7	269 31	209 56	217 38	49 20	226 54	197 59	318 24
	21	208 2	276 41	225 5	232 14	48 15	239 8	199 12	317 52
	31	218 1	284 1	239 3	245 20	47 00	251 21	200 24	317 19
Nov.	10	228 2	291 28	250 32	254 56	45 38	263 31	201 35	316 48
	20	238 7	299 1	256 30R	254 10	44 18	275 39	202 40	316 18
	30	248 14	306 36	248 6	242 9	43 5	287 43	203 42	315 44
Dec.	10	258 23	314 16	240 18D	242 27	42 6	299 40	204 37	315 12
	20	268 34	321 58	247 8	253 9	41 24	311 31	205 27	314 40
	30	278 45	329 42	259 52	268 26	41 1	323 10	206 9	314 10

Ayanamsa: 21° 44' 28"

Longitude of the Moon

1952	Sun.	Tue.	Thur.	Sat.	Mon.	Wed.	Fri.
Jan. 1		335 53	3 32	29 37	54 33	78 46	102 35
13	126 15	150 00	174 1	199 17	225 50	254 11	284 4
27	314 31	344 14	12 21				
Feb. 1							25 43
3	51 18	75 43	99 31	123 9	146 59	171 15	196 13
17	222 11	249 24	277 58	307 35	337 25	6 25	33 53
March 1				46 59	72 4	96 7	119 45
9	143 33	167 54	193 5	219 9	246 7	273 55	302 27
23	331 25	0 16	28 15	54 52	80 2		
April 1		92 11	115 59	139 40	163 53	189 6	215 28
13	242 49	270 46	298 59	327 15	355 23	23 4	49 53
27	75 23	100 3					
May 1			123 50	147 32	171 50	197 21	224 20
11	252 33	281 19	309 58	338 6	5 37	32 30	58 36
25	83 48	108 6	131 49	155 29			
June 1	167 30	192 23	218 50	246 59	276 18	305 51	334 45
15	2 35	29 21	55 13	80 16	104 35	128 21	151 55
29	175 48						
July 1		200 38	227 1	255 15	284 58	315 7	344 37
13	12 45	39 26	64 54	89 27	112 25	137 2	160 38
27	184 36	209 26	235 41				
Aug. 1							249 27
3	278 18	308 26	338 44	8 4	35 46	61 48	86 32
17	110 29	134 5	157 43	181 40	206 15	231 49	258 42
31	287 7						
Sep. 1					301 50	331 54	1 53
7	30 42	57 46	83 9	107 21	130 59	154 36	178 38
21	203 20	228 49	255 13	282 39	311 10		
Oct. 1						340 33	10 4
5	38 47	65 56	91 25	115 38	139 15	162 58	187 19
19	212 35	238 47	265 45	293 20	321 28	350 4	18 46
Nov. 1				32 57	60 33	86 43	111 31
9	135 22	158 59	183 5	208 13	234 37	262 3	290 6
23	318 18	346 28	14 28	42 4			
Dec. 1					68 54	94 40	119 18
7	143 9	166 45	190 52	216 6	242 52	271 2	299 59
21	328 57	357 23	25 2	51 53	77 54	103 3	

Ayanamsa: 21° 44′ 28″

Longitudes of Planets

1953		Sun	Mars.	Merc.	Merc.	Jupit.	Venus	Saturn	Rahu
Jan.	5	284 52	334 20	268 26	275 53	40 58R	330 2	206 29	313 50
	15	295 3	342 2	283 32	291 25	41 7D	341 15	206 55	313 20
	25	305 14	349 42	299 31	307 52	41 41	352 2	207 12	312 46
Feb.	4	315 23	357 19	316 31	325 28	42 36	2 17	207 18	312 15
	14	325 30	4 53	334 35	343 38	43 38	11 37	207 14R	311 44
	24	335 35	12 24	352 1	358 40	45 00	19 52	206 58	311 12
March	6	345 37	19 51	2 27	2 35R	46 35	26 24	206 33	310 40
	16	355 37	27 14	359 30	355 00	48 21	30 29	206 1	310 7
	26	5 32	34 32	351 19	349 49	50 17	31 6R	205 22	309 37
April	5	15 25	41 46	350 33D	353 25	52 21	27 45	204 43	309 5
	15	25 14	48 55	357 44	3 13	54 31	21 46	203 52	308 33
	25	34 59	55 59	9 42	17 2	56 45	16 37	203 7	308 00
May	5	44 42	62 58	24 40	34 5	59 2	15 00D	202 24	307 31
	15	54 22	69 53	43 48	54 14	61 22	17 9	201 46	306 57
	25	63 59	76 44	65 7	75 31	63 43	22 13	201 15	306 25
June	4	73 34	83 31	86 23	95 52	66 4	29 16	200 52	305 55
	14	83 8	90 14	104 18	111 40	68 22	37 38	200 37	305 22
	24	92 41	96 53	117 53	122 50	70 40	46 59	200 33D	304 50
July	4	102 13	103 25	126 21	128 11	72 52	56 57	200 38	304 20
	14	111 45	110 3	128 3R	126 3	75 00	67 27	200 53	303 48
	24	121 18	116 34	122 47	119 26	77 2	78 16	201 18	303 15
Aug.	3	130 52	123 2	117 37	118 14D	78 56	89 24	201 51	302 43
	13	140 27	129 28	121 39	127 42	80 42	100 45	202 32	302 11
	23	150 4	135 52	135 50	145 12	82 16	112 19	203 22	301 40
Sep.	2	159 44	142 15	154 59	164 39	83 38	124 4	204 17	301 5
	12	169 26	148 36	173 56	182 46	84 47	135 58	205 18	300 36
	22	179 11	154 54	191 10	199 9	85 39	148 00	206 23	300 5
Oct.	2	189 00	161 12	206 47	214 1	86 13	160 10	207 33	299 33
	12	198 52	167 29	220 52	227 13	86 26	172 26	208 45	299 00
	22	208 48	173 44	232 55	237 30	86 22R	184 47	208 55	298 29
Nov.	1	218 46	179 58	240 18	240 18R	85 58	197 11	211 7	297 58
	11	228 48	186 10	236 10	230 59	85 15	209 41	212 19	297 26
	21	238 53	192 20	225 11	226 16D	84 14	222 13	213 29	296 54
Dec.	1	249 00	198 22	228 49	234 00	83 2	234 45	214 36	296 23
	11	259 10	204 33	241 15	248 26	81 42	247 19	215 38	295 51
	21	269 20	210 38	255 54	263 00	80 22	259 54	216 35	295 18
	31	279 31	216 37	271 14	279 5	79	271 14	217 25	294 46

Ayanamsa: 21° 45' 18"

Longitude of the Moon

1953	Sun.	Tue.	Thur.	Sat.	Mon.	Wed.	Fri.
Jan. 1			115 19	139 19	162 56	186 40	211 11
11	237 5	264 41	293 50	323 43	353 17	21 45	48 53
25	74 47	99 43	123 57	147 44			
Feb. 1	159 33	183 12	207 16	232 16	258 44	286 57	316 44
15	347 8	16 55	45 11	71 42	96 47	120 57	144 40
March 1	168 17	192 6	216 22	241 25	267 39	295 26	324 49
15	355 9	25 16	53 56	80 42	105 47	129 48	153 24
29	177 5	201 10				213 26	238 26
April 1							
5	264 14	291 5	319 13	348 35	18 32	47 55	75 46
19	101 46	126 19	150 4	173 42	197 46	222 34	
May 1							248 9
3	274 30	301 36	329 33	358 18	27 27	56 13	83 46
17	109 44	134 19	158 8	181 52	206 7	231 18	257 31
31	284 37						
June 1	224 3	248 38			298 25	326 22	354 40
7	23 6	51 18	78 44	105 1	130 4	154 10	177 53
21	201 52	226 42	252 46	280 7	308 24		
July 1						337 6	5 42
5	33 51	61 18	87 53	113 30	138 12	162 12	185 54
19	209 52	234 41	260 52	288 36	317 38	347 11	16 23
Aug. 1				30 37	58 13	84 38	110 2
9	134 39	158 41	182 24	206 9	230 24	255 43	282 36
23	311 15	341 13	11 26	40 43	68 25		
Sep. 1		81 39	107 1	131 37	155 34	179 17	203 00
13	227 00	251 40	277 30	305 00	334 18	4 47	35 9
27	64 6	91 7					
Oct. 1			116 28	140 44	164 29	188 10	212 2
11	236 16	261 5	286 51	314 2	342 52	13 1	43 21
25	72 31	99 46	125 14	149 28			
Nov. 1	161 21	185 1	208 54	233 15	258 11	283 49	310 21
15	338 3	6 59	36 40	66 7	94 17	120 43	145 37
29	169 35						
Dec. 1		193 18	217 19	242 1	267 32	293 52	320 57
13	348 45	17 12	45 59	74 31	102 7	128 24	153 22
27	177 26	201 11	225 15				

Ayanamsa: 21° 45′ 18″

Longitudes of Planets

1954		Sun	Mars	Merc.	Merc.	Jupit.	Venus	Saturn	Rahu
Jan.	5	284 37	219 36	279 5	287 6	78 30R	278 47	217 43	294 30
	15	294 49	225 30	295 18	303 43	77 32	291 21	218 26	294 00
	25	304 59	231 19	312 18	321 1	76 51	303 55	218 53	293 26
Feb.	4	315 8	237 1	329 35	337 23	76 29	316 29	219 14	292 55
	14	325 16	242 36	343 22	346 3	76 26D	329 4	219 19	292 23
	24	335 21	248 1	344 41R	340 03	76 46	341 34	219 18R	291 52
March	6	345 23	253 15	335 15	332 14	77 22	354 2	219 6R	291 20
	16	355 22	258 14	331 48D	333 53	78 17	6 29	218 43	290 49
	26	5 18	262 54	337 37	342 39	79 27	18 53	218 12	290 17
April	5	15 10	267 12	348 43	355 35	80 52	31 15	217 35	289 45
	15	24 59	271 00	3 10	11 27	82 27	43 34	216 53	289 13
	25	34 45	274 13	20 24	30 4	84 13	55 49	216 7	288 42
May	5	44 28	276 41	40 23	51 10	86 8	68 2	215 22	288 10
	15	54 8	278 9	61 59	72 16	88 10	80 11	214 39	287 38
	25	63 45	278 32R	81 36	89 44	90 17	92 16	214 1	287 5
June	4	73 21	277 30	96 36	102 6	92 29	104 17	213 29	286 33
	14	82 54	275 35	106 4	108 20	94 42	116 12	213 2	286 2
	24	92 27	272 42	108 44R	107 21	96 58	127 2	212 46	285 30
July	4	101 59	269 40R	104 40	101 38	99 15	139 44	212 37	284 59
	14	111 31	267 10	99 38	99 31D	101 30	151 18	212 41D	284 27
	24	121 3	265 47	101 44	106 19	103 44	162 42	212 54	283 55
Aug.	3	130 37	265 45	113 4	121 39	105 54	173 55	213 17	283 23
	13	140 12	267 8	131 22	141 31	108 2	184 57	213 48	282 51
	23	149 50	269 41	151 31	161 4	110 4	195 26	214 27	282 20
Sep.	2	159 29	273 15	170 6	178 39	111 58	205 38	215 14	281 49
	12	169 12	277 39	186 39	194 14	113 44	215 10	216 8	281 16
	22	178 57	282 43	201 23	207 56	115 20	223 54	217 6	280 46
Oct.	2	188 46	288 19	213 54	219 2	116 46	231 24	218 11	280 12
	12	198 38	294 20	222 52	224 43	117 57	237 00	219 17	279 40
	22	208 33	300 38	223 33R	218 55	118 53	239 56	220 28	279 9
Nov.	1	218 32	307 12	212 44	209 7	119 31	239 8R	221 36	278 37
	11	228 34	314 00	210 4D	214 32	119 54	234 42	222 52	278 6
	21	238 38	320 57	220 53	228 7	119 55R	229 20	224 3	277 34
Dec.	1	248 45	328 00	235 42	243 31	119 35	225 5	225 9	277 2
	11	258 54	335 7	251 11	258 59	118 57	225 16D	226 19	276 31
	21	269 5	342 17	266 51	274 46	118 00	229 5	227 21	276 00
	31	279 16	349 28	281 49	290 53	116 54	235 27	228 17	275 26

Ayanamsa: 21° 46′ 8″

Longitude of the Moon

1954		Sun.	Tue.	Thurs.	Sat.	Mon.	Wed.	Fri.
Jan.	1							237 24
	3	262 58	289 39	317 17	345 31	13 57	42 13	70 6
	17	97 17	123 33	148 51	173 15	198 7	220 55	245 23
	31	270 30						
Feb.	1					284 10	311 58	340 54
	7	10 13	39 3	66 46	93 46	119 56	144 56	169 20
	21	193 18	217 4	240 58	265 46			
March	1					292 5	319 57	349 31
	7	19 42	49 17	77 18	103 52	129 16	153 53	178 2
	21	201 53	225 38	249 38	274 14	300 13	328 1	
April	1			342 40	12 57	43 33	72 43	100 24
	11	126 17	151 6	175 3	197 51	223 38	246 34	270 46
	25	296 12	322 54	351 17				
May	1				21 18	51 52	81 22	109 6
	9	135 17	159 56	182 59	207 41	231 32	255 41	280 30
	23	305 49	332 49	0 41	30 17	60 11		
June	1		75 1	103 41	130 44	156 11	181 37	204 19
	13	228 9	254 24	277 19	303 2	329 38	356 14	25 42
	27	54 43	83 41					
July	1			111 53	138 43	164 13	188 38	212 27
	11	236 20	260 47	286 11	312 38	340 5	8 10	36 5
	25	65 1	93 5	120 28	146 52			
Aug.	1	159 41	184 28	208 30	232 16	256 23	281 27	307 34
	15	335 54	4 20	33 20	61 47	89 30	116 27	142 40
	29	168 1	192 36					
Sep.	1						204 38	228 23
	5	252 10	276 52	302 29	330 5	359 11	28 56	57 15
	19	86 16	113 23	139 20	164 28	189 2	213 2	
Oct.	1							236 43
	3	260 27	284 48	310 32	338 5	7 31	37 54	68 1
	17	96 28	123 29	149 6	173 48	197 58	221 47	245 26
	31	269 14						
Nov.	1					281 16	306 7	332 39
	7	0 48	30 15	61 20	91 13	119 24	145 49	170 49
	21	195 1	218 47	242 28	266 19	290 34		
Dec.	1						315 37	341 52
	5	9 48	39 7	69 16	99 11	127 42	154 3	179 35
	19	203 43	227 21	251 6	275 14	300 00	325 36	352 4

Ayanamsa: 21° 46′ 8″

RAMAN'S EPHEMERIS

Longitudes of Planets

1955		Sun	Mars	Merc.	Merc.	Jupit.	Venus	Saturn	Rahu
Jan.	5	284 22	353 1	290 59	299 14	116 46	239 22	228 23	275 11
	15	294 34	0 14	307 33	315 35	114 58R	248 10	229 31	274 40
	25	304 44	7 23	322 47	327 58	113 37	257 55	230 10	274 8
Feb.	4	314 54	14 31	329 36	326 50R	112 24	268 21	230 40	273 36
	14	325 1	21 36	321 20	316 29	111 21	278 45	231 00	273 4
	24	335 6	28 39	314 25	315 14D	110 34	290 28	231 10	2~~ ~2
March	6	345 9	35 39	318 13	324 51	110 4	301 55	231 10R	272 00
	16	355 8	42 36	328 19	334 45	109 54	313 33	231 00	271 30
	26	5 4	49 28	341 54	349 38	110 2D	325 18	230 39	270 58
April	5	14 56	56 18	357 59	8 47	110 30	337 10	230 10	270 25
	15	24 45	63 4	16 27	26 36	111 15	349 4	229 35	269 53
	25	34 30	69 47	37 12	47 52	112 16	1 3	228 56	269 21
May	5	44 14	76 28	58 00	67 5	113 31	13 3	228 10	268 50
	15	53 54	83 5	74 47	80 56	115 00	25 6	227 25	268 18
	25	63 32	89 30	85 24	88 5	116 36	36 40	226 41	267 45
June	4	73 7	96 12	88 49R	87 44	118 24	49 16	226 2	267 15
	14	82 41	102 42	85 21	82 35	120 19	61 23	225 27	266 43
	24	92 14	109 10	80 37	80 16D	122 18	73 32	224 59	266 10
July	4	101 46	115 36	81 54	85 34	124 24	85 17	224 41	265 38
	14	111 18	122 00	91 8	98 32	126 32	97 56	224 31	265 9
	24	120 50	128 24	107 27	117 28	128 44	110 12	224 31D	264 36
Aug.	3	130 24	134 47	127 54	138 12	130 56	122 29	224 41	264 5
	13	139 59	141 9	148 2	157 16	133 8	134 49	225 1	263 31
	23	149 36	147 31	165 54	173 57	135 18	147 11	225 31	263 00
Sep.	2	159 16	153 53	181 28	188 23	137 26	159 34	226 7	262 28
	12	168 58	160 15	194 42	200 13	139 32	172 00	226 50	261 57
	22	178 43	166 37	204 43	207 44	141 33	184 26	227 43	261 25
Oct.	2	188 32	173 00	208 34	206 25R	143 26	196 53	228 41	260 54
	12	198 23	179 23	201 22	195 45	145 12	209 21	229 43	260 22
	22	208 19	185 47	193 12	195 5D	146 49	221 50	230 48	259 49
Nov.	1	218 17	192 13	200 18	207 17	148 14	234 18	231 58	259 17
	11	228 19	198 39	215 2	223 00	149 26	246 46	233 10	258 47
	21	238 24	205 26	231 16	238 56	150 23	259 22	234 22	258 14
Dec.	1	248 31	211 36	246 48	254 40	151 3	271 41	235 33	257 42
	11	258 40	218 6	262 26	270 18	151 25	284 7	236 43	257 11
	21	268 50	224 36	278 20	286 17	151 29R	296 33	237 48	256 39
	31	279 1	231 7	294 7	301 37	151 15	308 56	238 50	256 6

Ayanamsa: 21° 46′ 59″

Longitude of the Moon

1955		Sun.	Tue.	Thur.	Sat.	Mon.	Wed.	Fri.
Jan.	1				5 46	33 58	63 1	92 27
	9	121 23	148 34	175 8	199 52	224 46	247 24	271 30
	23	296 22	322 14	349 2	16 2	44 37		
Feb.	1		58 48	87 16	115 38	143 20	170 2	195 25
	13	219 40	243 24	269 14	291 38	317 38	343 47	12 55
	27	41 25						
March	1		69 44	97 50	125 14	152 8	178 14	203 50
	13	227 32	251 14	275 1	299 33	325 42	353 21	22 21
	27	51 41	80 32	108 40				
April	1							122 00
	3	148 38	174 26	199 27	223 47	247 33	271 9	295 13
	17	320 23	347 22	16 10	46 5	75 46	104 37	132 25
May	1	158 10	183 46	208 27	232 25	256 7	279 45	303 51
	15	328 29	355 45	24 20	54 20	84 40	114 7	142 2
	29	168 24	193 18					
June	1						205 32	229 30
	5	253 6	276 45	300 47	325 21	351 23	18 47	47 13
	19	77 50	107 58	136 59	164 21	190 3	214 29	
July	1							238 15
	3	261 52	285 42	310 5	335 4	2 6	28 39	57 20
	17	86 36	116 17	145 17	172 42	198 30	222 47	246 29
	31	270 27						
Aug.	1					282 13	306 46	331 37
	7	358 21	25 43	53 12	81 42	110 37	139 25	167 17
	21	193 51	218 55	242 56	266 36	290 31	315 20	
Sep.	1			328 11	354 44	22 9	50 4	78 14
	11	106 28	134 37	162 17	189 1	212 32	238 55	262 18
	25	286 20	310 51	336 27				
Oct.	1				3 5	31 53	60 36	89 10
	9	117 15	144 48	171 40	197 41	222 43	246 55	270 34
	23	294 14	318 37	344 21	11 47	40 41		
Nov.	1		58 20	85 1	113 55	141 45	168 29	194 10
	13	219 9	243 24	267 4	290 39	314 32	339 29	5 51
	27	33 57	63 40					
Dec.	1			93 56	123 34	151 49	178 30	203 50
	11	228 15	252 6	275 52	296 22	323 22	348 16	14 16
	25	43 3	71 23	101 54	132 6			

Ayanamsa: 21° 46' 59"

RAMAN'S EPHEMERIS

Longitudes of Planets

1956		Sun	Mars	Merc.	Merc.	Jupit.	Venus	Saturn	Rahu
Jan.	5	284 7	234 23	301 37	308 9	159 58R	315 7	239 20	255 52
	15	294 19	240 56	312 32	313 5R	150 14	327 25	240 15	255 20
	25	304 30	247 29	309 9	303 1	149 15	339 40	241 2	254 47
Feb.	4	315 39	254 2	298 39	297 40	148 3	351 48	241 41	254 17
	14	324 46	260 36	299 32D	303 23	146 46	3 48	242 12	253 45
	24	334 52	267 10	308 31	314 34	145 27	15 38	242 35	253 13
March	5	344 54	273 44	321 16	328 35	144 14	27 16	242 47	252 43
	15	354 53	280 16	326 25	344 45	143 9	38 36	242 45R	252 9
	25	4 49	286 47	352 36	3 00	142 19	49 38	242 41	251 36
April	4	14 42	293 15	12 56	23 17	141 46	60 13	242 22	251 5
	14	24 31	299 41	33 42	43 38	141 31	70 12	241 55	250 33
	24	33 19	306 3	52 21	59 27	141 34D	79 24	241 21	250 00
May	4	44 00	312 18	64 39	67 49	141 56	87 28	240 41	249 29
	14	53 40	318 27	68 52	67 56R	142 35	93 56	239 58	249 00
	24	63 18	324 23	65 33	62 49	143 30	98 1	239 13	248 28
June	3	72 53	330 4	60 46	60 17D	144 39	98 52R	238 30	247 54
	13	82 27	335 29	61 40	65 41	146 00	95 49	237 49	247 22
	23	92 00	340 29	69 44	76 10	147 32	90 3	237 14	246 51
July	3	101 31	344 55	83 34	93 18	149 14	84 38	236 44	246 19
	13	111 4	348 38	103 32	114 12	151 4	82 30D	236 24	245 47
	23	120 36	351 28	124 45	134 48	153 00	84 10	236 14	245 16
Aug.	2	130 10	353 12	144 11	152 54	155 2	88 51	236 10D	244 43
	12	139 45	353 38R	160 58	168 22	157 8	95 39	236 17	244 11
	22	149 22	352 45	175 6	181 4	159 15	103 54	236 35	243 40
Sep.	1	159 1	350 42	186 5	189 52	161 24	113 10	237 2	243 9
	11	168 44	348 00	191 57	191 44R	163 34	123 12	237 37	242 37
	21	178 29	345 24	188 40R	183 29	165 44	133 46	238 20	242 5
Oct.	1	188 17	343 41	178 44	177 22D	167 50	144 48	239 9	241 33
	11	198 9	343 9D	180 11	186 2	169 54	156 10	240 5	241 2
	21	208 4	343 57	193 43	202 55	171 54	167 47	241 7	240 30
	31	218 3	345 56	210 16	218 32	173 46	179 38	242 12	239 57
Nov.	10	228 5	348 56	226 37	234 39	175 32	191 39	243 20	239 26
	20	238 ·9	352 39	242 21	250 18	177 8	203 49	244 31	238 54
	30	248 16	357 9	258 3	265 34	178 33	216 6	245 43	238 23
Dec.	10	258 5	2 3	273 21	280 46	179 44	228 28	246 53	237 50
	20	268 35	7 19	287 41	293 32	180 41	240 53	248 3	237 20
	30	277 48	13 25	297 2	295 49R	181 25	253 21	249 8	236 48

Ayanamsa: 21° 47′ 49″

Longitude of the Moon

1956	Sun.	Tue.	Thur.	Sat.	Mon.	Wed.	Fri.
Jan. 1	146 42	174 35	206 38	225 15	249 7	272 44	296 22
15	320 16	345 6	10 36	37 21	65 18	94 48	124 58
29	154 42	182 52					
Feb. 1						196 12	221 42
5	246 51	269 27	293 6	317 14	342 10	7 39	34 00
19	61 15	89 29	118 40	147 38	176 58	204 7	
March 1			217 7	241 56	266 48	289 27	313 26
11	338 18	4 8	30 49	58 24	86 2	114 21	142 56
25	171 18	198 16	224 54	249 43			
April 1	261 46	285 28	309 16	333 51	359 34	25 16	54 24
15	82 45	111 9	139 22	167 11	194 14	220 22	245 27
29	269 37						
May 1		293 23	317 12	341 47	7 39	35 00	63 38
13	92 40	121 53	150 12	177 32	203 53	229 16	255 52
27	277 51	301 28	325 23				
June 1							337 32
3	2 24	29 13	57 29	86 58	117 4	146 24	174 22
17	200 54	226 12	250 40	274 36	298 19	322 4	346 12
July 1	11 14	37 38	65 45	95 28	125 54	155 46	184 4
15	210 34	235 37	259 46	283 29	307 10	331 4	355 25
29	20 30	46 44					
Aug. 1						60 26	89 4
5	119 5	149 32	178 54	206 30	232 15	256 41	280 28
19	304 9	328 6	352 25	17 33	43 22	70 19	98 29
Sep. 1				113 5	142 55	172 40	201 12
9	227 55	253 00	277 4	300 54	324 37	349 15	14 24
23	40 22	67 6	94 42	123 8			
Oct. 1					152 12	181 11	208 46
7	235 51	260 58	285 5	308 50	332 49	357 35	23 20
21	50 4	77 35	105 36	133 57	162 19	190 21	
Nov. 1			204 7	234 50	256 25	280 57	304 44
11	328 25	352 55	19 21	45 7	73 7	102 21	130 42
25	159 5	186 44	213 32				
Dec. 1				239 29	264 34	288 54	312 44
9	336 31	0 43	26 2	52 57	81 31	111 10	140 53
23	169 44	197 13	223 26	248 90	273 16		

Ayanamsa: 21° 47' 49"

Longitudes of Planets

1957		Sun	Mars.	Merc.	Merc.	Jupit.	Venus	Saturn	Rahu
Jan.	5	284 54	16 17	296 24R	291 19	181 37	260 49	249 47	236 30
	15	295 5	22 8	284 16	281 24	181 47	273 19	250 47	235 57
	25	305 16	28 8	282 6D	285 21	181 39R	285 49	251 42	235 24
Feb.	4	315 26	34 13	290 10	296 2	181 15	298 19	252 28	234 52
	14	325 32	40 23	302 33	309 38	180 27	310 49	253 10	234 21
	24	335 37	46 36	317 8	325 4	179 28	323 19	253 41	233 50
March	6	345 40	52 51	333 27	342 17	178 18	335 47	254 3	233 18
	16	355 38	59 8	351 35	1 22	177 11	348 15	254 15	232 45
	26	5 34	64 50	11 28	21 32	175 54	‘ 0 42	254 17R	232 15
April	5	15 7	71 41	30 55	38 52	174 34	13 6	254 10	231 41
	15	25 16	77 59	44 48	48 20	173 31	25 30	253 53	231 10
	25	35 1	84 15	49 27	48 44R	172 40	37 52	253 29	230 38
May	5	44 44	90 32	45 32R	42 34	172 8	50 12	252 55	230 8
	15	54 24	96 50	40 28	40 7	171 52	62 31	252 16	229 35
	25	64 1	103 5	41 35D	44 47	171 54D	74 48	251 33	229 3
June	4	73 36	109 21	49 32	55 19	172 14	87 4	250 50	228 31
	14	83 10	115 37	63 1	71 33	172 51	99 19	250 6	228 00
	24	92 43	121 53	81 13	91 42	173 45	111 32	249 25	227 28
July	4	102 15	128 10	102 3	113 13	174 53	123 43	248 49	226 56
	14	111 47	134 25	123 19	132 41	176 12	135 53	248 18	226 24
	24	121 20	140 43	141 18	149 9	177 43	148 1	247 57	225 53
Aug.	3	130 53	147 31	156 15	162 30	179 24	160 6	247 44	225 21
	13	140 28	153 21	167 50	171 58	181 11	172 10	247 41D	224 49
	23	150 16	160 42	174 34	175 10R	183 6	184 10	247 47	224 18
Sep.	2	159 45	166 5	173 19R	169 13	185 1	196 6	248 3	223 46
	12	169 28	172 29	164 23	161 24	187 11	207 56	248 28	223 14
	22	179 13	178 56	162 5D	166 29	189 17	219 41	249 3	222 42
Oct.	2	189 2	185 25	173 29	181 48	191 27	231 19	249 45	222 10
	12	198 54	191 56	190 30	199 14	193 37	242 48	250 34	221 40
	22	208 49	198 30	207 43	216 00	195 46	254 7	251 29	221 6
Nov.	1	218 48	205 6	224 4	231 54	197 54	265 8	252 30	220 35
	11	228 50	211 46	239 38	247 13	199 58	275 50	253 34	220 4
	21	238 55	218 28	254 38	261 52	201 55	286 3	254 43	219 31
Dec.	1	249 2	225 14	268 45	274 54	203 49	295 31	255 52	218 59
	11	259 11	232 3	279 36	281 31	205 33	303 10	257 4	218 30
	21	269 22	238 56	279 35R	272 55	207 8	310 43	258 14	217 56
	31	279 33	245 51	267 12	265 14	208 31	315 9	259 23	217 24

Ayanamsa: 21° 48′ 39″

Longitude of the Moon

1957	Sun	Tue.	Thur.	Sat.	Mon.	Wed.	Fri.
Jan. 1		285 20	309 14	332 56	356 48	21 21	47 10
13	74 46	104 16	134 46	165 3	193 4	220 24	245 51
27	270 14	294 11	318 58				
Feb. 1							330 50
3	353 39	17 50	42 28	69 14	97 9	127 26	158 8
17	188 9	216 12	242 26	267 15	291 14	314 57	
March 1							338 45
3	2 46	27 14	52 26	78 57	106 36	135 58	166 11
17	196 12	224 23	250 53	275 50	300 51	324 35	347 27
31	11 49						
April 1					24 10	49 29	75 35
7	102 48	131 5	160 18	189 42	218 28	245 43	271 28
21	296 2	320 25	343 44	7 59	33 1		
May 1						59 2	85 47
5	113 38	141 57	170 27	198 59	226 53	254 43	279 52
19	303 55	328 51	351 41	16 2	41 24	68 5	95 49
June 1				110 2	138 40	167 13	195 16
9	222 38	249 14	275 16	299 48	324 54	347 42	11 46
23	36 30	62 44	90 35	119 42			
July 1					149 10	178 1	205 52
7	232 43	258 36	283 45	308 15	332 13	356 55	19 54
21	44 36	70 58	99 3	128 37	158 48	188 16	
Aug. 1			202 28	229 43	255 38	280 39	305 00
11	328 59	352 43	16 26	40 39	66 00	93 9	122 2
25	152 17	182 43	211 55	239 17			
Sep. 1	252 29	277 44	302 5	326 00	349 45	13 31	37 35
15	62 25	88 26	116 7	145 30	175 50	205 49	234 2
29	261 23						
Oct. 1		286 42	311 00	334 48	358 32	22 31	46 59
13	72 14	98 23	125 51	155 9	184 20	213 52	242 29
27	269 38	295 5	319 25				
Nov. 1							331 20
3	355 10	18 59	43 36	69 1	95 20	122 47	150 31
17	179 40	208 2	236 33	264 9	290 17	315 18	339 17
Dec. 1	2 59	27 3	52 00	78 4	105 17	133 16	161 30
15	189 45	217 47	245 23	272 20	298 17	323 4	347 4
29	10 46	34 8					

Ayanamsa: 21° 48′ 39″

Longitudes of Planets

1958	Sun	Mars	Merc.	Merc.	Jupit.	Venus	Saturn	Rahu
Jan. 5	284 39	249 20	265 14	267 00	209 8	317 10	259 57	217 9
15	294 50	256 21	271 00	276 29	210 11	315 40R	201 2	216 37
25	305 1	263 25	282 45	289 35	210 58	310 26	262 2	216 6
Feb. 4	315 10	270 31	296 48	304 23	211 28	304 29	262 57	215 35
14	325 17	277 41	312 19	320 37	211 40	300 59	263 46	215 3
24	335 23	284 53	329 13	338 22	211 32R	301 28D	264 27	214 30
March 6	345 25	292 9	347 51	357 36	211 6	305 21	265 00	213 58
16	355 24	299 27	7 18	16 17	210 23	311 43	265 24	213 26
26	5 20	306 50	23 40	28 40	209 26	319 45	265 38	212 55
April 5	15 12	314 2	30 45	30 1	208 17	328 53	265 43R	212 24
15	25 2	321 28	27 10R	23 38	207 3	339 47	265 38	211 51
25	34 47	328 50	20 55	20 1	205 46	349 11	265 22	211 20
May 5	44 00	336 11	21 5D	23 52	204 32	0 03	264 58	210 47
15	54 10	343 30	28 20	34 00	203 30	11 6	264 26	210 15
25	63 47	350 48	40 48	48 37	202 40	22 23	263 49	209 44
June 4	73 23	358 3	57 25	67 12	202 6	33 50	263 9	209 11
14	82 57	5 9	77 45	88 43	201 49	45 25	262 23	208 40
24	92 29	12 9	99 31	109 43	201 48D	57 7	261 39	208 8
July 4	102 1	19 00	119 7	127 43	202 7	68 50	260 57	207 37
14	111 33	25 39	135 54	142 14	202 43	80 47	260 20	207 5
24	121 6	32 00	148 3	152 46	203 34	92 44	259 49	206 34
Aug. 3	130 40	38 5	156 3	157 37	204 40	104 46	259 26	206 2
13	140 15	43 44	157 34R	155 18	205 59	116 53	259 12	205 30
23	149 52	48 57	150 6	146 13	207 29	129 5	259 5	204 58
Sep. 2	159 31	53 33	144 42	146 32D	209 8	141 20	259 9D	204 27
12	169 14	57 25	151 50	159 24	210 58	153 41	259 24	203 55
22	178 59	60 20	168 12	177 22	212 53	166 4	259 47	203 22
Oct. 2	188 47	62 1	186 26	195 13	214 54	178 30	260 20	202 48
12	198 39	62 30R	203 40	211 50	217 00	190 59	261 00	202 19
22	208 35	61 26	219 43	227 22	219 39	203 00	261 48	201 47
Nov. 1	218 34	59 00	234 48	241 59	221 20	216 3	262 42	201 16
11	228 35	55 35	248 51	255 14	223 32	228 36	263 43	200 44
21	238 40	52 10	260 45	264 36	225 44	241 10	264 47	200 12
Dec. 1	248 47	49 00R	265 33	262 15R	227 52	253 44	265 53	199 40
11	258 56	47 6	255 45	250 32	229 58	266 18	267 4	199 9
21	269 7	46 36D	249 35D	252 15	231 59	278 52	268 14	198 36
31	279 18	47 23	257 4	263 4	233 54	291 26	269 26	198 4

Ayanamsa: 21° 49′ 30″

Longitude of the Moon

1958		Sun.	Tue.	Thurs.	Sat.	Mon.	Wed.	Fri.
Jan.	1						48 7	72 54
	5	100 14	128 52	157 53	187 5	214 5	241 47	268 15
	19	294 1	318 59	343 11	7 51	30 32	54 52	80 35
Feb.	1				94 17	122 36	152 22	182 12
	9	211 12	238 49	265 14	290 44	315 32	339 45	3 27
	23	27 2	50 53	75 42				
March	1				102 9	130 33	160 35	191 1
	9	220 38	248 49	275 7	300 18	324 41	348 31	18 11
	23	36 48	59 49	84 42	110 56	138 59		
April	1		153 39	183 51	214 14	243 36	270 39	296 34
	13	321 42	345 34	9 10	33 51	57 00	81 39	107 22
	27	134 21	162 43					
May	1			192 19	222 20	251 40	279 31	305 39
	11	330 20	354 9	18 43	41 34	66 3	91 23	117 37
	25	144 47	172 52	201 44	230 58			
June	1	245 30	273 53	300 50	326 15	350 9	14 7	37 51
	15	62 19	87 54	114 18	141 40	169 39	197 52	226 17
	29	254 36						
July	1		282 18	308 55	334 12	358 24	22 3	45 52
	13	70 29	96 27	123 12	151 57	180 26	208 52	236 53
	27	261 19	291 25	317 19				
Aug.	1							329 57
	3	354 25	18 11	41 53	65 59	91 12	118 23	146 53
	17	176 9	205 19	233 46	261 16	287 53	313 38	338 33
	31	2 43						
Sep.	1					13 31	38 10	61 56
	7	86 36	112 44	140 46	170 8	200 11	229 33	257 59
	21	284 54	310 36	335 22	359 28	23 9		
Oct.	1						46 43	70 31
	5	95 12	121 9	148 51	177 59	208 36	238 42	267 31
	19	294 35	320 6	344 32	8 19	31 55	55 37	79 42
Nov.	1				92 1	117 15	143 48	171 54
	9	201 29	231 47	261 39	290 00	316 27	341 20	5 13
	23	28 47	52 32	76 41	101 33			
Dec.	1					127 11	153 46	181 26
	7	210 20	239 58	269 33	297 29	324 37	349 39	14 31
	21	37 4	60 55	85 37	111 2	137 19	164 19	

Ayanamsa: 21° 49' 30"

Longitudes of Planets

1959		Sun	Mars	Merc.	Merc.	Jupit.	Venus	Saturn	Rahu
Jan.	5	284 24	48 12	263 5	269 44	234 48	297 42	270 00	197 50
	15	294 35	50 33	276 49	284 13	236 29	310 14	271 8	197 17
	25	304 46	53 41	291 52	299 45	238 00	322 45	272 13	196 45
Feb	4	314 55	57 27	307 57	316 28	239 19	335 14	273 15	196 13
	14	325 3	61 44	325 19	334 27	240 24	347 40	274 11	195 42
	24	335 8	66 22	343 47	353 6	241 13	0 4	275 00	195 10
March	6	345 10	71 18	1 36	8 20	241 44	12 23	275 43	194 38
	16	355 10	76 27	12 17	12 50R	241 58	24 38	276 16	194 6
	26	5 5	81 47	10 18	6 14	241 54R	6 40	276 42	193 34
April	5	14 58	87 16	2 35	0 45	241 31	48 40	276 57	193 4
	15	24 47	92 52	1 10D	3 31D	240 50	60 45	277 4	192 31
	25	34 33	98 34	7 28	12 46	239 53	72 31	277 00R	192 00
May	5	44 16	104 21	19 5	26 21	238 46	84 2	276 47	191 28
	15	53 56	110 12	34 28	43 27	237 33	95 29	276 24	190 56
	25	63 33	116 6	53 16	63 49	236 16	106 36	275 54	190 24
June	4	73 9	122 2	74 47	85 37	235 4	117 24	275 18	189 52
	14	82 43	128 3	95 54	105 17	233 49	127 47	274 36	189 21
	24	92 15	134 5	113 43	121 9	233 7	137 38	273 53	188 49
July	4	101 47	140 11	127 32	132 46	232 30	146 39	273 9	188 16
	14	111 20	146 20	136 37	138 35	232 11	154 38	272 27	187 46
	24	120 52	152 30	139 15R	137 34	232 9D	161 00	271 49	187 14
Aug.	3	130 26	158 44	134 15	130 31	232 26	165 5	271 15	186 43
	13	140 1	165 3	128 3	128 7D	233 2	166 00R	270 52	186 9
	23	149 38	171 24	131 13	137 17	233 50	163 3	270 35	185 39
Sep.	2	159 17	177 48	145 17	154 32	234 56	157 18	270 28	185 5
	12	168 59	184 16	164 7	173 32	236 16	152 00	270 30D	184 34
	22	178 44	190 47	182 35	191 14	237 47	149 53	270 42	184 2
Oct.	2	188 33	197 22	199 30	207 26	239 27	151 38D	271 4	183 32
	12	198 25	204 01	215 02	222 20	241 18	156 30	271 36	183 00
	22	208 20	210 45	229 16	235 45	243 16	163 32	272 15	182 28
Nov.	1	218 19	217 33	241 38	246 24	245 20	172 10	272 59	181 56
	11	228 21	224 26	249 25	249 23R	247 28	181 45	273 50	181 25
	21	238 25	231 22	245 16	238 43	249 41	192 07	274 53	180 51
Dec.	1	248 31	238 25	234 14	234 16D	251 55	203 3	275 57	180 21
	11	258 41	245 31	237 49	243 19	254 10	214 21	277 4	179 50
	21	268 52	252 42	249 51	256 54	256 25	225 58	278 13	179 16
	31	279 3	259 57	264 14	271 45	258 38	237 47	279 28	178 46

Ayanamsa : 21° 50' 20"

Longitude of the Moon

1959	Sun.	Tue.	Thur.	Sat.	Mon.	Wed.	Fri.
Jan. 1			178 3	206 1	234 37	263 31	292 00
11	319 19	345 23	9 30	33 12	56 53	81 12	106 40
25	133 17	160 48	188 50	217 00			
Feb. 1	231 6	259 15	287 5	314 14	340 18	5 13	29 9
15	52 45	76 43	101 38	128 00	155 47	184 32	213 28
March 1	242 4	269 58	296 36	323 23	348 45	13 16	37 7
15	60 45	84 40	109 31	135 51	163 53	193 20	223 6
29	252 24	280 33					
April 1						294 6	320 17
5	345 28	9 51	33 43	57 21	81 5	105 22	130 46
19	157 45	186 29	216 35	246 56	276 19	304 2	
May 1							330 4
3	354 50	18 50	42 30	66 8	90 1	114 26	139 42
17	166 30	194 53	223 47	255 20	285 7	313 9	339 23
31	3 55						
June 1					15 54	39 32	63 10
7	87 7	111 32	136 39	162 40	189 58	219 42	248 37
21	278 43	307 44	334 52	0 19	24 39		
July 1						48 8	71 52
5	96 1	120 58	146 35	172 56	200 19	228 40	257 53
19	287 18	315 55	343 00	8 26	32 40	56 21	80 11
Aug. 1				92 20	117 14	143 10	169 50
9	197 14	225 13	254 41	282 20	310 36	337 52	3 49
23	28 31	52 28	76 11	100 23	125 33		
Sep. 1		138 34	165 33	193 30	221 57	250 30	278 45
13	306 28	333 24	359 22	24 20	48 30	72 14	96 6
27	120 43	146 37					
Oct. 1			173 59	202 43	232 6	261 17	289 35
11	316 47	342 56	8 11	32 44	56 43	80 26	104 15
25	128 45	152 27	181 54	211 3			
Nov. 1	226 5	256 19	285 51	313 39	339 59	5 7	29 29
15	53 27	77 11	100 56	125 2	149 54	176 10	204 15
29	234 6						
Dec. 1		264 48	294 51	323 9	349 32	14 27	39 2
13	62 17	86 2	109 37	134 15	159 11	185 15	212 54
27	242 17	272 46	302 58				

Ayanamsa: 21° 50′ 20″

Longitudes of Planets

1960		Sun	Mars	Merc.	Merc.	Jupit.	Venus	Saturn	Rahu
Jan.	5	284 9	263 36	271 45	279 27	259 43	243 46	280 00	178 30
	15	294 21	270 57	287 21	295 27	261 50	255 48	281 9	177 58
	25	304 31	278 24	303 47	312 22	263 52	267 56	282 19	177 25
Feb.	4	314 41	285 53	321 11	330 8	265 46	280 9	283 21	176 35
	14	324 48	293 26	338 56	346 55	267 33	292 23	284 23	176 23
	24	334 53	301 1	352 57	355 45	269 9	304 40	285 20	175 50
March	5	344 56	308 40	354 43R	350 42	270 31	316 58	286 13	175 19
	15	354 55	316 20	346 00	342 51	271 42	329 17	286 57	174 47
	25	4 51	324 2	342 10D	343 48	272 35	341 36	287 33	174 14
April	4	14 44	331 44	347 14	352 3	273 15	353 55	288 00	173 43
	14	24 33	339 26	357 56	5 42	273 34	6 14	288 18	173 12
	24	34 19	347 8	12 17	20 36	273 35R	18 32	288 25	172 40
May	4	44 2	354 48	29 38	39 26	273 17	30 49	288 23R	172 7
	14	53 42	2 26	49 55	60 48	272 41	43 6	288 12	171 37
	24	63 19	10 1	71 38	81 52	271 50	55 23	287 52	171 5
June	3	72 55	17 31	91 9	99 19	270 47	67 40	287 21	170 34
	13	82 29	24 57	106 19	112 4	269 35	79 57	286 47	170 00
	23	92 2	32 17	116 28	119 15	268 19	92 14	286 7	169 30
July	3	101 34	39 29	120 14	119 18R	267 7	104 31	285 26	168 58
	13	111 5	46 33	116 44	113 27	265 55	116 49	284 40	168 25
	23	120 38	53 29	110 49	110 00	265 00	129 8	283 57	167 54
Aug.	2	130 12	60 13	111 40D	115 57	264 20R	141 27	283 20	167 21
	12	139 46	66 45	122 36	131 8	263 54	153 46	282 45	166 50
	22	149 24	73 3	140 47	150 44	263 48D	166 5	282 18	166 18
Sep.	1	159 3	79 8	160 30	169 50	264 1	178 24	282 00	165 46
	11	168 45	84 48	178 42	187 5	264 32	190 42	281 51	165 16
	21	178 30	90 9	195 2	202 35	265 19	203 3	281 51D	164 43
Oct.	1	188 19	95 5	209 43	216 22	266 25	215 15	282 1	164 11
	11	198 10	99 28	222 30	227 48	267 44	227 31	282 20	163 40
	21	208 6	103 11	231 52	233 55	269 15	239 44	282 51	163 8
	31	218 4	106 4	232 53R	228 8	270 57	251 56	283 29	162 35
Nov.	10	228 6	107 58	221 47	218 11	272 49	264 5	284 14	162 4
	20	238 10	108 37R	219 11D	223 33	274 50	276 12	285 7	161 32
	30	248 17	108 1	229 43	236 45	276 59	288 14	286 5	161 1
Dec.	10	258 26	105 53R	244 9	252 44	279 11	300 10	287 8	160 30
	20	268 37	102 38	259 24	267 11	281 36	311 58	288 16	160 00
	30	278 48	98 44	275 4	283 1	283 44	323 31	289 25	159 27

Ayanamsa: 21° 51' 10″

Longitude of the Moon

1960		Sun.	Tue.	Thur.	Sat.	Mon.	Wed.	Fri.
Jan.	1							317 19
	3	345 4	10 45	35 21	59 8	82 51	106 56	131 15
	17	156 14	182 3	208 53	236 59	266 18	296 6	325 18
	31	350 59						
Feb.	1					6 10	31 25	56 31
	7	79 17	103 10	127 38	152 54	178 56	205 47	233 26
	21	261 49	290 36	319 12	347 3	13 34		
March	1		26 41	51 23	75 20	99 15	123 25	146 41
	13	175 46	202 7	230 11	258 36	286 55	315 5	343 8
	27	9 2	34 36	59 13				
April	1							71 14
	3	95 3	118 59	143 39	169 32	197 01	225 38	254 51
	17	283 46	311 51	336 57	5 1	31 2	55 12	79 20
May	1	103 8	127 2	151 35	177 29	205 10	234 26	264 27
	15	294 4	322 21	348 47	14 55	39 50	64 4	87 58
	29	111 42	135 22					
June	1						147 38	172 41
	5	199 20	227 54	258 2	288 23	318 1	343 49	11 57
	19	36 55	61 6	84 58	108 45	132 39	156 40	
July	1							179 43
	3	208 13	236 31	266 34	297 2	326 48	354 52	21 9
	17	46 3	70 8	93 54	117 40	141 38	166 8	191 26
	31	217 55						
Aug.	1					231 46	260 32	290 22
	7	320 37	349 32	16 40	42 20	66 48	90 39	114 25
	21	138 26	163 5	188 22	214 48	241 52	270 30	
Sep.	1			285 17	314 18	343 18	11 14	37 43
	11	62 49	86 55	110 42	134 38	160 16	184 54	211 39
	25	239 1	267 6	295 32				
Oct.	1				323 58	352 4	19 24	45 8
	9	70 41	94 48	118 34	142 26	167 22	193 30	220 58
	23	249 23	278 4	306 29	334 33	1 44		
Nov.	1		14 57	41 6	66 22	90 47	114 36	138 17
	13	162 34	187 55	215 9	244 11	273 51	302 58	331 15
	27	358 26	24 39					
Dec.	1			50 6	74 53	99 4	122 47	146 25
	11	170 42	196 00	223 10	252 16	282 29	312 33	341 21
	25	8 35	34 31	59 29	83 45			

Ayanamsa: 21° 51' 10″

Longitudes of Planets

1961		Sun	Mars	Merc.	Merc.	Jupit.	Venus	Saturn	Rahu
Jan.	5	284 55	96 24R	284 39	292 50	285 8	329 54	290 7	159 8
	15	295 7	93 35	301 11	309 43	287 28	341 31	291 18	158 36
	25	305 18	90 52	318 13	326 23	289 46	352 12	292 29	158 3
Feb.	4	315 26	90 1	333 27	338 7	292 2	2 14	293 38	157 32
	14	325 34	90 25D	338 57R	335 42	294 15	11 24	294 44	157 00
	24	335 39	91 56	330 23	326 00	296 21	19 19	295 46	156 28
March	6	345 41	94 21	324 21	325 21D	298 21	25 23	296 43	155 59
	16	355 40	97 29	328 25	332 57	300 12	28 44	297 34	155 25
	26	5 36	101 12	338 35	345 5	301 55	28 26R	298 19	154 53
April	5	15 28	105 21	352 18	0 11	303 24	24 13	298 55	154 22
	15	25 17	109 52	8 43	17 54	304 42	18 6	299 23	153 49
	25	35 3	114 41	27 43	38 10	305 44	13 39	299 41	153 17
May	5	44 45	119 43	48 57	59 36	306 30	12 57D	299 50	152 47
	15	54 25	124 57	69 32	78 23	306 59	15 55	299 50R	152 15
	25	64 1	130 21	85 54	91 59	307 9	21 31	299 39	151 42
June	4	73 38	135 54	96 32	99 25	307 1R	28 56	299 21	151 10
	14	83 12	141 35	100 26	99 37R	306 32	37 36	298 52	150 45
	24	92 45	147 23	97 19	94 24	305 48	47 6	298 17	150 6
July	4	102 17	153 15	92 6R	91 23D	304 48	57 12	297 37	149 35
	14	111 49	159 16	92 46	96 22	303 38	67 45	296 54	149 4
	24	121 22	165 20	102 35	109 44	302 22	78 39	296 10	148 32
Aug.	3	130 44	171 30	118 55	128 30	301 4	89 50	295 27	148 00
	13	140 29	177 46	139 17	149 17	299 52	101 15	294 47	147 28
	23	150 6	184 7	158 46	167 37	298 50	112 51	294 13	146 57
Sep.	2	159 46	190 34	176 8	183 58	298 2	124 37	293 45	146 25
	12	169 29	197 6	191 21	198 13	297 31	136 32	293 26	145 52
	22	179 14	203 44	204 29	209 59	297 19	148 36	293 16	145 20
Oct.	1	188 4	209 46	213 40	216 55	297 24D	159 34	293 15	144 52
	11	197 56	216 34	218 00	216 57R	297 50	171 49	293 23	144 21
	21	207 51	223 29	210 45R	204 57	298 33	184 10	293 42	143 50
	31	217 49	230 28	202 21	204 16D	299 35	196 36	294 9	143 16
Nov.	9	226 51	236 51	208 11	214 45	300 42	207 50	294 42	142 49
	19	236 56	244 4	221 40	229 53	302 12	220 21	295 26	142 17
	29	247 1	251 17	237 43	245 33	303 53	232 54	296 17	141 45
Dec.	9	257 10	258 38	253 24	261 15	305 45	244 57	297 15	141 14
	19	267 21	266 4	269 9	277 6	307 46	258 2	298 17	140 41
	29	277 32	273 35	285 9	293 17	309 54	270 37	299 24	140 10

Ayanamsa: 21° 52' 01"

Longitude of the Moon

1961		Sun	Tue.	Thur.	Sat.	Mon.	Wed.	Fri.
Jan.	1	95 48	119 34	143 11	167 4	191 43	217 45	245 38
	15	275 16	305 45	335 47	4 20	31 7	56 28	80 19
	29	104 40	128 20					
Feb.	1						140 11	164 6
	5	188 32	213 54	240 36	268 56	298 32	328 48	358 21
	19	26 22	52 39	77 32	101 29	125 9		
March	1						148 56	173 10
	5	198 6	223 56	250 45	278 43	307 39	337 6	351 46
	19	34 17	60 44	85 44	109 44	133 24	157 18	181 56
April	1				194 36	220 41	247 39	275 20
	9	303 32	332 5	0 37	28 40	55 38	81 17	105 44
	23	129 30	153 16	177 40	203 12			
May	1					230 2	257 51	286 10
	7	314 30	342 38	10 24	37 36	63 59	89 19	113 39
	21	137 23	161 8	185 35	211 23	238 46	267 23	
June	1			281 57	311 00	339 29	6 41	34 3
	11	60 9	85 21	109 53	133 42	157 18	181 17	206 21
	25	233 3	261 29	291 6				
July	1				320 52	349 52	17 38	44 12
	9	69 44	94 27	118 32	141 56	165 47	189 48	214 48
	23	241 22	269 46	299 35	329 51	359 24		
Aug.	1		13 39	40 58	66 48	91 32	115 32	139 13
	13	162 48	186 40	211 13	236 54	264 6	292 58	323 1
	27	352 15	22 31	50 7				
Sep.	1							63 16
	3	88 26	112 24	136 13	159 50	183 46	208 17	233 36
	17	260 00	287 41	316 39	346 29	16 13	44 51	71 46
Oct.	1	97 00	121 7	144 43	168 27	192 44	217 47	243 40
	15	270 22	297 55	326 19	355 22	24 31	52 50	79 44
	29	105 3	129 11					
Nov.	1						141 1	164 40
	5	188 49	213 57	240 7	267 10	294 48	322 47	351 3
	19	19 23	47 24	74 32	100 24	125 1	148 49	
Dec.	1							172 29
	3	196 43	222 7	248 53	276 47	305 15	333 44	1 54
	17	29 37	56 45	83 6	108 28	132 52	156 39	180 18
	31	204 30						

Ayanamsa: 21° 52' 01"

Longitudes of Planets

1962	Sun	Mars.	Merc.	Merc.	Jupit.	Venus	Saturn	Rahu
Jan. 5	284 40	278 53	296 32	304 36	311 33	279 26	300 16	139 48
15	294 52	286 32	312 12	318 35	313 46	292 1	301 23	139 16
25	305 2	294 13	322 23	323 2R	316 7	304 34	302 34	138 42
Feb. 4	315 11	301 59	317 31R	311 42	318 30	317 9	303 45	138 12
14	325 19	309 46	307 59	307 24D	320 53	329 41	304 54	137 40
24	335 24	317 35	309 28	313 23	323 16	342 11	306 1	137 9
March 6	345 26	325 26	318 1	324 38	325 37	354 40	307 5	136 37
16	355 26	333 17	331 26	338 50	327 54	7 7	308 3	136 5
26	5 21	341 7	346 49	355 20	330 8	19 32	308 56	135 33
April 5	15 14	348 57	4 26	14 8	332 14	31 54	309 42	135 1
15	25 3	356 44	24 22	34 56	334 14	44 13	310 20	134 30
25	34 49	4 29	45 24	55 8	336 5	56 28	310 50	133 58
May 5	44 31	12 11	63 37	70 32	337 45	68 39	311 10	133 26
15	54 11	19 49	75 42	79 1	339 14	80 48	311 22	132 54
25	63 49	27 22	80 21	80 2R	340 28	92 52	311 23R	132 22
June 4	73 24	34 51	77 40R	74 56	341 27	104 52	311 15	131 52
14	82 58	42 14	72 41	71 51	342 11	116 46	310 58	131 20
24	92 31	49 32	72 53D	75 52D	342 35	128 34	310 32	130 48
July 4	102 3	56 42	80 41	87 14	342 41R	140 15	309 58	130 15
14	111 35	63 45	94 52	104 50	342 27	151 47	309 19	129 44
24	121 7	70 41	115 10	125 43	341 54	163 9	308 36	129 4
Aug. 3	130 41	77 29	136 00	145 43	341 5	174 17	307 52	128 40
13	140 16	84 9	154 48	163 16	340 1	185 9	307 8	128 9
23	149 53	90 39	171 8	178 24	338 46	195 39	306 27	127 38
Sep. 2	159 33	96 59	185 2	190 57	337 28R	205 41	305 51	127 3
12	169 15	103 09	195 26	199 41	336 10	215 3	305 22	126 34
22	179 00	109 1	201 38	201 5R	335 00	223 29	305 00	126 2
Oct. 2	189 49	114 49	197 32R	191 57	334 00	230 31	304 48	125 30
12	198 41	120 16	187 26	186 51D	333 18	235 33	304 46D	124 58
22	208 36	125 24	190 24	196 40	332 54	237 37	304 54	124 26
Nov. 1	218 35	130 10	204 14	212 16	332 50	236 54R	305 12	123 55
11	228 37	134 27	230 24	228 29	333 7	230 46	305 39	123 22
21	238 41	138 12	236 28	244 22	333 42	225 6	306 15	122 50
Dec. 1	248 48	141 16	252 13	260 2	334 37	222 18D	307 1	122 20
11	258 57	143 28	267 52	275 41	335 49	223 28D	307 52	121 48
21	269 8	144 39	283 27	291 2	337 16	227 59	308 50	121 14
31	279 19	144 37R	298 2	303 42	338 55	234 53	308 53	120 42

Ayanamsa: 21° 52′ 51″

Longitude of the Moon

1962		Sun.	Tue.	Thur.	Sat.	Mon.	Wed.	Fri.
Jan.	1					217 1	243 12	270 59
	7	300 1	329 26	358 30	26 31	53 38	79 35	104 44
	21	129 9	153 1	176 37	200 28	225 5	251 5	
Feb.	1			264 44	293 18	323 9	353 15	22 31
	11	50 19	76 37	101 42	125 59	269 47	173 26	197 11
	25	221 25	246 33					
March	1			273 6	301 20	331 7	1 32	31 22
	11	59 37	86 2	110 56	134 57	158 35	183 15	206 15
	25	230 45	256 2	282 25	310 14			
April	1	324 43	354 32	24 44	54 2	81 37	107 21	131 43
	15	155 26	179 4	203 7	227 45	253 4	279 17	306 15
	29	334 24						
May	1		3 35	33 10	62 9	89 15	115 30	139 58
	13	163 43	187 28	211 43	236 49	262 46	289 32	316 57
	27	345 49	13 38	42 24				
June	1							56 38
	3	84 22	110 46	135 46	159 49	183 33	207 37	232 32
	17	258 35	285 41	313 35	341 50	10 13	38 26	
July	1	93 6	118 58	143 45	167 44	191 29	215 34	240 34
	15	266 56	294 38	323 20	352 24	21 9	49 11	76 15
	29	102 22	127 35					
Aug.	1						139 53	164 1
	5	187 45	211 33	235 59	261 34	288 45	317 31	347 16
	19	17 1	45 48	73 14	99 18	124 22	148 41	172 35
Sep.	1				184 26	208 9	232 10	256 59
	9	283 9	311 4	340 39	11 5	41 3	69 33	96 14
	23	121 28	145 45	169 34	193 16			
Oct.	1					217 5	241 13	266 2
	7	291 59	319 34	348 53	19 20	49 37	78 27	105 21
	21	130 33	154 43	178 25	202 9	226 10	250 37	
Nov.	1			263 3	288 33	315 8	343 10	12 36
	11	42 44	72 19	100 20	126 31	151 12	175 5	198 47
	25	222 49	247 24	272 41				
Dec.	1				298 41	325 32	353 21	22 7
	9	51 23	80 20	108 6	134 19	159 9	183 7	206 53
	23	231 1	255 57	281 51	308 39	336 11		

Ayanamsa: 21° 52′ 51″

Longitudes of Planets

1963		Sun	Mars.	Merc.	Merc.	Jupit.	Venus	Saturn	Rahu
Jan.	5	284 25	144 6R	303 42	306 35	339 49	238 57	310 26	120 38
	15	294 36	142 34	305 17R	299 47R	341 46	248 00	311 34	119 57
	25	304 47	138 51	293 45	290 51	343 50	257 57	312 46	119 24
Feb.	4	314 57	134 57	291 23D	294 24	346 2	268 32	313 57	118 51
	14	325 4	131 6	299 00	304 42	348 20	279 32	315 8	118 24
	24	335 9	127 58	311 8	318 11	350 42	290 49	316 20	117 48
March	6	345 12	126 00R	325 41	333 42	353 6	302 20	317 27	117 18
	16	355 11	125 21	342 10	351 9	355 31	314 1	318 32	116 45
	26	5 7	125 51D	0 40	10 39	357 56	325 49	319 32	116 14
April	5	15 00	127 31	20 57	31 9	0 20	337 11	320 26	115 43
	15	24 49	130 00	40 36	48 37	2 41	349 38	321 14	115 10
	25	34 35	133 11	54 45	58 46	4 59	1 37	321 54	114 38
May	5	44 18	136 56	60 31	60 6R	7 12	13 39	322 26	114 6.
	15	53 58	141 9	58 58R	55 6	9 18	25 42	322 49	113 34
	25	63 35	145 44	52 48	51 44D	11 17	37 47	323 2	113 2
June	4	73 11	150 37	52 33	55 12	13 7	49 54	323 7R	112 32
	14	82 44	155 46	59 31	65 20	14 46	62 1	323 1	112 00
	24	92 17	161 9	72 33	81 4	16 13	74 11	322 45	111 27
July	4	101 49	166 43	90 45	101 17	17 26	86 22	322 21	110 57
	14	111 21	172 29	112 3	122 32	18 24	98 35	321 50	110 24
	24	120 54	178 24	132 27	141 40	19 3	110 51	321 12	109 52
Aug.	3	130 27	184 27	150 10	157 44	19 25	123 9	320 29	109 15
	13	140 2	190 40	165 5	171 26	19 28R	135 29	319 44	108 48
	23	149 39	197 00	176 55	180 31	19 10	147 51	319 00	108 17
Sep.	2	159 19	203 29	184 11	185 8	18 36	160 14	318 20	107 45
	12	169 1	210 5	183 29R	179 21	17 40	172 39	317 40	107 13
	22	178 46	216 48	174 11	170 51	16 32	185 6	317 9	106 40
Oct.	2	188 35	223 39	171 24D	175 47	15 19	197 33	316 46	106 10
	12	198 26	230 37	182 41	190 48	13 54	210 00	316 32	105 38
	22	208 22	237 42	199 11	207 45	12 36	222 28	316 27	105 6
Nov.	1	218 20	244 53	216 6	224 14	11 30	234 56	316 33D	104 34
	11	228 22	252 11	232 13	240 4	10 31	247 24	316 48	104 3
	21	238 27	259 32	247 48	255 26	9 52	259 52	317 15	103 31
Dec.	1	248 34	267 4	263 00	270 24	9 35	272 19	317 49	103 00
	11	258 42	274 41	277 29	283 52	9 36D	284 45	318 34	102 27
	21	268 53	282 19	288 45	290 43	10 1	297 10	319 25	101 56
	31	279 4	290 3	288 11R	282 2R	10 41	309 33R	320 22	101 24

Ayanamsa: 21° 53' 41"

1963		Sun.	Tue.	Thurs.	Sat.	Mon.	Wed.	Fri.
Jan.	1		350 10	18 25	46 51	75 6	102 41	129 13
	13	154 35	178 57	203 47	226 41	251 14	276 55	303 56
	27	332 3	0 46	29 27				
Feb.	1							43 37
	3	71 28	98 32	124 47	150 11	174 48	198 47	222 34
	17	246 38	271 39	298 7	326 15	355 37	25 17	
March	1							54 17
	3	82 3	108 34	134 7	158 56	183 12	207 6	230 51
	17	254 52	279 43	306 3	334 14	4 3	34 26	64 3
	31	92 6						
April	1					105 29	131 12	155 55
	7	180 5	203 57	227 42	251 35	275 59	301 23	328 23
	21	357 15	27 33	58 1	87 19	114 47		
May	1						140 32	165 7
	5	189 5	212 50	236 40	260 46	285 23	310 54	337 45
	19	6 15	36 5	66 19	95 39	123 19	149 15	173 54
June	1				185 54	209 41	233 31	257 41
	9	282 25	307 53	334 20	1 56	30 41	60 10	89 31
	23	117 49	144 36	169 55	194 13			
July	1					218 1	241 56	266 22
	7	292 7	317 48	344 52	12 44	41 11	69 54	98 23
	21	126 5	152 36	177 54	202 13	226 2	249 59	
Aug.	1			262 12	287 20	313 41	341 9	9 26
	11	37 57	66 18	94 14	121 31	147 59	174 1	198 8
	25	222 5	245 51	270 4	295 21			
Sep.	1	308 33	336 8	4 57	34 14	63 5	91 3	118 3
	15	144 12	169 36	194 19	218 22	242 4	265 53	290 28
	29	316 30						
Oct.	1		344 22	13 49	43 53	73 22	101 32	128 15
	13	153 54	178 45	203 3	226 55	250 34	274 17	298 54
	27	324 41	352 25	22 3				
Nov.	1							37 12
	3	67 40	97 4	124 47	150 55	175 51	200 4	223 53
	17	247 34	271 19	295 30	320 33	347 4	15 22	45 14
Dec.	1	75 42	105 27	133 35	159 57	184 54	208 58	232 40
	15	256 23	280 24	304 57	330 19	356 50	24 41	53 51
	29	83 41	113 14					

Ayanamsa : 21° 53' 41"

RAMAN'S EPHEMERIS

Longitudes of Planets

1964		Sun	Mars	Merc.	Merc.	Jupit.	Venus	Saturn	Rahu
Jan.	5	284 10	293 57	282 2R	276 26	11 10	315 43	320 53	101 15
	15	294 21	301 46	274 31D	276 4	12 19	328 1	321 58	100 37
	25	304 32	309 37	279 55	285 10	13 44	340 14	323 7	100 4
Feb.	4	314 42	317 30	291 18	298 2	15 22	352 21	324 18	99 33
	14	324 49	325 25	305 14	312 50	17 11	4 19	325 30	99 2
	24	334 55	333 19	320 49	329 13	19 10	16 7	326 43	98 29
March	5	344 57	341 12 ·	338 3	348 19	21 16	27 42	327 54	97 58
	15	354 56	349 5	357 2	7 00	23 30	38 59	329 3	97 25
	25	4 52	356 54	16 53	25 57	25 48	49 55	330 9	97 25
April	4	14 45	4 41	33 25	38 37	28 9	60 23	331 10	96 23
	14	24 34	12 25	41 13	41 23	30 32	69 58	332 6	95 51
	24	34 20	20 4	39 30R	35 47	32 56	79 12	332 56	95 18
May	4	44 3	27 40	33 2	31 34	35 20	86 58	333 39	94 46
	14	53 43	35 10	32 5D	34 26	37 42	92 58	334 14	94 15
	24	63 21	42 35	38 24	43 45	40 1	96 25	334 40	93 43
June	3	72 56	49 55	50 20	58 4	42 16	96 28R	334 55	93 11
	13	82 30	57 9	66 53	76 44	44 26	92 30	335 2	92 40
	23	92 3	64 17	87 20	98 15	46 30	86 27	335 00R	92 8
July	3	101 35	71 19	108 55	119 00	48 26	81 38	334 47	91 36
	13	111 7	78 15	128 16	136 45	50 13	80 26D	334 25	91 4
	23	120 10	85 06	144 27	151 20	51 50	82 53	333 56	90 33
Aug.	2	130 13	91 50	157 17	162 12	53 13	88 10	333 19	90 00
	12	139 48	98 28	165 49	167 44	54 22	95 18	332 35R	89 29
	22	149 25	105 00	167 33R	164 58R	55 15	103 48	331 50	88 57
Sep.	1	159 5	111 24	160 34	156 15	55 50	113 16	331 5	88 26
	11	168 47	117 42	154 17	156 2	56 7	123 24	330 24	87 54
	21	178 32	123 51	161 12	168 42	56 4R	134 5	329 43	87 22
Oct.	1	188 20	129 53	177 19	186 15	55 40	145 11	329 9	86 50
	11	198 12	135 46	195 4	203 39	54 57	156 36	328 44	86 18
	21	208 7	141 28	211 58	220 2	53 58	168 17	328 28	85 40
	31	218 6	146 59	227 52	235 32	52 47	180 10	328 21	85 15
Nov.	10	228 8	152 17	243 2	250 20	51 27	192 13	328 25	84 44
	20	238 12	157 19	257 22	263 56	50 6	204 25	328 39	84 11
	30	248 19	162 00	269 39	273 44	48 48	216 42	329 4	83 40
Dec.	10	258 28	166 18	274 50R	271 17	47 43	229 4	329 37	83 8
	20	268 38	170 8	264 49	259 40	46 51	241 30	330 19	82 36
	30	278 50	173 23	258 44D	261 15	46 19	253 58	331 9	82 3

Ayanamsa: 21° 54′ 32″

Longitude of the Moon

1964	Sun.	Tue.	Thur.	Sat.	Mon.	Wed.	Fri.
Jan. 1						127 36	155 6
5	180 55	205 27	229 15	252 57	276 59	301 42	327 16
19	353 45	21 5	49 14	78 1	106 58	135 27	162 49
Feb. 1				175 58	201 13	225 23	249 5
9	272 57	297 36	323 20	350 12	17 54	46 1	74 15
23	102 24	130 17	157 33	183 51			
March 1	196 34	221 11	245 2	268 45	292 59	318 24	345 20
15	13 31	42 20	71 2	99 11	126 39	153 28	179 33
29	204 48	229 11					
April 1						241 9	264 48
5	288 38	313 25	339 42	7 43	37 2	66 41	95 42
19	123 35	150 22	176 13	201 16	225 39	249 30	
May 1							273 6
3	296 57	321 40	347 52	15 55	45 31	75 43	105 19
17	133 35	160 23	185 54	210 31	234 31	258 12	281 50
31	305 48						
June 1					318 3	343 25	10 20
7	38 59	68 57	99 13	128 39	156 30	182 40	207 33
21	231 34	255 14	278 53	302 52	327 28		
July 1						353 00	19 48
5	48 3	77 32	107 34	137 2	165 6	191 21	216 19
19	240 15	263 52	287 40	312 1	337 7	3 6	30 2
Aug. 1				43 53	72 19	101 30	130 51
9	160 28	186 42	212 17	236 38	260 21	284 5	308 25
23	333 40	359 53	26 57	54 37	82 47		
Sep. 1		97 00	125 35	153 57	181 28	207 40	232 33
13	256 28	280 9	304 13	329 18	355 41	23 9	51 18
27	79 37	107 48					
Oct. 1			135 45	163 16	190 4	215 48	240 28
11	264 20	287 57	312 3	337 16	4 00	32 11	61 41
25	90 12	118 41	146 20	173 10			
Nov. 1	186 17	211 52	236 35	260 35	284 11	307 55	332 25
15	358 17	25 55	55 4	84 58	114 32	143 2	170 11
29	196 5						
Dec. 1		221 3	245 18	269 5	292 39	316 25	340 51
13	6 30	33 51	62 56	93 9	123 23	152 30	179 55
27	205 38	230 18	254 12				

Ayanamsa: 21° 54′ 32″

Longitudes of Planets

1965		Sun	Mars	Merc.	Merc.	Jupit.	Venus	Saturn	Rahu
Jan.	5	284 57	175 00R	262 3	266 57	46 9R	261 27	331 43	81 46
	15	295 8	177 00	272 56	279 34	46 9D	273 57	332 43	81 14
	25	305 19	177 59	286 38	294 2	46 29	286 28	333 48	80 40
Feb.	4	315 28	177 46	301 46	309 48	47 10	298 58	334 57	80 10
	14	325 35	176 16	317 39	318 9	48 8	311 28	336 9	79 38
	24	335 40	173 33	335 59	345 59	49 22	323 58	337 22	79 6
March	6	345 42	169 55	355 3	4 20	50 51	336 27	338 35	78 37
	16	355 42	166 00	12 46	19 6	52 31	348 55	330 50	78 3
	26	5 37	162 32	22 38	23 2R	54 22	1 21	340 57	77 30
April	5	15 30	160 3	20 43R	16 59	56 21	13 46	342 4	77 00
	15	25 19	158 51	13 36	11 50	58 27	26 10	343 7	76 27
	25	35 4	158 55D	12 12	14 29D	60 39	38 32	344 5	75 55
May	5	44 47	160 8	18 23D	23 36	62 54	50 52	344 56	75 24
	15	54 27	162 19	29 56	37 15	65 13	63 10	345 41	74 52
	25	64 4	165 19	45 31	54 44	67 33	75 28	346 17	74 20
June	4	73 40	168 58	64 49	75 35	69 53	87 43	346 45	73 49
	14	83 14	173 9	86 33	97 13	72 12	99 57	347 4	73 18
	24	93 46	177 46	107 12	116 19	74 29	112 10	347 13	72 45
July	4	102 18	182 46	124 32	131 50	76 43	124 22	347 12R	72 13
	14	111 50	188 6	138 9	143 22	78 54	136 31	347 00	71 42
	24	121 23	193 42	147 16	149 35	80 58	148 39	346 40	71 9
Aug.	3	130 57	200 9	149 58R	148 11	83 1	160 44	346 11	70 39
	13	140 32	205 37	144 38	140 34	84 46	172 46	345 35	70 6
	23	150 4	211 54	137 55	138 10D	86 25	184 44	344 54	69 34
Sep.	2	159 49	218 22	141 41	148 6	87 53	196 38	344 8	69 00
	12	169 31	225 00	156 26	165 37	89 8	208 27	343 23	68 31
	22	179 16	231 48	174 57	184 04	90 6	220 9	342 38	68 00
Oct.	2	189 5	238 45	192 52	201 18	90 50	231 45	342 00	67 24
	12	198 57	245 51	209 23	217 11	91 14	243 11	341 23	66 56
	22	208 52	253 4	224 44	232 00	91 19R	254 25	340 56	66 24
Nov.	1	218 51	260 25	238 58	245 32	91 3	265 22	340 38	65 53
	11	228 53	267 53	251 26	256 11	90 28	275 57	340 30	65 21
	21	238 58	275 27	258 51	258 3R	89 35	285 59	340 32D	64 49
Dec.	1	249 5	283 7	253 2	246 29	88 28	295 14	340 45	64 18
	11	259 14	290 52	243 00	243 50D	87 11	303 18	341 9	63 46
	21	269 25	298 39	247 43D	253 17	85 49	309 36	341 42	63 14
	31	279 36	306 30	259 45	266 44	84 30	313 18	342 25	62 42

Ayanamsa: 21° 55′ 22″

Longitude of the Moon

1965		Sun	Tue.	Thur.	Sat.	Mon.	Wed.	Fri.
								266 1
Jan.	1							
	3	289 37	313 23	337 36	2 37	28 50	56 35	85 55
	17	116 13	146 19	175 4	201 55	227 6	251 8	274 44
	31	208 20						
Feb.	1					310 20	334 41	359 39
	7	25 26	52 14	80 16	110 1	139 23	168 48	196 47
	21	222 56	247 34	271 20	294 57			
March	1					318 58	343 44	9 19
	7	35 40	62 45	90 36	119 11	148 13	176 59	204 38
	21	230 45	255 27	279 18	303 1	327 12	352 19	
April	1			5 18	32 1	59 29	87 20	115 39
	11	143 58	172 5	199 33	225 55	251 5	275 16	298 59
	25	322 55	347 39	13 38				
May	1				40 57	69 17	98 1	126 37
	9	154 46	182 11	208 48	234 28	299 14	283 17	306 59
	23	330 55	355 39	21 47	49 19	78 17		
June	1		93 4	122 34	151 25	179 7	205 38	231 5
	13	255 44	279 48	303 32	327 17	351 31	16 45	43 29
	27	71 55	101 43					
July	1			131 55	161 20	189 13	215 31	240 33
	11	264 47	288 35	312 17	336 8	0 26	25 36	52 8
	25	80 20	110 7	140 34	170 24			
Aug.	1	184 44	211 18	237 29	261 51	285 38	309 19	333 12
	15	357 29	22 23	48 11	75 17	103 55	133 51	164 2
	29	193 14	220 36					
Sep.	1						233 37	258 31
	5	282 28	306 9	330 3	354 26	18 27	45 9	71 43
	19	99 23	128 12	157 44	187 5	215 14	241 44	
Oct.	1							266 42
	3	290 42	314 27	338 29	2 49	28 48	55 12	82 18
	17	110 6	138 31	167 15	195 44	223 19	249 34	274 31
	31	299 36						
Nov.	1					310 28	334 20	358 48
	7	24 17	50 58	78 36	106 50	135 16	163 34	191 26
	21	218 36	244 51	270 7	294 28	318 18		
Dec.	1						342 8	6 33
	5	32 8	59 10	87 39	116 51	146 1	174 26	201·49
	19	228 10	253 41	279 27	302 37	326 24	350 10	14 28

Ayanamsa: 21° 55′ 22″

Longitudes of Planets

1966		Sun	Mars	Merc.	Merc.	Jupit.	Venus	Saturn	Rahu
Jan.	5	284 42	310 26	266 43	274 1	83 54R	313 49	342 48	62 25
	15	294 53	318 19	281 22	289 17	82 48	311 50R	343 41	61 52
	25	305 4	326 13	297 16	305 30	81 58	306 28	344 41	61 21
Feb.	4	315 13	334 7	314 2	322 52	81 27	300 51	345 46	60 51
	14	325 20	342 00	331 57	341 10	81 15	298 17	346 55	60 18
	24	335 26	349 51	350 5	357 53	81 24D	299 41D	348 7	59 46
March	6	345 28	357 39	3 25	5.41	81 52	304 18	349 20	59 15
	16	355 27	5 24	4 24R	0 35	82 37	311 10	350 34	58 43
	26	5 23	13 5	356 13	353 4	83 41	319 31	351 48	58 11
April	5	15 15	20 42	352 50D	354 26	84 58	328 53	352 59	57 40
	15	25 4	28 14	357 51	2 39	86 28	338 55	354 12	57 6
	25	34 50	35 42	8 34	15 24	88 9	349 27	355 14	56 36
May	5	44 33	43 4	25 5	31 34	89 59	0 21	356 13	56 14
	15	54 15	50 22	40 51	50 55	91 57	11 30	357 7	52 22
	25	63 51	57 34	61 38	72 7	94 00	22 50	357 54	55 00
June	4	73 26	64 41	82 48	93 17	96 9	33 20	358 34	54 29
	14	83 00	71 42	101 48	102 18	98 21	45 57	359 5	53 58
	24	92 33	78 38	117 12	117 12	100 35	57 40	359 27	53 25
July	4	102 5	85 29	127 23	130 17	102 51	69 29	359 39	52 53
	14	111 37	92 16	131 24	130 32R	105 6	81 22	359 41R	32 22
	24	121 10	98 58	127 54R	127 54	107 21	93 21	359 33	51 50
Aug.	3	130 43	105 36	121 22	120 21	109 32	105 24	359 15R	51 18
	13	140 18	112 9	122 5D	127 53	111 41	117 31	358 49	50 46
	23	149 56	118 37	133 41	142 27	113 45	129 44	358 14	50 14
Sep.	2	159 35	125 1	152 4	161 47	115 42	142 00	357 36	49 40
	12	169 17	131 20	171 13	180 16	117 33	154 21	356 49	49 5
	22	179 3	137 35	188 51	197 3	119 13	166 44	356 3	48 39
Oct.	1	187 52	143 8	203 19	210 51	120 35	177 57.	355 22	48 10
	11	197 44	149 14	218 1	224 47	121 53	190 25	354 39	47 39
	21	207 39	155 14	231 3	236 33	122 58	202 55	354 1	47 7
	31	217 37	161 9	240 51	243 7	123 46	215 27	353 30	46 34
Nov.	10	227 38	166 56	242 8R	237 14	124 17	228 00	353 9	46 4
	20	237 43	172 35	230 48	227 17	124 29	240 34	352 57	45 31
	30	247 49	178 5	228 18D	232 31	124 21R	253 8	352 56D	45 00
Dec.	10	257 58	183 25	238 27	245 18	123 54	265 42	353 5	44 29
	20	268 9	188 33	252 33	259 51	123 7	278 16	353 25	43 57
	30	279 21	193 58	267 38	276 57	121 58	292 4	353 59	43 25

Ayanamsa: 21° 56′ 12″

Longitude of the Moon

1966		Sun.	Tue.	Thur.	Sat.	Mon.	Wed.	Fri.
Jan.	1				26 59	53 11	81 9	110 42
	9	140 53	170 28	198 37	225 13	250 37	275 12	299 17
	23	323 6	346 49	10 46	35 25	61 19		
Feb.	1		74 56	103 39	133 47	164 28	194 00	221 41
	13	247 36	272 18	296 19	320 4	343 50	7 47	32 8
	27	57 19						
March	1		83 51	112 8	142 0	172 31	202 17	230 19
	13	256 18	281 13	305 9	328 52	352 43	16 56	41 42
	27	67 12	93 47	121 43				
April	1							136 12
	3	165 52	195 39	224 30	251 41	277 15	301 38	325 27
	17	349 16	13 30	38 25	64 14	90 42	118 12	146 32
May	1	175 27	204 23	232 36	259 34	285 10	309 38	333 30
	15	357 23	21 48	47 9	73 35	100 59	129 5	157 30
	29	185 54						
June	1						227 43	254 39
	5	280 32	305 25	329 32	353 20	17 26	42 26	69 14
	19	96 27	125 9	154 7	182 43	210 31	297 29	
July	1							263 38
	3	289 00	313 37	337 37	1 22	25 25	50 24	76 53
	17	105 6	134 36	164 20	193 20	221 3	247 33	273 8
	31	297 56						
Aug.	1					310 8	334 11	357 55
	7	21 42	46 3	71 38	99 00	128 13	158 30	188 35
	21	217 20	244 27	270 11	294 57	319 8	342 59	
Sep.	1			354 50	18 35	42 37	67 29	93 46
	11	121 52	151 39	182 10	212 3	240 19	266 49	291 56
	25	316 11	340 00	3 44				
Oct.	1				27 37	51 56	77 00	103 14
	9	131 00	160 16	190 24	220 12	248 41	275 26	300 39
	23	324 52	348 37	12 24	36 34	61 22		
Nov.	1		74 3	100 4	127 8	155 18	184 21	213 43
	13	242 34	270 10	296 15	320 59	344 56	8 40	32 46
	27	57 38	83 40					
Dec.	1			110 19	137 53	166 00	194 24	222 50
	11	250 52	278 4	304 2	328 49	352 46	16 29	40 37
	25	65 49	92 20	121 3	148 29			

Ayanamsa: 21° 56' 12"

Longitudes of Planets

1967		Sun	Mars	Merc.	Merc.	Jupit.	Venus	Saturn	Rahu
Jan.	5	284 27	196 11	276 57	284 53	121 23R	298 21	354 18	43 6
	15	294 38	200 31	293 00	301 20	120 6	310 53	355 2	42 35
	25	304 49	205 25	309 52	318 36	118 45	323 24	355 55	42 2
Feb.	4	314 58	207 47	327 22	335 45	117 28	335 52	356 54	41 30
	14	325 6	210 28	342 57	348 10	116 20	348 19	357 58	40 58
	24	335 11	212 20	348 38R	345 44R	115 25	0 42	359 8	40 26
March	6	345 13	213 9	341 48	336 31	114 47	13 00	0 19	39 55
	16	355 13	212 49R	334 36	335 16D	114 29	25 14	1 33	39 24
	26	5 9	211 11	337 1D	342 18	114 28D	37 22	2 48	38 52
April	5	15 1	208 24	347 45	354 9	114 48	49 24	4 2	38 20
	15	24 50	204 49	1 29	9 14	115 24	61 18	5 16	37 48
	25	34 36	200 4	17 49	27 7	116 18	73 2	6 26	37 15
May	5	44 19	197 53	37 7	47 43	117 27	84 35	7 33	36 45
	15	53 59	195 47	58 36	69 14	118 49	95 56	8 36	36 12
	25	63 37	195 00	79 8	79 8	120 21	106 59	9 32	35 40
June	4	73 12	195 30	95 35	101 54	122 3	117 42	10 23	35 9
	14	82 46	197 11	107 50	110 13	123 54	127 58	11 6	34 37
	24	92 19	199 51	111 51	111 35R	125 52	137 38	11 41	34 5
July	4	101 51	203 21	109 36R	106 35	127 54	146 27	12 6	33 34
	14	111 3	207 30	103 45	102 18	130 1	154 5	12 22	33 2
	24	120 56	212 12	102 2D	106 10	132 10	160 00	12 28	32 30
Aug.	3	130 29	217 24	111 41	119 17	134 22	163 26	12 24R	31 58
	13	140 4	222 58	127 56	138 24	136 34	163 26R	12 9	31 27
	23	149 41	228 53	148 29	158 15	139 50	159 37	11 45	0 55
Sep.	2	159 21	235 07	167 31	176 17	140 54	153 39	11 13	30 22
	12	169 3	241 36	184 33	192 22	141 1	148 54	10 34	29 51
	22	178 48	248 18	199 44	206 38	145 4	147 44D	9 49	29 20
Oct.	2	188 37	255 13	213 00	218 42	147 00	150 18	9 3	28 45
	12	198 29	262 19	223 22	223 22	148 49	155 45	8 16	28 16
	22	208 24	269 34	227 12R	224 30	150 30	163 12	7 32	27 43
Nov.	1	218 22	276 57	218 42	213 8	152 00	172 1	6 53	27 13
	11	228 24	284 27	211 32D	214 13	153 17	181 50	6 20	26 42
	21	238 29	292 4	219 38	226 26	154 21	192 20	5 56	26 10
Dec.	1	248 6	299 45	233 48	241 25	155 9	203 22	5 42	25 37
	11	258 45	307 28	249 8	256 54	155 39	214 45	5 39D	25 6
	21	268 55	315 15	264 43	272 36	155 50	226 25	5 47	24 33
	31	279 6	323 3	280 35	288 44	155 42R	238 17	6 5	24 1

Ayanamsa: 21° 57' 03″

Longitude of the Moon

1967		Sun.	Tue.	Thur.	Sat.	Mon.	Wed.	Fri.
Jan.	1	162 46	181 9	219 5	246 32	273 21	299 24	324 30
	15	358 42	12 24	36 11	60 46	86 46	114 29	143 31
	29	172 27	201 52					
Feb.	1						215 58	243 23
	5	269 54	295 36	320 38	344 57	8 44	32 19	56 20
	19	81 26	108 16	136 58	166 56	196 59		
March	1						226 2	253 39
	5	279 54	305 8	329 39	353 37	17 18	40 54	64 56
	19	89 58	116 34	145 2	175 2	205 28	235 5	263 7
April	1				276 29	302 9	326 43	350 39
	9	14 18	37 57	61 56	86 34	112 19	139 35	168 27
	23	198 27	228 35	257 45	285 16			
May	1					311 5	335 38	359 26
	7	23 2	46 51	71 12	96 18	122 21	149 32	177 55
	21	207 14	236 51	265 51	293 28	319 26	344 2	
June	1			355 59	19 37	43 24	68 19	93 5
	11	119 18	146 22	174 10	202 35	231 23	260 5	288 1
	25	314 39	339 53	4 1				
July	1				27 41	51 35	76 17	102 10
	9	129 9	156 56	185 7	213 22	241 32	269 25	296 39
	23	322 50	347 31	11 56	35 35	59 32		
Aug.	1		71 49	97 22	123 24	152 39	181 27	210 29
	13	238 19	265 51	292 41	318 43	343 50	8 5	31 48
	27	55 28	79 47	105 24				
Sep.	1							118 51
	3	146 57	176 17	205 52	234 51	262 46	289 35	315 23
	17	340 21	4 37	28 22	51 57	75 51	100 40	126 59
Oct.	1	155 5	184 41	214 52	244 30	272 47	299 33	325 00
	15	349 30	13 24	37 3	60 41	84 43	109 32	135 38
	29	163 23	192 44					
Nov.	1						207 50	238 11
	5	267 43	295 37	321 44	34 29	10 24	34 00	57 42
	19	81 46	106 22	131 59	158 39	186 44	216 5	
Dec.	1							246 10
	3	275 47	303 58	330 19	355 6	18 57	42 31	66 23
	17	90 52	116 6	142 6	168 55	196 39	225 18	254 37
	31	290 49						

Ayanamsa: 21° 57′ 03″

13

Longitudes of Planets

1968		Sun	Mars	Merc.	Merc.	Jupit.	Venus	Saturn	Rahu
Jan.	5	284 12	326 57	288 44	296 59	155 32R	244 16	6 19	23 46
	15	294 24	334 45	305 20	313 38	154 54	256 20	6 52	23 15
	25	304 34	342 32	321 24	327 59	154 2	268 29	7 34	22 42
Feb.	4	314 44	350 17	331 49	331 32R	152 56	280 43	8 26	22 12
	14	324 51	357 59	327 17	321 43	151 40	292 59	9 24	21 40
	24	334 57	5 37	317 58	317 10D	150 21	305 17	10 27	21 8
March	5	344 59	13 8	318 57	322 36	149 4	317 36	11 36	20 35
	15	354 58	20 43	327 35	333 33	147 56	329 55	12 48	20 3
	25	4 54	28 10	340 16	347 39	147 00	342 15	14 2	19 31
April	4	14 47	35 32	355 42	4 19	146 18	354 34	15 17	19 1
	14	24 36	42 48	13 34	23 25	145 55	6 53	16 33	18 24
	24	34 22	50 00	33 21	44 34	145 50D	19 12	17 48	17 56
May	4	44 5	57 7	55 5	64 43	146 5	31 29	19 00	17 25
	14	52 45	64 9	73 19	80 23	146 36	43 47	20 9	16 59
	24	63 23	71 36	85 54	85 54	147 24	56 4	21 14	16 21
June	3	72 58	78 00	91 43	91 49	148 26	68 20	22 14	15 49
	13	82 32	84 48	90 13R	87 31	149 42	80 37	23 7	15 18
	23	92 5	91 32	84 53	83 22	151 10	92 54	23 54	14 52
July	3	101 37	98 13	83 41D	86 3	152 48	105 11	24 32	14 15
	13	111 9	104 51	90 28	96 49	154 33	116 59	25 2	13 42
	23	120 42	112 4	104 55	114 24	156 27	129 48	25 22	13 11
Aug.	2	130 15	117 56	124 39	135 2	158 28	142 6	25 32	12 39
	12	139 50	124 23	145 6	154 37	160 30	154 25	25 31R	12 7
	22	149 27	130 49	163 32	171 52	162 36	166 44	25 21	11 34
Sep.	1	159 7	137 11	179 41	186 57	164 45	179 3	25 00	11 2
	11	168 49	143 31	193 37	199 38	166 55	191 20	24 31	10 32
	21	178 34	149 49	204 49	208 48	169 6	203 37	23 53	10 00
Oct.	1	188 22	156 5	211 00	210 41R	171 13	215 53	23 10	9 27
	11	198 14	162 19	207 8R	201 20	173 19	228 3	22 23	8 56
	21	208 9	168 30	226 38	196 4D	175 20	240 20	21 36	8 24
	31	218 8	174 45	199 36D	205 45	177 15	252 31	20 50	7 52
Nov.	10	228 9	180 46	213 5	220 55	179 5	264 40	20 8	7 20
	20	238 14	186 49	228 51	236 46	180 45	276 45	19 32	6 50
	30	248 21	192 48	244 41	252 33	182 14	288 46	19 6	6 17
Dec.	10	258 30	198 43	260 24	268 17	183 32	300 40	18 49	5 47
	20	268 40	204 35	276 12	284 11	184 34	312 25	18 42	5 14
	30	278 52	210 20	292 10	301 19	182 22	323 57	18 46D	4 42

Ayanamsa: 21° 57′ 53″

Longitude of the Moon

1968		Sun.	Tue.	Thurs.	Sat.	Mon.	Wed.	Fri.
Jan.	1					297 59	325 14	350 51
	7	15 10	38 50	62 34	86 58	112 21	138 43	165 48
	21	193 26	221 29	249 52	278 18	306 14	333 6	
Feb.	1			346 1	10 53	34 48	58 27	82 33
	11	107 39	1 34 3	161 36	189 51	218 17	246 34	274 29
	25	301 53	328 30	354 8				
March	1							6 33
	3	30 45	54 27	78 14	102 45	128 35	155 58	184 39
	17	213 57	243 3	271 22	299 42	325 1	350 25	14 59
	31	38 58						
April	1					50 48	74 28	98 31
	7	123 32	150 1	178 13	207 48	237 53	267 20	295 27
	21	322 3	347 24	11 51	35 45	59 25		
May	1						83 8	107·15
	5	132 11	158 27	186 25	215 30	246 25	276 25	304 56
	19	331 39	356 47	20 58	44 39	68 18	92 10	116 30
June	1				128 54	154 27	181 18	209 44
	9	239 34	269 55	299 19	327 19	353 17	17 50	41 38
	23	65 15	89 20	113 34	138 36			
July	1					164 26	191 17	219 21
	7	248 37	278 26	307 45	335 34	1 36	26 14	50 3
	21	73 46	97 52	122 42	148 19	174 42	201 51	
Aug.	1			215 44	244 6	273 4	302 00	330 6
	11	356 47	22 2	46 13	69 58	93 56	118 38	143 52
	25	171 5	198 36	226 39	254 59			
Sep.	1	269 12	297 28	325 11	351 56	17 32	42 6	65 59
	15	89 47	114 7	139 29	166 12	194 8	232 51	251 41
	29	280 9						
Oct.	1		307 53	334 46	0 43	25 49	50 9	74 00
	13	97 47	122 1	147 20	174 12	202 40	232 13	261 54
	27	290 47	318 22	344 40				
Nov.	1							357 26
	3	22 20	46 37	70 31	94 14	118 8	142 43	168 33
	17	196 8	225 29	255 52	285 58	314 40	341 36	7 2
Dec.	1	31 31	55 30	79 15	103 3	127 2	151 36	177 14
	15	204 26	233 30	263 53	294 21	323 31	350 45	16 13
	29	40 34	64 21					

Ayanamsa : 21° 57′ 53″

Longitudes of Planets

1969		Sun	Mars.	Merc.	Merc.	Jupit.	Venus	Saturn	Rahu
Jan.	5	284 59	213 44	301 29	308 31	185 42	330 45	18 54	4 23
	15	295 10	219 18	313 53	316 1	186 1	341 46	19 16	3 51
	25	305 21	224 42	313 37R	307 51	186 1R	352 19	19 48	3 20
Feb.	4	315 30	229 55	302 33	300 18	185 43	3 11	20 29	2 49
	14	325 37	234 56	301 11D	304 20	185 5	11 7	21 19	2 16
	24	335 43	229 39	309 1	314 43	184 12	18 39	22 16	1 46
March	6	345 45	244 1	321 12	328 19	183 6	24 9	23 20	1 12
	16	355 44	247 58	335 57	344 6	181 51	26 44	24 28	0 40
	26	5 40	251 21	352 48	2 3	180 34	25 30R	25 40	0 9
April	5	15 32	254 4	11 51	22 7	179 18	20 33	26 54	359 37
	15	25 21	255 55	32 37	42 49	178 11	14 31	28 10	359 5
	25	35 7	256 44	52 3	59 48	177 15	10 52	29 26	358 33
May	5	44 49	256 22R	65 36	69 48	176 35	11 6	30 42	358 00
	15	54 29	254 43	71 47	71 43R	171 12	14 47	31 56	357 30
	25	64 7	252 1	69 56	67 13	176 6D	20 54	33 9	356 57
June	5	74 39	248 21	66 21R	63 25D	176 22	29 30	34 20	356 23
	15	84 13	245 9	64 19	67 4	176 54	38 29	35 22	355 51
	24	93 46	242 49	71 34	77 42	177 42	48 13	36 17	355 19
July	4	103 18	241 45	85 15	94 23	178 43	58 31	37 6	354 49
	15	112 50	242 4D	103 58	115 6	180 00	69 11	37 47	354 16
	25	122 23	243 41	125 39	125 39	181 27	80 15	38 20	353 43
Aug.	4	131 56	246 26	145 12	153 59	183 4	91 26	38 42	353 12
	14	141 32	250 08	162 8	169 38	184 50	102 55	38 54	352 41
	24	151 9	254 37	176 29	182 36	186 43	114 34	38 56R	352 9
Sep.	3	160 49	259 43	187 50	191 54	188 42	126 23	38 48	351 37
	13	170 32	265 20	194 23	194 21R	190 45	138 20	38 29	351 5
	23	180 17	271 22	194 4R	185 57	192 52	150 25	38 1	330 34
Oct.	3	190 6	297 46	181 57	179 52R	195 1	162 38	37 24	349 56
	13	199 59	284 25	182 4D	188 57	197 11	174 56	36 41	349 29
	23	209 55	291 18	194 56	204 41	199 21	187 19	35 54	349 00
Nov.	2	219 54	298 22	211 19	219 33	201 29	199 45	35 7	348 27
	12	229 56	305 34	227 40	235 39	203 35	212 15	34 20	347 47
	22	240 1	313 7	243 32	251 21	205 36	224 47	33 36	347 13
Dec.	2	250 8	320 15	259 6	266 49	207 30	237 20	33 1	346 50
	12	260 18	327 41	274 30	282 1	209 18	249 55	32 31	346 19
	22	270 28	335 8	289 7	295 16	210 56	262 30	32 12	345 48

Ayanamsa: 21° 58' 43"

Longitude of the Moon

1969		Sun	Tue.	Thur.	Sat.	Mon.	Wed.	Fri.
Jan.	1						76 12	100 1
	5	124 6	148 38	173 50	200 7	227 50	257 5	287 15
	19	317 6	345 30	12 2	37 00	61 3	84 46	108 40
Feb.	1				120 48	145 29	170 52	197 1
	9	224 6	252 15	281 19	310 40	339 23	6 45	32 34
	23	57 8	81 1	104 50				
March	1				129 7	154 14	180 17	207 13
	9	234 53	263 6	291 36	320 00	347 50	14 41	40 20
	23	64 55	88 51	112 42	137 3	162 24		
April	1		175 34	202 50	231 5	259 47	288 22	316 24
	13	343 44	10 16	35 56	60 46	84 53	108 40	132 39
	27	157 25	183 34					
May	1			211 20	240 26	270 1	299 48	327 3
	11	353 54	19 44	44 40	69 15	93 13	116 57	140 51
	25	165 32	191 37	219 31	249 6			
June	1	264 14	294 22	323 24	350 50	16 49	41 48	66 8
	15	90 4	113 47	137 33	161 46	186 59	213 47	242 32
	29	272 44						
July	1		303 14	332 41	0 22	26 21	51 8	75 14
	13	98 55	122 44	146 39	171 2	196 19	223 00	251 23
	27	281 16	311 37	341 16				
Aug.	1							355 22
	3	22 23	48 11	72 9	95 57	119 42	143 41	168 9
	17	193 20	219 30	246 55	275 37	305 13	334 50	3 29
	31	30 26						
Sep.	1					43 33	68 28	92 30
	7	116 14	140 13	164 47	190 11	216 28	243 39	271 40
	21	300 18	329 10	357 41	25 14	51 28		
Oct.	1						76 26	100 30
	5	124 16	148 20	173 13	189 15	226 23	254 21	282 40
	19	311 00	339 3	6 40	33 32	59 26	84 19	108 21
Nov.	1				120 13	134 00	168 28	194 10
	9	221 25	249 57	279 00	307 47	335 50	4 2	29 31
	23	55 35	80 13	104 27	129 12			
Dec.	1					151 54	176 16	201 57
	7	229 27	258 36	288 31	318 2	346 21	13 21	39 17
	21	64 24	88 55	112 54	136 34	160 15	184 22	

Ayanamsa: 21° 58′ 43″

Longitudes of Planets

1970		Sun	Mars	Merc.	Merc.	Jupit.	Venus	Saturn	Rahu
Jan.	5	284 44	345 36	295 50R	296 22R	212 55	280 7	32 3D	345 4
	15	294 56	353 2	290 1	285 9	214 4	292 41	32 10	344 31
	25	305 6	0 26	283 55D	285 49	214 58	305 16	32 29	344 00
Feb.	4	315 15	7 49	289 48	295 5	215 36	317 49	32 58	343 28
	14	325 23	15 8	301 13	307 59	215 55	330 21	33 37	342 58
	24	335 28	22 24	315 14	322 57	215 56R	342 52	34 24	342 24
March	6	345 30	29 36	330 6	339 42	215 38	355 21	35 19	341 54
	16	354 29	36 44	348 47	358 22	215 2	7 48	36 21	341 20
	26	5 25	43 48	8 21	18 33	214 10	20 12	37 28	340 50
April	5	15 18	50 48	28 27	37 18	213 6	32 34	38 40	340 14
	15	25 7	57 43	44 28	49 27	211 53	44 52	39 54	349 45
	25	34 52	64 35	52 3	52 17R	210 36	57 7	41 10	339 13
May	5	44 38	71 24	50 29R	47 35	209 22	69 18	42 35	338 42
	15	54 15	78 9	44 50	43 19	208 14	78 9	43 44	338 10
	25	63 53	84 50	43 36D	45 43	207 17	84 50	44 59	337 40
June	4	73 28	91 28	49 31	54 47	206 36	105 28	46 13	337 7
	14	83 2	98 3	61 23	69 15	206 11	117 21	47 22	336 35
	24	92 35	104 36	78 18	88 23	206 4D	129 7	48 27	336 3
July	4	102 7	111 6	97 6	109 55	206 15	140 47	49 27	335 30
	14	111 39	117 34	120 19	130 4	206 44	152 16	50 20	335 00
	24	121 11	124 00	139 4	147 19	207 28	163 35	51 6	334 28
Aug.	3	130 45	130 25	154 50	161 33	208 28	174 39	51 43	333 56
	13	140 20	136 49	167 39	172 47	209 42	185 26	52 11	333 24
	23	149 57	143 11	176 18	177 50	211 5	195 49	52 29	332 59
Sep.	2	159 37	149 33	177 29R	174 31	212 43	205 42	52 37	332 20
	12	169 19	155 55	169 50	165 22	214 28	214 51	52 34R	331 49
	22	179 4	162 15	163 48D	163 48D	216 22	222 59	52 20	331 18
Oct.	2	188 53	168 36	171 55	179 35	218 22	229 36	51 57	330 43
	12	198 45	174 57	188 6	196 47	220 26	233 57	51 23	330 13
	22	208 40	181 18	205 21	213 43	222 34	235 9R	50 43	329 42
Nov.	1	218 39	187 39	221 51	229 49	224 45	232 27	50 00	329 9
	11	228 41	194 00	237 36	245 15	226 57	227 1	49 10	328 38
	21	238 45	200 21	252 48	252 48	229 9	221 39	48 22	328 6
Dec.	1	248 53	206 42	267 21	274 1	231 20	219 46D	47 35	327 35
	11	259 2	213 3	279 43	283 26	233 28	222 52	46 55	327 1
	21	269 12	219 24	283 35R	283 35R	235 31	227 3	46 21	326 31
	31	279 24	225 44	272 36	268 24	237 24	234 23	45 58	325 59

Ayanamsa : 21° 59′ 34″

Longitude of the Moon

1970		Sun.	Tue.	Thur.	Sat.	Mon.	Wed.	Fri.
Jan.	1			197 4	223 27	251 46	281 43	312 9
	11	341 46	9 48	36 15	61 28	85 52	109 47	133 28
	25	157 10	181 12	206 2	232 12			
Feb.	1	245 56	274 44	304 53	335 13	4 33	32 12	58 8
	15	82 49	106 44	130 24	160 8	178 15	202 59	228 38
March	1	255 33	283 50	313 17	343 11	12 28	40 22	66 33
	15	91 21	115 15	138 53	162 46	187 17	212 37	238 51
	29	266 00	294 00					
April	1						308 19	337 17
	5	6 17	34 35	61 35	87 6	111 25	135 9	158 55
	19	183 22	208 49	235 22	262 48	290 47	319 1	
May	1							347 19
	3	15 28	43 3	69 38	95 1	119 18	143 5	166 50
	17	191 26	217 18	244 33	272 51	301 32	333 00	358 00
	31	25 26						
June	1					38 55	65 19	90 58
	7	115 20	139 11	162 48	186 55	212 12	239 6	267 34
	21	296 55	326 14	354 48	22 21	48 57		
July	1						74 40	99 34
	5	123 45	147 28	171 4	195 9	220 23	247 17	275 58
	19	305 49	335 48	4 53	32 37	58 58	84 12	108 38
Aug.	1				120 37	144 20	167 54	191 44
	9	216 19	242 12	269 49	299 5	329 21	359 27	28 20
	23	55 33	81 12	105 43	129 33	153 9		
Sep.	1		164 58	188 47	213 15	238 27	265 00	273 3
	13	322 32	352 43	22 29	50 52	77 27	102 28	126 28
	27	150 4	173 45					
Oct.	1			197 55	232 45	248 25	274 27	302 44
	11	331 33	1 6	30 35	58 58	85 41	110 46	134 47
	25	158 23	182 14	206 46	232 13			
Nov.	1	245 17	271 58	279 20	327 21	355 54	24 43	53 8
	15	80 26	106 17	130 46	154 31	178 12	202 32	227 57
	29	254 35						
Dec.	1		282 6	310 7	338 15	6 25	34 24	61 56
	13	88 36	114 6	138 32	162 16	185 58	210 19	235 56
	27	263 2	291 23	320 16				

Ayanamsa: 21° 59′ 34″

Longitudes of Planets

1971	Sun	Mars	Merc.	Merc.	Jupit.	Venus	Saturn	Rahu
Jan. 5	284 30	228 54	268 19R	268 7D	238 26	238 48	45 50R	325 43
15	294 42	235 14	271 01	275 44	240 12	247 58	45 42	325 5
25	304 51	241 32	281 32	288 3	241 49	258 06	45 45D	324 39
Feb. 4	315 02	247 49	295 05	301 57	243 13	268 47	46 00	324 07
14	325 09	254 03	310 11	318 17	244 25	279 52	46 26	323 36
24	335 14	260 16	326 47	335 42	245 21	291 14	47 01	322 58
March 6	345 16	266 23	345 00	354 41	246 01	302 47	47 46	322 26
16	355 15	272 28	4 32	14 04	246 23	314 31	48 38	322 00
26	5 11	278 27	22 01	28 27	246 27R	326 20	49 38	321 29
April 5	15 04	284 19	32 48	33 45R	246 12	338 15	50 44	320 57
15	24 53	290 02	32 08	28 53	245 38	350 12	51 54	320 25
25	34 38	295 33	25 40	23 27	245 49	1 43	53 07	329 53
May 5	44 22	300 51	23 18D	25 16	243 46	14 17	54 23	319 22
15	54 01	305 49	28 31	33 24	342 35	26 21	55 41	318 43
25	63 38	310 22	39 31	46 14	241 19	38 25	56 58	318 18
June 4	73 14	314 25	55 01	64 12	240 04R	55 00	58 15	317 46
14	82 48	317 45	74 24	85 13	238 56	74 24	59 30	317 15
24	92 20	320 26	96 08	106 43	237 57	75 22	60 42	316 36
July 4	101 53	321 40	116 43	125 34	237 13	87 03	61 49	316 11
14	111 24	321 54R	133 45	141 04	236 46	99 17	62 52	315 39
24	120 57	320 51	147 29	152 55	236 36	111 42	63 50	315 02
Aug. 3	130 31	318 46R	157 07	159 48	236 45	123 50	64 39	314 35
13	140 17	316 09	160 31R	159 06	237 11	136 10	65 21	314 04
23	149 43	313 44	155 31	151 05	237 55	148 32	65 54	313 32
Sep. 2	159 22	312 13	147 51	147 41D	238 53	160 56	66 17	313 00
12	169 04	311 57D	151 06	157 30	240 07	173 20	66 29	312 28
22	178 49	313 00	165 14	174 44	241 33	185 48	66 31R	311 57
Oct. 2	188 39	315 17	183 49	192 43	243 10	198 15	66 21	311 25
12	198 30	318 44	200 49	209 36	244 58	210 42	66 03	310 53
22	208 23	322 39	217 38	225 20	246 51	223 10	65 33	310 21
Nov. 1	218 24	327 25	232 58	240 19	248 56	235 36	64 55	309 50
11	228 35	332 35	247 24	254 09	251 02	248 05	64 12	309 18
21	238 31	338 17	260 17	265 15	253 15	260 32	63 23	308 40
Dec. 1	248 38	344 13	268 06	267 12R	255 29	272 59	62 34	308 14
11	258 46	350 26	262 04	255 42	257 44	285 25	61 46	307 43
21	268 57	356 43	252 02	252 52D	260 00	297 48	61 04	307 10
31	278 08	3 04	256 37	–	262 15	310 10	60 27	306 39

Ayanamsa : 22° 0' 24"

Longitude of the Moon

1971		Sun.	Tue.	Thurs.	Sat.	Mon.	Wed.	Fri.
Jan.	1							334 43
	3	358 15	31 12	58 20	84 38	110 4	134 37	158 29
	17	182 1	205 50	230 36	256 54	284 55	314 39	344 17
	31	13 39						
Feb.	1					27 54	55 21	81 32
	7	106 43	131 8	155 00	178 36	202 17	226 30	258 5
	21	285 22	307 21	337 27	7 55			
March	1					37 25	65 44	91 19
	7	116 4	128 39	163 43	187 21	211 13	235 35	260 51
	21	287 25	315 40	345 28	16 1	45 58	74 11	
April	1			87 32	114 25	137 5	160 44	184 18
	11	209 12	232 39	258 47	283 46	310 56	339 27	8 13
	25	39 19	68 30	96 53				
May	1				121 23	143 36	169 12	191 36
	9	217 2	241 58	267 40	294 8	321 25	349 36	28 39
	23	47 58	76 38	104 52	129 25	153 40		
June	1		168 38	190 4	213 11	238 4	263 59	290 49
	13	318 19	346 21	14 44	43 17	71 29	98 47	124 47
	27	149 31	173 26					
July	1			198 6	221 12	246 17	272 39	300 13
	11	328 38	357 18	25 49	53 52	81 11	107 38	132 4
	25	157 34	181 25	206 5	229 10			
Aug.	1	241 34	267 20	299 42	323 27	352 58	22 19	50 47
	15	78 5	104 25	129 28	153 57	177 52	202 31	225 18
	29	249 44	275 22					
Sep.	1						288 56	317 4
	5	346 51	17 11	46 50	74 54	101 20	126 29	150 48
	19	171 42	198 23	222 5	246 10	271 00	297 13	
Oct.	1							325 12
	3	355 1	25 44	55 57	84 55	110 54	135 51	159 52
	17	184 34	108 15	231 9	255 25	280 23	306 25	334 1
	31	3 20						
Nov.	1					33 30	49 7	78 48
	7	106 33	132 20	156 45	180 29	204 6	228 4	252 30
	21	277 31	303 16	330 00	355 2	27 20		
Dec.	1						57 16	86 39
	5	114 27	140 26	164 59	188 45	212 27	236 33	261 24
	19	287 3	312 30	340 11	8 40	37 19	66 15	94 45

Ayanamsa : 22° 0' 24"

Longitudes of Planets

1972		Sun	Mars	Merc.	Merc.	Jupit.	Venus	Saturn	Rahu
Jan.	5	284 11	6 18	262 1	268 18	263 21	315 50	60 11R	306 23
	15	294 27	12 49	275 9	282 22	265 31	328 37	59 49	305 51
	25	304 38	19 24	289 52	297 37	267 35	340 50	59 37	305 19
Feb.	4	314 47	25 59	305 41	314 02	269 34	352 54	59 35D	304 48
	14	324 54	30 39	322 44	331 41	271 25	4 51	59 46	304 16
	24	334 59	39 11	341 7	350 44	273 20	16 37	60 8	303 46
March	5	345 1	45 47	359 39	6 8	274 36	28 9	60 39	303 13
	15	355 1	52 21	13 14	15 47	275 52	39 21	61 21	302 34
	25	4 57	58 54	15 00R	11 42	276 54	50 13	62 10	302 9
April	4	14 49	65 26	7 37	4 36	277 40	60 31	63 7	301 37
	14	24 39	71 54	3 43D	4 51	278 9	70 14	64 11	301 05
	24	34 25	78 24	7 52	12 23	278 19	78 59	65 18	300 33
May	4	44 8	84 51	18 3	24 52	278 11R	86 23	66 32	300 2
	14	53 47	91 16	32 24	40 53	277 44	91 54	67 47	299 30
	24	63 25	97 40	50 15	60 27	277 00	94 37	69 4	298 58
June	3	73 00	104 2	71 16	82 15	276 2	93 40R	70 22	398 26
	13	82 34	110 24	92 53	102 45	274 52	89 2	71 40	397 55
	23	92 6	116 43	111 43	119 42	273 37	82 56	72 56	397 23
July	3	101 38	123 3	126 44	132 40	272 21	78 51	74 10	296 51
	13	111 11	129 23	137 24	140 43	271 10	78 33D	75 21	296 19
	23	120 43	135 43	142 18	141 51R	270 6	81 44	76 27	295 48
Aug.	2	130 17	142 3	139 25	135 38	269 18	87 29	77 26	295 16
	12	139 52	148 23	132 4	130 26	268 45	95 2	78 20	294 38
	22	149 29	154 44	131 44D	136 7	268 30	103 47	79 6	294 12
Sep.	1	159 8	161 6	143 8	151 50	268 34D	113 44	79 44	293 40
	11	168 50	167 29	161 17	170 47	268 57	123 41	80 11	293 9
	21	178 35	173 55	180 00	188 49	269 38	134 27	80 29	292 37
Oct.	1	188 24	179 44	197 16	205 22	270 36	145 37	80 36	292 5
	11	198 16	186 49	213 9	220 35	271 47	157 5	80 31R	291 34
	21	208 11	193 19	227 46	234 37	273 14	168 48	80 16	291 1
	31	218 10	199 51	240 51	246 23	274 52	180 43	79 51	290 30
Nov.	10	228 13	206 25	250 37	252 30	276 40	192 49	79 17	289 58
	20	238 16	213 2	250 43R	246 17	278 39	205 1	78 35	289 26
	30	248 24	219 41	238 40	236 10	280 41	217 21	77 49	288 55
Dec.	10	258 33	226 22	237 58D	242 31	282 55	229 44	76 58	288 23
	20	268 44	233 6	248 41	255 15	285 10	242 10	76 10	287 51
	30	278 55	239 52	263 53	—	287 42	254 38	75 25	287 19

Ayanamsa: 22° 1' 14"

Longitude of the Moon

1972		Sun.	Tue.	Thur.	Sat.	Mon.	Wed.	Fri.
Jan.	1				108 37	135 18	160 36	184 47
	9	209 30	232 22	256 58	282 39	308 30	337 14	5 32
	23	33 58	62 14	90 3	117 7	143 14		
Feb.	1		155 54	180 32	205 26	229 9	251 48	277 27
	13	303 4	332 10	1 16	30 31	59 9	86 46	113 26
	27	139 12	163 15					
March	1						176 31	200 37
	5	224 21	248 9	272 34	298 20	325 51	354 8	25 19
	19	55 8	83 36	110 30	136 8	160 57	185 12	210 8
April	1				221 00	244 43	268 45	293 38
	9	320 2	348 23	18 29	49 12	78 59	106 59	133 10
	23	158 5	182 15	206 3	229 49			
May	1					253 39	277 50	302 46
	7	328 30	357 3	27 51	57 31	87 30	115 46	142 15
	21	167 41	191 14	214 57	239 42	260 45	287 16	
June	1			299 47	325 33	352 35	21 9	50 55
	11	80 59	110 7	137 36	163 21	187 48	211 39	236 23
	25	259 27	284 7	309 32				
July	1				335 51	3 10	31 28	60 32
	9	89 45	118 18	145 35	171 23	195 57	219 48	244 4
	23	267 47	292 52	319 00	346 8	14 4		
Aug.	1		28 13	56 41	85 9	113 12	140 29	166 21
	13	191 44	215 53	239 35	263 31	288 16	314 19	341 46
	27	10 17	39 11	67 47				
Sep.	1							81 50
	3	109 25	136 15	162 19	187 32	211 56	236 45	259 24
	17	283 36	309 00	336 37	4 55	34 39	64 10	92 39
Oct.	1	119 51	146 3	171 28	196 12	220 20	244 1	267 40
	15	291 42	316 59	344 4	13 8	43 31	73 47	102 46
	29	130 4	155 57					
Nov.	1						168 31	193 4
	5	217 9	240 53	264 29	288 17	312 48	338 42	6 32
	19	36 15	66 58	97 12	125 53	152 39	177 55	
Dec.	1							192 13
	3	226 2	250 40	273 25	297 27	322 12	348 4	15 30
	17	44 37	74 51	105 6	133 4	161 15	186 43	210 59
	31	234 39						

Ayanamsa: 22° 1′ 14″

Longitudes of Planets

1973		Sun	Mars.	Merc.	Merc.	Jupit.	Venus	Saturn	Rahu
Jan.	5	285 2	243 59	271 20	278 58	288 59	262 8	74 59R	287 00
	15	295 13	250 49	286 49	294 50	291 12	275 38	74 24	286 28
	25	305 24	257 42	303 6	311 38	293 32	287 19	73 57	285 57
Feb.	4	315 33	264 37	320 27	329 27	295 50	299 39	73 42	285 25
	14	325 41	271 34	338 26	346 51	298 5	312 10	73 38D	284 53
	24	335 46	278 34	354 47	357 19	300 15	324 40	73 45	284 21
March	6	345 47	285 36	358 21R	356 4	302 18	337 9	74 3	283 49
	16	355 46	292 39	351 2	346 40	304 15	349 37	74 31	283 18
	26	5 42	299 45	345 00	345 46D	306 1	2 2	75 9	232 52
April	5	15 34	306 51	348 32	352 50	307 38	14 27	75 57	282 20
	15	25 22	313 57	358 18	4 43	309 2	26 51	76 51	281 42
	25	35 8	321 3	12 00	20 3	310 12	39 13	77 52	281 11
May	5	44 51	328 8	28 50	38 24	311 8	51 33	78 59	280 45
	15	54 31	335 9	48 41	59 31	311 46	63 52	80 11	280 8
	25	64 8	342 8	70 27	80 56	312 5	76 9	81 26	279 35
June	4	73 43	349 2	90 34	99 10	312 5R	88 29	82 42	279 4
	14	83 17	355 48	107 37	112 54	311 48	100 38	84 00	278 38
	24	92 50	2 23	118 23	121 23	311 10	112 51	85 18	278 00
July	4	102 22	8 45	123 12	123 3R	310 20	125 2	86 35	277 28
	14	111 54	14 49	121 6	117 53	309 13	137 11	87 50	277 3
	24	121 26	20 32	114 42	112 55	307 59	149 18	89 3	276 25
Aug.	3	131 00	25 45	113 31D	117 14	306 41	161 21	90 11	275 53
	13	140 40	30 23	122 33	130 30	305 26	173 20	91 13	275 21
	23	150 12	34 15	139 51	149 39	304 18	185 19	92 10	274 56
Sep.	2	159 52	37 8	159 33	169 59	303 22	197 12	93 00	274 18
	12	169 34	38 54	178 58	186 38	302 42	208 59	93 40	273 46
	22	179 21	39 13R	194 34	202 15	302 21	220 39	94 11	273 14
Oct.	2	189 9	38 7	209 31	216 24	302 19D	232 12	94 33	272 42
	12	199 1	35 51	219 00	228 27	302 37	243 35	95 44	272 10
	22	208 57	32 28	233 7	236 5	303 14	254 44	94 44R	271 39
Nov.	1	218 55	29 13	236 21R	232 51	304 7	265 36	94 32	271 7
	11	228 57	26 42	227 48	221 24	305 18	276 3	94 9	270 35
	21	239 3	25 25	220 39D	224 11	306 44	285 54	93 38	270 3
Dec.	1	249 10	25 32D	229 49	236 34	308 22	294 54	92 59	269 32
	11	259 19	26 50	243 49	251 18	310 00	302 35	92 14	269 6
	21	269 30	29 10	258 56	266 41	312 11	308 21	91 24	268 28
	31	279 41	32 22	274 31	—	314 19	311 16	90 34	267 56

Ayanamsa: 22° 2' 5"

Longitude of the Moon

1973		Sun	Tue.	Thur.	Sat.	Mon.	Wed.	Fri.
Jan.	1					246 28	270 13	294 24
	7	319 18	345 00	11 46	39 40	68 39	98 23	127 31
	21	155 39	182 9	207 8	231 5	254 34	278 32	
Feb.	1			290 41	315 43	341 46	8 44	36 24
	11	64 34	93 7	121 42	149 47	176 51	202 34	227 3
	25	250 46	274 25					
March	1			298 41	324 7	350 55	18 50	47 15
	11	75 39	103 44	131 28	158 39	185 4	211 29	234 52
	25	258 34	282 12	306 39	332 6			
April	1	345 31	13 36	42 46	72 2	100 9	128 21	155 10
	15	181 14	206 32	231 2	254 53	278 26	302 16	327 6
	29	353 34						
May	1		22 5	51 39	81 41	110 55	138 47	165 21
	13	190 52	215 35	239 42	263 24	286 57	310 50	335 38
	27	1 58	30 9	59 59				
June	1							68 13
	3	105 29	133 35	162 2	187 56	212 42	236 43	260 22
	17	283 57	307 47	332 15	357 46	24 47	53 41	83 32
July	1	113 52	143 19	171 5	197 7	221 44	245 34	269 8
	15	292 50	317 1	341 54	7 42	34 39	62 54	92 17
	29	122 12	151 34					
Aug.	1						165 44	192 46
	5	218 6	242 15	265 19	289 30	313 43	338 46	4 42
	19	31 29	59 5	87 28	116 27	145 32	173 53	194 50
Sep.	1				213 42	238 24	267 9	285 45
	9	309 49	344 51	1 3	28 14	55 59	84 5	112 21
	23	140 10	168 39	195 47	221 39			
Oct.	1					246 16	270 1	293 35
	7	317 44	343 2	9 48	37 49	66 28	95 5	123 19
	21	151 1	178 8	204 28	229 51	254 13	277 55	
Nov.	1			289 41	313 24	338 1	4 9	31 59
	11	61 9	90 47	119 53	148 00	175 1	201 2	226 11
	25	250 34	274 21	297 53				
Dec.	1				321 39	346 6	12 3	39 46
	9	69 43	99 32	129 30	158 7	185 10	210 46	235 21
	23	259 20	282 57	306 32	330 22	354 54		

Ayanamsa: 22° 2' 5"

Longitudes of Planets

1974		Sun	Mars	Merc.	Merc.	Jupit.	Venus	Saturn	Rahu
Jan.	5	284 47	34 24	282 27	290 36	315 24	311 17R	90 10R	267 41
	15	294 58	38 21	298 54	307 23	317 40	308 18	89 25	267 8
	25	305 9	42 54	315 58	324 29	320 00	302 30	88 47	266 37
Feb.	4	315 18	47 50	332 22	338 35	322 22	297 24	88 18	266 5
	14	325 26	53 1	341 45D	340 44R	324 46	295 50D	87 57	265 38
	24	335 30	58 24	336 15	331 1	327 11	298 8	87 47	264 55
March	6	345 32	63 57	327 29	327 14D	329 32	303 24	87 50D	264 30
	16	355 1	69 36	329 8	332 50	331 52	310 42	88 3	263 58
	26	5 22	75 23	337 51	343 52	334 8	319 20	88 27	263 32
April	5	15 20	81 14	350 40	358 12	336 19	328 55	89 00	262 55
	15	25 9	87 8	6 21	15 13	338 22	339 6	89 44	262 23
	25	34 54	93 4	24 44	34 53	340 18	349 46	90 35	261 51
May	5	44 37	99 4	45 34	56 23	342 4	0 43	91 33	261 19
	15	54 17	105 5	66 47	76 17	348 39	11 56	92 38	260 47
	25	63 54	111 9	84 35	91 32	345 1	23 20	93 47	260 16
June	4	73 30	117 15	97 3	100 55	346 9	34 51	95 00	259 44
	14	83 3	123 21	103 13	103 32R	347 2	46 30	96 15	259 12
	24	92 36	129 29	102 8	99 27	347 36	58 14	97 33	258 40
July	4	102 8	135 39	96 32	94 36	347 51	70 5	98 51	258 12
	14	111 40	141 51	94 29D	96 54	347 47R	81 59	100 9	257 37
	24	121 13	148 4	101 18	107 52	347 24	94 00	101 25	257 5
Aug.	3	130 47	154 19	116 15	125 56	346 43	106 2	102 39	256 33
	13	140 22	160 38	136 9	146 17	345 45	118 11	103 49	256 1
	23	149 59	166 59	156 2	165 13	344 36	130 24	104 54	255 36
Sep.	2	159 38	173 22	173 52	182 00	343 19	142 41	105 54	254 58
	12	169 20	179 49	189 39	196 50	342 00	155 1	106 47	254 26
	22	179 7	186 18	203 27	209 27	340 45	167 25	107 32	253 54
Oct.	2	188 55	192 51	214 35	218 31	339 39	179 53	108 3	253 29
	12	198 47	199 27	220 34	219 47R	338 48	192 22	108 34	252 51
	22	208 43	206 7	215 34	209 21	338 13	205 53	108 50	252 19
Nov.	1	218 40	213 16	205 11	205 36D	338 00	217 25	108 54	251 47
	11	228 44	219 38	209 46	216 5	338 6D	229 58	108 49R	251 22
	21	238 47	226 30	223 23	231 1	338 32	242 31	108 30	250 44
Dec.	1	248 55	233 25	238 49	246 37	339 18	255 5	108 2	250 12
	11	259 4	240 24	254 26	262 17	340 21	267 39	107 26	249 40
	21	269 15	247 29	270 11	278 9	341 41	280 12	106 42	249 8
	31	279 26	254 37	286 14	—	343 14	292 46	105 54	248 37

Ayanamsa: 22° 2' 55"

Longitude of the Moon

1974		Sun.	Tue.	Thur.	Sat.	Mon.	Wed.	Fri.
Jan.	1		7 23	34 00	62 15	92 8	122 14	152 45
	13	181 7	207 33	232 26	256 22	279 56	305 32	327 26
	27	351 22	17 5	43 22				
Feb.	1							57 6
	3	85 32	115 23	145 44	175 17	192 32	228 49	252 40
	17	276 46	300 24	324 15	348 50	14 9	40 15	
March	1							67 13
	3	95 15	124 19	153 58	183 10	210 55	236 52	261 19
	17	284 58	308 34	332 42	357 45	14 5	50 23	77 59
	31	105 57						
April	1					120 9	148 49	177 28
	7	205 23	231 53	257 00	281 2	131 12	328 32	353 19
	21	19 19	46 29	74 32	102 49			
May	1						159 23	187 11
	5	214 7	240 3	264 54	288 53	312 32	336 28	1 18
	19	27 31	55 13	84 1	112 29	142 7	170 14	197 21
June	1				210 33	236 14	261 3	285 10
	9	308 52	332 35	356 52	22 17	49 16	77 57	107 47
	23	137 43	166 45	194 21	220 31			
July	1					245 35	269 53	293 46
	7	317 26	341 12	5 29	30 46	57 35	86 12	116 17
	21	146 49	176 24	204 12	230 13	254 55	278 54	
Aug.	1			290 45	314 26	338 14	2 22	27 9
	11	53 2	80 26	109 33	139 59	170 23	199 57	226 30
	25	251 47	275 55	299 35	323 16			
Sep.	1	335 13	358 58	24 15	49 45	76 18	104 12	133 32
	15	163 39	193 23	221 32	247 46	272 27	296 16	320 54
	29	343 53						
Oct.	1		8 31	33 51	59 55	86 47	114 34	143 17
	13	172 35	201 37	229 26	255 39	280 26	304 20	328 1
	27	352 7	17 4	43 1				
Nov.	1							55 21
	3	83 6	111 22	139 45	168 12	196 29	224 7	250 39
	17	276 8	300 15	323 59	347 48	12 18	38 1	65 4
Dec.	1	93 16	122 5	150 50	179 5	206 35	233 14	259 2
	15	283 58	308 9	331 54	355 39	20 3	45 42	73 00
	29	101 55	131 43					

Ayanamsa: 22° 2′ 55″

Longitudes of Planets

1975		Sun	Mars	Merc.	Merc.	Jupit.	Venus	Saturn	Rahu
Jan.	5	284 32	258 12	294 25	302 5	344 5	299 2	105 30R	248 21
	15	294 43	265 26	310 36	317 52	345 57	311 34	104 40	247 49
	25	304 54	272 43	323 22	325 30	347 57	324 3	103 53	247 17
Feb.	4	315 3	280 4	323 10R	317 36	350 7	336 33	103 13	246 45
	14	325 11	287 30	312 22	310 00	352 21	348 59	102 38	246 14
	24	335 15	294 58	310 44D	313 33	354 40	1 22	102 14	245 42
March	6	345 17	302 28	318 1	323 36	357 3	13 39	102 1	245 10
	16	355 17	310 1	330 00	337 4	359 29	24 52	101 57D	244 38
	26	5 13	317 36	344 44	352 58	1 53	38 00	102 5	244 10
April	5	15 5	325 12	1 46	11 11	4 19	49 59	102 24	243 35
	15	24 55	332 49	21 10	31 39	6 41	61 50	102 53	243 3
	25	34 41	340 26	42 17	52 31	9 1	73 33	103 33	242 31
May	5	44 22	348 2	61 50	69 38	11 16	85 5	104 20	242 6
	15	54 4	355 36	75 52	80 21	13 27	96 22	105 14	241 28
	25	63 40	3 8	82 57	83 35R	15 29	107 22	106 15	240 56
June	4	73 16	10 34	82 25	79 58	17 24	117 58	107 23	240 24
	14	82 50	17 57	77 13	75 21	19 8	128 8	108 33	239 59
	24	92 22	25 14	75 7D	76 50	20 43	138 7	109 48	239 20
July	4	101 54	32 23	80 31	86 5	22 3	146 12	111 4	238 49
	14	111 27	39 22	93 16	102 1	23 9	153 29	112 22	238 17
	24	120 59	46 12	111 57	122 28	23 58	158 53	113 39	237 45
Aug.	3	130 33	52 48	132 55	142 53	24 29	161 35	114 56	237 13
	13	140 8	59 9	159 4R	161 4	24 42	160 41R	116 11	236 42
	23	149 45	65 14	169 14	177 50	24 35R	158 42	117 23	236 10
Sep.	2	159 24	70 57	183 49	190 11	24 8	153 39	118 31	235 38
	12	169 7	76 16	195 45	200 18	23 22	146 2	119 34	235 6
	22	178 51	81 4	203 26	204 23R	22 21	145 48D	120 29	234 35
Oct.	2	188 41	85 15	202 38	197 52	21 8	149 8	121 17	234 3
	12	198 33	88 41	192 9	189 6	19 48	155 5	121 58	233 31
	22	208 28	91 10	190 29D	195 27	18 28	162 55	122 28	232 59
Nov.	1	218 26	92 30	202 24	210 11	17 12	172 00	122 49	232 28
	11	228 28	92 29R	218 16	226 19	16 10	181 59	122 58	231 56
	21	238 34	91 3	234 20	242 16	15 22	192 36	122 56R	231 24
Dec.	1	248 41	88 15	250 7	257 58	14 53	203 43	122 43	230 52
	11	258 50	84 34	265 48	273 39	14 45D	215 10	122 19	230 21
	21	269 00	80 36	281 32	289 32	14 57	226 52	121 46	229 49
	31	279 11	77 19	296 45	—	15 32	238 47	121 6	229 17

Ayanamsa: 22° 3′ 45″

Longitude of the Moon

1975	Sun.	Tue.	Thur.	Sat.	Mon.	Wed.	Fri.
Jan. 1						146 38	176 00
5	203 34	230 5	255 34	277 19	304 31	328 21	352 2
19	15 56	40 42	66 54	95 3	124 56	155 36	185 28
Feb. 1				199 48	227 3	252 43	277 20
9	301 23	325 10	348 54	12 44	36 33	62 15	89 4
23	117 50	148 15	179 1				
March 1				208 40	236 16	262 1	286 30
9	310 22	334 3	357 51	21 55	46 27	71 49	98 27
23	126 16	156 36	187 3	216 42	244 34		
April 1		257 49	283 1	307 10	330 51	354 37	18 46
13	43 28	68 54	95 13	122 40	151 18	180 46	210 16
27	238 47	265 44					
May 1			291 7	315 22	339 7	2 56	27 19
11	52 32	78 41	105 44	133 54	161 59	190 43	219 13
25	247 2	273 38	299 1	323 20			
June 1	335 14	358 59	23 6	47 36	74 21	102 50	130 11
15	158 51	187 18	215 15	242 34	269 2	294 36	319 14
29	343 12						
July 1		6 54	31 00	56 5	82 43	110 55	140 12
13	169 35	196 44	225 50	252 25	278 12	303 12	327 4
27	351 25	15 5	39 5				
Aug. 1							51 27
3	77 14	104 22	134 17	164 32	194 16	222 38	249 29
17	275 13	299 59	324 16	348 8	11 48	35 34	59 58
31	85 37						
Sep. 1					99 7	127 38	157 51
7	188 31	218 9	245 58	272 10	297 6	321 18	345 8
21	8 50	32 36	56 45	81 45	108 6		
Oct. 1						136 18	156 10
5	196 45	226 38	254 52	281 14	306 10	330 13	353 55
19	17 38	41 40	66 13	91 32	117 59	144 49	174 59
Nov. 1				189 56	219 56	248 56	276 26
9	302 14	326 44	350 30	14 11	38 13	63 56	88 30
23	114 28	142 20	170 30	199 19			
Dec. 1					228 20	256 51	284 12
7	310 7	334 43	358 30	22 10	46 19	71 28	97 47
21	125 11	153 12	181 29	209 45	237 47	265 23	

Ayanamsa: 22° 3' 45"

Longitudes of Planets

1976	Sun	Mars	Merc.	Merc.	Jupit.	Venus	Saturn	Rahu
Jan. 5	284 18	76 18R	303 23	308 6	15 54	244 49	120 44R	229 1
15	294 29	74 54	309 8R	305 42	16 55	256 54	119 55	228 29
25	304 39	74 51D	299 27	294 42	18 12	269 5	119 7	227 58
Feb. 4	314 49	76 00	293 22D	295 1	19 42	281 19	118 17	227 26
14	324 51	78 9	298 47	304 23	21 26	293 36	117 35	226 54
24	335 00	81 4	309 54	316 35	23 20	304 41	116 57	226 22
March 5	345 3	84 37	323 51	331 34	25 23	318 14	116 29	225 51
15	355 2	88 41	339 49	348 33	27 32	330 34	116 10	225 18
25	4 58	93 7	357 48	7 34	29 47	342 54	116 2	224 47
April 4	14 51	97 53	17 47	28 10	32 6	355 14	116 4D	224 15
14	24 39	102 51	38 10	47 4	34 28	7 34	116 19	223 44
24	34 25	108 3	254 20	59 40	36 51	19 52	116 44	223 11
May 4	44 8	113 24	62 50	63 46	39 15	32 10	117 17	222 40
14	53 48	118 55	62 41R	60 10	41 39	44 27	118 1	222 8
24	63 26	124 31	57 22	55 22	43 58	56 44	118 52	221 36
June 3	73 2	130 15	55 00D	56 28	46 16	69 1	119 49	221 4
13	82 36	136 3	58 58	64 36	48 28	81 18	120 54	220 33
23	92 8	141 56	70 59	78 47	50 36	93 35	122 2	220 1
July 3	101 41	147 54	87 51	97 59	52 35	105 53	123 15	219 29
13	111 12	153 58	109 10	119 21	54 27	118 11	124 29	218 57
23	120 44	160 5	129 33	139 7	56 8	130 29	125 46	218 26
Aug. 2	130 19	166 17	148 00	156 10	57 37	142 47	127 4	217 54
12	139 53	172 32	163 40	170 27	58 54	155 6	128 21	217 22
22	149 30	178 53	177 29	181 34	59 55	167 24	129 36	216 50
Sep. 1	159 10	185 19	185 25	187 37	60 40	179 42	130 49	216 19
11	168 53	191 49	187 33R	184 47	61 6	192 00	131 59	215 47
21	178 38	198 23	179 48	174 55	61 12R	204 16	133 3	215 15
Oct. 1	187 28	205 3	173 5	175 27D	60 58	216 29	134 2	214 43
11	198 18	211 47	181 9	188 41	60 24	228 45	134 54	214 12
21	208 13	218 37	197 00	205 27	59 34	240 37	135 37	213 39
31	218 12	225 33	213 50	222 2	58 27	253 7	136 12	213 8
Nov. 10	228 13	232 33	230 5	237 58	57 11	265 15	136 36	212 36
20	238 19	239 38	245 47	253 29	55 50	277 17	136 49	212 5
30	248 26	246 50	261 8	268 40	54 30	289 17	136 52R	211 45
Dec. 10	258 35	254 5	276 2	282 57	53 17	301 9	136 43	211 1
20	268 45	261 26	288 52	292 44	52 18	312 50	136 23	210 29
30	278 56	268 52	292 52R	–	51 36	324 19	135 52	199 57

Ayanamsa: 22° 4' 36"

Longitude of the Moon

1976	Sun.	Tue.	Thurs.	Sat.	Mon.	Wed.	Fri.
Jan. 1			278 55	305 13	330 19	355 26	18 4
11	41 52	66 32	92 38	120 19	149 5	173 7	206 40
25	234 27	261 31	287 54	313 34			
Feb. 1	326 3	350 27	14 12	37 45	61 49	87 3	114 13
15	143 6	173 00	202 40	231 17	258 5	284 47	310 8
29	334 47						
March 1					346 54	10 44	34 17
7	57 58	82 28	108 28	136 35	166 9	196 39	226 34
21	255 00	281 47	306 46	331 47	355 46	19 25	
April 1			31 12	54 51	79 00	104 9	130 50
11	159 24	189 28	219 30	249 42	277 43	303 59	328 50
25	352 51	16 26	40 1				
May 1				63 56	88 25	113 48	140 27
9	168 35	197 56	228 8	257 49	286 7	312 37	337 34
23	1 29	25 1	48 43	73 00	96 1		
June 1		110 53	137 16	164 40	193 2	222 10	251 32
13	280 17	307 41	332 26	357 50	21 29	45 6	69 17
27	94 27	120 39					
July 1			147 46	175 31	203 43	232 12	260 42
11	288 45	315 44	341 22	5 47	29 30	53 6	77 27
25	103 1	129 57	157 55	186 21			
Aug. 1	200 36	228 53	256 51	284 22	311 10	336 56	1 42
15	25 34	49 7	73 3	98 4	124 41	152 51	181 50
29	211 12	239 48					
Sep. 1						253 47	281 3
5	307 31	333 9	357 54	21 55	45 29	69 6	93 27
19	119 10	146 42	175 52	205 55	235 38	264 14	
Oct. 1							291 25
3	317 24	342 23	6 40	30 26	53 59	77 9	102 1
17	127 34	154 51	183 55	214 13	244 33	273 46	301 13
31	327 3						
Nov. 1					339 36	3 41	27 22
7	50 57	74 40	98 51	123 49	149 59	177 44	207 3
21	237 25	267 36	296 25	323 18	348 28		
Dec. 1						12 30	36 3
5	59 40	83 41	108 18	133 40	159 55	187 13	215 56
19	245 37	275 28	304 22	331 29	356 48	20 50	44 23

Ayanamsa : 22° 4′ 36″

Longitudes of Planets

1977		Sun	Mars	Merc.	Merc.	Jupit.	Venus	Saturn	Rahu
Jan.	5	285 3	273 21	288 18R	281 49	51 21R	331 5	135 33R	209 38
	15	295 15	280 53	277 43	277 43D	51 10	342 1	134 52	209 6
	25	305 25	288 30	280 50	285 36	51 21D	352 26	134 4	208 32
Feb.	4	315 35	296 9	291 26	297 56	51 51	2 7	133 15	208 3
	14	325 42	303 53	304 58	312 26	52 44	10 46	132 27	207 31
	24	335 46	311 38	320 18	328 33	53 47	17 55	131 43	206 59
March	6	345 48	319 24	337 16	347 26	55 7	22 50	131 3	206 27
	16	355 47	327 12	356 3	6 2	56 42	24 33	130 32	205 40
	26	5 43	334 59	16 3	25 32	58 28	22 22R	130 10	205 25
April	5	15 35	342 46	33 42	39 50	60 22	17 28	129 59	204 58
	15	25 23	350 34	43 30	44 29R	62 25	11 33	129 58D	204 20
	25	35 9	358 21	43 18	40 1	64 33	8 18	130 8	203 49
May	5	44 52	6 2	37 13	35 7	66 46	9 27D	130 28	203 17
	15	54 32	13 42	34 48D	36 16	69 2	13 48	130 59	202 45
	25	64 10	21 17	39 23	44 24	71 21	20 23	131 39	202 13
June	4	73 45	28 48	50 30	57 46	73 40	28 28	132 27	201 42
	14	83 19	36 12	66 12	75 43	76 00	37 35	133 22	201 10
	24	92 52	43 32	85 37	97 00	78 18	47 25	134 24	200 35
July	4	102 24	50 44	107 48	118 3	80 33	57 45	135 30	200 6
	14	111 56	57 48	127 35	136 20	82 45	68 29	136 40	199 35
	24	121 29	64 46	144 19	151 29	84 53	79 31	137 54	199 3
Aug.	3	131 2	71 33	157 50	163 12	86 53	90 47	139 9	198 31
	13	140 37	78 12	167 23	170 4	88 46	103 27	140 26	197 59
	23	150 15	84 39	170 43R	169 7	90 30	113 58	141 42	197 28
Sep.	2	159 54	90 56	165 10	160 26	92 4	125 47	142 58	196 57
	12	169 36	96 58	157 15	157 31D	93 24	137 45	144 11	196 24
	22	179 23	102 45	161 34	168 23	94 31	149 51	145 22	195 52
Oct.	2	189 11	108 14	176 42	185 32	95 21	162 3	146 28	195 21
	12	199 3	113 23	194 21	203 00	95 54	174 21	147 27	194 48
	22	208 59	118 8	211 21	219 28	96 8	186 45	148 21	194 17
Nov.	1	218 57	122 21	227 23	235 6	96 2R	199 11	149 6	193 45
	11	228 59	125 58	241 15	250 4	95 36	211 41	149 44	193 13
	21	239 5	128 50	257 16	264 5	94 51	224 13	150 11	192 41
Dec.	1	249 12	130 36	270 17	275 8	93 49	236 46	150 26	192 10
	11	259 21	131 33	277 29	275 41R	92 37	249 20	150 33	191 38
	21	269 31	131 2R	270 55	264 37	91 17	261 55	150 28R	191 6
	31	279 43	129 10	261 5	–	89 56	274 30	150 11	190 34

Ayanamsa: 22° 5' 27"

Longitude of the Moon

1977		Sun	Tue.	Thur.	Sat.	Mon.	Wed.	Fri.
Jan.	1				56 9	80 7	104 53	130 31
	9	157 2	184 3	211 50	240 51	269 22	298 11	325 56
	23	352 7	16 48	40 33	64 4	88 12		
Feb.	1		100 37	126 19	153 8	180 46	208 46	236 57
	13	265 11	293 15	320 46	347 11	12 21	36 30	60 5
	27	83 51						
March	1		108 17	134 26	161 50	190 20	219 15	247 56
	13	276 4	303 27	329 32	355 52	20 26	44 26	68 3
	27	91 48	116 21	142 18				
April	1							155 53
	3	184 18	213 52	243 38	272 40	300 28	326 58	352 24
	17	16 58	40 59	64 37	88 16	112 21	137 35	163 58
May	1	192 20	222 10	252 40	282 22	310 30	336 53	1 54
	15	26 2	49 45	73 23	97 8	121 21	146 25	172 44
	29	200 45	230 28					
June	1						245 43	276 43
	5	305 41	333 10	358 48	23 8	46 20	70 24	94 14
	19	118 28	143 19	168 59	196 00	224 27	254 17	
July	1							284 30
	3	314 4	341 44	7 27	31 48	55 28	79 6	103 8
	17	127 47	153 9	179 16	206 19	234 27	263 38	293 14
	31	322 17						
Aug.	1					336 16	2 55	27 56
	7	51 54	75 32	99 28	124 8	149 41	176 27	204 17
	21	232 5	259 30	288 21	316 49	344 29	10 19	
Sep.	1			23 28	47 54	71 41	95 25	119 47
	11	145 17	171 51	199 31	227 49	256 21	284 43	312 40
	25	339 55	6 13	31 37				
Oct.	1				55 48	79 33	103 18	127 39
	9	153 9	180 8	208 34	237 52	267 7	295 10	323 8
	23	349 35	15 5	39 51	63 58	87 43		
Nov.	1		99 33	123 26	148 10	174 15	202 9	231 42
	13	261 59	291 43	319 00	345 39	12 1	36 34	60 37
	27	84 25	108 2					
Dec.	1			132 2	156 37	182 27	210 5	239 38
	11	269 51	300 44	329 31	356 18	21 28	45 42	.69 30
	25	93 13	117 3	141 10	165 52			

Ayanamsa: 22° 5' 27″

Longitudes of Planets

1978		Sun	Mars.	Merc.	Merc.	Jupit.	Venus	Saturn	Rahu
Jan.	5	284 48	127 46R	262 31	266 29	89 17R	280 48	149 58R	190 19
	15	295 00	124 12	271 55	278 10	88 7	293 23	149 27	189 47
	25	305 10	120 14	284 59	292 12	87 9	305 57	148 49	189 15
Feb.	4	315 20	116 35	299 45	307 37	86 28	318 30	148 3	188 43
	14	325 26	113 54	315 49	324 22	86 8	331 3	147 16	188 12
	24	335 31	112 29	333 19	342 38	86 6D	343 33	146 27	187 39
March	6	345 33	112 23D	352 15	1 53	86 25	356 1	145 41	187 8
	16	355 33	112 26	10 59	18 36	87 2	8 28	145 00	186 36
	26	5 28	115 26	23 44	26 5	87 57	20 52	144 26	186 5
April	5	15 22	118 16	25 20R	22 20	89 7	33 14	144 00	185 33
	15	25 9	121 41	10 36	15 47	90 31	45 32	143 45	185 1
	25	34 55	125 39	14 50	15 53D	92 6	58 16	143 39	184 29
May	5	44 38	130 00	18 51	23 15	93 52	69 57	143 45D	183 57
	15	54 18	134 41	28 55	35 43	95 45	82 3	144 00	183 25
	25	63 55	139 38	43 24	52 4	97 47	94 6	144 27	182 54
June	4	74 28	144 50	61 43	72 9	99 52	106 4	145 1	182 22
	14	83 5	150 12	83 5	93 59	102 2	117 56	145 46	181 50
	24	92 37	155 47	104 21	114 46	104 15	129 40	146 37	181 15
July	4	102 10	161 30	122 39	130 27	106 29	141 17	147 34	180 47
	14	111 42	167 21	137 21	143 15	108 44	152 44	148 38	180 15
	24	121 14	173 20	147 59	151 38	110 59	164 00	149 46	179 43
Aug.	3	130 48	179 28	152 58	152 29R	113 12	175 1	150 58	179 11
	13	140 23	185 42	149 52	145 48	115 22	185 42	152 12	178 40
	23	150 00	192 2	141 56	140 17	117 26	195 59	153 27	178 8
Sep.	2	159 40	198 31	141 55D	146 48	119 27	205 40	154 44	177 36
	12	169 22	205 5	154 12	162 59	121 21	214 37	155 59	177 4
	22	179 7	211 47	172 16	181 28	123 5	222 24	157 13	176 32
Oct.	2	188 57	218 34	190 24	198 59	124 40	228 32	158 24	176 1
	12	198 49	225 28	207 13	215 10	126 3	232 13	159 30	175 39
	22	208 44	232 30	222 52	230 17	127 12	232 27R	160 32	174 57
Nov.	1	218 43	239 37	237 31	244 19	128 6	228 50	161 28	174 25
	11	228 44	246 50	250 42	256 13	128 44	222 57	162 17	173 54
	21	238 50	254 8	260 17	261 35R	129 1	218 21	162 56	173 22
Dec.	1	248 57	261 34	258 56	252 35	129 00R	217 29D	163 27	172 50
	11	259 6	269 4	246 51	245 26D	128 39	220 26	163 47	172 18
	21	269 16	276 39	247 44	252 29	127 59	226 14	163 56	171 46
	31	279 28	284 19	258 28	—	127 3	233 58	63 54R	171 15

Ayanamsa: 22° 6' 17"

Longitude of the Moon

1978		Sun.	Tue.	Thur.	Sat.	Mon.	Wed.	Fri.
Jan.	1	179 1	204 55	233 5	262 58	293 38	323 36	351 46
	15	17 55	42 34	66 24	90 5	103 55	138 10	162 58
	29	188 27	214 55					
Feb.	1						228 37	257 7
	5	286 53	316 44	345 45	13 3	38 35	62 52	86 36
	19	110 21	134 35	159 34	185 20	211 54		
March	1						239 20	267 34
	5	296 26	325 24	353 43	20 46	46 20	70 46	94 34
	19	118 22	142 39	168 5	194 32	222 3	250 11	278 40
April	1				292 53	321 11	348 50	15 45
	9	41 43	66 29	90 34	114 17	138 17	163 9	189 23
	23	217 8	246 00	275 12	303 56			
May	1					331 48	358 44	24 48
	7	50 5	74 10	98 38	123 20	146 16	171 9	197 26
	21	225 29	255 7	285 10	314 29	342 22	8 53	
June	1			21 44	46 44	71 15	95 15	118 58
	11	142 40	176 54	192 15	219 23	248 30	278 27	309 24
	25	338 29	5 47	31 29				
July	1				56 12	80 18	104 2	127 48
	9	151 36	175 53	201 11	228 8	256 59	287 22	317 59
	23	347 56	15 1	40 47	65 24	89 19		
Aug.	1		101 9	124 51	148 44	172 59	197 58	224 5
	13	251 44	280 57	311 9	341 9	9 48	36 40	61 54
	27	86 4	109 49	133 31				
Sep.	1							145 32
	3	169 57	195 4	221 3	248 5	276 14	305 21	334 48
	17	3 44	31 26	57 2	82 17	106 11	129 52	153 54
Oct.	1	178 43	204 5	231 18	258 55	287 6	315 37	344 6
	15	12 12	39 24	65 23	90 9	114 5	137 45	161 49
	29	186 53	213 19					
Nov.	1						227 13	255 15
	5	283 55	312 24	340 25	7 53	34 44	60 46	85 52
	19	110 4	133 45	157 26	181 55	207 48	235 27	
Dec.	1							264 33
	3	294 9	323 13	351 13	18 7	44 12	69 33	94 14
	17	118 15	142 52	165 25	189 51	115 36	243 19	272 51
	31	303 14						

Ayanamsa: 22° 6′ 17″

Longitudes of Planets

1979		Sun	Mars	Merc.	Merc.	Jupit.	Venus	Saturn	Rahu
Jan.	5	284 34	288 10	265 4	272 13	126 29R	238 22	163 48R	170 59
	15	294 45	295 57	279 38	287 16	125 15	247 53	163 31	170 27
	25	304 56	303 45	295 7	303 13	123 56	258 13	163 3	169 55
Feb.	4	315 5	311 36	311 38	320 20	122 36	269 1	162 27	169 24
	14	325 11	319 28	329 21	338 35	121 23	280 11	161 45	168 52
	24	335 18	327 22	347 48	356 24	120 22	291 38	160 57	168 20
March	6	345 19	335 15	3 24	7 40	119 37	303 16	160 9	167 48
	16	355 18	343 8	8 26R	5 55	119 9	314 59	159 22	167 16
	26	5 14	350 59	1 38	357 46	119 00D	326 52	158 40	166 45
April	5	15 8	358 48	355 49	356 10D	119 11	338 48	158 3	166 19
	15	24 56	6 33	358 33	2 31	119 40	350 47	157 35	165 41
	25	34 41	14 16	7 46	14 4	120 26	2 48	157 15	165 9
May	5	44 24	21 55	21 15	29 17	121 28	14 53	157 5	164 44
	15	54 4	29 30	38 8	47 49	122 43	26 58	157 7D	164 6
	25	63 42	36 59	58 14	71 20	124 11	39 4	157 18	163 34
June	4	73 16	44 22	80 3	90 28	125 48	51 12	157 39	163 2
	14	82 50	51 40	100 2	108 36	127 35	63 20	158 10	162 31
	24	92 24	58 53	116 8	122 35	129 29	75 31	158 51	161 59
July	4	101 56	65 58	127 50	131 45	131 29	87 43	159 38	161 27
	14	111 28	72 58	134 1	134 21R	133 33	99 56	160 32	160 55
	24	121 00	79 51	132 57	129 33	135 55	112 12	161 32	160 23
Aug.	3	130 34	86 37	125 56	123 39	137 53	124 31	162 39	159 51
	13	140 9	93 16	123 28D	126 22	140 1	136 50	163 48	159 20
	23	149 46	99 49	132 4	140 00	142 15	149 14	164 59	158 48
Sep.	2	159 26	106 12	149 13	158 54	144 26	161 36	166 15	158 16
	12	169 9	112 28	168 29	177 42	146 34	174 1	167 30	157 44
	22	178 54	118 34	186 29	194 52	148 37	186 27	168 45	157 13
Oct.	2	188 42	124 31	202 51	210 30	150 36	198 55	169 59	156 41
	12	198 34	130 15	217 50	224 45	152 29	211 22	171 10	156 9
	22	208 29	135 47	231 15	237 8	154 13	223 50	172 17	155 37
Nov.	1	218 28	141 5	242 1	245 12	155 48	236 17	173 20	155 6
	11	228 29	146 6	245 34R	242 1	157 11	248 44	174 18	154 34
	21	238 25	150 44	235 29	230 27	158 20	261 11	175 9	154 2
Dec.	1	248 42	154 57	229 56D	233 13	159 14	273 36	177 00	153 30
	11	258 51	158 38	239 39	245 12	159 53	286 1	177 00R	152 59
	21	269 1	161 39	252 18	259 39	160 13	298 25	176 49	152 27
	31	279 13	163 54	267 12	—	160 13R	310 47	176 28	151 55

Ayanamsa: 22° 7' 7"

Longitude of the Moon

1979		Sun.	Tue.	Thurs.	Sat.	Mon.	Wed.	Fri.
Jan.	1					317 47	347 29	15 5
	7	41 17	66 28	90 57	114 56	133 38	162 14	186 8
	21	211 1	237 28	265 51	295 58	326 37	356 25	
Feb.	1			10 43	37 53	63 29	88 1	111 55
	11	135 33	159 13	183 11	207 43	233 20	260 25	289 12
	25	319 17	349 36					
March	1			18 56	46 31	72 21	96 51	120 37
	11	144 12	168 1	192 20	217 26	243 24	270 30	298 46
	25	328 2	357 43	26 48	55 30			
April	1	77 44	93 1	117 8	140 43	164 26	188 47	214 2
	15	240 18	267 25	295 14	323 35	352 17	20 56	48 55
	29	75 39						
May	1		100 56	125 5	148 51	173 28	197 3	222 52
	13	249 56	277 54	306 14	334 33	2 39	30 26	57 35
	27	83 48	108 54	132 58				
June	1							144 47
	3	168 23	192 32	217 56	244 54	273 17	302 21	331 17
	17	359 33	27 5	53 51	79 49	104 56	129 11	153 52
July	1	176 25	200 34	225 58	253 7	281 59	311 48	341 29
	15	10 9	37 35	63 53	89 12	113 46	137 43	161 17
	29	184 51	209 00					
Aug.	1						221 27	247 36
	5	275 35	305 13	335 37	5 30	33 59	60 51	86 20
	19	110 19	134 41	158 15	181 50	205 47	230 30	256 48
Sep.	1				270 6	298 39	323 38	359 7
	9	28 49	56 52	83 5	107 50	131 44	155 17	178 54
	23	202 54	227 30	253 00	279 39			
Oct.	1					307 43	337 6	7 13
	7	36 57	65 14	91 40	110 59	140 18	163 49	187 34
	21	211 59	237 10	263 10	290 2	317 46	346 27	
Nov.	1			1 5	30 28	59 16	86 38	112 18
	11	136 35	160 10	183 47	208 6	233 27	259 47	286 59
	25	314 38	342 42	11 4				
Dec.	1				39 32	67 33	94 30	120 2
	9	144 21	167 58	191 38	216 3	241 44	268 47	296 52
	23	325 21	353 45	21 51	49 30	76 35		

Ayanamsa : 22° 7' 7'

Longitudes of Planets

1980		Sun	Mars.	Merc.	Merc.	Jupit.	Venus	Saturn	Rahu
Jan.	5	284 14	164 39	274 54	282 45	160 5R	316 56	177 1	151 39
	15	294 30	165 21	290 46	300 40	159 37	329 13	176 57R	151 7
	25	304 41	164 48R	307 29	316 10	158 50	341 24	176 42	150 36
Feb.	4	314 50	162 56	325 00	333 45	157 50	353 27	176 17	150 4
	14	324 58	159 54	341 48	348 8	156 37	5 22	175 44	149 32
	24	335 2	156 4	351 22	350 30R	155 19	17 5	175 5	149 00
March	5	345 4	152 17	346 33	341 36	154 1	28 33	174 20	148 29
	15	355 3	148 55	338 13	337 28D	152 48	39 45	173 33	147 57
	25	5 00	146 45	338 50	342 22	151 46	50 28	172 46	147 25
April	4	14 52	145 53	347 10	353 1	150 59	60 40	172 00	146 53
	14	24 41	146 16D	359 45	7 14	150 28	70 9	171 22	146 22
	24	34 27	147 43	15 28	24 23	150 15	78 39	170 51	145 49
May	4	44 10	150 4	34 1	44 21	150 21D	85 42	170 28	145 18
	14	53 50	153 13	55 9	66 2	150 45	90 39	170 14	144 46
	24	63 28	156 57	76 25	85 51	151 24	92 35	170 12D	144 14
June	3	73 3	161 10	94 10	101 14	152 21	90 43R	170 19	143 42
	13	82 37	165 47	107 4	111 26	153 31	85 29	170 36	143 11
	23	92 10	170 47	114 13	115 9	154 53	79 33	171 4	142 39
July	3	101 42	176 1	114 12R	111 41	156 27	76 15	171 39	142 7
	13	111 14	181 33	108 30	105 57	158 10	76 51D	172 24	141 35
	23	120 46	187 12	105 15D	106 50	160 00	80 43	173 15	141 4
Aug.	2	130 20	193 13	110 56	117 24	161 56	86 56	174 12	140 32
	12	139 55	199 22	125 46	135 23	163 57	94 47	175 16	140 00
	22	149 32	205 40	145 27	155 21	166 2	103 46	176 22	139 28
Sep.	1	159 11	212 8	164 51	173 51	168 10	113 33	177 34	138 57
	11	168 53	218 44	182 22	190 25	170 21	123 58	178 46	138 25
	21	178 40	225 31	198 1	205 11	172 31	134 49	180 1	137 53
Oct.	1	188 28	232 25	211 53	218 2	174 40	146 2	181 15	137 21
	11	198 20	239 28	223 23	227 31	176 47	157 29	182 28	136 50
	21	208 15	246 38	229 49	229 10R	178 49	169 20	183 40	136 18
	31	218 13	253 54	224 49	218 27	180 48	181 16	184 49	135 46
Nov.	10	228 15	261 19	213 47	214 39D	182 40	193 23	185 52	135 14
	20	238 19	268 49	218 52	225 00	184 23	205 37	186 51	134 43
	30	248 27	275 39	232 3	239 30	185 58	217 56	187 43	134 11
Dec.	10	258 36	284 5	247 9	254 52	187 20	230 20	188 26	133 39
	20	268 47	291 50	262 38	270 28	188 29	242 43	189 2	133 7
	30	278 58	299 40	278 25	—	189 29	255 16	189 29	132 35

Ayanamsa: 22° 7' 57"

Longitude of the Moon

1980	Sun.	Tue.	Thur.	Sat.	Mon.	Wed.	Fri.
Jan. 1		89 49	115 30	140 9	164 00	187 33	211 36
13	236 29	262 22	281 11	320 25	349 50	18 9	46 27
27	73 16	99 7	124 6				
Feb. 1							136 20
3	160 18	183 55	207 35	231 54	257 27	284 44	313 44
17	343 51	13 54	42 51	70 15	96 10	121 00	145 7
March 1				157 1	180 35	204 19	228 20
9	253 10	279 16	307 4	336 39	7 11	36 54	66 6
23	92 56	118 5	142 11	165 50	189 27		
April 1		201 9	225 22	249 59	275 28	302 9	330 21
13	0 7	30 31	60 19	88 24	114 29	139 2	162 16
27	186 18	210 9					
May 1			234 35	259 39	285 31	312 16	340 10
11	9 14	39 2	68 27	96 30	122 41	147 19	171 6
25	194 42	218 44	243 33	269 15			
June 1	282 24	309 15	336 48	5 3	33 54	62 48	90 58
15	117 47	143 5	167 14	190 54	214 44	239 22	265 4
29	291 53						
July 1		319 33	347 42	16 6	44 27	72 29	99 46
13	126 59	151 1	175 8	198 49	222 41	247 22	273 20
27	300 43	329 14	358 10				
Aug. 1							12 44
3	41 20	69 9	86 4	122 1	147 3	170 50	195 5
17	218 42	242 55	268 8	294 54	323 20	353 00	22 53
31	51 59						
Sep. 1					66 1	93 4	118 51
7	143 41	167 55	191 44	215 22	239 14	263 43	289 28
21	316 55	346 15	16 44	44 3	75 58		
Oct. 1						103 00	128 29
5	152 55	176 49	200 30	224 13	248 11	272 44	298 17
19	325 25	254 39	24 53	55 32	84 54	112 14	137 42
Nov. 1				149 57	173 52	197 29	221 15
9	245 18	269 19	294 59	321 12	348 50	18 5	47 21
23	78 25	106 29	143 34	158 28			
Dec. 1					182 25	206 2	229 53
7	254 16	279 18	305 1	331 33	359 5	27 44	57 8
21	86 26	114 42	140 51	166 26	190 29	214 9	

Ayanamsa: 22° 7′ 57″

Longitudes of Planets

1981		Sun	Mars	Merc.	Merc.	Jupit.	Venus	Saturn	Rahu
Jan.	5	285 05	304 22	288 08	296 24	189 48	262 46	189 37	132 16
	15	295 16	312 45	304 47	313 12	190 15	275 17	189 46	131 44
	25	305 27	320 09	321 19	328 30	190 23R	287 48	189 44R	131 13
Feb.	4	315 35	328 04	333 30	334 48R	190 12	300 19	189 32	130 41
	14	325 43	335 58	331 51	326 26	189 42	312 49	189 09	130 09
	24	335 48	343 52	321 48	319 53D	188 56	325 19	188 38	129 37
March	6	345 50	351 43	320 45	323 43	187 55	337 48	187 59	129 06
	16	355 49	359 32	328 13	333 49	186 43	350 16	187 15	128 34
	26	5 44	7 17	340 16	347 26	185 27	2 43	186 29	128 02
April	5	15 37	14 59	355 14	3 39	184 10	15 08	185 42	127 30
	15	25 26	22 36	12 42	22 23	182 59	27 31	184 58	126 58
	25	35 11	30 09	32 40	43 22	181 58	39 53	184 18	126 27
May	5	44 54	37 31	54 03	64 07	181 11	52 13	183 45	125 55
	15	54 33	45 00	73 06	80 43	180 40	64 32	183 21	125 23
	25	64 11	52 17	86 52	91 26	180 27D	76 48	183 05	124 51
June	4	73 46	59 29	94 18	95 12	180 32	89 04	182 59	124 20
	14	83 20	66 36	94 18R	91 58	180 55	101 18	183 04	123 48
	24	92 52	73 37	89 08	86 58	181 34	113 29	183 18	123 16
July	4	102 24	80 32	86 23D	87 49	182 29	125 40	183 43	122 44
	14	111 57	87 23	91 23	97 00	183 38	137 48	184 16	122 12
	24	121 29	94 08	104 28	113 31	184 59	149 54	184 57	121 41
Aug.	3	131 03	100 48	123 33	133 56	186 31	161 57	185 46	121 09
	13	140 38	107 22	144 05	153 44	188 12	173 57	186 42	120 37
	23	150 15	113 52	162 49	171 20	190 02	185 52	187 43	120 05
Sep.	2	159 55	120 16	179 19	186 46	191 58	197 43	188 49	119 34
	12	169 38	126 35	193 40	199 58	193 59	209 28	189 58	119 02
	22	179 23	132 48	205 31	210 01	196 05	221 07	191 10	118 30
Oct.	2	189 12	138 55	213 01	213 46R	198 13	232 37	192 23	117 58
	12	199 04	144 56	211 25	206 06	200 23	243 56	193 37	117 26
	22	209 00	150 50	200 29	198 17	202 33	255 01	194 50	116 55
Nov.	1	218 59	156 35	200 30D	205 52	204 43	265 47	196 01	116 23
	11	229 01	162 12	212 51	220 29	206 50	276 05	197 09	115 51
	21	239 05	167 38	228 22	236 16	208 53	285 45	198 13	115 19
Dec.	1	249 13	172 52	244 09	252 00	210 51	294 27	199 12	114 48
	11	259 22	177 51	259 52	267 45	212 43	301 44	200 04	114 16
	21	269 32	182 32	275 41	283 41	214 27	306 52	200 49	113 44
	31	279 42	186 51	291 44	—	216 00	308 53	201 25	113 12

Ayanamsa : 22° 8' 47''

Longitude of the Moon

1981	Sun.	Tues.	Thurs.	Sat.	Mon.	Wed.	Fri.
Jan. 1			221 05	250 22	270 00	301 33	328 28
11	356 05	24 14	52 41	81 06	108 59	135 52	161 33
25	186 09	210 05	233 54	258 14			
Feb. 1	270 45	296 44	323 59	352 14	20 55	49 28	77 30
15	104 50	131 23	157 04	181 54	206 03	234 50	253 47
March 1	278 31	304 35	332 17	1 21	30 58	60 08	88 11
15	115 01	140 51	165 54	190 21	214 20	238 05	261 59
29	286 36	312 32					
April 1						326 10	354 50
5	240 53	55 07	84 19	111 52	137 55	162 53	187 12
19	211 09	234 55	258 44	282 56	308 02	334 39	
May 1							3 07
3	33 12	63 45	93 22	121 14	147 21	172 11	196 17
17	32 04	243 51	267 49	292 14	317 28	343 59	12 08
31	41 48						
June 1					56 57	87 05	116 01
7	143 11	168 43	193 07	216 57	240 44	264 46	289 17
21	314 30	340 38	7 57	36 30	65 57		
July 1						95 30	124 10
5	151 21	176 60	201 28	225 20	249 10	273 25	298 25
19	324 17	351 03	18 41	47 01	75 47	104 28	132 29
Aug. 1				146 05	172 20	197 20	221 28
9	245 16	269 20	294 12	320 12	347 21	15 22	43 48
23	72 12	100 17	127 50	154 37	180 28		
Sep. 1		193 00	217 26	241 16	265 05	289 32	315 11
13	342 22	10 52	40 01	68 57	97 07	124 22	150 47
27	176 27	201 23					
Oct. 1			225 36	249 21	273 05	297 25	323 04
15	350 29	19 36	49 34	79 12	107 37	134 41	160 36
29	185 41	210 09	234 08	257 48			
Nov. 1	269 37	293 30	318 17	344 36	12 52	42 48	73 18
15	103 01	131 07	157 34	182 46	207 10	231 05	254 46
29	278 28						
Dec. 1		302 28	327 14	353 21	21 14	50 50	81 18
15	111 20	139 54	166 40	191 54	216 08	239 54	263 38
29	287 27	311 48	336 54				

Ayanamsa : 22° 8' 47''

Longitudes of Planets

1982		Sun	Mars	Merc.	Merc.	Jupit.	Venus	Saturn	Rahu
Jan.	5	284 50	188 51	299 41	307 16	216 42	308 26R	201 40	112 56
	15	295 01	192 27	313 46	317 56	217 58	304 33	202 01	112 25
	25	305 12	195 27	318 08R	313 56	218 58	298 35	202 13	111 53
Feb.	4	315 21	197 39	307 57	303 51	219 43	294 12	202 13R	111 21
	14	325 28	198 56	303 01D	304 56	220 10	293 37D	202 04	110 49
	24	335 33	199 05R	308 46	313 54	220 19	296 46	201 44	110 18
March	6	345 35	197 59	319 57	326 42	220 09R	302 37	201 15	109 46
	16	355 34	195 37	334 02	341 55	219 41	310 18	200 38	109 14
	26	5 30	192 14	350 21	359 19	218 56	319 13	199 56	108 42
April	5	15 22	188 24	8 51	18 56	217 56	328 58	199 11	108 10
	15	25 11	184 49	29 24	39 52	216 47	339 18	198 25	107 39
	25	34 57	182 06	49 43	58 21	215 31	350 03	197 40	107 07
May	5	44 40	180 38	65 24	70 37	214 15	1 06	196 60	106 35
	15	54 19	180 28D	73 54	75 09R	213 04	12 22	196 25	106 03
	25	63 57	181 30	74 26	72 15	212 02	23 48	195 58	105 32
June	4	73 32	183 36	69 30	67 20	211 14	35 22	195 39	105 00
	14	83 06	186 34	66 38D	67 47	210 42	47 02	195 30	104 28
	24	92 39	190 15	70 49	75 37	210 27	58 49	195 31D	103 56
July	4	102 11	194 31	82 04	90 03	210 30D	70 40	195 42	103 24
	14	111 43	199 17	99 23	109 40	210 51	82 35	196 03	102 53
	24	121 16	204 28	119 47	130 43	211 29	94 36	196 33	102 21
Aug.	3	130 49	210 00	140 36	149 51	212 22	106 41	197 12	101 49
	13	140 24	215 51	158 27	166 25	213 30	118 50	197 58	101 17
	23	150 02	221 58	173 46	180 27	214 51	126 03	198 51	100 46
Sep.	2	159 41	228 19	186 24	191 26	216 23	143 21	199 50	100 14
	12	169 23	234 54	195 14	197 18	218 05	155 42	200 53	99 42
	22	179 9	241 40	196 59	193 45	219 55	168 06	202 01	99 10
Oct.	2	188 58	248 38	188 23	183 40	221 52	180 33	203 11	98 39
	12	198 50	255 45	182 35D	185 43	223 55	193 02	204 24	98 07
	22	208 45	263 01	191 47	199 20	226 02	205 33	205 37	97 35
Nov.	1	218 44	270 24	207 27	215 41	228 13	218 06	206 49	97 03
	11	228 46	277 55	223 51	231 54	230 25	230 38	208 00	96 31
	21	238 51	285 31	239 51	247 42	232 37	243 12	209 08	96 00
Dec.	1	248 58	293 13	255 30	263 17	234 49	255 45	210 13	95 28
	11	259 07	300 58	271 02	278 44	236 58	268 19	211 12	94 56
	21	269 18	308 46	286 14	293 14	239 04	280 52	212 06	94 24
	31	279 29	316 37	299 01	—	241 05	293 25	212 52	93 53

Ayanamsa : 22° 9' 38"

Longitude of the Moon

1982		Sun.	Tues.	Thurs	Sat.	Mon.	Wed.	Fri.
Jan.	1							349 50
	3	16 39	44 54	74 22	104 19	133 40	161 35	187 48
	17	212 36	236 32	260 11	284 04	308 34	333 51	0 02
	31	27 07						
Feb.	1					40 59	69 21	98 17
	7	127 17	155 37	182 40	208 16	232 38	256 23	280 09
	21	304 32	329 57	356 28	23 54			
March	1					51 53	80 05	108 20
	7	136 25	163 58	190 36	216 03	240 26	264 11	287 58
	21	312 28	338 14	5 27	33 47	62 32	91 04	
April	1			105 07	132 48	159 52	186 14	211 46
	11	236 23	260 18	283 56	307 58	333 05	359 49	28 18
	25	57 38	87 06	115 46				
May	1				143 22	169 56	195 38	220 35
	9	244 50	268 36	292 13	316 13	341 17	7 59	36 30
	23	66 20	96 25	125 40	153 30	179 56		
June	1		192 42	217 32	241 43	265 28	289 04	312 54
	13	337 25	3 09	30 34	59 40	89 51	119 59	148 60
	27	176 22	202 09					
July	1			226 45	250 40	278 14	297 59	322 04
	11	346 50	12 39	39 50	68 30	98 17	128 19	157 30
	25	185 07	211 01	235 34	259 22			
Aug.	1	271 10	294 53	319 02	343 53	9 34	36 13	63 55
	15	92 38	122 02	151 22	179 44	206 31	231 44	255 50
	29	279 29	303 19					
Sep.	1						315 28	340 27
	5	6 22	33 09	60 36	88 39	117 09	145 50	174 08
	19	201 24	227 16	251 51	275 38	299 20	323 38	
Oct.	1							349 01
	3	15 39	58 15	71 22	99 36	127 45	155 41	183 09
	17	209 46	235 17	259 43	283 28	307 09	331 28	357 03
	31	24 10						
Nov.	1					38 14	67 01	96 01
	7	124 35	152 27	179 32	205 49	231 14	255 48	279 41
	21	303 16	327 08	351 56	18 15	46 18		
Dec.	1						75 42	105 32
	5	134 49	162 56	189 46	215 27	240 15	264 23	288 06
	19	311 41	335 34	0 15	26 19	54 08	83 36	113 56

Ayanamsa : 22° 9′ 38″

Longitudes of Planets

1983		Sun	Mars	Merc.	Merc.	Jupit.	Venus	Sat.	Rahu
Jan.	5	284 35	320 32	302 18	301 26R	242 03	299 42	213 12	93 37
	15	294 46	328 24	296 15R	290 06	243 53	312 13	213 45	93 05
	25	304 57	336 15	286 47	287 01D	245 34	324 44	214 09	92 33
Feb.	4	315 06	344 04	289 54D	294 28	247 04	337 12	214 22	91 58
	14	325 13	351 52	300 08	306 32	248 21	349 37	214 26R	91 30
	24	335 18	359 37	313 31	320 59	249 25	1 59	214 18	90 58
March	6	345 21	7 18	328 54	337 16	250 12	14 16	214 01	90 26
	16	355 20	14 55	346 07	355 28	250 43	26 28	213 34	89 54
	26	5 16	22 28	5 18	15 29	250 55	38 34	213 00	89 22
April	5	15 08	29 56	25 39	35 12	250 48R	50 33	212 20	88 51
	15	24 57	37 20	43 24	49 42	250 23	62 23	211 36	88 19
	25	34 43	44 38	53 46	55 28	249 41	74 03	210 50	87 47
May	5	44 26	51 52	54 56R	52 40R	248 44	85 32	210 05	87 15
	15	54 06	59 00	49 43	47 20	247 36	96 45	209 24	86 44
	25	63 43	66 04	46 25	47 21D	246 22	107 41	208 47	86 12
June	4	73 18	73 02	50 04D	54 25	245 06	118 12	208 18	85 40
	14	82 52	79 56	60 13	67 21	243 53	128 13	207 57	85 08
	24	92 25	86 46	75 44	85 17	242 50	137 31	207 45	84 37
July	4	101 57	93 31	95 43	106 32	241 59	145 50	207 43D	84 05
	14	111 29	100 12	117 10	127 15	241 24	152 44	207 51	83 33
	24	121 02	106 49	136 38	145 16	241 06	157 35	208 09	83 01
Aug.	3	130 45	113 22	153 11	160 23	241 06D	159 29	208 36	82 29
	13	140 11	119 52	166 48	172 19	241 25	157 39R	209 12	81 58
	23	149 48	126 19	176 44	179 42	242 01	152 28	209 55	81 26
Sep.	2	159 27	132 42	180 44R	179 19R	242 53	146 36	210 46	80 54
	12	169 09	139 02	175 26	170 23	244 01	143 24	211 43	80 22
	22	178 55	145 19	166 51	166 58D	245 22	144 04D	212 44	79 51
Oct.	2	188 43	151 33	170 58D	177 41	246 55	148 05	213 51	79 19
	12	198 35	157 44	185 48	194 23	248 38	154 32	215 00	78 47
	22	208 31	163 51	202 59	211 25	250 31	162 40	216 11	78 15
Nov.	1	218 29	169 54	219 38	227 41	252 30	171 59	217 23	77 43
	11	228 31	175 54	235 33	243 17	254 36	182 08	218 35	77 12
	21	238 36	181 48	250 54	258 25	256 47	192 52	219 46	76 40
Dec.	1	248 43	187 38	265 46	272 48	259 00	204 04	220 55	76 08
	11	258 52	193 21	279 11	284 13	261 16	215 36	221 60	75 36
	21	269 03	198 56	286 36	284 43	263 32	227 21	222 60	75 05
	31	279 14	204 24	278 48R	—	265 48	239 18	223 54	74 33

Ayanamsa : 22° 10' 28"

Longitude of the Moon

1983		Sun.	Tues.	Thurs.	Sat.	Mon.	Wed.	Fri.
Jan.	1				129 03	158 29	181 18	212 27
	9	237 19	256 22	285 02	308 39	332 29	356 51	22 06
	23	48 41	76 54	106 36	136 00	166 52		
Feb.	1		181 14	208 32	234 04	258 20	281 59	305 35
	13	392 29	353 55	19 02	45 01	72 07	100 32	130 06
	27	160 02						
March	1		189 12	216 43	242 25	266 45	290 25	314 05
	13	338 15	3 10	28 53	54 21	82 34	105 38	139 29
	27	168 38	197 15	224 34				
April	1							237 38
	3	262 38	286 38	310 18	334 19	359 10	25 04	51 54
	17	79 25	107 24	135 40	164 03	192 09	214 27	245 34
May	1	270 27	294 28	318 11	342 16	7 18	33 37	61 09
	15	89 31	118 11	146 40	169 40	201 59	228 26	253 56
	29	278 31	242 27					
June	1						314 19	338 08
	5	2 38	28 20	55 34	84 12	113 37	142 57	171 29
	19	198 53	225 09	250 26	274 57	298 56	322 39	
July	1							346 29
	3	10 56	36 31	63 43	92 35	122 34	152 36	181 36
	17	209 02	229 58	259 46	283 53	307 40	331 23	355 18
	31	19 46						
Aug.	1					32 21	58 31	86 21
	7	115 51	145 17	176 21	204 56	231 39	256 43	280 58
	21	304 43	328 26	352 22	16 45	41 47	67 52	
Sep.	1			81 26	109 45	139 30	169 49	199 22
	11	232 12	253 11	277 45	301 35	325 17	349 16	13 46
	25	38 52	64 42	91 30				
Oct.	1				119 29	148 37	178 18	207 30
	9	235 17	261 20	286 0	309 52	333 38	357 49	22 42
	23	48 25	74 55	102 08	130 06	158 39		
Nov.	1		173 04	201 46	229 42	256 21	281 38	305 52
	13	329 39	353 37	18 18	44 03	70 55	98 39	126 53
	27	155 17	183 31					
Dec.	1			211 18	238 20	264 24	289 28	313 41
	11	337 28	1 23	26 03	51 58	79 22	108 01	137 13
	25	166 10	194 19	221 27	247 39			

Ayanamsa : 22° 10' 28"

15

Longitudes of Planets

1984		Sun	Mars	Merc.	Merc.	Jupit.	Venus	Sat.	Rahu
Jan.	5	284 20	207 03	272 50	270 25R	266 55	245 20	224 18	74 17
	15	294 31	212 44	271 41D	275 25D	269 07	257 27	225 02	73 45
	25	304 42	217 10	280 38	286 45	271 14	269 39	225 37	73 13
Feb.	4	314 51	222 19	293 28	300 38	273 16	281 55	226 02	72 42
	14	324 59	226 07	308 11	316 06	275 11	294 13	226 17	72 10
	24	335 04	229 58	324 23	334 53	276 57	306 32	226 23R	71 38
March	6	346 07	233 34	344 06	353 44	278 41	320 06	226 17	71 03
	16	356 05	236 06	3 36	13 22	280 03	332 26	226 00	70 31
	26	6 01	237 45	22 18	30 45	281 10	344 47	225 35	70 00
April	5	15 53	238 20R	34 27	36 35	282 03	357 07	225 02	69 28
	15	25 42	237 43	36 01R	33 23R	282 38	9 26	224 23	68 56
	25	35 27	235 51	29 59	27 19	282 56R	21 45	223 40	68 24
May	5	45 10	232 53	26 18	27 15D	282 54	34 04	222 55	67 53
	15	54 50	229 21	29 59D	34 17	282 34	46 21	222 10	67 21
	25	64 27	225 55	39 53	46 39	281 56	58 38	221 28	66 49
June	4	74 02	223 17	54 31	63 25	281 03	70 56	220 51	66 17
	14	83 36	221 53	73 18	83 56	279 57	83 12	220 21	65 45
	24	93 08	221 51D	94 52	105 34	278 44	95 30	219 59	65 14
July	4	102 40	223 06	115 39	129 56	277 27	107 47	219 45	64 42
	14	112 12	225 30	133 24	141 02	276 13	120 05	219 42D	64 10
	24	121 45	228 51	147 48	153 38	275 06	132 23	219 48	63 38
Aug.	3	131 19	232 59	158 21	161 42	274 12	144 41	220 04	63 07
	13	140 54	237 46	163 18R	162 45R	273 33	156 60	220 29	62 35
	23	150 31	243 04	159 55	155 32	273 11	169 18	221 03	62 03
Sep.	2	160 11	248 50	151 32	150 03D	273 08D	181 35	221 45	61 31
	12	169 53	254 58	152 09D	157 34	273 25	193 52	222 34	60 60
	22	179 39	261 24	165 14	174 00	273 59	206 07	223 29	60 28
Oct.	2	189 28	268 07	183 02	191 58	274 51	218 22	224 30	59 56
	12	199 20	275 03	200 37	208 59	275 59	230 34	225 35	59 24
	22	209 16	282 09	217 04	224 55	277 20	242 45	226 44	58 52
Nov.	1	219 15	289 26	232 33	239 60	278 55	249 54	227 54	58 21
	11	229 17	296 49	247 13	254 08	280 41	266 60	229 06	57 49
	21	239 22	304 19	260 34	266 06	282 36	279 01	230 17	57 17
Dec.	1	249 29	311 52	269 53	270 33R	284 39	290 58	231 28	56 45
	11	259 38	319 29	266 50R	260 18	286 48	302 46	232 36	56 14
	21	269 49	327 07	255 23	254 46D	289 03	314 24	233 41	55 42
	31	280 00	334 46	257 34D	—	291 21	325 47	234 41	55 10

Ayanamsa : 22° 11' 18"

Longitude of the Moon

1984		Sun.	Tues.	Thurs.	Sat.	Mon.	Wed.	Fri.
Jan.	1	260 26	285 26	309 47	333 39	357 23	21 30	46 34
	15	73 12	101 37	131 23	161 28	190 40	218 24	244 40
	29	269 51	294 20					
Feb.	1						306 24	330 18
	5	354 02	17 52	42 17	67 50	95 07	124 18	154 46
	19	185 10	214 12	241 23	266 56	291 26	315 23	
March	1			327 16	351 01	14 52	39 04	63 59
	11	90 09	118 02	147 38	178 09	208 13	236 41	263 15
	25	288 16	312 22	336 06	359 53			
April	1	11 52	36 10	61 01	86 44	113 39	142 00	171 34
	15	201 30	230 41	258 18	284 14	308 50	332 44	356 30
	29	20 34						
May	1		45 15	70 42	96 59	124 13	152 22	181 16
	13	210 21	238 53	266 14	292 09	316 52	340 50	4 39
	27	28 52	53 56	80 01				
June	1							93 27
	3	120 59	149 08	177 35	205 58	233 58	261 12	287 25
	17	312 34	336 50	0 39	24 37	49 21	75 18	102 38
July	1	131 04	159 57	188 36	216 37	243 51	270 18	295 56
	15	320 46	344 54	8 40	32 35	57 18	83 24	111 12
	29	140 25	170 07					
Aug	1						184 48	213 25
	5	240 48	267 04	292 28	317 12	341 23	5 11	28 54
	19	53 03	78 18	105 15	134 04	164 12	194 23	223 27
Sep.	1				237 22	264 04	289 32	314 09
	9	338 16	2 04	25 22	49 40	74 16	100 09	127 51
	23	157 21	187 50	217 57	246 37			
Oct.	1					273 30	298 54	323 19
	7	347 12	10 56	34 44	58 52	83 40	109 34	136 58
	21	165 58	196 02	226 04	254 57	282 07	307 40	
Nov.	1			319 58	344 00	7 43	31 33	55 49
	11	80 44	106 28	133 14	161 08	190 03	219 30	248 38
	25	276 38	303 07	328 09				
Dec.	1				352 13	15 56	39 52	64 30
	9	90 03	116 33	143 53	171 50	200 12	228 44	257 01
	23	284 32	310 53	335 57	0 04	23 46		

Ayanamsa : 22° 11' 18"

Longitudes of Planets

1985		Sun	Mars	Merc.	Merc.	Jupit.	Venus	Sat.	Rahu
Jan.	5	285 06	338 35	262 24	268 22	292 30	331 22	235 09	54 54
	15	295 17	346 12	275 01	282 05	294 51	342 11	236 00	54 22
	25	305 28	353 47	289 28	297 08	297 11	352 28	236 43	53 51
Feb.	4	315 37	1 20	305 06	313 22	299 30	1 57	237 19	53 19
	14	325 45	8 50	321 59	330 57	301 47	10 18	237 45	52 47
	24	335 50	16 16	340 15	349 45	304 00	16 60	238 01	52 15
March	6	345 52	23 38	359 05	7 33	306 07	21 16	238 07	51 44
	16	355 21	30 56	14 09	17 56	308 07	22 08R	238 03R	51 12
	26	5 47	38 10	18 27R	16 05R	309 59	19 01	237 49	50 40
April	5	15 39	45 19	12 12	8 40	311 41	13 05	237 26	50 08
	15	25 28	52 23	6 51	7 11D	313 12	7 49	236 55	49 36
	25	35 13	59 23	9 28D	13 22	314 29	6 00D	236 17	49 05
May	5	44 56	66 19	18 35	24 53	315 32	8 00	235 35	48 33
	15	54 35	73 10	32 09	40 20	316 18	12 58	234 50	48 01
	25	64 13	79 58	49 24	59 21	316 47	19 57	234 06	47 29
June	4	73 48	86 42	69 59	80 58	316 57	28 19	233 23·	46 58
	14	83 22	93 22	91 45	101 53	316 49R	37 38	232 45	46 26
	24	92 55	99 59	111 10	119 30	316 21	47 36	232 14	45 54
July	4	102 27	106 34	126 53	133 15	315 36	58 02	231 49	45 22
	14	111 59	113 05	138 30	142 27	314 36	68 51	231 34	44 51
	24	121 32	119 34	144 47	145 13R	313 26	79 57	231 28	44 19
Aug.	3	131 05	126 01	143 32R	140 08	312 09	91 17	231 31D	43 47
	13	140 40	132 26	136 13	133 35	310 52	102 48	231 45	43 15
	23	150 18	138 50	133 38D	136 53D	309 39	114 30	232 07	42 43
Sep.	2	159 57	145 12	143 01	151 12	308 37	126 22	232 39	42 12
	12	169 40	151 33	160 26	169 53	307 49	138 21	233 19	41 40
	22	179 25	157 53	179 09	188 05	307 18	149 58	234 06	41 08
Oct.	2	189 14	164 12	196 37	204 48	307 07	162 41	235 00	40 36
	12	196 06	170 30	212 40	220 14·	307 15D	175 00	235 59	40 05
	22	209 02	176 47	227 31	234 29	307 43	187 24	237 03	39 33
Nov.	1	219 00	183 03	241 01	246 55	308 29	199 51	238 11	39 01
	11	229 02	189 19	251 44	254 38	309 33	212 21	239 20	38 29
	21	239 07	195 33	254 19R	249 50R	310 52	224 53	240 32	37 58
Dec.	1	249 14	201 46	243 13	239 08	312 25	237 26	241 43	37 26
	11	259 23	207 58	239 31D	243 11D	314 10	250 01	242 53	36 54
	21	269 34	214 08	248 42	255 11	316 05	262 36	244 02	36 22
	31	279 45	220 16	262 10	—	318 09	275 11	245 06	35 50

Ayanamsa : 22° 12′ 09″

Longitude of the Moon

1985		Sun.	Tues.	Thurs.	Sat.	Mon.	Wed.	Fri.
Jan.	1		35 40	60 01	85 30	112 17	140 10	168 35
	13	196 59	225 03	252 41	279 47	306 07	331 30	355 56
	27	19 43	43 24	67 44				
Feb.	1							80 20
	3	105 16	134 49	163 57	193 15	221 53	249 34	276 20
	17	302 19	327 34	352 05	15 59	39 35	63 26	
March	1							88 14
	3	114 37	142 53	172 35	202 39	231 57	259 53	286 28
	17	311 58	336 41	0 48	24 32	48 07	72 00	96 44
	31	122 56						
April	1					136 44	165 41	195 54
	7	226 12	255 24	282 58	308 58	333 46	357 50	21 32
	21	45 09	68 59	93 24	118 51	145 45		
May	1						174 17	204 08
	5	234 23	263 52	291 47	317 58	342 45	6 41	30 17
	19	54 00	78 10	103 01	128 47	155 40	183 48	213 01
June	1				227 51	257 29	286 12	313 23
	5	338 56	3 15	26 57	50 38	74 50	99 50	125 45
	23	152 32	180 08	208 26	237 16			
July	1					266 10	294 26	321 27
	7	346 59	11 20	35 02	58 49	83 16	108 48	135 28
	21	163 00	191 02	219 15	247 31	275 35	303 07	
Aug.	1			316 31	342 28	7 13	31 07	54 47
	11	78 55	104 08	130 47	158 42	187 20	216 01	244 18
	21	272 01	299 07	325 26	350 50			
Sep.	1	3 11	27 16	50 55	74 42	99 19	125 21	153 04
	15	182 07	211 38	240 45	268 54	295 59	322 05	347 17
	29	11 45						
Oct.	1		35 37	59 12	82 58	107 31	133 27	161 07
	13	190 25	220 33	250 21	278 58	306 04	331 49	356 32
	27	20 35	44 16	67 53				
Nov.	1							79 46
	3	103 56	129 01	155 32	183 44	213 28	243 51	273 40
	17	301 58	328 30	353 31	17 35	41 14	64 52	88 48
Dec.	1	113 16	138 31	164 52	192 36	221 45	251 48	281 42
	15	310 19	337 05	2 11	26 12	49 47	73 31	97 48
	29	122 47	148 32					

Ayanamsa : 22° 12' 09"

Longitudes of Planets

1986		Sun	Mars	Merc.	Merc.	Jupit.	Venus	Saturn	Rahu
Jan.	5	285 00	223 19	269 28	276 59	319 14	281 28	245 37	35 35
	15	295 03	229 23	284 43	292 38	321 27	294 03	246 35	35 03
	25	305 13	235 23	300 48	309 13	323 46	306 37	247 27	34 31
Feb.	4	315 22	241 19	317 55	326 53	326 08	319 11	248 12	33 59
	14	325 30	247 10	335 58	344 51	328 31	331 43	248 48	33 27
	24	335 35	252 54	352 46	358 37	330 55	344 14	249 16	32 56
March	6	345 37	258 30	1 13R	0 07	333 19	356 42	249 34	32 24
	16	355 36	263 56	356 12	351 41	335 40	9 09	249 41	31 52
	26	5 32	269 09	348 39	348 00D	337 58	21 33	249 39R	31 20
April	5	15 24	274 07	349 35	352 58	340 11	33 54	249 27	30 49
	15	25 13	278 46	357 45	3 37	342 19	46 11	249 06	30 17
	25	34 59	282 59	10 25	18 01	344 19	58 25	248 37	29 45
May	5	44 42	286 40	26 24	35 33	346 10	70 35	248 00	29 13
	15	54 22	289 41	45 29	56 04	347 51	82 41	247 19	28 42
	25	63 59	291 51	67 00	77 47	349 20	94 43	246 35	28 10
June	4	73 34	292 29	87 55	97 05	350 35	106 39	245 51	27 38
	14	83 08	292 55R	105 12	112 10	351 36	118 29	245 08	27 06
	24	92 41	291 37	117 57	122 24	352 19	130 12	244 29	26 34
July	4	102 13	289 18	125 18	126 24	352 44	141 47	243 56	26 03
	14	111 45	286 26	125 34R	123 00	352 51R	153 12	243 30	25 31
	24	121 18	283 46	119 35	116 44	352 38	164 24	243 12	24 59
Aug.	3	130 51	281 57	115 45D	117 22	352 05	175 20	243 04	24 27
	13	140 27	281 25D	121 42	128 31	351 16	185 55	243 05D	23 56
	23	150 04	282 16	137 09	146 46	350 12	196 04	243 16	23 24
Sep.	2	159 43	284 23	156 37	166 13	348 57	205 36	243 37	22 52
	12	169 26	287 36	175 24	184 08	347 38	214 16	244 07	22 20
	22	179 11	291 43	192 25	200 18	346 20	221 42	244 44	21 49
Oct.	2	189 00	296 32	207 48	214 55	345 09	227 17	245 30	21 17
	12	198 52	301 55	221 37	227 45	344 10	230 11	246 22	20 45
	22	208 47	307 44	233 05	237 09	343 27	229 27R	247 20	20 13
Nov.	1	218 46	313 53	239 06	237 47R	343 03	225 02	248 23	19 41
	11	228 48	320 18	232 42	226 22	342 59D	219 08	249 30	19 10
	21	238 52	326 54	223 10	224 30D	343 15	215 20	250 39	18 38
Dec.	1	248 59	333 39	228 59	235 09	343 52	215 28D	251 50	18 06
	11	259 09	340 31	242 07	249 27	344 47	219 11	253 01	17 34
	21	269 19	347 26	256 59	264 38	345 59	225 31	254 11	17 03
	31	279 31	354 24	272 24	—	347 26	233 39	255 20	16 31

Ayanamsa : 22° 12′ 59″

Longitude of the Moon

1986		Sun.	Tues.	Thurs.	Sat.	Mon.	Wed.	Fri.
Jan.	1						161 42	188 42
	5	216 41	245 38	275 04	304 06	331 49	357 49	22 23
	19	46 08	69 47	93 59	119 04	145 07	171 58	199 24
Feb.	1				213 18	241 28	269 58	298 27
	9	326 15	352 49	17 59	42 06	65 46	89 41	114 29
	23	140 31	167 45	195 46				
March	1			.	224 07	252 26	280 30	308 08
	9	335 03	0 59	25 52	48 55	73 36	97 31	122 20
	23	148 32	176 15	205 04	234 18	263 12		
April	1		277 21	304 57	331 34	357 14	22 03	46 12
	13	69 55	93 38	117 53	143 15	170 11	198 47	228 33
	27	258 29	287 35					
May	1			315 17	341 33	6 40	30 59	54 50
	11	78 30	102 16	126 32	151 47	178 30	206 57	236 52
	25	267 17	296 56	324 56	351 10			
June	1	3 44	28 06	51 53	75 32	99 19	123 28	148 17
	15	174 08	201 25	230 19	260 28	290 45	319 55	347 13
	29	12 43						
July	1		37 00	60 42	84 23	108 22	132 53	158 03
	13	184 04	211 12	239 40	269 16	299 10	328 11	355 32
	27	21 08	45 28	69 11				
Aug.	1							81 02
	3	105 01	129 37	154 58	181 04	207 58	235 43	264 20
	17	293 28	322 21	350 11	16 31	41 25	65 26	89 10
	31	113 17						
Sep.	1					125 38	151 03	177 27
	7	204 42	232 34	260 50	289 16	317 31	345 07	11 40
	21	37 00	61 21	85 10	109 03	133 36		
Oct.	1						159 18	186 18
	5	214 24	243 07	271 50	300 07	327 40	354 23	20 12
	19	45 09	69 21	93 08	116 59	141 27	167 08	194 24
Nov.	1				208 38	237 57	267 37	296 42
	9	324 35	351 12	16 46	41 33	65 46	89 36	113 20
	23	137 21	162 11	188 26	216 30			
Dec.	1					246 13	276 38	306 25
	7	334 37	1 07	26 17	50 38	74 33	98 19	122 07
	21	146 12	170 57	196 56	224 39	254 11	284 46	

Ayanamsa : 22° 12' 59''

Longitudes of Planets

1987		Sun	Mars	Merc.	Merc.	Jupit.	Venus	Sat.	Rahu
Jan.	5	284 36	357 54	280 18	288 25	348 14	238 11	255 53	16 15
	15	294 48	4 53	296 35	305 01	350 01	247 56	256 56	15 43
	25	304 58	11 52	313 37	322 16	351 57	258 23	257 54	15 11
Feb.	4	315 08	18 50	330 08	337 58	354 02	269 18	258 47	14 40
	14	325 15	25 47	343 01	344 25R	356 14	280 33	259 33	14 08
	24	335 20	32 43	341 46	336 43	358 32	292 03	260 10	13 36
March	6	345 23	39 33	332 11	330 03	0 53	303 43	260 39	13 04
	16	355 22	46 22	330 35D	333 16	3 17	315 30	260 59	12 33
	26	5 18	53 09	337 31	342 57	5 42	327 24	261 08	12 01
April	5	15 10	59 52	349 18	356 25	8 07	339 22	261 08R	11 29
	15	24 59	66 33	4 14	12 43	10 31	351 22	260 58	10 57
	25	34 45	73 11	21 53	31 44	12 52	3 25	260 38	10 25
May	5	44 28	79 47	42 11	53 01	15 10	15 29	260 11	9 54
	15	54 08	86 20	63 43	73 45	17 23	27 35	259 36	9 22
	25	63 46	92 51	82 43	89 57	19 29	39 42	258 56	8 50
June	4	73 21	99 20	96 50	101 47	21 28	51 51	258 13	8 18
	14	82 55	105 46	105 08	106 42R	23 18	64 00	257 28	7 47
	24	92 27	112 12	106 23	104 24	24 58	76 11	256 45	7 15
July	4	102 00	118 36	101 28	98 46	26 25	88 23	256 05	6 43
	14	111 32	124 59	97 26D	98 12	27 38	100 37	255 31	6 11
	24	121 04	131 21	101 17	106 38	28 36	112 54	255 03	5 40
Aug.	3	130 38	137 43	114 02	123 03	29 17	125 12	254 44	5 08
	13	140 13	144 04	133 01	143 13	29 39	137 32	254 33	4 36
	23	149 50	150 26	153 08	162 35	29 42R	149 54	254 32D	4 04
Sep.	2	159 29	156 48	171 29	179 53	29 25	162 18	254 41	3 32
	12	169 12	163 10	187 46	195 12	28 48	174 43	255 00	3 01
	22	178 57	169 33	202 08	208 32	27 54	187 09	255 28	2 29
Oct.	2	188 46	175 57	214 14	218 57	26 47	199 35	256 04	1 57
	12	198 37	182 22	222 11	223 09R	25 29	212 02	256 48	1 25
	22	208 33	188 49	220 52	215 24	24 08	224 29	257 39	0 54
Nov.	1	218 31	195 17	209 37	207 25D	22 50	236 56	258 36	0 22
	11	228 33	201 46	209 40	214 55	21 40	249 23	259 38	359 50
	21	238 38	208 17	221 41	229 07	20 44	261 50	260 44	359 18
Dec.	1	248 45	214 49	236 48	244 34	20 06	274 15	261 53	358 47
	11	258 54	221 23	252 22	255 11	19 47	286 40	263 03	358 15
	21	269 05	227 59	268 03	276 00	19 49D	299 03	264 14	357 43
	31	279 16	234 36	284 03	—	20 12	311 24	265 24	357 11

Ayanamsa : 22° 13' 49"

Longitude of the Moon

1987		Sun.	Tues.	Thurs	Sat.	Mon.	Wed.	Fri.
Jan.	1			300 01	329 34	357 15	23 05	47 39
	11	71 33	95 17	119 07	143 16	167 53	193 17	219 54
	25	248 04	277 43	307 59	337 34			
Feb.	1	351 46	18 45	44 03	68 16	92 00	115 49	140 03
	15	164 50	190 20	216 39	243 60	272 27	301 45	331 06
March	1	359 35	25 34	52 02	76 22	100 10	124 04	148 30
	15	173 47	199 59	227 03	254 50	283 09	311 43	340 07
	29	7 49	34 25					
April	1						47 16	72 07
	5	96 10	119 58	144 08	169 11	195 27	222 56	251 16
	19	279 55	308 22	336 17	3 30	29 54	55 25	
May	1							80 05
	3	109 06	127 52	151 60	177 05	203 38	231 45	261 00
	17	290 26	319 12	346 53	13 28	39 10	64 07	88 28
	31	112 22						
June	1					124 13	148 02	172 29
	7	198 12	225 41	254 54	285 04	314 55	343 29	10 29
	21	36 13	61 02	85 17	109 11	132 53		
July	1						156 42	181 06
	5	206 42	234 03	263 17	293 43	324 01	352 58	20 08
	19	45 46	70 21	94 21	118 06	141 50	165 48	190 20
Aug.	1				202 58	229 17	262 19	286 57
	9	317 22	347 13	15 33	42 05	67 09	91 19	115 04
	23	138 50	162 53'	187 27	212 48	239 14		
Sep.	1		252 57	281 25	310 56	340 43	9 44	37 15
	13	63 09	87 46	111 40	135 25	159 29	184 12	209 45
	27	236 11	263 32					
Oct.	1			291 44	320 32	349 28	17 52	45 10
	11	71 05	95 47	119 42	143 28	167 41	192 49	219 04
	25	246 22	274 22	302 40	330 58			
Nov.	1	345 02	12 05	40 02	66 16	91 25	115 38	139 22
	15	163 15	187 59	214 03	241 37	270 17	299 15	327 48
	29	355 38						
Dec.	1		22 42	49 04	74 42	99 31	123 37	147 17
	13	171 05	195 44	221 52	249 49	279 14	309 04	338 14
	27	6 11	32 54	58 39				

Avanamsa : 22° 13′ 49″

Longitudes of Planets

1988		Sun	Mars	Merc.	Merc.	Jupit.	Venus	Saturn	Rahu
Jan.	5	284 22	237 55	292 12	300 27	20 31	317 33	265 29	356 55
	15	294 33	244 34	308 39	316 28	21 23	329 48	267 06	356 24
	25	304 44	251 15	323 08	327 21	22 32	341 57	268 10	355 52
Feb.	4	314 53	257 57	327 34R	323 34	23 56	353 59	269 09	355 20
	14	325 00	264 40	317 50	313 46	25 34	5 52	270 02	354 48
	24	335 06	271 24	312 43D	314 57	27 23	17 32	270 49	354 17
March	6	346 08	278 49	318 51	324 04	29 33	30 05	271 31	353 42
	16	356 07	285 34	330 06	336 56	31 40	41 07	272 01	353 10
	26	6 03	292 19	344 23	352 25	33 53	51 43	272 21	352 38
April	5	15 55	299 03	1 02	10 16	36 11	61 44	272 31	352 06
	15	25 44	305 46	20 06	30 29	38 31	70 56	272 32R	351 34
	25	35 30	312 27	41 08	51 41	40 54	79 01	272 23	351 03
May	5	45 12	319 04	61 15	69 38	43 17	85 27	272 04	350 31
	15	54 52	325 36	76 30	81 43	45 40	89 31	271 37	349 59
	25	64 29	332 01	85 09	86 41R	48 01	90 16R	271 03	349 27
June	4	74 04	338 17	86 18	84 21	50 19	87 08	270 24	348 56
	14	83 38	344 19	81 36	79 13	52 34	81 16	269 41	348 24
	24	93 11	350 04	78 10D	78 59	54 43	75 56	268 57	347 52
July	4	102 43	355 26	81 48	86 34	56 45	73 55D	268 13	347 20
	14	112 15	0 18	93 09	101 23	58 40	75 42	267 33	346 49
	24	121 48	4 31	110 57	121 18	60 25	80 26	266 58	346 17
Aug.	3	131 21	7 55	131 45	141 53	61 60	87 16	266 29	345 45
	13	140 57	10 17	151 26	160 24	63 21	95 32	266 09	345 13
	23	150 34	11 23	168 45	176 32	64 29	104 48	265 58	344 42
Sep.	2	160 13	11 07R	183 45	190 21	65 20	114 48	265 56D	344 10
	12	169 56	9 30	196 16	201 16	65 53	125 21	266 04	343 38
	22	179 42	6 53	205 01	206 56R	66 07	136 20	266 21	343 06
Oct.	2	189 30	3 58	206 15	202 29	66 01R	147 38	266 48	342 34
	12	199 23	1 30	196 43	192 21	65 35	159 14	267 24	342 03
	22	209 18	0 05	192 08D	195 58	64 50	171 03	268 07	341 31
Nov.	1	219 17	359 60D	202 18	209 49	63 49	183 03	268 58	340 59
	11	229 19	1 10	217 45	225 47	62 36	195 12	269 55	340 27
	21	239 24	3 28	233 47	241 43	61 16	207 28	270 56	339 56
Dec.	1	249 31	6 40	249 35	257 26	59 54	219 48	272 02	339 24
	11	259 41	10 35	266 17	273 10	58 39	232 13	273 11	338 52
	21	269 51	15 03	281 04	288 56	57 34	244 41	274 21	338 20
	31	280 02	19 57	296 37	—	56 45	257 10'	275 32	337 48

Ayanamsa : 22° 14' 40''

Longitude of the Moon

1988		Sun.	Tues.	Thurs	Sat.	Mon.	Wed.	Fri.
Jan.	1							71 15
	13	95 57	120 05	148 48	167 26	191 29	216 39	243 32
	17	272 21	302 31	332 48	2 00	29 36	55 42	80 42
	31	104 59						
Feb.	1					116 57	140 41	164 20
	7	188 13	212 47	238 36	266 07	295 22	325 42	355 53
	21	24 48	51 57	77 32	101 58			
March	1		137 38	161 18	185 16	209 47	235 09	261 43
	13	289 42	318 59	348 55	18 30	46 47	73 23	98 27
	27	122 30	146 09	169 55				
April	1							186 59
	3	206 39	232 09	258 33	285 54	314 08	343 05	12 15
	17	40 51	68 15	94 07	118 41	142 29	166 10	190 23
May	1	215 32	241 45	268 55	296 43	324 53	353 09	21 34
	15	49 25	76 21	102 03	126 35	150 22	174 06	198 27
	29	223 58	250 51					
June	1						264 45	293 06
	5	321 40	350 00	17 54	45 16	71 57	97 43	122 31
	19	146 30	170 08	194 05	219 02	245 32	273 37	
July	1							302 45
	3	332 03	0 46	28 34	55 25	81 25	106 34	130 58
	17	154 46	178 20	202 16	227 11	253 41	281 57	311 35
	31	341 35						
Aug.	1					356 22	25 04	52 23
	7	78 26	103 29	127 47	151 34	175 09	198 52	223 13
	21	248 50	275 58	304 55	335 03	5 16	34 29	
Sep.	1			48 29	75 14	100 33	124 51	148 36
	11	172 11	195 55	220 06	245 06	271 18	299 01	328 15
	25	358 25	28 25	57 12				
Oct.	1				84 12	109 31	133 42	157 20
	9	180 51	204 57	229 34	254 56	281 15	308 41	337 18
	23	6 49	36 30	65 16	92 25	117 52		
Nov.	1		130 05	153 54	177 30	201 23	226 12	251 49
	13	278 14	305 22	333 12	1 40	30 34	59 15	86 57
	27	113 10	137 58					
Dec.	1			161 50	185 28	209 35	234 41	260 57
	11	288 12	316 02	344 07	12 17	40 24	68 49	95 10
	25	121 01	145 43	169 35	193 14			

Ayanamsa : 27° 14' 40''

RAMAN'S EPHEMERIS

Longitudes of Planets

1989		Sun	Mars	Merc.	Merc.	Jupit.	Venus	Sat.	Rahu
Jan.	5	285 08	22 31	303 40	309 14	56 28R	263 26	276 07	337 33
	15	295 20	27 53	311 50R	309 59	56 07	275 57	277 17	337 01
	25	305 30	33 27	304 22	298 44	56 08D	288 28	278 24	336 29
Feb.	4	315 39	39 11	296 06D	296 45	56 29	300 59	279 28	335 57
	14	325 47	45 03	299 48	304 25	57 09	313 30	280 28	335 26
	24	335 51	51 01	310 06	316 33	58 07	326 00	281 21	334 54
March	6	345 54	57 03	323 36	331 10	59 21	338 29	282 08	334 22
	16	355 53	63 08	339 14	347 49	60 49	350 57	282 48	333 50
	26	5 48	69 15	356 55	6 33	62 28	3 24	283 19	333 18
April	5	15 41	75 23	16 41	27 06	64 18	15 49	283 40	332 47
	15	25 30	81 33	37 19	46 41	66 17	28 12	283 53	332 15
	25	35 15	87 43	54 36	60 41	68 22	40 34	283 55R	331 43
May	5	44 58	93 54	64 45	66 40R	70 32	52 54	283 48	331 11
	15	54 38	100 06	66 29	64 34	72 47	65 12	283 31	330 40
	25	64 15	106 17	61 48	59 20	75 04	77 29	283 06	330 08
June	4	73 50	112 29	58 11D	58 48	77 23	89 44	282 33	329 36
	14	83 24	118 42	61 16	65 28	79 42	101 58	281 54	329 04
	24	92 57	124 55	71 14	78 29	82 00	114 09	281 12	328 33
July	4	102 29	131 09	87 06	96 54	84 17	126 19	280 28	328 01
	14	112 01	137 24	107 27	118 09	86 30	138 27	279 44	327 29
	24	121 34	143 40	128 31	138 16	88 39	150 02	279 03	326 57
Aug.	3	131 07	149 58	147 21	155 45	90 43	162 34	278 27	326 25
	13	140 43	156 17	163 29	170 32	92 39	174 32	277 57	325 54
	23	150 20	162 37	176 52	182 20	94 28	186 26	277 35	325 22
Sep.	2	160 00	169 00	186 43	189 38	96 06	198 16	277 21	324 50
	12	169 42	175 25	190 31R	188 48	97 33	209 59	277 18	324 18
	22	179 27	181 53	184 27	179 09	98 46	221 35	277 24D	323 47
Oct.	2	189 16	188 23	175 52	176 49D	99 44	233 02	277 40	323 15
	12	199 08	194 56	181 27	188 25	100 25	244 17	278 05	322 43
	22	209 04	201 32	196 28	204 51	100 48	255 17	278 39	322 11
Nov.	1	219 03	208 11	213 12	221 26	100 51	265 56	279 22	321 39
	11	229 05	214 53	229 30	237 26	100 34	276 06	280 11	321 08
	21	239 09	221 39	245 16	253 01	99 57	285 32	281 07	320 36
Dec.	1	249 17	228 28	260 43	268 20	99 03	293 56	282 08	320 04
	11	259 26	235 21	275 49	282 59	97 55	300 46	283 14	319 32
	21	269 36	242 18	289 24	294 11	96 38	305 13	284 22	319 01
	31	279 48	249 18	295 50R	—	95 16	306 19R	285 32	318 29

Ayanamsa : 22° 15′ 30″

1989		Sun.	Tues.	Thurs.	Sat.	Mon.	Wed.	Fri.
Jan.	1	205 12	229 50	255 47	283 11	311 39	340 29	9 06
	15	37 09	64 30	91 05	116 47	141 36	165 40	189 19
	29	213 06	237 40					
Feb.	1						250 26	277 10
	15	305 33	335 02	4 42	33 40	61 26	87 58	113 27
	19	138 06	162 09	185 51	209 32	233 37		
March	1						258 40	285 11
	5	313 26	343 11	13 29	43 08	71 18	96 18	122 56
	19	147 09	170 55	194 34	218 23	242 37	267 40	293 57
April	1				307 40	336 23	6 26	36 48
	9	66 13	93 51	119 40	144 09	167 56	191 33	215 23
	23	239 41	264 36	290 21	317 13			
May	1					345 29	15 00	45 04
	7	74 27	102 15	128 12	152 43	176 29	200 09	224 12
	21	248 55	274 21	300 33	327 36	355 36	24 31	
June	1			39 11	68 25	96 43	123 29	148 41
	11	172 48	196 30	220 27	245 07	270 44	297 14	324 29
	25	352 19	20 38	49 12				
July	1				82 34	105 10	131 31	156 36
	9	180 43	204 28	228 29	253 21	279 23	306 35	334 39
	23	3 09	31 39	59 49	87 24	114 08		
Aug.	1		127 08	152 23	176 44	200 34	224 22	248 44
	13	274 14	301 12	329 33	358 46	28 03	56 39	84 14
	27	110 43	136 14	160 57				
Sep.	1							173 04
	3	196 58	220 40	244 37	269 23	295 31	323 20	352 43
	17	22 51	52 32	80 55	107 44	133 14	157 49	181 51
Oct.	1	265 36	229 19	253 18	277 58	303 51	331 27	0 51
	15	31 20	61 36	90 25	117 21	142 40	166 58	190 46
	29	214 28	239 19					
Nov.	1						250 20	274 45
	5	299 57	326 23	354 30	24 18	54 42	84 35	112 46
	19	139 01	169 46	187 41	211 22	235 14	259 31	
Dec.	1							284 20
	3	309 50	336 18	4 03	33 06	62 56	92 29	120 40
	17	147 07	172 01	196 01	219 44	243 44	268 21	293 45
	31	319 54						

Ayanamsa : 22° 15' 30''

RAMAN'S EPHEMERIS

1990 A.D.

Longitudes of Planets

1990		Sun	Mars	Merc.	Merc.	Jupit.	Venus	Saturn	Rahu
Jan.	5	284 53	252 49	292 55R	286 39	94 36R	305 21R	286 08	318 13
	15	295 05	259 55	281 21	279 43D	93 21	300 41	287 19	317 41
	25	305 15	267 04	281 24	285 17	92 18	294 46	288 29	317 09
Feb.	4	315 25	279 16	290 31	296 38	91 29	291 14	289 37	316 38
	14	325 32	281 31	303 22	310 35	90 59	291 39D	290 41	316 06
	24	335 37	288 50	318 14	326 18	90 48	295 34	291 42	315 34
March	6	345 39	296 11	334 47	343 44	90 58D	301 57	292 36	315 02
	16	355 38	303 35	353 09	3 00	91 26	310 00	293 25	314 31
	26	5 34	311 01	13 06	23 00	92 13	319 10	294 05	313 59
April	5	15 26	318 28	32 00	39 21	93 16	329 06	294 38	313 27
	15	25 15	325 57	44 29	47 08	94 33	339 33	295 01	312 55
	25	35 01	333 25	47 17R	45 21	96 02	350 23	295 16	312 23
May	5	44 44	340 53	42 19	39 30	97 43	1 30	295 20R	311 52
	15	54 24	348 20	38 01	38 22	99 33	12 49	295 15	311 20
	25	64 01	355 44	40 34D	44 24	101 30	24 18	295 00	310 48
June	4	73 37	3 04	49 41	56 14	103 33	35 54	294 36	310 16
	14	83 10	10 19	64 00	72 55	105 40	47 36	294 05	309 45
	24	92 43	17 28	82 53	93 33	107 52	59 24	293 27	309 13
July	4	102 15	24 27	104 25	114 59	110 05	71 16	292 46	308 41
	14	111 47	31 16	124 53	134 02	112 20	83 13	292 02	308 09
	24	121 20	37 52	142 26	150 03	114 34	95 14	291 18	307 38
Aug.	3	130 54	44 12	156 53	162 50	116 47	107 20	290 36	307 06
	13	140 29	50 13	167 46	171 24	118 58	119 29	289 58	306 34
	23	150 06	55 51	173 21R	173 08	121 06	131 44	289 26	306 02
Sep.	2	159 46	60 59	170 28	165 54	123 08	144 01	289 03	305 31
	12	169 28	65 32	161 28	159 36D	125 04	156 23	288 48	304 59
	22	179 14	68 51	161 34	166 57	126 53	168 47	288 42	304 27
Oct.	2	189 02	72 16	174 31	183 05	128 32	181 14	288 46D	303 55
	12	198 54	74 04	191 53	200 35	130 01	193 44	289 00	303 23
	22	208 50	74 32R	209 03	217 17	131 16	206 15	289 24	302 52
Nov.	1	218 48	73 33	225 17	233 05	132 17	218 47	289 57	302 20
	11	228 50	71 10	240 45	248 16	133 02	231 19	290 38	301 48
	21	238 55	67 44	255 37	262 43	133 28	243 53	291 27	301 16
Dec.	1	249 02	63 59	269 22	275 06	133 35R	256 26	292 22	300 45
	11	259 11	60 44	279 04	279 44R	133 23	269 00	293 23	300 13
	21	269 21	58 34	275 54	269 18	132 51	281 33	294 28	299 41
	31	279 33	57 45	264 34	—	132 01	294 06	295 36	299 09

Ayanamsa : 22° 16' 20"

Longitude of the Moon

1990		Sun.	Tues.	Thurs.	Sat.	Mon.	Wed.	Fri.
Jan.	1					330 17	0 38	33 47
	7	57 34	86 28	114 45	141 48	167 27	191 56	215 47
	21	239 38	264 04	289 26	315 55	343 21	11 25	
Feb.	1			25 35	53 58	82 09	109 50	136 45
	11	162 40	187 34	211 41	235 28	259 31	284 26	310 40
	25	338 20	7 06					
March	1			36 12	64 55	92 48	119 44	145 49
	11	171 06	195 42	219 43	243 29	267 28	292 16	318 31
	25	346 30	15 58	45 56	75 16			
April	1	89 27	116 44	142 44	167 49	192 16	216 18	240 05
	15	263 53	288 08	313 27		9 16	39 31	69 53
	29	99 05						
May	1		126 33	152 26	177 12	201 20	225 10	248 56
	13	272 50	297 11	322 28	349 14	17 49	47 53	78 21
	27	107 51	135 36	161 35				
June	1							174 04
	3	183 12	222 11	245 57	269 54	292 46	319 18	345 23
	17	12 52	41 49	71 45	101 35	130 15	157 14	182 39
July	1	206 58	230 47	254 37	271 48	303 37	329 13	355 43
	15	23 16	51 49	81 00	110 07	138 23	165 17	190 46
	29	215 09	239 00					
Aug	1						250 54	275 00
	5	299 51	325 40	352 29	20 07	48 19	76 47	105 13
	19	133 10	160 14	186 11	211 01	235 03	258 50	282 59
Sep.	1				295 23	321 06	348 10	16 19
	9	45 00	73 35	101 40	129 07	155 51	181 47	206 51
	23	231 06	254 52	278 41	303 13			
Oct.	1					329 05	356 39	25 38
	7	55 14	79 18	112 23	139 22	165 25	190 43	215 21
	21	239 24	263 05	286 49	311 13	337 00	4 39	
Nov	1			19 11	49 10	79 22	108 34	136 14
	11	162 29	187 40	212 10	236 11	259 53	283 32	307 31
	25	332 24	358 51	27 12				
Dec.	1				57 13	87 46	117 31	145 37
	9	172 00	197 03	221 16	245 03	268 43	292 30	316 43
	23	341 43	8 00	35 54	65 22	95 38		

Ayanamsa : 22° 16′ 20″

Longitudes of Planets

1991		Sun	Mars	Merc.	Merc.	Jupit.	Venus	Sat.	Rahu
Jan.	5	284 38	57 51D	263 57D	266 35	131 31	300 22	296 11	298 53
	15	294 50	58 56	271 13	277 00	130 21	312 54	297 22	298 22
	25	305 01	61 03	283 30	290 29	129 03	325 24	298 34	297 50
Feb.	4	315 10	64 00	297 50	305 32	127 43	337 51	299 44	297 18
	14	325 17	67 36	313 34	321 57	126 27	350 16	300 53	296 46
	24	335 22	71 42	330 43	339 53	125 20	2 37	301 58	296 15
March	6	345 24	76 12	349 24	359 09	124 27	14 54	302 59	295 43
	16	355 24	81 00	8 40	17 14	123 51	27 05	303 55	295 11
	26	5 20	86 04	23 54	27 55	123 34	39 10	304 45	294 39
April	5	15 12	91 18	28 58 R	27 17	123 36D	51 07	305 27	294 07
	15	25 01	96 43	23 55	20 28	123 57	62 56	306 02	293 36
	25	34 47	102 15	18 20	18 10	124 35	74 34	306 27	293 04
May	5	44 30	107 53	19 58D	23 27	125 29	85 59	306 44	292 32
	15	54 10	113 36	28 21	34 27	126 38	97 09	306 50	292 00
	25	63 47	119 25	41 35	49 44	128 00	108 00	306 47R	291 29
June	4	73 23	125 17	58 51	68 53	129 33	118 25	306 34	290 57
	14	82 57	131 13	79 37	90 35	131 16	128 18	306 12	290 25
	24	92 29	137 13	101 15	111 16	133 07	137 24	305 42	289 53
July	4	102 01	143 16	120 26	128 44	135 04	145 26	305 06	289 21
	14	111 34	149 22	136 09	142 39	137 06	151 55	304 25	288 50
	24	121 06	155 32	148 06	152 20	139 13	156 10	303 41	288 18
Aug.	3	130 40	161 46	155 03	155 53R	141 22	157 14R	302 57	287 46
	13	140 15	168 03	154 32	151 10	143 33	154 30	302 14	287 14
	23	149 52	174 23	146 54	143 42	145 44	148 50	301 35	286 43
Sep.	2	159 32	180 47	143 19D	146 23	147 55	143 20	301 02	286 11
	12	169 14	187 16	152 28	160 35	150 03	141 01	300 36	285 39
	22	178 59	193 48	169 37	168 50	152 09	142 32D	300 19	285 07
Oct.	2	188 48	200 25	187 52	196 35	154 10	147 12	300 12	284 36
	12	198 40	207 06	204 59	213 04	156 05	154 06	300 14D	284 04
	22	208 35	213 52	220 53	228 28	157 53	162 32	300 27	283 32
Nov.	1	218 34	220 43	235 48	242 52	159 32	172 03	300 49	283 00
	11	228 36	227 38	249 34	255 41	161 00	182 21	301 20	282 28
	21	238 40	234 38	260 43	263 48R	162 15	193 12	302 00	281 57
Dec.	1	248 47	241 43	263 29	258 52	163 17	204 28	302 48	281 25
	11	258 56	248 52	252 13	248 16D	164 02	216 03	303 43	280 53
	21	269 07	256 07	248 37	252 08	164 29	227 51	304 43	280 21
	31	279 18	263 26	257 28		164 37	239 50	305 48	279 50

Ayanamsa : 22° 17′ 11″

Longitude of the Moon

1991	Sun.	Tues.	Thurs.	Sat.	Mon.	Wed.	Fri.
Jan. 1		110 42	139 59	167 35	193 28	218 03	241 54
13	265 33	289 24	313 44	338 46	4 43	31 44	59 57
27	89 09	118 42	147 44				
Feb. 1							161 47
3	188 42	214 04	238 17	261 59	285 45	310 07	335 22
17	1 34	28 38	56 23	84 41	113 17	141 50	
March 1							169 44
3	196 29	221 53	246 10	269 53	293 42	318 17	344 03
17	11 04	38 59	67 18	95 35	123 37	151 18	178 23
31	204 37						
April 1					217 20	241 59	265 53
7	289 33	313 42	339 00	5 52	34 09	63 13	92 11
21	120 30	148 00	174 43	200 40	225 49		
May 1						250 11	273 58
5	297 36	321 43	347 01	14 00	42 42	72 26	102 07
19	130 54	158 24	184 45	210 07	234 45	258 46	282 26
June 1				294 10	318 03	342 40	8 40
9	36 27	65 52	96 07	125 59	154 34	181 34	207 12
23	231 48	255 46	279 25	303 04			
July 1					327 03	351 47	17 43
7	45 14	74 21	104 29	134 33	163 30	190 45	216 23
21	237 50	264 37	293 14	312 03	336 22	1 26	
Aug. 1			14 20	41 00	68 58	98 09	127 59
11	157 30	185 46	212 19	237 20	261 20	284 57	308 46
25	333 11	358 24	24 29	51 24			
Sep. 1	65 11	93 23	122 17	151 26	180 02	207 21	233 06
15	257 32	281 16	305 00	329 20	354 39	21 01	48 14
29	76 00						
Oct. 1		104 06	132 25	160 43	188 35	215 26	241 00
13	264 54	289 08	312 52	337 20	3 01	30 04	58 08
27	86 39	115 04	143 09				
Nov. 1							157 01
3	184 21	210 58	236 38	261 18	285 12	308 48	332 47
17	357 49	24 24	52 33	81 45	111 07	139 52	167 41
Dec. 1	194 28	220 20	245 21	269 38	293 23	316 58	340 54
15	5 48	32 13	60 25	90 03	120 11	149 42	177 52
29	204 32	229 56					

Ayanamsa : 22° 17′ 11″

Longitudes of Planets

1992		Sun	Mars	Merc.	Merc.	Jupit.	Venus	Saturn	Rahu
Jan.	5	284 24	267 07	263 45	270 36	164 34R	245 52	306 22	279 34
	15	294 35	274 32	277 49	285 17	164 14	258 01	307 31	279 02
	25	304 46	282 01	293 01	301 00	163 35	270 15	308 43	278 30
Feb.	4	314 55	289 35	309 16	317 50	162 40	282 31	309 54	277 58
	14	325 03	297 11	326 44	335 56	161 32	294 50	311 06	277 27
	24	335 08	304 50	345 16	356 04	160 16	307 10	312 15	276 55
March	6	346 10	313 18	3 46	9 09	158 50	320 45	313 28	276 20
	16	356 09	321 02	11 16R	9 59	157 35	333 06	314 30	275 48
	26	6 05	328 46	6 18	2 09	156 29	345 26	315 26	275 16
April	5	15 57	336 32	359 23	358 49	155 36	357 47	316 17	274 45
	15	25 46	344 16	0 22D	3 42	154 59	10 07	317 01	274 13
	25	35 31	352 00	8 27	14 20	154 40	22 26	317 36	273 41
May	5	45 14	359 42	21 11	28 54	154 40D	34 44	318 03	273 09
	15	54 54	7 21	37 28	46 52	154 57	47 02	318 21	272 37
	25	64 31	14 56	57 04	67 52	155 32	59 19	318 29	272 06
June	4	74 06	22 27	78 50	89 27	156 23	71 37	318 27R	271 34
	14	83 40	29 53	99 18	108 13	157 29	83 54	318 15.	271 02
	24	93 13	37 12	116 08	123 00	158 47	96 11	317 54	270 30
July	4	102 45	44 25	128 46	133 15	160 16	108 28	317 26	269 59
	14	112 17	51 30	136 15	137 27R	161 56	120 46	316 50	269 27
	24	121 49	58 26	136 39	133 59	163 43	133 04	316 09	268 55
Aug.	3	131 23	65 12	130 18	127 08	165 38	145 22	315 25	268 23
	13	140 58	71 47	125 59D	127 43	167 37	157 40	314 40	267 52
	23	150 36	78 09	132 25	139 37	169 42	169 58	313 57	267 20
Sep.	2	160 16	84 17	148 26	157 59	171 49	182 15	313 17	266 48
	12	169 58	90 08	167 34	176 52	173 58	194 31	312 43	266 16
	22	179 44	95 40	185 46	194 15	176 08	206 46	312 16	265 44
Oct.	2	189 33		202 21	210 07	178 17	218 60	311 58	265 13
	12	199 25	105 30	217 33	224 38	180 25	231 11	311 49	264 41
	22	209 20	109 38	231 20	237 30	182 29	243 21	311 51D	264 09
Nov.	1	219 19	113 05	242 51	246 48	184 29	255 29	312 03	263 37
	11	229 21	115 41	248 21R	246 15	186 23	267 33	312 24	263 06
	21	239 26	117 15	240 26	234 24	188 10	279 33	312 55	262 34
Dec.	1	249 33	117 34R	232 13D	234 17	189 47	291 28	313 35	262 02
	11	259 42	116 31	239 03	245 13	191 13	303 14	314 23	261 30
	21	269 53	114 06	252 05	259 20	192 27	314 48	315 17	260 58
	31	280 05	110 36	266 48	—	193 26	326 07	316 18	260 27

Ayanamsa : 22° 18' 01''

Longitude of the Moon

1992		Sun.	Tues.	Thurs	Sat.	Mon.	Wed.	Fri.
Jan.	1						242 16	266 25
	5	290 09	313 46	337 32	1 53	27 18	54 15	82 57
	19	113 02	143 27	172 58	200 47	226 48	251 28	275 21
Feb.	1				287 09	310 45	334 34	358 51
	9	23 51	49 52	77 15	106 10	136 13	166 23	195 25
	23	222 36	248 01	272 10	295 47			
March	1	307 35	331 25	355 49	20 54	46 45	73 28	101 16
	15	130 09	159 44	189 05	217 11	243 33	268 22	292 15
	29	315 53	339 54					
April	1						352 11	17 26
	5	43 33	70 25	97 55	126 03	154 42	183 27	211 35
	19	238 29	263 57	288 16	312 00	335 51	0 26	
May	1							26 06
	3	52 53	80 33	108 43	137 02	165 19	193 15	220 30
	17	246 45	271 54	296 08	319 53	343 47	8 25	34 18
	31	61 35						
June	1					75 42	104 30	133 31
	7	162 08	189 59	216 55	242 54	268 00	292 20	316 10
	21	339 54	4 04	29 14	55 13	84 08		
July	1						113 37	143 25
	5	172 34	200 28	226 59	252 22	276 56	300 57	324 41
	19	348 27	12 37	37 40	64 09	92 22	122 07	152 29
Aug.	1				167 29	196 29	223 46	249 26
	9	274 00	297 57	321 40	345 26	9 28	34 05	59 42
	23	86 46	115 33	145 41	176 05	205 25		
Sep.	1		219 24	245 57	270 55	294 58	318 40	342 26
	13	6 33	31 09	56 26	82 43	110 19	139 21	169 22
	27	199 12	227 43					
Oct.	1			254 24	279 27	303 30	327 13	351 07
	11	15 33	40 39	66 27	93 03	120 36	149 08	178 21
	25	207 31	235 41	262 19	287 27			
Nov.	1	299 36	323 28	347 16	11 35	36 46	62 52	89 50
	15	117 27	145 35	174 01	202 25	230 18	257 10	282 49
	29	307 23						
Dec.	1		331 16	355 06	19 27	44 50	71 31	99 21
	13	127 53	156 35	184 55	212 38	239 34	265 39	290 52
	27	315 17	339 09	2 56				

Ayanamsa : 22° 18' 01''

Longitudes of Planets

1993		Sun	Mars	Merc.	Merc.	Jupit.	Venus	Saturn	Rahu
Jan.	5	285 10	108 38R	274 26	282 13	193 50	331 39	316 50	260 11
	15	295 21	104 44	290 12	298 23	194 24	342 22	317 57	259 39
	25	305 32	101 30	306 48	315 29	194 40	352 29	319 07	259 07
Feb.	4	310 41	99 25	324 20	333 13	194 37R	1 44	320 19	258 36
	14	325 49	98 40	341 39	348 45	194 15	9 45	321 31	258 04
	24	335 54	99 11D	353 14	354 00R	193 36	15 58	322 43	257 32
March	6	345 56	100 46	351 05	346 17	192 40	19 32	323 53	257 00
	16	355 55	103 13	342 10	340 21D	191 33	19 29R	325 00	256 28
	26	5 50	106 24	341 01	343 43	190 18	15 29	326 03	255 57
April	5	15 43	110 07	347 58	353 25	189 01	9 22	326 32	255 25
	15	25 32	114 18	359 49	7 02	187 47	4 45	327 54	254 53
	25	35 17	118 49	14 59	23 40	186 41	3 54D	328 40	254 21
May	5	45 00	123 39	33 05	43 13	185 48	6 42	329 18	253 50
	15	54 40	128 42	53 55	64 50	185 10	12 14	329 47	253 18
	25	64 17	133 58	75 26	85 13	184 49	19 37	330 07	252 46
June	4	73 52	139 23	93 56	101 29	184 46D	28 14	330 18	252 14
	14	83 26	144 58	107 49	112 49	185 01	37 44	330 18R	251 42
	24	92 59	150 41	116 18	118 04R	185 34	47 50	330 09	251 11
July	4	102 31	156 31	117 56	116 00	186 22	58 22	329 51	250 39
	14	112 03	162 27	112 55	109 54	187 25	69 15	329 24	250 07
	24	121 36	168 31	108 15D	108 49	188 41	80 25	328 50	249 35
Aug.	3	131 09	174 40	111 56	117 32	190 08	91 47	328 10	249 04
	13	140 45	180 55	125 16	134 30	191 46	103 21	327 26	248 32
	23	150 22	187 16	144 25	154 22	193 32	115 05	326 41	248 00
Sep.	2	160 02	193 43	163 58	173 06	195 26	126 57	325 56	247 28
	12	169 44	200 16	181 45	189 56	197 25	138 58	325 15	246 57
	22	179 30	206 55	197 41	205 00	199 29	151 06	324 39	246 25
Oct.	2	189 18	213 40	211 54	218 16	201 37	163 20	324 10	245 53
	12	199 10	220 30	223 58	228 40	203 46	175 40	323 50	245 21
	22	209 06	227 27	231 46	232 19R	205 56	188 04	323 39	244 49
Nov.	1	219 05	234 30	229 18	223 16	208 06	200 31	323 39D	244 18
	11	229 07	241 38	217 53	216 42D	210 15	213 02	323 48	243 46
	21	239 12	248 52	219 39	225 09	212 20	225 34	324 08	243 14
Dec.	1	249 19	256 12	231 53	239 12	214 21	238 08	324 38	242 42
	11	259 28	263 37	246 44	254 24	216 16	250 42	325 16	242 11
	21	269 39	271 07	262 08	269 57	218 03	263 17	326 03	241 39
	31	279 50	278 42	277 52	—	219 41	275 52	326 57	241 07

Ayanamsa : 22° 18' 51"

Longitude of the Moon

1993		Sun.	Tues.	Thurs.	Sat.	Mon.	Wed.	Fri.
Jan.	1							14 57
	3	39 41	65 46	93 29	122 34	152 14	181 27	209 33
	17	236 24	262 12	287 12	311 35	335 33	359 16	23 09
	31	47 42						
Feb.	1					60 27	87 11	115 48
	7	145 52	176 13	205 33	233 13	259 17	284 13	305 28
	21	332 22	356 07	19 55	44 04			
March	1					69 05	95 33	123 53
	7	153 55	184 34	214 23	242 26	268 38	293 28	317 31
	21	341 16	5 02	29 00	53 24	78 33	101 54	
April	1			118 40	147 27	177 31	207 45	236 54
	11	264 15	289 53	314 18	338 07	1 52	25 53	50 25
	25	75 37	101 40	128 50				
May	1				157 14	186 34	216 07	244 54
	9	272 14	298 00	322 33	346 25	10 14	34 28	59 25
	23	85 16	112 01	139 36	167 53	196 35		
June	1		210 57	239 22	266 54	293 13	318 19	342 30
	13	6 19	30 21	55 09	81 04	108 10	136 11	164 40
	27	193 09	22 16					
July	1			248 48	275 34	301 25	326 19	350 28
	11	14 15	38 16	63 09	89 24	117 11	146 06	175 20
	25	204 04	231 54	258 47	284 49			
Aug.	1	297 32	322 28	346 43	10 32	34 17	58 35	84 06
	15	111 19	140 17	170 14	199 59	228 35	255 46	281 45
	29	306 51	331·20					
Sep.	1						343 23	7 14
	5	45 54	54 49	79 33	105 45	133 50	163 38	194 07
	19	233 54	252 00	278 41	303 56	328 21	352 19	
Oct.	1							16 03
	3	39 47	63 49	88 36	114 39	142 27	171 56	202 21
	17	232 23	260 58	287 46	313 03	337 20	1 09	24 52
	31	48 48						
Nov.	1					60·55	85 36	111 11
	7	137 59	166 12	195 39	225 34	254 52	282 45	308 58
	21	333 47	357 45	21 27	45 23	69 54		
Dec.	1						95 12	121 22
	5	148 27	176 25	205 07	234 09	262 51	290 32	316 50
	19	341 45	50 46	29 28	53 30	72 23	164 22	131 24

Ayanamsa : 22° 18' 51''

Longitudes of Planets

1994		Sun	Mars	Merc.	Merc.	Jupit.	Venus	Saturn	Rahu
Jan.	5	284 55	282 31	285 55	294 08	220 26	282 10	327 26	240 51
	15	295 07	290 11	302 30	310 59	221 47	294 45	328 29	240 19
	25	305 17	297 56	319 23	327 16	222 54	307 19	329 36	239 48
Feb.	4	315 27	305 43	334 41	337 15R	223 46	319 52	330 46	239 16
	14	325 34	313 32	336 41	332 22	224 21	332 24	331 58	238 44
	24	335 39	321 23	326 59	323 25	224 37	343 55	333 11	238 12
March	6	345 41	329 15	322 43D	324 31	224 36R	357 23	334 24	237 40
	16	355 40	337 07	328 09	333 08	224 15	9 50	335 35	237 09
	26	5 36	344 58	339 05	345 50	223 37	22 13	336 43	236 37
April	5	15 28	352 48	353 17	1 22	222 43	34 33	337 48	236 05
	15	25 17	0 35	10 05	19 27	221 37	46 51	338 49	235 33
	25	35 03	8 20	29 27	40 00	220 24	59 04	339 43	235 02
May	5	44 46	16 01	50 47	61 16	219 07	71 14	340 31	234 30
	15	54 26	23 38	70 54	79 19	217 54	83 19	341 12	233 58
	25	64 03	31 10	86 21	91 54	216 47	95 18	341 44	233 26
June	4	73 38	38 38	95 50	98 00	215 53	107 14	342 07	232 54
	14	83 12	45 59	98 17R	96 48	215 13	119 03	342 20	232 23
	24	92 45	53 15	94 09	91 23	214 51	130 44	342 24R	231 51
July	4	102 17	60 24	89 38	89 44	214 46D	142 17	342 17	231 19
	14	111 49	67 27	91 57D	96 20	214 59	153 39	342 01	230 47
	24	121 22	74 22	102 44	110 56	215 30	164 47	341 37	230 16
Aug.	3	130 55	81 10	120 30	130 44	216 17	175 38	341 04	229 44
	13	140 31	87 50	141 01	150 55	217 19	186 08	340 25	229 12
	23	150 08	94 21	160 16	169 04	218 35	196 08	339 42	228 40
Sep.	2	159 47	100 44	177 18	180 02	220 02	205 28	338 56	228 09
	12	169 30	106 56	192 15	198 55	221 40	213 53	338 11	227 37
	22	179 15	112 57	204 56	210 07	223 27	220 54	337 28	227 05
Oct.	2	189 04	118 46	214 06	216 17	225 22	225 54	336 51	226 33
	12	198 56	124 21	215 48R	212 00	227 23	227 59	336 20	226 01
	22	208 51	129 40	206 01	201 31	229 29	226 17R	335 57	225 30
Nov.	1	218 50	134 39	201 19D	205 08	231 38	221 11	335 44	224 58
	11	228 52	139 15	211 19	218 37	233 50	215 30	335 41D	224 26
	21	238 57	143 22	226 20	234 12	236 03	212 35	335 48	223 54
Dec.	1	249 04	146 55	242 04	249 55	238 16	213 40D	336 06	223 23
	11	259 13	149 46	257 46	265 38	240 27	218 06	336 34	222 51
	21	269 23	151 43	273 33	281 33	242 35	224 56	337 11	222 19
	31	279 35	152 37	289 37	—	244 38	233 24	337 57	221 47

Ayanamsa : 22° 19' 42"

Longitude of the Moon

1994		Sun.	Tues.	Thurs.	Sat.	Mon.	Wed.	Fri.
Jan.	1				145 13	173 14	201 28	229 41
	9	257 42	285 11	311 46	337 13	1 37	25 23	49 09
	23	73 37	99 22	126 36	155 00	183 51		
Feb.	1		198 12	226 30	254 08	281 07	307 24	332 54
	13	357 32	21 27	45 04	69 02	94 04	120 44	149 08
	27	178 41						
March	1		208 18	237 05	264 41	291 12	316 50	341 44
	13	5 59	29 45	53 21	77 16	102 12	128 44	157 11
	27	187 05	217 20	246 45				
April	1							260 55
	3	288 06	313 55	338 44	2 54	26 38	50 14	74 01
	17	98 25	124 00	151 14	180 14	210 26	240 42	269 53
May	1	297 24	323 17	347 56	11 51	35 28	59 09	83 10
	15	107 52	133 35	160 37	189 09	218 51	248 53	278 11
	29	305 58	332 01					
June	1						344 30	8 41
	5	32 20	56 00	80 06	104 54	130 34	157 10	184 49
	19	213 24	242 43	272 00	300 25	327 22	352 45	
July	1							16 57
	3	40 37	64 24	88 50	114 13	140 34	167 46	195 34
	17	223 51	252 25	280 55	308 45	335 25	0 43	24 55
	31	48 36						
Aug.	1					60 28	84 40	109 56
	7	136 29	164 06	192 19	220 38	248 50	276 45	304 10
	21	330 48	356 22	20 53	44 41	68 21	92 36	
Sep.	1			105 09	131 22	159 06	187 54	216 58
	11	245 38	273 33	300 41	326 59	352 27	17 03	40 58
	25	64 34	88 24	113 09				
Oct.	1				139 22	167 20	196 42	226 36
	9	255 05	284 02	310 55	336 40	1 32	25 43	49 27
	23	73 02	96 54	121 34	147 36	175 22		
Nov.	1		189 55	219 53	250 10	279 34	307 25	333 38
	13	358 34	22 41	46 22	69 60	93 50	118 11	143 27
	27	170 02	198 13					
Dec.	1			227 52	258 12	288 01	316 17	342 41
	11	7 34	31 29	55 05	78 48	102 57	127 43	153 15
	25	179 46	207 29	236 28	266 16			

Ayanamsa : 22° 19' 42''

Longitudes of Planets

1995		Sun	Mars	Merc.	Merc.	Jupit.	Venus	Sat.	Rahu
Jan.	5	284 41	152 37R	297 43	305 37	245 37	238 04	338 23	221 31
	15	294 52	151 37	312 54	318 36	247 31	248 01	339 19	220 60
	25	305 03	149 18	321 12R	319 23	249 17	258 36	340 21	220 28
Feb.	4	315 12	145 53	313 59	308 31	250 52	269 37	341 28	219 56
	14	325 19	141 57	305 49D	306 13	252 16	280 56	342 38	219 24
	24	335 24	138 12	309 01	313 25	253 26	292 29	343 50	218 53
March	6	345 27	135 17	318 57	325 18	254 21	304 12	345 04	218 21
	16	355 26	133 35	332 19	339 54	254 59	316 02	346 17	217 49
	26	5 22	133 11D	348 02	356 43	255 19	327 57	347 30	217 17
April	5	15 14	133 58	5 59	15 49	255 21R	339 56	348 40	216 45
	15	25 03	135 47	26 09	36 43	255 04	351 58	349 47	216 14
	25	34 49	138 25	47 00	56 23	254 30	4 01	350 49	215 42
May	5	44 32	141 45	64 23	70 42	253 39	16 07	351 46	215 10
	15	54 12	145 37	75 12	77 45	252 36	28 13	352 36	214 38
	25	63 49	149 55	78 18R	77 01	251 23	40 21	353 20	214 07
June	4	73 25	154 36	74 31	71 51	250 07	52 29	353 55	213 35
	14	82 59	159 35	70 06	70 00D	248 53	64 39	354 21	213 03
	24	92 31	164 50	71 49	75 31	247 45	76 50	354 38	212 31
July	4	102 04	170 18	80 58	88 04	246 48	89 03	354 45	211 59
	14	111 35	175 59	96 40	106 29	246 05	101 18	354 41R	211 28
	24	121 08	181 50	116 58	127 31	245 39	113 34	354 28	210 56
Aug.	3	130 42	187 52	137 41	147 15	245 32D	125 53	354 06	210 24
	13	140 17	194 03	156 10	164 27	245 42	138 13	353 35	209 52
	23	149 54	200 23	172 08	179 13	246 11	150 05	352 58	209 21
Sep.	2	159 33	206 51	185 37	191 13	246 56	162 59	352 15	208 49
	12	169 15	213 28	195 48	198 59	247 58	175 24	351 30	208 17
	22	179 01	220 12	200 10R	198 38	249 13	187 50	350 44	207 45
Oct.	2	188 49	227 04	194 14	188 39	250 41	200 16	349 59	207 13
	12	198 41	234 03	185 14D	186 04	252 21	212 43	349 20	206 42
	22	208 37	241 10	190 41	197 31	254 10	225 09	348 46	206 10
Nov.	1	218 35	248 24	205 21	213 29	256 07	237 36	348 21	205 38
	11	228 37	255 44	221 39	229 44	258 11	250 03	348 05	205 06
	21	238 42	263 10	237 43	245 36	260 20	262 29	347 59	204 35
Dec.	1	248 49	270 42	253 26	261 14	262 33	274 54	348 04D	204 03
	11	258 58	278 19	269 02	276 49	264 49	287 18	348 20	203 31
	21	269 08	286 01	284 30	291 54	267 05	299 40	348 46	202 59
	31	279 20	293 47	298 32	—	269 22	312 00	349 22	202 27

Ayanamsa : 22° 20' 32"

Longitude of the Moon

1995		Sun.	Tues.	Thurs.	Sat.	Mon.	Wed.	Fri.
Jan.	1	281 11	310 20	337 52	3 37	27 60	51 40	75 19
	15	99 29	124 36	150 12	176 42	203 56	231 56	260 39
	29	289 42	318 18					
Feb.	1						332 11	358 45
	5	23 49	47 49	71 27	95 26	120 17	146 13	173 09
	19	200 45	228 44	256 55	285 11	313 12		
March	1						340 29	6 38
	5	31 34	55 35	79 15	103 16	128 15	154 34	182 11
	19	210 40	239 24	267 54	295 51	323 06	349 31	15 01
April	1				27 25	51 38	75 22	99 07
	9	123 31	149 08	176 19	204 59	234 31	263 58	292 36
	23	320 03	346 20	11 36	36 05			
May	1					60 02	83 42	107 29
	7	131 50	157 19	184 23	213 10	243 10	273 19	302 31
	21	330 07	356 09	20 59	45 04	68 48	92 28	
June	1			104 22	128 28	153 18	179 21	207 01
	11	236 22	266 45	296 56	325 45	352 41	17 58	42 10
	25	65 52	89 32	113 27				
July	1				137 48	162 51	188 53	216 16
	9	245 10	275 13	305 20	334 16	1 21	26 42	50 53
	23	74 34	98 19	122 30	147 17	172 46		
Aug	1		185 48	212 35	240 29	269 28	299 04	328 17
	13	356 11	22 23	47 08	71 02	94 46	118 53	143 45
	27	169 28	195 59	223 14				
Sep.	1							237 07
	3	265 23	294 06	322 48	350 45	17 27	42 47	67 04
	17	90 51	114 47	139 26	165 09	191 59	219 43	247 58
Oct.	1	276 24	304 40	332 30	359 34	25 40	50 43	74 56
	15	98 43	122 38	147 18	173 11	200 32	229 07	258 17
	29	287 16	315 29					
Nov.	1						329 13	355 57
	5	21 46	46 46	71 05	94 57	118 42	142 49	167 54
	19	194 30	222 50	252 32	282 35	311 49	339 37	
Dec.	1							5 57
	3	31 10	55 39	79 41	103 28	127 14	151 19	176 13
	17	202 32	230 43	310 36	291 11	321 04	349 15	15 36
	31	40 34						

Ayanamsa : 22° 20′ 32″

Longitudes of Planets

1996		Sun	Mars	Merc.	Merc.	Jupit.	Venus	Sat.	Rahù
Jan.	5	284 25	297 41	303 28	305 06	270 30	318 09	349 43	202 12
	15	294 37	305 32	302 09R	296 00	272 44	330 23	350 31	201 40
	25	304 48	313 25	290 50	289 07D	274 54	342 31	351 26	201 08
Feb.	4	314 57	321 19	290 36	294 15	276 59	354 32	352 28	200 36
	14	325 04	329 13	299 19	305 18	275 57	6 22	353 34	200 05
	24	335 10	337 07	311 57	319 09	280 48	17 60	354 44	199 33
March	6	346 12	345 48	328 24	336 38	282 38	30 28	356 05	198 58
	16	356 11	353 39	345 21	354 33	284 06	41 25	357 19	198 26
	26	6 07	1 27	4 17	14 25	285 21	51 55	358 33	197 54
April	5	15 59	9 13	24 42	34 34	286 21	61 46	359 47	197 22
	15	25 48	16 54	43 21	50 24	287 05	70 45	0 58	196 51
	25	35 33	24 31	55 23	58 06	287 31	78 31	2 06	196 19
May	5	45 16	32 04	58 31R	56 58	287 39R	84 29	3 10	195 47
	15	54 56	39 31	54 13	51 29	287 28	87 51	4 09	195 15
	25	64 33	46 53	49 51D	49 56	286 58	87 44R	5 02	194 44
June	4	74 08	54 10	51 51	55 30	286 12	83 46	5 47	194 12
	14	83 42	61 21	60 42	67 18	285 12	77 41	6 25	193 40
	24	93 15	68 27	75 13	84 23	284 01	72 58	6 54	193 08
July	4	102 46	75 26	94 33	105 17	282 45	71 52D	7 13	192 36
	14	112 19	82 20	116 00	126 16	281 29	74 25	7 23	192 05
	24	121 51	89 09	136 52	144 44	280 18	79 43	7 22R	191 33
Aug.	3	131 25	95 51	152 53	160 21	279 17	86 55	7 11	191 01
	13	141 00	102 24	167 04	172 57	278 30	95 27	6 51	190 29
	23	150 38	108 58	177 51	181 27	278 00	104 54	6 22	189 58
Sep.	2	160 17	115 22	183 20R	182 55	277 49D	115 02	5 45	189 26
	12	169 60	121 40	179 54	174 57	277 56	125 41	5 03	188 54
	22	179 45	127 51	170 27	169 04D	278 23	136 44	4 17	188 22
Oct.	2	189 34	133 55	171 44	177 38	279 07	148 07	3 31	187 50
	12	199 26	139 50	185 20	193 45	280 08	159 45	2 45	187 19
	22	209 22	145 37	202 19	210 46	281 24	171 36	2 04	186 47
Nov.	1	219 21	151 13	219 02	227 07	282 53	183 37	1 29	186 15
	11	229 23	156 37	235 01	242 48	284 35	195 48	1 02	185 43
	21	239 28	161 48	250 29	258 04	286 26	208 04	0 44	185 12
Dec.	1	249 35	166 42	265 31	272 45	288 26	220 26	0 36	184 40
	11	259 44	171 16	279 29	285 11	290 34	232 52	0 40D	184 08
	21	269 55	175 25	288 44R	288 30	292¦46	245 20	0 54	183 36
	31	280 06	179 04	283 45	—	295 03	257 49	1 18	183 05

Ayanamsa : 22° 21' 22"

Longitude of the Moon

1996	Sun.	Tues.	Thurs.	Sat.	Mon.	Wed.	Fri.
Jan. 1					52 43	76 39	100 25
7	124 13	148 14	172 46	198 12	225 05	253 45	283 53
21	314 23	343 49	11 24	37 09	61 37	85 27	
Feb. 1			97 18	121 07	145 14	169 05	195 06
11	221 18	248 47	277 40	307 29	337 13	5 45	32 34
25	57 48	81 58	105 43				
March 1							117 37
3	141 44	166 28	191 58	218 16	245 26	273 29	302 15
17	331 16	359 48	27 11	53 09	77 53	101 51	125 40
31	149 53						
April 1					162 18	187 54	214 33
7	242 07	270 17	298 42	327 02	354 58	22 09	48 21
21	73 30	97 47	121 36	145 33	170 14		
May 1						196 08	223 27
5	251 56	280 56	309 42	337 47	4 60	31 22	56 56
19	81 43	105 52	129 39	153 32	178 09	204 08	231 49
June 1				246 16	275 55	305 39	334 28
9	361 58	28 15	53 36	78 17	102 26	126 13	149 57
23	174 03	199 11	225 56	254 35			
July 1					284 41	315 02	344 20
7	12 00	38 07	63 06	87 24	111 19	135 02	158 48
21	182 57	208 02	234 38	263 05	293 07	323 39	
Aug. 1			338 40	7 31	34 34	60 03	84 29
11	108 23	132 06	155 55	180 03	204 50	230 40	257 58
25	286 51	316 52	346 56	15 53			
Sep. 1	29 45	56 09	81 07	105 12	128 56	152 46	177 01
15	201 54	227 37	254 21	282 15	311 10	340 36	9 43
29	37 44						
Oct. 1		64 14	89 19	113 26	137 11	161 08	185 43
13	211 14	237 42	265 01	293 01	321 26	350 00	18 16
27	45 46	72 05	97 11				
Nov. 1							109 21
3	133 13	156 59	181 19	206 45	233 28	261 18	299 44
17	318 12	346 20	13 59	41 03	67 22	92 45	117 13
Dec. 1	141 02	164 45	189 03	214 36	241 48	270 28	299 50
15	328 55	357 07	24 19	50 40	76 16	101 10	125 24
29	149 08	172 47					

Ayanamsa : 22° 21′ 22″

Longitudes of Planets

1997		Sun	Mars	Merc.	Merc.	Jupit.	Venus	Saturn	Rahu
Jan.	5	285 12	180 40	277 15R	273 24	296 13	264 05	1 34	182 49
	15	295 23	183 20	273 27	276 22	298 34	276 36	2 14	182 17
	25	305 34	185 08	281 05	286 53	300 55	289 08	3 01	181 45
Feb.	4	315 43	185 54	293 22	300 22	303 15	301 39	3 56	181 13
	14	325 59	185 27R	307 47	315 35	305 34	314 10	4 57	180 42
	24	335 55	183 44	323 46	332 21	307 49	326 40	6 04	180 10
March	6	345 57	180 48	341 22	350 50	309 59	339 10	7 14	179 38
	16	355 57	177 05	1 09	10 36	312 04	351 38	8 27	179 06
	26	5 52	173 14	20 08	28 27	314 00	4 05	9 42	178 34
April	5	15 44	169 56	34 46	38 33	315 48	16 30	10 57	178 03
	15	25 33	167 42	39 37R	38 11	317 25	28 53	12 11	177 31
	25	35 19	166 46	35 13	31 59	318 49	41 15	13 24	176 59
May	5	45 02	167 05D	29 53	29 36D	320 00	53 35	14 35	176 27
	15	54 42	168 33	31 13	34 33	320 55	65 53	15 41	175 56
	25	64 19	170 57	39 20	45 24	321 33	78 09	16 42	175 24
June	4	73 54	174 08	52 37	60 56	321 53	90 24	17 38	174 52
	14	83 28	177 57	70 18	80 34	321 54R	102 37	18 27	174 20
	24	93 00	182 18	91 24	102 17	321 36	114 48	19 08	173 48
July	4	102 33	187 05	112 42	122 24	321 00	126 57	19 41	173 17
	14	112 05	192 14	131 18	139 23	320 07	139 04	20 04	172 45
	24	121 37	197 43	146 39	153 03	319 01	151 09	20 18	172 13
Aug.	3	131 11	203 28	158 27	162 41	317 47	163 10	20 21R	171 41
	13	140 46	209 28	165 24	166 12R	316 29	175 07	20 14	171 10
	23	150 23	215 42	164 41	161 01	315 13	186 60	19 57	170 38
Sep.	2	160 03	222 08	156 26	153 12	314 05	198 47	19 31	170 06
	12	169 45	228 45	153 10D	156 48	313 09	210 28	18 56	169 34
	22	179 31	235 33	163 20	171 35	312 30	222 02	18 15	169 02
Oct.	2	189 20	242 30	180 29	189 27	312 08	233 25	17 30	168 31
	12	199 12	249 37	198 12	206 36	312 07D	244 37	16 43	167 59
	22	209 07	256 51	214 53	222 51	312 26	255 31	15 56	167 27
Nov.	1	219 06	264 13	230 36	238 10	313 03	266 03	15 13	166 55
	11	229 08	271 43	245 32	252 40	313 59	276 03	14 35	166 24
	21	239 12	279 18	259 28	265 37	315 11	285 16	14 05	165 52
Dec.	1	249 20	286 58	270 34	273 13	316 38	293 19	13 44	165 20
	11	259 29	294 43	272 01R	266 32	318 17	299 38	13 33	164 48
	21	269 39	302 31	260 09	257 09D	320 08	303 21	13 33D	164 17
	31	279 51	310 23	258 12	—	322 09	303 29R	13 44	163 45

Ayanamsa : 22° 22' 13''

Longitude of the Moon

1997		Sun.	Tues.	Thurs.	Sat.	Mon	Wed.	Fri.
Jan.	1						184 46	209 29
	5	235 47	263 59	293 42	323 50	353 11	21 08	47 42
	19	73 11	97 53	122 03	145 50	169 27	193 18	217 58
Feb.	1				230 47	257 47	286 40	316 54
	9	347 16	16 32	44 07	70 08	94 57	119 03	142 47
	23	166 26	190 17	214 40				
March	1				240 01	266 47	295 12	324 59
	9	355 14	24 47	52 46	79 01	103 52	127 50	151 28
	23	175 13	199 23	224 14	249 58	276 46		
April	1		290 38	319 13	348 40	18 13	46 56	74 14
	13	99 53	124 17	148 01	171 43	195 54	220 54	246 50
	27	273 40	301 16					
May	1			329 30	358 12	26 57	55 09	82 12
	11	107 51	132 17	156 02	179 47	204 11	229 41	256 22
	25	284 00	312 08	340 24	8 36			
June	1	22 37	50 21	77 21	103 18	128 08	152 05	175 45
	15	199 48	224 55	251 29	279 27	308 13	337 04	5 27
	29	33 10						
July	1		60 11	86 27	111 50	136 20	160 10	183 46
	13	207 48	232 57	259 42	288 07	317 36	347 11	16 01
	27	43 43	70 19	95 57				
Aug	1							108 27
	3	132 54	156 46	180 21	204 04	228 32	254 21	281 56
	17	311 10	341 19	11 14	39 59	67 12	93 01	117 47
	31	141 50						
Sep.	1					153 42	177 18	200 57
	7	225 05	250 08	276 35	304 45	334 25	364 46	34 37
	21	63 01	89 39	114 46	138 53	162 32		
Oct.	1						186 08	210 02
	5	234 28	259 42	286 04	313 48	342 55	12 55	42 46
	19	71 24	98 16	123 27	147 31	171 06	194 49	219 02
Nov.	1				231 25	256 46	282 55	309 57
	9	337 57	6 52	36 15	65 16	93 00	119 05	143 42
	23	167 28	191 07	215 15	240 18			
Dec.	1					266 20	293 12	320 40
	7	348 36	16 55	45 26	73 39	100 55	126 51	151 28
	21	175 16	198 57	223 12	248 34	275 13	302 57	

Ayanamsa : 22° 22' 13"

Longitudes of Planets

1998		Sun	Mars	Merc.	Merc.	Jupit.	Venus	Sat.	Rahu
Jan.	5	284 57	314 19	262 00	267 22	323 12	302 01R	13 54	163 29
	15	295 08	322 12	273 37	280 26	325 23	296 43	14 21	162 57
	25	305 18	330 05	287 38	295 09	327 40	291 05	14 58	162 25
Feb.	4	315 28	337 58	302 57	311 04	330 01	288 30	15 43	161 54
	14	325 35	345 49	319 31	328 20	332 24	289 53D	16 37	161 22
	24	335 40	353 39	337 30	346 59	334 48	294 30	17 37	160 50
March	6	345 43	1 25	356 32	5 38	337 13	301 23	18 42	160 18
	16	355 42	9 08	13 26	18 54	339 36	309 45	19 52	159 46
	26	5 37	16 46	21 22R	20 40	341 56	319 09	21 05	159 15
April	5	15 30	24 21	17 35	13 43	344 12	329 14	22 20	158 43
	15	25 19	31 50	10 47	9 48D	346 23	339 48	23 36	158 11
	25	35 05	39 15	10 54	13 50	348 27	350 44	24 52	157 39
May	5	44 48	46 34	18 15	23 54	350 23	1 55	26 06	157 08
	15	54 27	53 49	30 35	38 15	352 10	13 17	27 18	156 36
	25	64 05	60 58	46 49	56 18	353 46	24 48	28 27	156 04
June	4	73 40	68 02	66 37	77 29	355 09	36 26	29 31	155 32
	14	83 14	75 01	88 26	98 56	356 17	48 10	30 30	155 00
	24	92 47	81 55	108 41	117 32	357 10	59 59	31 22	154 29
July	4	102 19	88 44	125 27	132 25	357 45	71 52	32 07	153 57
	14	111 51	95 29	138 22	143 08	358 02	83 50	32 44	153 25
	24	121 24	102 09	146 30	148 09R	357 59R	95 52	33 12	152 53
Aug.	3	130 57	108 45	147 45	145 17	357 37	107 58	33 30	152 22
	13	140 32	115 17	141 24	137 42	356 56	120 08	33 37	151 50
	23	150 10	121 44	135 59D	137 21	355 59	132 23	33 34R	151 18
Sep.	2	159 49	128 08	141 54	149 03	354 49	144 41	33 21	150 46
	12	169 31	134 28	157 47	167 08	353 32	157 03	32 58	150 14
	22	179 17	140 44	176 28	185 33	352 12	169 28	32 26	149 43
Oct.	2	189 05	146 55	194 15	202 36	350 56	181 55	31 47	149 11
	12	198 57	153 02	210 37	218 20	349 50	194 24	31 02	148 39
	22	208 53	159 05	225 47	232 57	348 58	206 55	30 15	148 07
Nov.	1	218 51	165 02	239 47	246 07	348 24	219 27	29 27	147 36
	11	228 53	170 54	251 40	255 50	348 10	232 00	28 42	147 04
	21	238 58	176 39	257 32R	255 23	348 16D	244 33	28 02	146 32
Dec.	1	249 05	182 16	249 25	243 24	348 43	257 07	27 28	146 00
	11	259 14	187 45	241 19D	243 20	349 28	269 40	27 04	145 29
	21	269 24	193 03	247 55	253 53	350 32	282 13	26 49	144 57
	31	279 36	198 08	260 35	—	351 52	294 46	26 46D	144 25

Ayanamsa : 22° 23' 34"

Longitude of the Moon

1998		Sun.	Tues.	Thurs.	Sat.	Mon.	Wed.	Fri.
Jan.	1			317 02	345 24	13 40	41 41	69 17
	11	96 13	122 13	147 09	171 13	194 52	218 44	243 30
	25	269 40	297 23	326 15	355 30			
Feb.	1	10 02	38 32	66 06	92 42	118 25	143 17	167 27
	15	191 10	214 51	239 02	264 19	291 11	319 45	349 31
March	1	19 29	48 38	76 23	102 41	127 50	152 11	176 03
	15	199 43	223 28	247 41	272 51	299 27	327 46	357 36
	29	28 00	57 45					
April	1						72 03	99 16
	5	124 51	149 15	173 03	196 41	220 28	244 38	269 27
	19	295 14	322 22	351 04	21 02	51 18	80 35	
May	1							108 04
	3	133 44	158 05	181 48	205 27	229 27	253 60	279 13
	17	305 14	332 17	0 34	29 56	59 42	88 46	116 16
	31	142 02						
June	1					154 22	178 21	202 02
	7	225 58	250 35	275 59	302 12	329 09	1 51	25 19
	21	54 16	83 04	110 56	137 20	162 20		
July	1						186 23	210 07
	5	234 12	259 05	285 03	311 59	339 39	7 48	36 10
	19	64 30	92 25	119 30	145 27	170 16	194 17	218 03
Aug.	1				230 01	254 32	280 11	307 10
	9	335 19	4 06	32 55	61 16	88 52	115 35	141 23
	23	166 17	190 27	214 13	238 03	262 30		
Sep.	1		275 08	301 32	329 33	358 50	28 34	57 45
	13	85 47	112 30	136 05	162 50	187 00	210 47	234 30
	27	258 31	283 21					
Oct.	1			309 35	337 35	7 13	37 36	67 27
	11	95 48	122 25	147 38	171 58	195 51	219 34	243 20
	25	267 26	292 12	318 11	345 51			
Nov.	1	0 22	30 31	61 06	90 44	118 30	144 25	169 00
	15	192 53	216 34	240 23	264 32	289 10	314 34	341 08
	29	9 15						
Dec.	1		38 51	69 07	98 47	126 47	152 55	177 36
	13	201 28	225 10	249 09	273 40	298 48	324 40	351 25
	27	19 15	48 08	77 35				

Ayanamsa : 22° 23' 34''

1999		Sun	Mars	Merc.	Merc.	Jupit.	Venus	Sat.	Rahu
Jan.	5	284 41	200 35	267 41	275 04	352 37	301 02	26 48	144 09
	15	294 53	205 16	282 41	290 30	354 18	313 33	27 02	143 37
	25	305 04	209 35	298 32	306 50	356 09	326 02	27 25	143 06
Feb.	4	315 13	213 29	315 25	324 18	358 10	338 30	27 60	142 34
	14	325 20	216 50	333 24	342 31	0 19	350 54	28 43	142 02
	24	335 25	219 30	351 09	358 20	2 34	3 15	29 34	141 30
March	6	345 28	221 21	2 54	3 56R	4 54	15 31	30 33	140 58
	16	355 27	222 10	⸱ 32	357 10	7 16	27 41	31 37	140 27
	26	5 23	221 48R	353 08	351 03D	9 41	39 45	32 46	139 54
April	5	15 15	220 10	351 19	353 39	12 06	51 41	33 59	139 23
	15	25 05	217 23	357 37	2 50	14 31	63 27	35 14	138 51
	25	34 51	213 48	9 06	16 14	16 54	75 03	36 30	138 20
May	5	44 33	210 08	24 10	32 54	19 13	86 26	37 47	137 48
	15	54 13	207 03	42 46	52 42	21 29	97 32	39 03	137 16
	25	63 51	205 05	63 32	74 29	23 39	108 18	40 16	136 44
June	4	73 26	204 27D	85 00	94 43	25 42	118 36	41 27	136 12
	14	83 00	205 07	103 25	111 03	27 37	129 19	42 34	135 41
	24	92 33	206 57	117 34	122 51	29 22	137 13	43 36	135 09
July	4	102 05	209 47	126 44	129 00	30 56	144 56	44 32	134 37
	14	111 37	213 25	129 23R	127 49	32 17	150 57	45 21	134 05
	24	121 10	217 45	124 45	121 18	33 23	154 32	46 01	133 34
Aug.	3	130 43	222 37	118 57	118 54	34 13	154 44R	46 34	133 02
	13	140 18	227 58	121 38D	127 04	34 46	151 08	46 56	132 30
	23	149 55	233 43	134 46	143 55	34 59	145 11	47 08	131 58
Sep.	2	159 35	239 48	153 40	163 23	34 52R	140 14	47 10R	131 27
	12	169 17	246 11	172 45	181 41	34 25	138 50D	47 01	130 55
	22	179 02	252 49	190 11	198 16	33 40	146 10	46 42	130 23
Oct.	2	188 51	259 40	205 58	213 18	32 39	146 25	46 13	129 51
	12	198 43	266 43	220 16	226 45	31 25	153 43	45 36	129 19
	22	208 38	273 56	232 38	237 32	30 06	162 25	44 53	128 48
Nov.	1	218 37	281 18	240 52	241 34	28 45	172 08	44 06	128 16
	11	228 39	288 46	238 31R	232 19	27 30	182 34	43 18	127 44
	21	238 43	296 21	226 55	225 48D	26 26	193 31	42 31	127 12
Dec.	1	248 50	303 60	228 43	234 02	25 38	204 51	41 48	126 41
	11	258 59	311 42	240 34	247 41	25 09	216 30	41 11	126 09
	21	269 10	319 26	250 05	262 39	25 00D	228 21	40 43	125 37
	31	279 21	328 10	270 15	—	25 11	240 21	40 25	125 07

Ayanamsa : 22° 23' 53''

Longitude of the Moon

1999		Sun.	Tues.	Thurs.	Sat.	Mon.	Wed.	Fri.
Jan.	1							92 14
	3	120 48	147 51	173 20	197 40	221 27	245 19	269 46
	17	295 04	321 16	348 18	16 00	44 15	72 47	101 12
	31	128 57						
Feb.	1					142 26	168 28	193 20
	7	217 23	241 10	265 19	290 22	316 37	344 05	12 24
	21	41 02	69 28	97 23	124 36			
March	1					151 00	176 32	201 13
	7	225 15	249 02	273 07	298 08	324 36	352 40	21-53
	21	51 23	80 15	107 59	134 35	160 15	185 12	
April	1			197 27	221 34	245 22	269 11	293 34
	11	319 08	346 26	15 32	45 42	75 42	104 26	131 33
	25	157 19	182 08	206 22				
May	1				230 17	254 02	277 53	302 15
	9	327 42	354 49	23 49	54 09	84 34	113 43	141 04
	23	166 48	191 24	215 24	239 11	262 59		
June	1		274 57	299 11	324 09	350 19	18 07	47 32
	13	77 51	107 47	136 16	162 57	188 07	212 19	236 06
	27	259 54	284 01					
July	1			308 38	334 00	0 23	28 02	56 56
	11	86 36	116 04	144 25	171 12	201 29	220 44	244 32
	25	268 26	292 49	317 57	343 58			
Aug.	1	357 20	24 42	52 53	81 38	110 28	138 48	166 03
	15	191 59	216 44	240 43	264 31	288 44	313 51	340 06
	29	7 25	35 29					
Sep.	1						49 40	78 05
	5	106 18	134 05	161 11	187 20	212 27	236 42	260 28
	19	284 23	309 05	335 07	2 38	31 18	60 22	
Oct.	1							89 04
	3	166 58	144 03	170 22	195 55	220 42	244 47	268 29
	17	292 18	316 55	343 00	10 53	40 17	70 12	99 30
	31	127 31						
Nov.	1					141 02	167 14	192 34
	7	217 13	241 21	265 04	288 42	312 44	337 51	4 41
	21	33 28	63 40	94 02	123 19	150 57		
Dec.	1						177 03	202 02
	5	226 18	250 09	273 49	297 31	321 39	346 42	13 15
	19	41 39	71 36	102 06	131 50	159 55	186 14	

RAMAN'S EPHEMERIS 2000 A.D.
Longitudes of Planets

2000		Sun	Mars	Merc.	Merc.	Jupit.	Venus	Saturn	Rahu
Jan.	5	284 27	331 04	278 09	286 08	25 27	246 25	40 20R	124 50
	15	294 38	338 49	294 17	302 39	26 09	258 35	40 17D	124 18
	25	304 48	346 32	311 17	319 56	27 09	270 49	40 28	123 47
Feb.	4	314 58	354 13	328 35	336 40	28 23	283 07	40 48	123 15
	14	325 06	1 52	343 12	346 48	29 56	295 26	41 18	122 43
	24	335 11	9 27	346 26R	342 32	31 39	307 47	41 58	122 11
March	6	346 13	I7 43	336 30	333 23	33 44	321 22	42 53	121 36
	16	356 12	25 10	333 25D	334 48	35 47	333 44	43 50	121 03
	26	6 07	32 31	338 28	343 28	37 57	346 05	44 53	120 33
April	5	16 00	39 49	349 28	356 18	40 12	358 26	46 01	120 01
	15	25 49	47 01	3 51	12 06	42 31	10 46	47 13	119 29
	25	35 35	54 09	21 02	30 37	44 52	23 05	48 29	118 57
May	5	45 17	61 11	41 03	51 45	47 14	35 24	49 45	118 25
	15	54 57	68 09	62 34	73 24	49 37	47 42	51 03	117 52
	25	64 34	75 03	82 16	90 28	51 59	59 59	52 19	117 22
June	4	74 10	81 53	97 24	102 57	54 18	72 17	53 34	116 50
	14	83 44	88 38	107 00	109 33	56 34	84 34	54 47	116 18
	24	93 16	95 20	109 45R	109 01	58 46	96 51	55 56	115 47
July	4	102 48	101 59	105 55	102 54	60 51	109 08	57 00	115 15
	14	112 20	108 34	100 48	100 34D	62 51	121 51	57 59	114 43
	24	121 53	115 06	102 40	107 08	64 41	133 44	58 51	114 11
Aug.	3	131 27	121 35	113 48	122 18	66 21	146 02	59 35	113 40
	13	141 02	128 02	131 59	142 07	67 49	158 19	60 11	113 08
	23	150 39	134 26	152 07	163 33	69 04	170 46	60 37	112 36
Sep.	2	160 19	140 59	170 45	179 17	70 03	182 53	60 53	112 04
	12	170 01	147 10	187 20	194 55	70 45	195 09	60 59R	111 32
	22	179 47	153 27	202 03	208 40	71 09	207 23	60 53	111 01
Oct.	2	189 35	159 44	214 40	219 51	71 13	219 36	60 37	110 29
	12	199 28	166 00	223 45	225 43	70 57	231 47	60 11	110 00
	22	209 23	172 13	225 16R	220 13	70 22	243 55	59 37	109 25
Nov.	1	219 22	178 54	214 09	210 13	69 28	256 02	58 55	108 54
	11	229 24	184 34	210 58D	215 19	68 20	268 05	58 08	108 22
	21	239 29	190 41	221 37	228 49	67 03	280 04	57 20	107 50
Dec.	1	249 36	196 46	236 23	244 06	65 41	292 07	56 32	107 18
	11	259 45	202 47	251 51	259 39	64 22	303 39	55 47	106 46
	21	269 56	208 45	267 30	275 25	63 11	315 10	55 08	106 15
	31	280 08	214 39	283 28	—	62 13	326 25	54 37	105 43

Ayanamsa : 22° 24′ 44″

Longitude of the Moon

2000		Sun.	Tues.	Thurs.	Sat.	Mon.	Wed.	Fri.
Jan.	1				223 18	247 08	270 48	294 35
	9	318 45	343 35	9 26	36 37	65 16	95 00	124 57
	23	154 02	181 32	207 32	231 58	255 39		
Feb.	1		267 28	291 10	315 31	340 32	6 26	33 14
	13	61 05	89 34	118 40	147 39	175 46	202 28	227 43
	27	251 52	276 03					
March	1						287 25	311 35
	5	336 40	2 52	30 01	57 49	85 58	114 16	142 30
	19	170 20	197 18	223 05	247 42	271 33	295 13	319 31
April	1				332 03	358 10	25 39	54 02
	9	82 42	111 04	138 56	166 14	192 53	218 27	243 34
	23	267 37	291 17	315 09	339 58			
May	1					6 17	34 17	63 27
	7	92 53	121 44	149 35	176 36	202 24	227 35	252 02
	21	275 54	299 31	323 23	348 09	14 27	42 33	
June	1			57 12	87 10	117 03	145 53	173 20
	11	199 27	224 33	248 54	272 44	296 21	320 04	344 22
	25	9 47	36 48	65 34				
July	1				95 36	125 50	155 09	182 53
	9	209 00	233 52	257 55	271 35	305 13	328 39	253 41
	23	19 11	46 02	74 24	104 03	134 11		
Aug	1		149 04	177 54	205 01	230 30	254 47	278 29
	13	292 08	326 08	350 44	16 09	42 30	69 56	98 28
	27	127 51	157 22	186 06				
Sep.	1							199 55
	3	226 11	251 07	275 02	298 39	322 37	347 20	12 57
	17	39 27	66 41	94 33	123 00	151 47	180 21	208 00
Oct.	1	234 14	259 05	283 00	306 39	330 45	355 49	22 06
	15	49 24	77 20	105 30	133 40	161 44	189 27	218 24
	29	242 15	266 57					
Nov.	1						278 57	302 37
	5	326 24	351 22	16 58	44 24	72 55	101 50	130 28
	19	158 31	186 01	212 24	238 06	262 55	286 58	
Dec.	1							310 35
	3	334 19	358 51	24 45	52 23	81 28	111 14	140 40
	17	169 04	196 12	222 11	247 13	271 32	295 16	318 57
	31	342 38						

Ayanamsa : 22° 24′ 44″

RAMAN'S EPHEMERIS
Longitudes of Uranus
on the First of each Month

Year	Jan.	Feb.	Mar.	Apr.	May	June	July	Aug.	Sep.	Oct.	Nov.	Dec.
1891	210 52	211 24	211 8	210 9	208 53	207 47	207 18	207 37	208 41	210 17	212 12	213 59
1892	215 24	216 3	215 53	214 58	213 44	212 35	212 00	212 11	213 10	214 44	216 36	218 26
1893	219 54	220 40	220 37	219 48	218 35	217 23	216 42	216 46	217 37	219 5	220 57	222 47
1894	224 21	225 13	225 17	224 37	223 26	222 12	221 24	221 19	222 5	223 26	225 16	227 7
1895	228 44	229 45	229 56	229 21	223 14	226 59	226 5	225 54	226 31	227 47	229 33	231 25
1896	233 5	234 11	234 32	234 1	233 00	231 42	230 47	230 28	230 58	232 9	233 51	235 44
1897	237 23	238 39	239 3	238 42	237 43	236 27	235 26	234 59	235 21	236 27	238 6	239 57
1898	241 43	243 00	243 32	243 19	242 24	241 9	240 5	239 32	239 45	240 44	242 20	244 9
1899	245 58	247 21	247 58	247 52	247 4	245 50	244 42	244 3	244 10	245 2	246 33	248 20
1900	250 10	251 38	252 22	252 23	251 41	250 29	249 19	248 34	248 33	249 18	250,43	252 29
1901	254 21	255 52	256 43	256 51	256 15	255 6	253 55	253 4	252 55	253 33	254 54	256 37
1902	258 29	260 4	261 00	261 17	260 47	259 41	258 29	257 33	257 17	257 48	259 2	260 43
1903	262 34	264 14	265 15	266 38	265 15	264 14	263 12	262 00	261 33	262 2	263 10	264 46
1904	266 38	268 20	269 28	269 57	269 39	268 42	267 30	266 26	265 58	266 15	267 19	268 53
1905	270 44	272 27	273 37	274 18	274 2	273 9	271 58	270 51	270 16	270 27	271 24	272 54
1906	274 43	276 29	277 43	278 26	278 21	277 34	276 24	275 15	274 34	274 38	275 28	276 53
1907	278 42	280 29	281 47	282 36	282 38	281 56	280 49	279 38	278 51	278 48	279 32	280 52
1908	282 38	284 27	285 51	286 45	286 52	286 15	285 10	283 57	283 7	282 58	283 37	284 55
1909	286 37	288 26	289 50	290 50	291 4	290 33	289 31	288 18	287 23	287 7	287 39	288 50
1910	290 32	292 21	293 48	294 53	295 14	294 49	293 51	292 37	291 38	291 16	291 41	292 47
1911	294 25	296 14	297 43	298 54	299 21	299 3	298 8	296 55	295 53	295 25	295 42	296 48
1912	298 17	300 6	301 40	302 54	303 26	303 13	302 23	301 10	300 5	299 23	299 45	300 40
1913	302 12	304 00	305 33	306 52	307 30	307 23	306 27	305 27	304 19	303 41	303 45	304 35
1914	306 3	307 49	309 24	310 47	311 31	311 31	310 50	309 42	308 32	307 48	307 46	308 30
1915	309 53	311 38	313 13	314 40	315 30	315 37	315 2	313 55	312 44	311 56	311 47	312 24
1916	313 43	315 26	317 5	318 35	319 29	319 41	319 9	318 5	316 53	316 1	315 48	316 20
1917	317 35	319 16	320 53	322 25	323 25	323 43	323 17	322 16	321 4	320 8	319 48	320 14
1918	321 24	323 2	324 39	326 14	327 18	327 43	327 23	326 26	325 13	324 14	323 48	324 7
1919	325 12	326 47	328 28	330 2	331 10	331 14	331 28	330 35	329 23	328 20	327 48	328 1
1920	329 00	330 32	332 11	333 51	335 3	335 39	335 30	334 40	333 29	332 24	331 47	331 56
1921	332 50	334 19	335 55	337 36	338 53	339 34	339 31	338 47	337 37	336 30	335 48	335 50
1922	336 38	338 4	339 38	341 21	342 41	343 29	343 32	342 53	341 45	340 34	339 49	339 44
1923	340 27	341 48	343 21	345 5	346 29	347 22	347 32	346 58	345 53	344 43	343 51	343 40
1924	344 16	345 33	347 7	348 52	350 18	351 16	351 30	351 1	349 58	348 47	347 52	347 36
1925	348 7	349 21	350 50	352 36	354 5	355 8	355 28	355 5	354 6	352 55	351 55	351 33
1926	351 58	353 7	354 34	356 19	357 52	359 00	359 26	359 9	358 13	357 0	355 59	355 32
1927	355 50	356 53	358 18	0 3	1 38	2 51	3 23	3 12	2 21	1 11	0 5	359 31
1928	359 43	0 41	2 6	3 50	5 27	6 43	7 21	7 14	6 27	5 18	4 9	3 32
1929	3 38	4 32	5 51	7 35	9 13	10 34	11 17	10 35	9 27	8 16	7 33	7 33
1930	7 33	8 21	9 37	11 19	12 59	14 24	15 13	15 20	14 42	13 37	12 25	11 37

Longitudes of Uranus

Year	Jan.	Feb.	Mar.	Apr.	May	June	July	Aug.	Sep	Oct.	Nov.	Dec.
1931	11 29	12 11	13 22	15 4	16 45	18 13	19 8	19 22	18 50	17 48	16 34	15 41
1932	15 27	16 3	17 13	18 53	20 34	22 6	23 4	23 23	22 56	21 56	20 42	19 46
1933	19 27	19 57	21 1	22 39	24 21	25 56	26 59	27 24	27 4	26 7	24 51	23 52
1934	23 28	23 51	24 51	26 26	28 8	29 46	30 55	31 26	31 12	30 21	29 5	28 1
1935	27 30	27 47	28 42	30 14	31 56	33 37	34 50	35 28	35 21	34 32	33 19	32 12
1936	31 35	31 45	32 37	34 36	35 48	37 31	38 48	39 30	39 28	38 44	37 31	36 23
1937	35 42	35 46	36 32	37 57	39 38	41 22	42 44	43 33	43 38	42 58	41 48	40 38
1938	39 51	39 53	40 30	41 50	43 30	45 15	46 41	47 36	47 47	47 14	46 7	44 54
1939	44 2	43 52	44 27	45 43	47 23	49 9	50 38	51 39	51 58	51 31	50 26	49 13
1940	48 16	47 59	43 29	49 43	51 10	53 7	54 40	55 45	56 9	55 47	54 45	53 31
1941	52 30	52 2	52 32	53 41	55 15	57 3	58 33	59 50	60 20	60 5	59 8	57 54
1942	56 49	56 21	56 38	57 41	59 13	61 1	62 38	63 56	64 33	64 24	63 32	62 20
1943	61 10	60 35	60 46	61 44	63 12	64 59	66 39	68 2	68 46	68 44	67 57	66 46
1944	65 33	64 53	64 58	65 49	67 15	69 3	70 43	72 11	73 1	73 5	72 21	71 11
1945	69 57	69 13	69 12	69 57	71 18	73 3	74 49	76 19	77 14	77 26	76 50	75 41
1946	74 25	73 35	73 26	74 6	75 23	77 7	78 52	80 28	81 30	81 47	81 18	80 14
1947	78 56	78 00	77 45	78 17	79 29	81 11	82 58	84 36	85 45	86 11	85 48	84 47
1948	83 29	82 27	82 6	82 33	83 42	85 21	87 8	88 50	90 4	90 34	90 17	89 21
1949	88 1	86 57	86 31	86 50	87 52	89 30	91 16	93 00	94 21	94 59	94 49	93 57
1950	92 40	91 31	90 58	91 9	92 6	93 40	95 26	97 14	98 39	99 23	99 23	98 36
1951	97 21	96 7	95 28	95 32	96 23	97 53	99 38	101 27	102 57	103 50	103 56	103 16
1952	102 1	100 45	100 2	99 59	100 46	102 11	103 55	105 46	107 19	108 16	108 30	107 55
1953	106 43	105 26	104 38	104 28	105 7	106 28	108 11	110 2	111 42	112 49	113 6	112 35
1954	111 29	110 11	109 19	109 1	109 31	110 48	112 27	114 20	116 2	117 13	117 42	117 22
1955	116 18	114 59	114 1	113 36	114 00	115 9	116 46	118 39	120 24	121 42	122 19	122 5
1956	121 7	119 48	118 45	118 14	118 31	119 36	121 11	123 3	124 51	126 13	126 56	126 50
1957	125 56	124 37	123 33	122 55	123 4	124 3	125 33	127 24	129 15	130 41	131 32	131 34
1958	130 47	129 31	128 23	127 38	127 39	128 30	129 55	131 45	133 38	135 10	136 10	136 20
1959	135 39	134 24	133 15	132 23	132 17	133 00	134 20	136 9	138 5	139 40	140 46	141 3
1960	141 31	139 20	138 7	137 10	136 57	137 35	138 51	140 37	142 32	144 12	145 24	145 48
1961	145 22	144 15	143 2	142 00	141 39	142 8	143 19	145 3	146 58	148 41	150 00	150 32
1962	150 15	149 11	147 59	146 52	146 24	146 44	147 49	149 29	151 24	153 11	154 35	155 15
1963	155 5	154 9	152 57	151 46	151 11	151 23	152 21	153 57	155 51	157 39	159 10	159 58
1964	159 58	159 7	157 54	156 40	155 59	156 4	156 57	158 28	160 21	162 12	163 46	164 41
1965	164 47	164 2	162 54	161 37	160 50	160 47	161 32	162 59	164 49	166 41	168 20	169 22
1966	169 37	169 00	167 55	166 36	165 43	165 31	166 9	167 29	169 17	171 10	172 53	174 2
1967	174 26	173 56	172 54	171 35	170 37	170 17	170 47	172 1	173 46	175 30	177 26	178 41
1968	179 13	178 52	177 52	176 33	175 31	175 5	175 27	176 36	178 18	180 11	182 00	183 21
1969	183 59	183 45	182 52	181 33	180 26	179 53	180 7	181 9	182 47	184 39	186 31	187 57
1970	188 43	188 38	187 50	186 33	185 23	184 43	184 48	185 44	187 16	189 6	191 00	192 31
1971	193 25	193 29	192 48	191 33	190 20	190 33	189 31	190 18	191 45	193 33	195 28	197 4
1972	198 6	198 17	197 41	196 29	195 15	194 23	194 14	194 55	196 17	198 3	199 59	201 37
1973	202 45	203 3	202 34	201 27	200 11	199 13	198 57	199 29	200 45	202 28	204 24	206 6
1974	207 21	207 47	207 26	206 22	205 6	204 3	203 40	204 3	205 13	206 52	208 48	210 33
1975	211 54	212 28	212 14	211 16	210 1	208 53	208 22	208 38	209 41	211 15	213 10	214 58
1976	216 24	217 6	216 59	216 5	214 51	213 41	213 5	213 13	214 11	215 41	217 35	219 24
1977	220 54	221 42	221 42	220 55	219 45	218 30	217 47	217 48	218 38	220 3	221 55	223 45
1978	225 20	226 15	226 22	225 42	224 33	223 18	222 30	222 22	223 4	224 24	226 13	228 4
1979	229 43	230 45	231 0	230 27	229 21	228 5	227 11	226 56	227 30	228 45	230 31	232 22
1980	234 4	235 13	235 34	235 8	234 5	232 49	231 51	231 30	231 58	233 7	234 50	236 41

Longitudes of Uranus
on the first of each month

Year	Jan.	Feb.	March	April	May	June	July	Aug.	Sep.	Oct.	Nov.	Dec.
1981	238 30	239 40	240 06	239 47	238 49	237 33	236 31	236 03D	236 23	237 27	239 05	240 56
1982	242 43	244 02	244 36R	244 24	243 31	242 16	241 10	240 36D	240 48	241 45	243 20	245 08
1983	246 57	248 22	249 02R	248 58	248 11	246 57	245 49	245 08D	245 13	246 03	247 32	249 19
1984	251 10	252 39	253 26	253 28	252 46	251 34	250 24	249 38	249 37	250 21	251 47	253 32
1985	255 24	256 56	257 47	257 56	257 20	256 12	255 00	254 09	254 00	254 37	255 57	257 40
1986	259 32	261 08	262 05	262 21	261 52	260 47	259 34	258 38	258 22	258 52	260 06	261 46
1987	263 38	265 17	266 19	266 43	266 20	265 20	264 07	263 06	262 43	263 06	264 14	265 50
1988	267 42	269 24	270 33	271 03	270 45	269 48	268 36	267 32	267 03	267 20	268 23	269 56
1989	271 47	273 31	274 41	275 18	275 08	274 15	273 04	271 57	271 22	271 32	272 29	273 58
1990	275 47	277 33	278 48	279 31	279 27	278 40	277 31	276 22	275 40	275 43	276 33	277 58
1991	279 46	281 33	282 52	283 42	283 44	283 03	281 56	280 45	279 58	279 54	280 37	281 57
1992	283 43	285 31	286 56	287 50	287 59	287 22	286 17	285 04	284 14	284 04	284 42	285 58
1993	287 42	289 31	290 55	291 56	292 10	291 40	290 39	289 25	288 30	288 14	288 45	289 56
1994	291 37	293 26	294 53	295 59	296 21	295 57	294 59	293 45	292 46	292 23	292 47	293 52
1995	295 30	297 19	298 49	300 00	300 28	300 10	299 17	298 04	297 01	296 32	296 49	297 49
1996	299 23	301 14	302 46	304 01	304 34	304 21	303 31	302 19	301 13	300 40	300 51	301 47
1997	303 18	305 06	306 39	307 58	308 37	308 31	307 46	306 35	305 27	304 48	304 53	305 42
1998	307 09	308 55	310 30	311 53	312 38	312 39	311 59	310 50	309 40	308 56	308 53	309 36
1999	310 59	312 44	314 19	315 47	316 37	316 45	316 10	315 04	313 52	313 03	312 54	313 31
2000	314 47	316 29	318 09	319 39	320 35	320 48	320 18	319 15	318 02	317 10	316 54D	317 25

RAMAN'S EPHEMERIS
Longitudes of Neptune
on the First of each Month

Year	Jan.	Feb.	Mar.	Apr.	May	June	July	Aug.	Sept.	Oct.	Nov.	Dec.
1890	62 12	61 47	61 52	62 26	63 22	63 31	65 34	66 24	66 48	66 41	66 6	65 18
1891	64 30	64 2	64 5	64 37	65 32	66 40	67 44	68 36	69 2	68 58	68 25	67 36
1892	66 48	66 18	66 19	66 50	67 44	68 52	69 56	70 49	71 17	71 14	70 42	69 54
1893	69 5	68 34	68 33	69 2	69 54	71 1	72 6	73 00	73 30	73 30	73 00	72 13
1894	71 24	70 51	70 48	71 13	72 5	73 10	74 16	75 12	75 44	75 46	75 20	74 32
1895	73 42	73 7	73 2	73 25	74 14	75 20	76 26	77 23	77 58	78 2	77 37	76 51
1896	76 00	75 24	75 16	75 38	76 26	77 32	78 37	79 36	80 12	89 18	79 53	79 10
1897	78 19	77 41	77 31	77 51	78 37	79 40	80 46	81 46	82 24	82 34	82 12	81 27
1898	80 36	79 56	79 44	80 2	80 46	81 49	82 56	83 56	84 36	84 47	84 28	83 46
1899	82 54	82 13	81 59	82 13	82 55	83 57	85 4	86 6	86 48	87 2	86 44	86 4
1900	85 12	84 30	84 13	84 25	85 4	86 5	87 12	88 15	88 59	89 16	89 1	88 22
1901	87 30	86 45	86 27	86 37	87 15	88 14	89 21	90 25	91 11	91 29	91 17	90 40
1902	89 48	89 3	88 42	88 49	89 25	90 23	91 29	92 34	93 22	93 43	93 33	92 58
1903	92 6	91 20	90 57	91 1	91 34	92 32	93 37	94 43	95 33	95 56	95 49	95 15
1904	94 23	93 37	93 12	93 14	93 46	94 42	95 48	96 54	97 45	98 9	98 4	97 31
1905	96 41	95 53	95 26	95 26	95 56	96 51	97 56	99 3	99 55	100 22	100 19	99 48
1906	98 59	98 10	97 42	97 39	98 7	99 00	100 4	101 12	102 6	102 35	102 35	102 6
1907	101 17	100 27	99 58	99 52	100 18	101 9	102 13	103 21	104 16	104 48	104 50	104 23
1908	103 35	102 45	102 13	102 6	102 30	103 20	104 23	105 31	106 28	107 1	107 5	106 39
1909	105 52	105 1	104 28	104 19	104 41	105 29	106 32	107 40	108 38	109 13	109 19	108 56
1910	108 10	107 19	106 44	106 33	106 52	107 38	108 40	109 48	110 48	111 25	111 34	111 12
1911	110 27	109 36	109 00	108 46	109 2	109 47	110 48	111 56	112 57	113 36	113 48	113 29
1912	112 45	111 53	111 15	110 59	111 14	111 58	112 58	114 6	115 8	115 48	116 1	115 43
1913	115 00	114 9	113 31	113 13	113 25	114 7	115 6	116 14	117 16	117 59	118 14	117 59
1914	117 18	116 26	115 47	115 26	115 37	116 15	117 13	118 21	119 25	120 9	120 27	120 15
1915	119 35	118 43	118 3	117 40	117 47	118 24	119 21	120 29	121 33	122 19	122 40	122 30
1916	121 15	121 00	120 17	119 53	119 59	120 35	121 31	122 39	123 44	124 31	124 53	124 44
1917	124 7	123 16	122 34	122 7	122 11	122 45	123 39	124 46	125 52	126 41	127 5	126 59
1918	126 24	125 33	124 50	124 22	124 23	124 54	125 47	126 54	128 00	128 51	129 18	129 13
1919	128 40	127 50	127 6	126 36	126 35	127 4	127 55	129 1	130 8	131 00	131 30	131 28
1920	130 57	130 7	129 21	128 50	128 47	129 15	130 5	131 11	132 18	133 11	133 42	133 42
1921	138 12	132 23	131 38	131 4	130 59	131 24	132 13	133 18	134 26	135 20	135 53	135 56
1922	135 28	134 40	133 54	133 19	133 11	133 34	134 21	135 26	136 33	137 29	138 5	138 9
1923	137 43	136 56	136 11	135 33	135 23	135 44	136 29	137 32	138 41	139 38	140 15	140 22
1924	139 59	139 13	138 25	137 47	137 36	137 54	138 38	139 41	140 50	141 48	142 26	142 35
1925	142 13	141 27	140 41	140 1	139 48	140 4	140 46	141 48	142 56	143 55	144 36	144 47
1926	144 27	143 14	142 57	142 16	142 00	142 13	142 54	143 55	145 3	146 3	146 46	147 00
1927	146 42	145 59	145 13	144 30	144 12	144 23	145 1	146 1	147 9	148 11	148 55	149 11
1928	148 56	148 15	147 27	146 44	146 24	146 34	147 11	148 10	149 18	150 20	151 6	151 23
1929	151 9	150 29	149 43	148 58	148 37	148 44	149 19	150 17	151 24	152 27	153 15	153 35
1930	153 24	152 45	151 59	151 13	150 49	150 54	151 27	152 23	153 31	154 34	155 24	155 46

Longitudes of Neptune

Year	Jan.	Feb.	Mar.	Apr.	May	June	July	Aug.	Sept.	Oct.	Nov.	Dec.
1931	155 38	155 2	154 16	153 29	153 3	153 4	153 35	154 30	155 37	156 41	157 33	157 57
1932	157 52	157 18	156 31	155 43	155 16	155 16	155 45	156 39	157 46	158 50	159 43	160 9
1933	160 5	159 31	158 47	157 59	157 29	157 27	157 54	158 46	159 53	160 58	161 52	162 20
1934	162 18	168 47	161 3	160 14	159 42	159 58	160 2	160 53	161 59	163 4	164 00	164 30
1935	164 31	164 2	163 18	162 29	161 56	161 49	162 10	163 00	164 5	165 11	166 8	166 40
1936	166 45	166 17	165 33	164 43	164 9	164 00	164 21	165 8	166 12	167 18	168 16	168 51
1937	168 57	168 30	167 48	166 58	166 22	166 11	166 29	167 15	168 18	169 24	170 24	171 00
1938	171 8	170 44	170 3	169 12	168 36	168 22	168 38	169 22	170 25	171 31	172 31	173 10
1939	173 20	172 58	172 17	171 27	170 49	170 33	170 47	171 28	172 30	173 36	174 38	175 18
1940	175 31	175 11	174 32	173 41	173 1	172 44	172 56	173 36	174 37	175 43	176 45	177 28
1941	177 42	177 24	176 46	175 55	175 15	174 54	175 5	175 44	176 44	177 49	178 53	179 36
1942	179 53	179 37	179 1	178 10	177 28	177 7	177 14	177 50	178 49	179 55	181 00	181 45
1943	182 4	181 51	181 15	180 24	179 44	179 19	179 23	179 57	180 55	182 1	183 6	183 53
1944	184 15	184 3	183 29	182 49	181 55	181 29	181 34	182 6	183 3	184 9	185 15	186 2
1945	186 26	186 16	185 43	184 54	184 9	183 42	183 43	184 13	185 9	186 15	187 21	188 11
1946	188 36	188 29	187 59	187 10	186 24	185 54	185 53	186 22	187 16	188 19	189 28	190 19
1947	190 47	190 42	190 13	189 24	188 37	188 8	188 4	188 30	189 22	190 26	191 33	192 27
1948	192 56	192 55	192 26	191 38	190 51	190 19	190 14	190 39	191 30	192 33	193 42	194 36
1949	195 7	195 6	194 40	193 53	193 5	192 32	192 24	192 48	193 36	194 39	195 47	196 42
1950	197 16	197 18	196 54	196 7	195 20	194 45	194 35	194 55	195 42	196 45	197 53	198 49
1951	199 26	199 30	199 7	198 22	197 35	196 58	196 46	197 3	197 49	198 51	199 58	200 56
1952	201 33	201 41	201 20	200 36	199 47	199 10	198 56	199 12	199 56	200 56	202 6	203 4
1953	203 42	203 52	203 33	202 50	202 2	201 21	201 6	201 20	202 4	203 2	204 12	205 9
1954	205 48	205 59	205 46	205 5	204 15	203 36	203 18	203 30	204 9	205 7	206 15	207 16
1955	208 00	208 15	208 00	207 18	206 31	205 48	205 28	205 37	206 15	207 14	208 22	209 24
1956	210 9	210 25	210 10	209 32	208 44	208 00	207 40	207 48	208 25	209 20	210 30	211 32
1957	212 18	212 36	212 24	211 47	211 00	210 15	209 52	209 57	210 32	211 27	212 36	213 39
1958	214 26	214 47	214 36	214 1	214 13	212 29	212 4	212 6	212 39	213 33	214 40	215 44
1959	216 34	216 57	216 50	216 15	215 28	214 42	214 16	214 17	214 46	215 39	216 46	217 45
1960	218 42	219 7	219 2	218 28	217 41	216 55	216 27	216 26	216 55	217 46	218 54	219 58
1961	220 51	221 17	221 14	220 42	219 55	219 9	218 39	218 34	219 1	219 51	220 58	222 3
1962	222 58	223 27	223 26	222 56	222 10	221 22	220 51	220 40	221 8	221 57	223 3	224 9
1963	225 5	225 36	225 38	225 10	224 25	223 37	223 3	222 54	223 15	224 3	225 8	226 15
1964	227 12	227 45	227 48	227 22	226 38	225 49	225 15	225 4	225 24	226 11	227 15	228 22
1965	229 20	229 55	230 00	229 36	228 52	228 3	227 27	227 14	227 32	228 16	229 19	230 27
1966	231 27	232 5	232 10	231 49	231 6	230 17	229 40	229 25	229 40	230 22	231 25	232 31
1967	233 33	234 12	234 21	234 2	233 21	232 31	231 53	231 35	231 48	232 29	233 30	234 35
1968	235 39	236 20	236 32	236 14	235 34	234 44	234 4	233 46	233 57	234 37	235 38	236 45
1969	237 48	238 30	238 43	238 27	237 48	236 58	236 18	235 57	236 6	236 43	237 43	238 50
1970	239 54	240 38	240 53	240 40	240 3	239 13	238 31	238 9	238 15	238 50	239 49	240 55
1971	242 1	242 47	243 4	242 53	242 17	241 28	240 45	240 20	240 24	240 57	241 55	243 1
1972	244 7	244 55	245 15	245 5	244 30	243 41	242 58	242 32	242 34	243 6	244 2	245 9
1973	246 15	247 4	247 25	247 18	246 45	245 56	245 12	244 44	244 44	245 13	246 8	247 14
1974	248 21	249 12	249 35	249 31	248 59	248 11	247 26	246 56	246 54	247 21	248 14	249 19
1975	250 27	251 20	251 45	251 43	251 13	250 26	249 40	249 8	249 3	249 28	250 20	251 24
1976	252 33	253 27	253 55	253 54	253 26	252 39	251 52	251 20	251 13	251 37	252 27	253 32
1977	254 40	255 35	256 4	256 6	255 39	554 53	254 6	253 32	253 23	253 44	254 33	255 37
1978	256 46	257 42	258 13	258 17	257 53	257 8	256 20	255 44	255 33	255 52	256 39	257 42
1979	258 51	259 49	260 22	260 29	260 6	259 22	258 35	257 57	257 44	258 00	258 45	259 47
1980	260 56	261 56	262 31	262 40	262 19	261 36	260 48	260 9	259 54	260 9	260 53	261 55

Longitudes of Neptune
on the first of each month

Year	Jan.	Feb.	March	April	May	June	July	Aug.	Sep.	Oct.	Nov.	Dec.
1981	263 05	264 05	264 41	264 51	264 32	263 50	263 02	262 22	262 05	262 18	263 00	264 00
1982	265 10	266 12	266 50	267 03	266 45	266 05	265 17	264 36	264 17	264 27	265 07	266 07
1983	267 16	268 19	268 58	269 14	268 59	268 20	267 32	266 50	266 29	266 37	267 15	268 13
1984	269 22	270 26	271 09	271 26	271 12	270 34	269 46	269 03	268 40	268 47	269 24	270 21
1985	271 31	272 35	273 17	273 37	273 26	272 49	272 02	271 17	270 53	270 57	271 31	272 28
1986	273 37	274 42	275 26	275 48	275 39	275 04	274 17	273 32	273 05	273 07	273 19	274 34
1987	275 43	276 49	277 35	277 59	277 53	277 19	276 33	275 46	275 18	275 17	275 47	276 40
1988	277 49	278 56	279 45	280 10	280 05	279 33	278 46	278 00	277 30	277 28	277 56	278 22
1989	279 57	281 04	281 52	282 21	282 18	281 48	281 02	280 15	279 43	279 38	280 05	280 55
1990	282 03	283 11	284 00	284 31	284 31	284 02	283 18	282 29	281 56	281 49	282 13	282 37
1991	284 09	285 17	286 08	286 41	286 43	286 17	285 33	284 44	284 09	283 00	284 21	284 44
1992	286 15	287 24	288 18	288 52	288 55	288 30	287 47	286 58	286 22	286 11	286 31	287 17
1993	288 23	289 32	290 25	291 02	291 08	290 45	290 03	289 14	288 36	288 23	288 40	289 25
1994	290 29	291 39	292 33	293 12	293 20	292 59	292 19	291 29	290 50	290 35	290 49	291 32
1995	292 36	293 46	294 41	295 22	295 33	295 15	294 35	293 45	293 04	292 47	292 59	293 40
1996	294 42	295 52	296 51	297 33	297 45	297 28	296 49	295 00	295 18	294 59	295 10	295 49
1997	296 51	298 01	298 59	299 43	299 58	299 43	299 05	298 16	297 33	297 12	297 20	297 58
1998	298 58	300 08	301 06	301 52	302 10	301 57	301 21	300 32	299 48	299 25	299 31	300 06
1999	301 05	302 15	303 14	304 02	304 22	304 12	303 27	302 49	302 03	301 38	301 41	302 14
2000	303 11	304 20	305 22	306 12	306 34	306 26R	305 53	305 04	304 18	303 51	303 52D	304 23

RAMAN'S EPHEMERIS
Longitudes of Pluto
on the First of each Month

Year	Jan.	Feb.	Mar.	Apr.	May	June	July	Aug.	Sep.	Oct.	Nov.	Dec.
1890	65 00	65 00	65 00	65 00	66 00	67 00	67 00	68 00	68 00	68 00	67 00	67 00
1891	66 00	66 00	66 00	66 00	67 00	67 00	68 00	69 00	69 00	69 00	68 00	68 00
1892	67 00	67 00	67 00	67 00	68 00	68 00	69 00	69 00	70 00	70 00	69 00	69 00
1893	68 00	68 00	68 00	68 00	69 00	69 00	70 00	70 00	71 00	71 00	70 00	70 00
1894	69 00	69 00	69 00	69 00	70 00	70 00	71 00	71 00	72 00	72 00	71 00	71 00
1895	70 00	70 00	70 00	70 00	71 00	71 00	72 00	72 00	73 00	79 00	72 00	72 00
1896	71 00	71 00	71 00	71 00	71 00	72 00	73 00	73 00	74 00	74 00	73 00	73 00
1897	72 00	72 00	72 00	72 00	72 00	73 00	74 00	74 00	74 00	74 00	74 00	74 00
1898	73 00	73 00	73 00	73 00	73 00	74 00	75 00	75 00	76 00	76 00	75 00	75 00
1899	74 00	74 00	74 00	74 00	74 00	75 00	76 00	76 00	77 00	77 00	76 00	76 00
1900	75 00	75 00	75 00	75 00	75 00	76 00	77 00	77 00	78 00	78 00	77 00	77 00
1901	76 00	76 00	76 00	76 00	76 00	77 00	78 00	78 00	79 00	79 00	78 00	78 00
1902	77 00	77 00	77 00	77 00	77 00	78 00	79 00	79 00	80 00	80 00	79 00	79 00
1903	78 00	78 00	78 00	78 00	78 00	79 00	80 00	80 00	81 00	81 00	80 00	80 00
1904	79 00	79 00	79 00	79 00	79 00	80 00	81 00	81 00	82 00	82 00	81 00	81 00
1905	80 00	80 00	80 00	80 00	80 00	81 00	82 00	82 00	83 00	83 00	82 00	82 00
1906	81 00	81 00	81 00	81 05	81 00	82 00	83 00	83 00	84 00	84 00	83 00	83 00
1907	82 00	82 00	82 00	82 00	82 00	83 00	84 00	84 00	85 00	85 00	84 00	84 00
1908	83 00	83 00	83 00	83 00	83 00	84 00	85 90	85 00	86 00	86 00	86 00	85 00
1909	84 00	84 00	84 00	84 00	84 00	85 00	86 00	86 00	87 00	87 00	87 00	86 00
1910	86 00	85 00	85 00	85 00	85 00	86 00	87 00	87 00	88 00	88 00	88 00	87 00
1911	87 00	86 00	86 00	86 00	86 00	87 00	88 00	88 00	89 00	89 00	89 00	88 00
1912	88 00	87 00	87 00	87 00	87 00	88 00	89 00	89 00	90 00	90 00	90 00	89 00
1913	89 00	88 00	88 00	88 00	88 00	89 00	90 00	90 00	91 00	91 00	91 00	90 00
1914	90 00	89 00	89 00	89 00	89 00	90 00	91 00	91 00	92 00	92 00	92 00	92 00
1915	91 00	90 00	90 00	90 00	91 00	91 00	92 00	93 00	93 00	93 00	93 00	93 00
1916	92 00	92 00	91 00	91 00	92 00	92 00	93 00	94 00	94 00	94 00	94 00	94 00
1917	93 00	93 00	92 00	92 00	93 00	93 00	94 00	95 00	95 00	95 00	95 00	95 00
1918	94 00	94 00	93 00	93 00	94 00	94 00	95 00	96 00	96 00	97 00	96 00	96 00
1919	95 00	95 00	95 00	95 00	95 00	95 00	96 00	97 00	97 00	98 00	98 00	97 00
1920	97 00	96 00	96 00	96 00	96 00	97 00	97 00	98 00	99 00	99 00	99 00	98 00
1921	98 00	97 00	97 00	97 00	97 00	98 00	98 00	99 00	100 00	100 00	100 00	100 00
1922	99 00	98 00	98 00	98 00	98 00	99 00	100 00	100 00	101 00	101 00	101 00	101 00
1923	100 00	100 00	99 00	99 00	99 00	100 00	101 00	101 00	102 00	102 00	102 00	101 00
1924	101 00	101 00	100 00	100 00	101 00	101 00	102 00	103 00	103 00	103 00	103 00	103 00
1925	103 00	102 00	102 00	101 00	102 00	102 00	103 00	104 00	104 00	105 00	105 00	104 00
1926	104 00	103 00	103 00	103 00	103 00	103 00	104 00	105 00	106 00	106 00	106 00	106 00
1927	105 00	104 00	104 00	104 00	104 00	105 00	105 00	106 00	107 00	107 00	107 00	107 00
1928	106 00	106 00	105 00	105 00	105 00	106 00	107 00	107 00	108 00	108 00	108 00	108 00
1929	107 00	107 00	106 00	106 00	106 00	107 00	108 00	108 00	109 00	110 00	110 00	109 00
1930	109 00	108 00	108 00	107 00	108 00	108 00	109 00	110 00	110 00	111 00	111 00	111 00

Longitudes of Pluto

Year	Jan.	Feb.	Mar.	Apr.	May	June	July	Aug.	Sep	Oct	Nov.	Dec.
1931	110 00	109 00	109 00	109 00	109 00	109 00	110 00	111 00	112 00	112 00	112 00	112 00
1932	111 00	111 00	110 00	110 00	110 00	111 00	111 00	112 00	113 00	113 00	113 00	113 00
1933	113 00	112 00	111 00	111 00	111 00	112 00	113 00	113 00	114 00	114 00	115 00	114 00
1834	114 00	113 00	113 00	113 00	113 00	113 00	114 00	115 00	115 00	116 00	116 00	116 00
1935	115 00	115 00	114 00	114 00	114 00	114 00	115 00	116 00	117 00	117 00	117 00	117 00
1936	117 00	116 00	115 00	115 00	115 00	116 00	116 00	117 00	118 00	119 00	119 00	119 00
1937	118 00	117 00	117 00	116 00	117 00	117 00	118 00	119 00	119 00	120 00	120 00	120 00
1938	119 00	119 00	118 00	118 00	118 00	118 00	119 00	120 00	121 00	121 00	122 00	121 00
1939	121 00	120 00	120 00	119 00	119 00	120 00	120 00	121 00	122 00	123 00	123 00	123 00
1940	122 00	122 00	121 00	121 00	121 00	121 00	122 00	123 00	124 00	124 00	124 00	124 00
1941	124 00	123 00	122 00	122 00	122 00	123 00	123 00	124 00	125 00	126 00	126 00	126 00
1942	125 00	124 00	124 00	124 00	124 00	124 00	125 00	125 00	126 00	127 00	127 00	127 00
1943	127 00	126 00	125 00	125 00	125 00	125 00	126 00	127 00	128 00	128 00	129 00	129 00
1944	128 00	128 00	127 00	126 00	126 00	127 00	127 00	128 00	129 00	130 00	130 00	130 00
1945	130 00	129 00	128 00	128 00	128 00	128 00	129 00	130 00	131 00	131 00	132 00	132 00
1946	131 00	131 00	130 00	130 00	129 00	130 00	130 00	131 00	132 00	133 00	133 00	133 00
1947	133 00	132 00	132 00	131 00	131 00	131 00	132 00	133 00	134 00	134 00	135 00	135 00
1948	134 00	134 00	133 00	133 00	133 00	133 00	134 00	134 00	135 00	136 00	136 00	136 00
1949	136 00	135 00	135 00	134 00	134 00	134 00	135 00	136 00	137 00	138 00	138 00	138 00
1950	138 00	137 00	136 00	136 00	136 00	136 00	137 00	138 00	139 00	139 00	140 00	140 00
1951	140 00	139 00	138 00	138 00	137 00	137 00	138 00	139 00	140 00	141 00	142 00	142 00
1952	141 00	141 00	140 00	139 00	139 00	139 00	140 00	141 00	142 00	143 00	143 00	143 00
1953	143 00	142 00	142 00	141 00	141 00	141 00	142 00	143 00	144 00	144 00	145 00	145 00
1954	145 00	144 00	143 00	143 00	143 00	143 00	143 00	144 00	145 00	146 00	147 00	147 00
1955	147 00	146 00	145 00	145 00	144 00	144 00	145 00	146 00	147 00	148 00	149 00	149 00
1956	148 00	148 00	147 00	146 00	146 00	146 00	147 00	148 00	149 00	150 00	150 00	150 00
1957	150 00	150 00	149 00	148 00	148 00	148 00	149 00	149 00	151 00	152 00	152 00	152 00
1958	152 00	151 00	151 00	150 00	150 00	150 00	150 00	151 00	152 00	153 00	154 00	154 00
1959	154 00	154 00	153 00	152 00	152 00	152 00	152 00	153 00	154 00	155 00	156 00	156 00
1960	156 00	156 00	155 00	154 00	154 00	154 00	154 00	155 00	156 00	157 00	158 00	158 00
1961	158 00	157 00	157 00	156 00	156 00	156 00	156 00	157 00	158 00	159 00	160 00	160 00
1962	160 00	160 00	159 00	158 00	157 00	157 00	158 00	159 00	160 00	161 00	162 00	162 00
1963	162 00	161 00	161 00	160 00	160 00	160 00	160 00	161 00	162 00	163 00	164 00	164 00
1964	164 00	164 00	163 00	162 00	162 00	162 00	162 00	163 00	164 00	165 00	166 00	166 00
1965	166 00	166 00	165 00	165 00	164 00	164 00	164 00	165 00	166 00	167 00	168 00	169 00
1966	169 00	168 00	168 00	167 00	166 00	166 00	167 00	167 00	168 00	169 00	170 00	171 00
1967	171 00	170 00	170 00	169 00	169 00	168 00	169 00	169 00	170 00	171 00	172 00	173 00
1968	173 00	173 00	172 00	171 00	171 00	170 00	170 00	171 00	172 00	173 00	174 00	175 00
1969	175 00	175 00	174 00	173 00	173 00	173 00	173 00	174 00	176 00	176 00	178 00	180 00
1970	177 00	177 00	177 00	176 00	175 00	175 00	175 00	176 00	176 00	178 00	179 00	180 00
1971	179 42	179 27	178 51	178 1	177 20	176 59	177 8	177 45	178 45	179 52	180 57	181 43
1972	182 3	181 50	181 14	180 24	179 42	179 19	179 26	180 3	181 2	182 10	183 16	184 3
1973	184 25	184 14	183 40	182 50	182 7	181 42	181 46	182 21	183 19	184 26	185 34	186 24
1974	186 49	186 41	186 8	185 19	184 34	184 6	184 8	184 40	185 37	186 45	187 54	188 46
1975	189 13	189 8	188 38	187 48	187 2	186 33	186 32	187 2	187 57	189 5	190 15	191 9
1976	191 39	191 37	191 7	190 18	189 31	189 00	188 58	189 26	190 21	191 28	192 39	193 35
1977	194 7	194 7	193 40	192 51	192 4	191 31	191 25	191 51	192 45	193 51	195 3	196 1
1978	196 36	196 39	196 14	195 26	194 37	194 3	193 55	194 17	195 9	196 15	197 28	198 28
1979	199 5	199 12	198 49	198 2	197 15	196 36	196 26	196 46	197 36	198 41	199 55	200 56
1980	201 36	201 46	201 25	200 38	199 49	199 11	198 58	199 17	200 5	201 10	202 24	203 26

Longitudes of Pluto
on the first of each month

	Jan.	Feb.	March	April	May	June	July	Aug.	Sep.	Oct.	Nov.	Dec.
1981	204 10	204 20	204 01	203 17	202 27	201 47	201 32	201 48	202 34	203 38	204 52	205 57
1982	206 42	206 56	206 50	205 57	205 06	204 24	204 07	204 20	205 04	206 07	207 21	208 27
1983	209 15	209 32	209 18	208 37	207 47	207 03	206 43	206 53	207 34	208 36	209 50	210 57
1984	211 48	212 08	211 56	211 17	210 26	209 42	209 10	209 28	210 07	211 08	212 22	213 31
1985	214 22	214 44	214 35	213 57	213 08	212 22	211 57	212 02	212 39	213 38	214 52	216 01
1986	216 56	217 21	217 14	216 39	215 49	215 02	214 35	214 37	215 11	216 08	217 21	218 32
1987	219 28	219 56	219 53	219 20	218 31	217 43	217 13	217 12	217 43	218 39	219 51	221 02
1988	222 01	222 31	222 30	221 59	221 11	220 21	219 51	219 48	220 16	221 11	222 23	223 34
1989	224 34	225 07	225 08	224 39	223 52	223 02	222 29	222 23	222 50	223 42	224 52	226 04
1990	227 06	227 42	227 45	227 19	226 33	225 43	225 08	224 59	225 22	226 11	227 21	228 34
1991	229 37	230 15	230 21	229 58	229 14	228 23	227 46	227 34	227 54	228 41	229 50	231 02
1992	232 06	232 48	232 57	232 35	231 52	231 01	230 23	230 09	230 27	231 13	232 20	233 32
1993	234 37	235 20	235 31	235 12	234 30	233 39	233 00	232 43	232 58	233 41	234 47	235 59
1994	237 06	237 51	238 04	237 48	237 08	236 17	235 36	235 17	235 29	236 10	237 14	238 25
1995	239 33	240 21	240 37	240 24	239 46	238 55	238 13	237 51	237 00	238 38	239 40	240 51
1996	241 59	242 48	243 07	242 56	242 19	241 29	240 46	240 22	240 29	241 05	242 06	243 17
1997	244 26	245 16	245 36	245 27	244 53	244 03	243 19	242 53	242 57	243 31	244 29	245 39
1998	246 47	247 41	248 03	247 57	247 25	246 36	245 51	245 22	245 23	245 54	246 51	247 59
1999	249 08	250 04	250 28	250 25	249 54	249 06	248 21	247 50	247 49	248 16	249 11	250 19
2000	251 27	252 23	252 52	252 51	252 22	251 35	250 49	250 17	250 12	250 38	251 ··	252 37

TABLE I

Sidereal Time on January 1 of each year at Ujjain at *12 Mean Noon

Year	Sid. Time	Year	Sid. Time	Year	Sid. Time
1891	18 42 33	1921	18 41 30	1951	18 40 27
2	18 41 36	22	18 40 33	52	18 39 30
3	18 44 35	23	18 39 36	53	18 42 20
4	18 43 38	24	18 38 40	54	18 41 30
5	18 42 41	25	18 41 37	55	18 40 34
6	18 41 34	26	18 40 40	56	18 39 37
7	18 44 44	27	18 39 43	57	18 42 34
8	18 43 47	28	18 38 47	58	18 41 37
9	18 42 50	29	18 41 44	59	18 40 41
1900	18 41 53	1930	18 40 47	1960	18 39 44
1	18 40 56	31	18 39 50	61	18 42 41
2	18 39 59	32	18 38 54	62	18 41 44
3	18 39 2	33	18 41 51	63	18 40 48
4	18 38 5	34	18 40 54	64	18 39 51
5	18 41 2	35	18 39 57	65	18 42 48
6	18 40 5	36	18 39 1	66	18 41 51
7	18 39 8	37	18 41 58	67	18 40 55
8	18 38 12	38	18 41 1	68	18 39 58
9	18 41 9	39	18 40 4	69	18 42 55
1910	18 40 12	1940	18 39 8	1970	18 41 55
11	18 39 15	41	18 42 6	71	18 41 2
12	18 38 19	42	18 41 9	72	18 40 5
13	18 41 16	43	18 40 12	73	18 43 2
14	18 40 12	44	18 39 15	74	18 42 5
15	18 39 22	45	18 42 13	75	18 41 9
16	18 38 26	46	18 41 16	76	18 40 12
17	18 41 23	47	18 40 20	77	18 43 9
18	18 40 26	48	18 39 23	78	18 42 12
19	18 39 29	49	18 42 20	79	18 41 16
20	18 38 33	50	18 41 23	80	18 40 19

* By adding 51 seconds, Sidereal Time at G.M.N. (Greenwich Mean Noon) is obtained.

Example : 1-1-1926: From Table 18-40-40 adding 51s. we get
18-41-31 as S.T. at G.M.N.

TABLE II

Date-wise motion in Sidereal Time

Date	January hr m s	February hr m s	March hr m s	April hr m s	May hr m s	June hr m s
1	0 0 0	2 2 13	3 52 37	5 54 50	7 53 7	9 55 21
2	0 3 57	2 6 9	3 56 33	5 58 47	7 57 4	9 59 17
3	0 7 53	2 10 6	4 0 30	6 2 43	8 1 0	10 3 14
4	0 11 50	2 14 2	4 4 26	6 6 40	8 4 57	10 7 10
5	0 15 46	2 17 59	4 8 23	6 10 36	8 8 53	10 11 7
6	0 19 43	2 21 55	4 12 19	6 14 33	8 12 50	10 15 3
7	0 23 39	2 25 52	4 16 16	6 18 29	8 16 46	10 19 0
8	0 27 36	2 29 48	4 20 12	6 22 26	8 20 43	10 22 56
9	0 31 32	2 33 45	4 24 9	6 26 22	8 24 39	10 26 53
10	0 35 29	2 37 42	4 28 5	6 30 19	8 28 36	10 30 49
11	0 39 25	2 41 39	4 32 2	6 34 16	8 32 32	10 34 46
12	0 43 22	2 45 35	4 35 59	6 38 13	8 36 29	10 38 42
13	0 47 18	2 49 32	4 39 56	6 42 9	8 40 25	10 42 39
14	0 51 18	2 53 28	4 43 52	6 46 6	8 44 22	10 46 35
15	0 55 12	2 57 25	4 47 49	6 50 2	8 48 18	10 50 32
16	0 59 8	3 1 21	4 51 45	6 53 59	8 52 15	10 54 28
17	1 3 4	3 5 18	4 55 42	6 57 55	8 56 11	10 58 25
18	1 7 1	3 9 14	4 59 38	7 1 52	9 0 8	11 2 21
19	1 10 57	3 13 11	5 3 35	7 5 48	9 4 4	11 6 18
20	1 14 54	3 17 8	5 7 31	7 9 45	9 8 1	11 10 15
21	1 18 51	3 21 5	5 11 28	7 13 41	9 11 58	11 14 12
22	1 22 48	3 25 1	5 15 25	7 17 38	9 15 55	11 18 8
23	1 26 44	3 28 58	5 19 22	7 21 34	9 19 51	11 22 5
24	1 30 41	3 32 54	5 23 18	7 25 31	9 23 48	11 26 1
25	1 34 37	3 36 51	5 27 15	7 29 28	9 27 44	11 29 58
26	1 38 34	3 40 47	5 31 11	7 33 24	9 31 41	11 33 54
27	1 42 30	3 44 44	5 35 8	7 37 20	9 35 37	11 37 51
28	1 46 27	3 48 40	5 39 5	7 41 17	9 39 34	11 41 47
29	1 50 23		5 43 1	7 45 13	9 43 30	11 45 44
30	1 54 20		5 46 58	7 49 10	9 47 27	11 49 41
31	1 58 16		5 50 54		9 51 24	

TABLE II (contd.)

Date-wise motion in Sidereal Time

Date	July			August			September			October			November			December		
	hr	m	s	hr	m	s	hr	m	s	hr	m	s	hr	m	s	hr	m	s
1	11	53	38	13	55	50	15	58	4	17	56	21	19	58	34	21	56	50
2	11	57	34	13	59	47	16	2	0	18	0	17	20	2	31	22	0	47
3	12	1	31	14	3	44	16	5	57	18	4	14	20	6	27	22	4	43
4	12	5	27	14	7	40	16	9	53	18	8	10	20	10	24	22	8	40
5	12	9	24	14	11	36	16	13	50	18	12	7	20	14	20	22	12	36
6	12	13	21	14	15	33	16	17	46	18	16	3	20	18	17	22	16	33
7	12	17	17	14	19	29	16	21	43	18	20	0	20	22	13	22	20	30
8	12	21	14	14	23	26	16	25	40	18	23	57	20	26	10	22	24	27
9	12	25	10	14	27	23	16	29	37	18	27	54	20	30	6	22	28	23
10	12	29	6	14	31	20	16	33	33	18	31	50	20	34	3	22	32	20
11	12	33	3	14	35	16	16	37	30	18	35	47	20	38	0	22	36	16
12	12	36	59	14	39	13	16	41	26	18	39	43	20	41	56	22	40	13
13	12	40	56	14	43	9	16	45	23	18	43	40	20	45	52	22	44	9
14	12	44	52	14	47	6	16	49	19	18	47	37	20	49	49	22	48	6
15	12	48	49	14	51	2	16	53	16	18	51	33	20	53	45	22	52	2
16	12	52	45	14	54	59	16	57	12	18	55	30	20	57	42	22	55	59
17	12	56	42	14	58	55	17	1	9	18	59	26	21	1	39	22	59	56
18	13	0	38	15	2	52	17	5	5	19	3	22	21	5	36	23	3	53
19	13	4	35	15	6	48	17	9	2	19	7	19	21	9	32	23	7	49
20	13	8	32	15	10	45	17	12	58	19	11	15	21	13	29	23	11	46
21	13	12	29	15	14	41	17	16	55	19	15	12	21	17	25	23	15	42
22	13	16	25	15	18	38	17	20	51	19	19	8	21	21	22	23	19	39
23	13	20	22	15	22	34	17	24	48	19	23	5	21	25	18	23	23	35
24	13	24	18	15	26	31	17	28	44	19	27	1	21	29	15	23	27	32
25	13	28	15	15	30	27	17	32	41	19	30	58	21	33	11	23	31	00
26	13	32	11	15	34	24	17	36	37	19	34	54	21	37	8	23	35	25
27	13	36	8	15	38	20	17	40	34	19	38	51	21	41	4	23	39	21
28	13	40	4	15	42	17	17	44	31	19	42	48	21	45	1	23	43	18
29	13	44	1	15	46	14	17	48	28	19	46	45	21	48	57	23	47	14
30	13	48	57	15	50	11	17	52	24	19	50	41	21	52	57	23	51	11
31	13	51	54	15	54	7				19	54	38				23	55	7

Note :—In case of leap year, sidereal motion for the date next to that in question should be taken after 28th February.

TABLE III

Tables of Houses—Sayana

Sid. T. H.M.	0°	10°	20°	30°	40°	50°	60°	Tenth House For all Lats.
	♋	♋	♋	♑	♋	♋	♌	♈
0 0	0 0	4 1	8 14	12 56	18 28	25 22	4 34	0 0
0 16	3 40	7 40	11 49	16 24	21 45	28 21	7 3	4 22
						♌		
0 32	7 21	11 18	15 23	19 51	24 59	1 17	9 31	8 43
0 48	11 2	14 56	18 56	23 16	28 12	4 12	11 58	13 3
					♌			
1 4	14 44	18 35	22 29	26 40	1 24	7 6	14 25	17 22
				♌				
1 20	18 28	22 13	26 1	0 3	4 34	9 59	16 52	21 38
1 36	22 13	25 53	29 32	3 25	7 44	12 51	19 18	25 53
			♌					♉
1 52	26 0	29 40	3 6	6 48	10 53	15 42	21 45	0 6
		♌						
2 8	29 50	3 16	6 39	10 10	14 2	18 33	24 11	4 16
	♌							
2 24	3 41	6 59	10 13	13 33	17 11	21 24	26 38	8 23
2 40	7 35	10 45	13 48	16 56	20 20	24 15	29 5	12 27
							♍	
2 56	11 32	14 31	17 24	20 19	23 28	27 5	1 32	16 28
3 12	15 32	18 20	21 1	23 43	26 37	29 56	3 59	20 26
						♍		
3 28	19 35	22 11	24 39	27 8	29 47	2 47	6 27	24 22

TABLE III—(contd.)   235

Tables of Houses—Sayana

H.M. Sid. T.	0°	10°	20°	30°	40°	50°	60°	Tenth House For all Lat.
	♌	♌	♌	♍	♍	♍	♍	
3 44	23 41	26 3	28 18	0 33	2 56	5 38	8 55	28 15
			♍					♊
4 00	27 49	29 58	1 58	3 59	6 6	8 29	11 23	2 5
	♍	♍						
4 16	2 00	3 54	5 40	7 25	9 16	11 21	13 51	5 54
4 32	6 14	7 52	9 23	10 53	12 27	14 13	16 20	9 40
4 48	10 30	11 51	13 06	14 20	15 38	17 5	18 48	13 24
5 4	14 48	15 52	16 51	17 49	18 49	19 57	21 18	17 7
5 20	19 7	19 53	20 36	21 17	22 1	22 49	23 47	20 49
5 36	23 28	23 56	24 21	24 46	25 12	25 41	26 16	24 30
5 52	27 49	27 59	28 7	28 15	28 24	28 34	28 45	28 10
	♎	♎	♎	♎	♎	♎	♎	♋
6 8	2 11	2 2	1 53	1 45	1 36	1 26	1 15	1 50
6 24	6 32	6 4	5 39	5 14	4 48	4 19	3 44	5 30
6 40	10 53	10 7	9 24	8 43	7 59	7 11	6 13	9 11
6 56	15 12	14 8	13 9	12 11	11 11	10 3	8 43	12 53
7 12	19 30	18 9	16 54	15 40	14 22	12 55	11 12	16 36
7 28	23 46	22 8	20 37	19 7	17 33	15 47	13 40	20 20
7 44	28 00	26 6	24 20	22 35	20 44	18 39	16 9	24 6
	♏	♏						
8 00	2 11	0 2	28 2	2 26	1 23 54	21 31	18 37	27 55
			♏					♌
8 16	6 19	3 57	1 42	29 27	27 4	24 22	21 6	1 45
				♏	♏			
8 32	10 25	7 49	5 21	2 52	0 13	27 13	23 33	5 38
						♏		
8 48	14 28	11 40	8 59	6 17	3 23	0 4	26 1	9 34
9 4	18 27	15 29	12 36	9 41	6 32	2 55	28 28	13 32
							♏	
9 20	22 25	19 16	16 12	13 4	9 40	5 45	0 55	17 33
9 36	26 19	23 1	19 47	16 27	12 49	8 36	3 22	21 37
	♐							
9 52	0 11	26 44	23 21	19 50	15 58	11 27	5 49	25 44
	♐							
10 8	4 00	0 26	26 54	23 12	19 7	14 18	8 15	29 54

18

TABLE III—(contd.)

Tables of Houses—Sayana

Sid T. H.M.	0° ♐	10° ♐	20° ♐	30° ♏	40° ♏	50° ♏	60° ♏	Tenth House For all Lat.
10 24	7 47	4 7	0 27	26 35	22 16	17 9	10 42	4 7 ♏
10 40	11 32	7 47	3 59 ♐	29 57	25 26	20 1	13 9	8 22
10 56	15 16	11 26	7 31	3 21 ♐	28 36	22 54	15 35	12 39
11 12	18 58	15 4	11 4	6 44 ♐	1 48	25 48	18 1	16 57
11 28	22 39	18 42	14 37	10 9	5 1 ♐	28 43	20 29	21 17
11 44	26 20 ♑	22 21 ♐	18 11 ♐	13 36 ♐	8 15 ♐	1 39 ♐	22 57 ♏	25 38 ♎
12 00	0 00	25 59	21 46	17 4	11 32	4 38	25 26	0 00
12 16	3 40	29 39 ♑	25 22	20 34	14 52	7 39	27 57 ♐	4 22
12 32	7 21	3 20 ♑	29 1	24 7	18 14	10 43	0 27	8 43
12 48	11 2	7 2	2 41 ♑	27 43	21 41	13 51	3 00	13 3
13 4	14 44	10 46	6 25	1 23	25 11	17 2	5 36	17 21
13 20	18 28	14 32	10 12	5 7 ♑	28 47	20 19	8 14	21 38
13 36	22 13	18 21	14 2	8 55	2 28 ♑	23 42	10 55	25 53 ♏
13 52	26 00	22 13	17 57	12 50	6 16	27 11 ♑	13 41	0 6
14 8	29 50	26 8	21 56	16 50	10 11	0 49	16 33	4 16
14 24	3 41 ♒	0 6 ♒	26 00	20 56	14 15	4 36	19 30	8 23
14 40	7 35	4 9	0 9 ♒	25 10	18 28	8 35	22 36	12 27
14 56	11 32	8 15	4 24	29 32	22 52	12 47	25 53	16 28
15 12	15 32	12 26	8 45	4 3 ♒	27 29	17 14	29 22	20 26
15 28	19 35	16 41	13 12	8 42	2 18 ♒	22 00	3 9 ♑	24 22

(TABLE III—(contd.) 237

Tables of Houses—Sayana

Sid H. H.M.	0°	10°	20°	30°	40°	50°	60°	Tenth House For all Lat.
	≈	≈	≈	≈	≈	♑	♑	
15 44	23 41	21 00	17 46	13 31	7 21	27 7	7 17	28 15 ♐
						≈		
16 00	27 49	25 23	22 25	18 29	12 39	2 39	11 54	2 5
	♓							
16 16	2 00	29 51	27 11	23 37	18 14	8 38	17 10	5 54
		✳	✳	≈	≈	≈	♑	
16 32	6 14	4 22	2 3	28 54	24 4	15 9	23 20	9 40
				✳	✳	≈		
16 48	10 30	8 56	7 00	4 20	1 00	22 12	0 42	13 24
17 4	14 48	13 34	12 1	9 53	6 30	29 49	9 44	17 7
						✳		
17 20	19 7	18 14	17 7	15 33	13 3	7 59	21 00	20 49
							✳	
17 36	23 28	22 57	22 15	21 18	19 46	16 35	4 55	24 30
17 52	27 49	27 38	27 25	27 6	26 35	25 30	21 17	28 10
	♈	♈	♈	♈	♈	♈	♈	♑
18 8	2 11	2 22	2 35	2 54	3 26	4 30	8 43	1 50
18 24	6 32	7 4	7 45	8 42	10 14	13 25	25 5	5 30
							♉	
18 40	10 53	11 46	12 54	14 27	16 57	22 1	9 00	9 11
						♉		
18 56	15 12	16 26	17 59	20 7	23 30	0 11	20 16	12 53
19 12	19 30	21 4	23 00	25 40	29 50	7 48	29 18	16 36
				♉	♉		♊	
19 28	23 46	25 38	27 57	1 6	5 56	14 51	6 41	20 20
		♉	♉					
19 44	28 00	1 00	2 49	6 32	11 46	21 22	12 50	24 6
	♉							
20 00	2 11	4 37	7 35	11 31	17 21	27 21	18 6	27 55
						♊		≈
20 16	6 19	9 00	12 15	16 29	22 39	2 53	22 43	1 45
20 32	10 25	13 38	16 48	21 18	27 42	8 00	26 51	5 33
					♊		♋	
20 48	14 28	17 34	21 15	25 58	2 32	12 46	0 38	9 34
	♉	♉	♉	♊	♊	♊	♋	
21 4	18 28	21 45	25 36	0 28	7 8	17 13	4 7	13 32

TABLE III—(contd.)

Tables of Houses—Sayana

Sid T. H.M.	0° ♉	10° ♉	20° ♉	30° ♊	40° ♊	50° ♊	60° ♋	Tenth House For all Lat.
21 20	22 25	25 51	29 51	4 50	11 32	21 25	7 24	17 33
21 36	26 19	29 54 ♊	4 1	9 4	15 45	25 24	10 30	21 37
21 52	0 11 ♊	3 52 ♊	8 4	13 10	19 49	29 11	13 27	25 44
22 8	4 00	7 47	12 4	17 10	23 44 ♋	2 49	16 19	29 54 ♓
22 24	7 47	11 39	15 58	21 5	27 32	6 19	19 5	4 7
22 40	11 32	15 28	19 48	24 53	1 13 ♋	9 41	21 46	8 22
22 56	15 16	19 14	23 35	28 37	4 49	12 58	24 25	12 39
23 12	18 58	22 58	27 19	2 17 ♋	8 19	16 10	27 00	16 57
23 28	22 39	26 41 ♋	1 00	5 53	11 46	19 17	29 33	21 17
23 44	26 20	0 21 ♋	4 38	9 25	15 8	22 21	2 4 ♌	25 38
24 00								30 00

TABLE IV 239

Nakshatras and their Longitudes

No.	Rasi (Sign)	Nakshatra (Constellation)	Padas (Quarters)	Space on the ecliptic from 0° Aries	
1.	Áries	1. Aswini	4	13	20
		2. Bharani	4	26	40
		3. Krittika	1	30	0
2.	Taurus	Krittika	3	40	0
		4. Rohini	4	53	20
		5. Mrigasira	2	60	0
3.	Gemini	Mrigasira	2	66	40
		6. Aridra	4	80	0
		7. Punarvasu	3	90	0
4.	Cancer	Punarvasu	1	93	20
		8. Pushyami	4	106	40
		9. Aslesha	4	120	0
5.	Leo	10. Makha	4	133	20
		11. Pubba	4	146	40
		12. Uttara	1	150	0
6.	Virgo	Uttara	3	160	0
		13. Hasta	4	173	20
		14. Chitta	2	180	0
7.	Libra	Chitta	2	186	40
		15. Swati	4	200	0
		16. Visakha	3	210	0
8.	Scorpio	Visakha	1	213	20
		17. Anuradha	4	226	40
		18. Jyeshta	4	240	0
9.	Sagittarius	19. Moola	4	253	20
		20. Poorvashadha	4	266	40
		21. Uttarashadha	1	270	0
10.	Capricorn	Uttarashadha	3	280	0
		22. Sravana	4	293	20
		23. Dhanishta	2	300	0
11.	Aquarius	Dhanishta	2	306	40
		24. Satabhisha	4	320	0
		25. Poorvabhadra	3	330	0
12.	Pisces	Poorvabnadra	1	333	20
		26. Uttarabhadra	4	346	40
		27. Revati	4	360	0

TABLE V
The following is reproduced from Mr. N. C. Lahiri's
Indian Ephemeris

Balance of Vimsottari Dasa by Longitude of the Moon

In the example given the Moon is in Aquarius
25° 59′ 46′ or 26°: For this balance of Jupiter's
Dasa is Yrs. 8-9-18.

Long. of Moon		Moon in Mesha, Simha, Dhanus			Moon in Vrishabha, Kanya, Makara			Moon in Mithuna, Thula, Kumbha			Moon in Kataka, Vrischika, Meena		
		Balance of Dasa			Balance of Dasa			Balance of Dasa			Balance of Dasa		
°	′	*y*	*m*	*d*	*y*	*m*	*d*	*y*	*m*	*d*	*y*	*m*	*d*
			Kethu			*Sun*			*Mars*			*Jupiter*	
0	0	7	0	0	4	6	0	3	6	0	4	0	0
0	20	6	9	27	4	4	6	3	3	27	3	7	6
0	40	6	7	24	4	2	12	3	1	24	3	2	12
1	0	6	5	21	4	0	18	2	11	21	2	9	18
1	20	6	3	18	3	10	24	2	9	18	2	4	24
1	40	6	1	15	3	9	0	2	7	15	2	0	0
2	0	5	11	12	3	7	6	2	5	12	1	7	6
2	20	5	9	9	3	5	12	2	3	9	1	2	12
2	40	5	7	6	3	3	18	2	1	6	0	9	18
3	0	5	5	3	3	1	24	1	11	3	0	4	24
												Saturn	
3	20	5	3	0	3	0	0	1	9	0	19	0	0
3	40	5	0	27	2	10	6	1	6	27	18	6	9
4	0	4	10	24	2	8	12	1	4	24	18	0	18
4	20	4	8	21	2	6	18	1	2	21	17	6	27
4	40	4	6	18	2	4	24	1	0	18	17	1	6
5	0	4	4	15	2	3	0	0	10	15	16	7	15
5	20	4	2	12	2	1	6	0	8	12	16	1	24
5	40	4	0	9	1	11	12	0	6	9	15	8	3
6	0	3	10	6	1	9	18	0	4	6	15	2	12
6	20	3	8	3	1	7	24	0	2	3	14	8	21

TABLE V (contd.)

Long. of Moon	Moon in Mesha, Simha, Dhanus			Moon in Vrishabha, Kanya, Makara			Moon in Mithuna, Thula, Kumbha			Moon in Kataka, Vrischika, Meena		
	Balance of Dasa			Balance of Dasa			Balance of Dasa			Balance of Dasa		
	Ketu			*Sun*			*Rahu*			*Saturn*		
6 40	3	6	0	1	6	0	18	0	0	14	3	0
7 0	3	3	27	1	4	6	17	6	18	13	9	9
7 20	3	1	24	1	2	12	17	1	6	13	3	18
7 40	2	11	21	1	0	18	16	7	24	12	9	27
8 0	2	9	18	0	10	24	16	2	12	12	4	6
8 20	2	7	15	0	9	0	15	9	0	11	10	15
8 40	2	5	12	0	7	6	15	3	18	11	4	24
9 0	2	3	9	0	5	12	14	10	6	10	11	3
9 20	2	1	6	0	3	18	14	4	24	10	5	12
9 40	1	11	3	0	1	24	13	11	12	9	11	21
	Kethu			*Moon*								
10 0	1	9	0	10	0	0	13	6	0	9	6	0
10 20	1	6	27	9	9	0	13	0	18	9	0	9
10 40	1	4	24	9	6	0	12	7	6	8	6	18
11 0	1	2	21	9	3	0	12	1	24	8	0	27
11 20	1	0	18	9	0	0	11	8	12	7	7	6
11 40	0	10	15	8	9	0	11	3	0	7	1	15
12 0	0	8	12	8	6	0	10	9	18	6	7	24
12 20	0	6	9	8	3	0	10	4	6	6	2	3
12 40	0	4	6	8	0	0	9	10	24	5	8	12
13 0	0	2	3	7	9	0	9	5	12	5	2	21
	Venus											
13 20	20	0	0	7	6	0	9	0	0	4	9	0
13 40	19	6	0	7	3	0	8	6	18	4	3	9
14 0	19	0	0	7	0	0	8	1	6	3	9	18
14 20	18	6	0	6	9	0	7	7	24	3	3	27
14 40	18	0	0	6	6	0	7	2	12	2	10	6
15 0	17	6	0	6	3	0	6	9	0	2	4	15
15 20	17	0	0	6	0	0	6	3	18	1	10	24
15 40	16	6	0	5	9	0	5	10	6	1	5	3
16 0	16	0	0	5	6	0	5	4	24	0	11	12
16 20	15	6	0	5	3	0	4	11	12	0	5	21

Long. of Moon	Moon in Mesha, Simha, Dhanus Balance of Dasa			Moon in Vrishabha, Kanya, Makara Balance of Dasa			Moon in Mithuna, Thula, Kumbha Balance of Dasa			Moon in Kataka, Vrischika, Meena Balance of Dasa		
	Venus			*Moon*			*Rahu*			*Mercury*		
16 40	15	0	0	5	0	0	4	6	0	17	0	0
17 0	14	6	0	4	9	0	4	0	18	16	6	27
17 20	14	0	0	4	6	0	3	7	6	16	1	24
17 40	13	6	0	4	3	0	3	1	24	15	8	21
18 0	13	0	0	4	0	0	2	8	12	15	3	18
18 20	12	6	0	3	9	0	2	3	0	14	10	15
18 40	12	0	0	3	6	0	1	9	18	14	5	12
19 0	11	6	0	3	3	0	1	4	6	14	0	9
19 20	11	0	0	3	0	0	0	10	24	13	7	6
19 40	10	6	0	2	9	0	0	5	12	13	2	3
	Venus			*Moon*			*Jupiter*			*Mercury*		
20 0	10	0	0	2	6	0	16	0	0	12	9	0
20 20	9	6	0	2	3	0	15	7	6	12	3	27
20 40	9	0	0	2	0	0	15	2	12	11	10	24
21 0	8	6	0	1	9	0	14	9	18	11	5	21
21 20	8	0	0	1	6	0	14	4	24	11	0	18
21 40	7	6	0	1	3	0	14	0	0	10	7	15
22 0	7	0	0	1	0	0	13	7	6	10	2	12
22 20	6	6	0	0	9	0	13	2	12	9	9	9
22 40	6	0	0	0	6	0	12	9	18	9	4	6
23 0	5	6	0	0	3	0	12	4	24	8	11	3
				Mars								
23 20	5	0	0	7	0	0	12	0	0	8	6	0
23 40	4	6	0	6	9	27	11	7	6	8	0	27
24 0	4	0	0	6	7	24	11	2	12	7	7	24
24 20	3	6	0	6	5	21	10	9	18	7	2	21
24 40	3	0	0	6	3	18	10	4	24	6	9	18
25 0	2	6	0	6	1	15	10	0	0	6	4	15
25 20	2	0	0	5	11	12	9	7	6	5	11	12
25 40	1	6	0	5	9	9	9	2	12	5	6	9
26 0	1	0	0	5	7	6	8	9	18	5	1	6
26 20	0	6	0	5	5	3	8	4	24	4	8	3

TABLE V (contd.)   243

Long. of Moon	Moon in Mesha, Simha, Dhanus	Moon in Vrishabha, Kanya, Makara	Moon in Mithuna, Thula, Kumbha	Moon in Kataka, Vrischika, Meena
	Balance of Dasa	Balance of Dasa	Balance of Dasa	Balance of Dasa
	Sun	Mars	Jupiter	Mercury
26 40	6 0 0	5 3 0	8 0 0	4 3 0
27 0	5 10 6	5 0 27	7 7 6	3 9 27
27 20	5 8 12	4 10 24	7 2 12	3 4 24
27 40	5 6 18	4 8 21	6 9 18	2 11 21
28 0	5 4 24	4 6 18	6 4 24	2 6 18
28 20	5 3 0	4 4 15	6 0 00	2 1 15
28 40	5 1 6	4 2 12	5 7 6	1 8 12
29 0	4 11 12	4 0 9	5 2 12	1 3 9
29 20	4 9 18	3 10 6	4 9 18	0 10 6
29 40	4 7 24	3 8 3	4 4 24	0 5 3
30 0	4 6 0	3 6 0	4 0 0	0 0 0

Proportional Parts for Dasas of Planets

	Kethu		Venus		Sun		Moon		Mars		Rahu		Jupit.		Saturn		Merc.		
'	m	d	m	d	m	d	m	d	m	d	m	d	m	d	m	d	m	d	'
1	0	3	0	9	0	3	0	5	0	3	0	8	0	7	0	9	0	8	1
2	0	6	0	18	0	5	0	9	0	6	0	16	0	14	0	17	0	15	2
3	0	9	0	27	0	8	0	14	0	9	0	24	0	22	0	26	0	23	3
4	0	13	1	6	0	11	0	18	0	13	1	2	0	29	1	4	1	1	4
5	0	16	1	15	0	14	0	23	0	16	1	11	1	6	1	13	1	8	5
6	0	19	1	24	0	16	0	27	0	19	1	19	1	13	1	21	1	16	6
7	0	22	2	3	0	19	1	2	0	22	1	27	1	20	2	0	1	24	7
8	0	25	2	12	0	22	1	6	0	25	2	5	1	28	2	8	2	1	8
9	0	28	2	21	0	24	1	11	0	28	2	13	2	5	2	17	2	9	9
10	1	1	3	0	0	27	1	15	1	1	2	21	2	12	2	26	2	17	10
15	1	17	4	15	1	11	2	8	1	17	4	2	3	18	4	8	3	25	15
20	2	3	6	0	1	24	3	0	2	3	5	12	4	24	5	21	5	3	20

TABLE VI

Table of Yogas

Sl. No.	Yoga		Joint longitude of Sun and Moon
			Upto
1	Vishkambha	...	13° 20′
2	Priti	...	26 40
3	Ayushman	...	40 00
4	Saubhagya	...	53 20
5	Sobhana	...	66 40
6	Atiganda	...	80 00
7	Sukarman	...	93 20
8	Dhriti	...	106 40
9	Soola	...	120 00
10	Ganda	...	133 20
11	Vriddhi	...	146 40
12	Dhruva	...	160 00
13	Vyaghata	...	173 20
14	Harshana	...	186 40
15	Vajra	...	200 00
16	Siddhi	...	213 20
17	Vyatipata	...	226 40
18	Variyan	...	240 00
19	Parigha	...	253 20
20	Siva	...	266 40
21	Siddha	...	280 00
22	Sadhya	...	293 20
23	Subha	...	306 40
24	Sukla	...	320 00
25	Brahma	...	333 20
26	Indra	...	346 40
27	Vaidhriti	...	360 00

EXPLANATION

Suppose the sum of the longitudes of the Sun and the Moon is 281°. Reference to the above table reveals Siddha-yoga lasting from 280° to 293° 20′. Therefore one degree has elapsed in this yoga.

TABLE VII

Terrestrial Latitudes and Longitudes

Name of Place	Name of Country	Latitude			Longitude		
Aberdeen	Scotland	57	N	10	2	W	6
Abyssinia State	Africa	10	N	0	40	E	0
Abu Mount	India	24	N	41	72	E	50
Acapulco	Mexico	16	N	59	100	W	00
Achin	Sumatra	5	N	0	96	E	30
Addis Ababa	Ethiopia	9	N	2	38	E	42
Adelaide	South Australia	34	S	55	138	E	32
Aden	Southern Yemen	12	N	50	45	E	00
Adilabad	India	19	N	33	78	E	35
Adoni	India	15	N	28	77	E	16
Agartala	India	23	N	50	91	E	23
Agin Court	France	53	N	29	2	E	9
Agra	India	27	N	17	78	E	13
Ahmedabad	India	23	N	0	72	E	40
Ahmednagar	India	19	N	08	74	E	48
Aix-la-Chapelle	Germany	50	N	46	6	E	2
Ajanta	India	20	N	31	75	E	48
Ajjaccio	France	41	N	55	8	E	44
Ajmer	India	26	N	28	74	E	37
Akyab	Burma	20	N	18	92	E	45
Alaska	N. America	65	N	0	150	W	0
Alcola	India	20	N	32	77	E	02
Alexandria	Egypt	31	N	12	30	E	10
Algeriers	Algeria	36	N	42	3	E	8
Aligarh	India	27	N	55	78	E	10
Allahabad	India	25	N	25	81	E	58
Alleppey	India	9	N	30	76	E	28
Almora	India	29	N	38	79	E	42
Alwar	India	27	N	38	76	E	34
Amarapur	Burma	2	N	50	96	E	2
Ambala	India	30	N	22	76	E	50
Amraoti	India	20	N	58	77	E	56

Name of Place	Name of Country	Latitude			Longitude		
Amritsar	India	31	N	35	74	E	57
Amsterdam	Netherlands	52	N	22	4	E	53
Amona	Italy	43	N	28	13	E	32
Anantapur	India	14	N	39	77	E	42
Ankara	Turkey	40	N	0	32	E	54
Antwerp	Belgium	51	N	13	4	E	24
Anuradhapura	Ceylon	8	N	26	80	E	20
Arakan	Burma	20	N	46	93	E	12
Aravali (Hills)	India	25	N	25	73	E	30
Arcot	India	12	N	55	79	E	20
Argentina	S. America	36	S	0	65	W	0
Arkonam	India	13	N	7	79	E	43
Athens	Greece	37	N	58	23	E	46
Atlanta	U. S. A.	33	N	53	84	W	19
Augsburgh	Germany	48	N	18	10	E	53
Aurangabad	India	19	N	52	75	E	22
Babylon	Mesopotamia	32	N	30	44	E	35
Bagdad	Iraq	33	N	20	44	E	30
Bahama Islands	West Indies	23	N	0	74	W	0
Baharain Island	Persian Gulf	26	N	0	50	E	35
Balasore	India	21	N	35	87	E	3
Balsar	India	20	N	35	73	E	5
Baltic Sea	Europe	57	N	0	18	E	0
Baltimore	Ireland	51	N	28	9	W	19
Baltimore	U. S. A.	39	N	35	76	W	36
Baluchistan (State)	Asia	28	N	4	65	E	0
Banda	India	25	N	28	80	E	20
Bangalore	India	12	N	59	77	E	40
Bangkok	Thailand	13	N	45	100	E	35
Barbados	West Indies	13	N	40	59	W	50
Bareilly	India	28	N	22	79	E	27
Baroda	India	22	N	21	73	E	13
Bastar	India	19	N	25	81	E	40
Batavia	Java	6	N	0	106	E	58
Bavanahotte	India	22	N	18	86	E	10
Beirut	Lebanon	35	N	34	35	E	28
Belgaum	India	15	N	55	74	E	35

Name of Place	Name of Country	Latitude			Longitude		
Belgium	Europe	51	N	0	4	E	30
Belgrade	Yugoslavia	44	N	57	20	E	37
Belize	British Honduras	17	N	30	88	W	20
Bellary	India	15	N	10	76	E	56
Belur	India	12	N	58	76	E	44
Benaras	India	25	N	20	83	E	0
Berhampore	India	24	N	2	88	E	27
Berlin	East Germany	53	N	32	13	E	24
Berne	Switzerland	46	N	57	7	E	28
Bethlehem	Palestine	31	N	41	35	E	15
Bhagalpur	India	25	N	11	87	E	15
Bharatpur	India	27	N	15	77	E	30
Bhatinda	India	30	N	15	74	E	57
Bhavnagar	India	21	N	49	77	E	10
Bhopal	India	23	N	15	77	E	30
Bhubaneshwar	India	20	N	13	85	E	50
Bhuj	India	23	N	12	69	E	54
Bidar	India	17	N	55	77	E	35
Bijapur	India	16	N	50	75	E	55
Bijnour	India	29	N	22	78	E	9
Bikaner	India	28	N	2	73	E	18
Bilaspur	India	22	N	2	82	E	15
Bismark	U. S. A.	46	N	50	100	W	50
Bodh Gaya	India	24	N	48	85	E	1
Bombay	India	18	N	55	72	E	50
Bonn	East Germany	50	N	43	7	E	6
Boordere	India	25	N	25	76	E	0
Boston	U. S. A.	42	N	20	71	W	0
Brindisi	Italy	40	N	39	17	E	56
Brisbane	Queensland	27	S	25	152	E	54
Broach	India	21	N	47	73	E	0
Brunswick	Germany	52	N	15	10	E	22
Bruxelles	Belgium	50	N	51	4	E	21
Bucharest	Rumania	44	N	27	26	E	10
Budapest	Hungary	47	N	29	19	E	5
Buenos Aires	Argentina	34	S	30	58	W	20
Bulsar	India	20	N	40	72	E	58

Name of Place	Name of Country	Latitude			Longitude		
Burdwan	India	23	N	16	87	E	54
Bushire	Persia	29	N	0	50	E	50
Cairo	Egypt	30	N	1	31	E	14
Calais	France	50	N	57	1	E	51
Calcutta	India	22	N	36	88	E	24
Calicut	India	11	N	15	75	E	47
Cambridge	England	52	N	12	0	E	8
Canberra	Australia	35	S	15	149	E	8
Cannanore	India	11	N	53	75	E	27
Cantebury	England	51	N	16	1	E	4
Canton	China	23	N	25	113	E	32
Cape Town	C. of G. Hope	33	S	59	18	E	25
Caracas	Venezuela	10	N	30	66	W	50
Chandernagore	India	22	N	48	88	E	31
Chandigarh	India	30	N	30	76	E	58
Charleston	U. S. A.	32	N	54	80	W	0
Chicago	U. S. A.	41	N	56	87	E	50
Chickmagalur	India	13	N	10	75	E	48
Chitradurg	India	14	N	14	76	E	26
Chittagong	Bangla Desh	22	N	19	91	E	55
Chittoor	India	13	N	15	79	E	5
Chota Nagpur	India	23	N	0	83	E	0
Cochin	India	9	N	55	76	E	22
Coimbatore	India	11	N	2	76	E	59
Cologne	Germany	50	N	56	6	E	58
Colombo	Ceylon	7	N	0	79	E	45
Constantinople	Turkey	41	N	1	28	E	55
Copenhagen	Denmark	55	N	40	12	E	34
Corsica I	France	42	N	10	9	E	0
Costa Rica	Central America	10	N	0	84	W	0
Croydon	England	51	N	22	0	W	6
Croydon	Queensland	18	S	10	142	E	0
Cuddalore	India	11	N	46	79	E	45
Cuddapah	India	14	N	30	78	E	47
Cuttack	India	20	N	25	85	E	57
Dacca	Bangla Desh	23	N	43	90	W	26
Dakoth N-Sb.	U. S. A.	47	N	0	100	W	0

Name of Place	Name of Country	Latitude			Longitude		
Daman	India	20	N	25	72	E	57
Damascus	Syria	33	N	30	36	E	18
Dar-es-Salam	Tanganika	6	S	50	39	E	12
Daranga	India	26	N	51	91	E	26
Darbhanga	India	26	N	15	86	E	13
Darjeeling	India	27	N	3	88	E	18
Datia	India	25	N	40	78	E	30
Dartmoor	England	50	N	38	3	W	58
Delhi	India	28	N	38	77	E	17
Derby	England	52	N	50	1	W	28
Davenport	England	50	N	22	4	W	12
Dhanbad	India	23	N	48	86	E	24
Dharwar	India	15	N	29	75	E	5
Dhubri	India	26	N	2	90	E	2
Dibrugarh	India	27	N	30	95	E	0
Dublin	Ireland	53	N	20	6	W	18
Dunkirk	France	51	N	3	2	E	26
Durban	S. Africa	29	S	58	30	E	53
Durg	India	21	N	11	81	E	20
East London	C. of G. Hope	32	S	58	27	E	52
Ellichpur	India	21	N	12	77	E	8
Elluru	India	16	N	43	81	E	9
Emdem	Germany	53	N	22	7	E	13
Entebbe	Uganda	0	N	3	32	E	30
Ernakulam	India	9	N	59	76	E	19
Fatehabad	India	29	N	31	75	E	30
Fatehpur	India	25	N	56	80	E	56
Fiji Islands	Pacific Ocean	17	S	20	179	E	0
Florence	Italy	43	N	47	11	E	20
Fyzabad	India	26	N	44	82	E	22
Gangotri	India	30	N	58	78	E	59
Gangtok	Sikkim	27	N	20	88	E	40
Gauhati	India	26	N	5	91	E	55
Gaya	India	24	N	45	85	E	5
Geneva	Italy	44	N	25	8	E	35
Georgia	U. S. A.	32	N	0	82	W	0
Georgetown	British Guineas	6	N	50	58	W	12

Name of Place	Name of Country	Latitude			Longitude		
Georgetown	Malaysia	5	N	25	100	E	19
Ghazipur	India	25	N	34	83	E	35
Ghazni	Afghanistan	33	N	37	68	E	17
Gibraltar	Spain	36	N	7	5	W	12
Glasgow	Scotland	55	N	51	4	W	16
Goa	India	15	N	33	73	E	59
Golconda	India	17	N	30	78	E	2
Gorakhpur	India	26	N	47	83	E	32
Greenwich	England	51	N	29	0	E	0
Gulbarga	India	17	N	20	76	E	50
Guntur	India	16	N	23	80	E	30
Gwalior	India	26	N	12	78	E	10
Hague	Netherland	52	N	7	4	E	17
Haiifax	England	53	N	43	1	W	52
Hamilton	New Zealand	37	S	47	175	E	19
Havana	Cuba	23	N	0	82	W	30
Helsinki	Finland	60	N	15	25	E	3
Hiroshima	Japan	34	N	30	132	E	30
Hissar	India	29	N	12	75	E	45
Hobart	Tasmania	42	S	50	147	E	15
Hong-kong	China	22	N	16	114	E	9
Hubli	India	15	N	22	75	E	15
Hyderabad	India	17	N	10	78	E	20
Imphal	India	24	N	15	94	E	0
Indore	India	22	N	42	75	E	53
Jabalpur	India	23	N	10	79	E	57
Jaffna	Ceylon	9	N	45	80	E	2
Jagannath	India	19	N	59	86	E	2
Jaipur	India	26	N	54	75	E	52
Jaisalmer	India	26	N	56	70	E	55
Jalgaon	India	21	N	0	75	E	42
Jamkhandi	India	16	N	30	75	E	17
Jammu	India	32	N	47	74	E	50
Jamnagar	India	22	N	26	70	E	2
Jeddah	Saudi Arabia	21	N	29	39	E	16
Jerusalem	Palestine	31	N	47	35	E	10
Jhansi	India	25	N	30	78	W	36

Name of Place	Name of Country	Latitude			Longitude		
Jodhpur	India	26	N	23	73	E	2
Johannesburg	U. of S. Africa	26	S	10	28	E	8
Jorhat	India	26	N	45	94	E	20
Jullundur	India	31	N	20	75	E	40
Jwalamukhi	India	32	N	44	74	E	54
Kabba	Nigeria	7	N	45	6	E	45
Kabul	Afghanistan	34	N	28	69	E	18
Kandla	India	23	N	3	70	E	10
Kandy	Ceylon	7	N	18	80	E	43
Kanpur	India	26	N	35	80	E	20
Kansas City	U. S. A.	39	N	3	94	E	39
Kanyakumari	India	8	N	4	77	E	36
Karachi	Pakistan	24	N	53	67	E	0
Karaikal	India	11	N	0	79	E	39
Kathmandu	Nepal	27	N	43	85	E	19
Khartoum	Sudan	15	N	31	32	E	35
Kobe	Japan	34	N	45	135	E	10
Kohima	Nagaland	23	N	35	94	E	10
Kolar	India	13	N	12	78	E	15
Kolhapur	India	16	N	43	74	E	15
Kuala Lumpur	Malaysia	3	N	9	101	E	41
Kuching	Sarawak	1	N	33	110	E	25
Kumbakonam	India	11	N	0	78	E	40
Kurnool	India	15	N	50	78	E	5
Kuwait	Saudi Arabia	29	N	30	47	E	30
Lahore	Pakistan	31	N	32	74	E	22
Lancaster	England	54	N	3	2	E	28
Laos	Vietnam	17	N	45	105	E	0
La Paz	Bolivia	16	S	20	68	W	10
Lashkar	India	26	N	0	77	E	0
Leh	India	34	N	15	77	E	35
Leipzig	Germany	51	N	20	12	E	21
Leningrad	U. S. S. R.	59	N	55	30	E	20
Leopoldville	Belgian Congo	4	S	20	15	E	15
Lima	Peru	12	S	0	77	W	0
Limbdi	India	22	N	36	71	E	54
Livingstone	N. Rhodesia	17	N	50	25	E	50

19

Name of Place	Name of Country	Latitude			Longitude		
London	England	51	N	30	0	W	5
Los Angeles	U. S. A.	34	N	0	118	W	10
Lucknow	India	26	N	50	81	E	0
Ludhiana	India	30	N	57	75	E	56
Madras	India	13	N	8	80	E	19
Madrid	Spain	40	N	25	3	W	45
Madurai	India	9	N	50	78	E	10
Mahabaleshwar	India	17	N	56	73	E	43
Mahe	India	11	N	33	75	E	35
Mahendragarh	India	28	N	24	76	E	12
Malacca	Malaysia	2	N	15	102	E	15
Mandalay	Burma	22	N	0	96	E	15
Mandi	India	31	N	39	76	E	58
Mangalore	India	12	N	55	74	E	47
Manila	Phillippines	14	N	40	121	E	3
Mantua	Italy	45	N	10	10	E	48
Maskat and Oman	Saudi Arabia	23	N	35	56	E	48
Masulipatam	India	16	N	15	81	E	12
Mathura	India	27	N	30	77	E	40
Mecca	Saudi Arabia	21	N	30	39	E	54
Meerut	India	29	N	1	77	E	50
Melbourne	Victoria	37	S	40	145	E	0
Mercara	India	12	N	30	75	E	45
Mexico City	Mexico	19	N	20	99	W	10
Midnapore	India	22	N	25	87	E	21
Mirzapur	India	25	N	10	82	E	45
Moradabad	India	28	N	50	78	E	50
Moscow	U. S. S. R.	55	N	45	37	E	35
Multan	India	30	N	15	71	E	30
Murshidabad	India	24	N	2	88	E	0
Muzaffarpur	India	26	N	7	85	E	32
Mysore	India	12	N	17	76	E	41
Nagapattinam	India	10	N	46	79	E	51
Nagasaki	Japan	32	N	47	129	E	50
Nagpur	India	21	N	8	79	E	10
Nairobi	Kenya	1	S	20	36	E	50
Nahan	India	30	N	23	77	E	21

Name of Place	Name of Country	Latitude		Longitude		
Nandyal	India	15	N	30	78	E	30
Naples	Italy	40	N	50	14	E	5
Nasik	India	20	N	2	73	E	50
Natal	S. Africa	29	S	0	30	E	30
Nazareth	Israel	32	N	42	35	E	17
Nellore	India	14	N	27	79	E	59
New York	U. S. A.	40	N	45	74	W	0
Nicosia	Cyprus	35	N	10	33	E	25
Olympia	Greece	37	N	40	21	E	20
Osaka	Japan	34	N	40	135	E	30
Oslo	Norway	59	N	53	10	E	52
Ottawa	Canada	59	N	50	80	W	0
Oxford	England	51	N	45	1	W	15
Palghat	India	10	N	46	76	E	42
Panama City	Panama	9	N	0	79	W	25
Panipat	India	29	N	25	77	E	2
Panjim	India	15	N	30	73	E	9
Paris	France	48	N	50	2	E	20
Patiala	India	30	N	23	76	E	26
Patna	India	25	N	35	85	E	18
Peking	China	39	N	50	116	E	20
Peshawar	Pakistan	34	N	2	71	E	37
Prague	Czechoslovakia	50	N	5	14	E	22
Pondicherry	India	11	N	59	79	E	50
Poona	India	18	N	29	73	E	57
Port Blair	Andaman Islands	11	N	40	92	E	30
Pretoria	U. of S. Africa	25	S	44	28	E	12
Punaka	Bhutan	27	N	30	90	E	0
Puri	India	19	N	50	85	E	58
Quebec	Canada	46	N	52	71	W	13
Quetta	Baluchistan	30	N	15	66	E	55
Quilon	India	8	N	54	76	E	38
Raichur	India	16	N	10	77	E	20
Raigarh	India	21	N	56	83	E	25
Rajahmundry	India	17	N	1	81	E	48
Rajkot	India	22	N	15	70	E	56
Rameswaram	India	9	N	18	79	E	28

Name of Place	Name of Country	Latitude			Longitude		
Ranchi	India	23	N	19	85	E	27
Rangoon	Burma	16	N	45	96	E	20
Rawalpindi	Pakistan	33	N	38	73	E	8
Rio de Janeiro	Brazil	23	S	0	43	W	12
Riyadh	Saudi Arabia	24	N	41	46	E	42
Rohtak	India	28	N	55	76	E	43
Rome	Italy	41	N	54	12	E	30
Saar, R	Germany	49	N	28	6	E	45
Saharanpur	India	29	N	58	77	E	33
Saigon		10	N	58	106	E	40
Salem	India	11	N	39	78	E	12
Salisbury	S. Rhodesia	17	S	50	31	E	2
Salt Lake City	U. S. A.	40	N	55	112	W	0
Samarkhand	Afghanistan	39	N	40	67	E	0
Sambalpur	India	21	N	30	84	E	3
San Francisco	U. S. A.	38	N	0	122	W	24
Sangli	India	16	N	55	74	E	33
Santiago	Chile	33	S	24	70	W	50
Sarnath	India	25	N	28	83	E	2
Seoul	Korea	37	N	31	127	E	6
Shangai	China	31	N	15	121	E	30
Sheffield	England	53	N	23	1	W	27
Shillong	India	25	N	30	92	E	0
Shimoga	India	13	N	57	75	E	32
Sholapur	India	17	N	43	75	E	56
Simla	India	31	N	2	77	E	15
Singapore	Singapore	1	N	17	103	E	51
Sofia	Bulgaria	42	N	45	23	E	20
Srinagar	India	34	N	12	74	E	50
Srirangapatnam	India	12	N	30	76	E	40
Stockholm	Sweden	59	N	17	18	E	3
Surat	India	21	N	12	72	E	55
Suva	Fiji	18	S	0	178	E	20
Sydney	New South Wales	33	S	53	151	E	10
Taihoku	Taiwan	25	N	2	121	E	31
Teheran	Iran	35	N	44	51	E	30
Tehri Garhwal	India	30	N	27	78	E	33

Name of Place	Name of Country	Latitude			Longitude		
Tejpur	India	26	N	37	92	E	50
Thanjavur	India	10	N	45	79	E	17
Tirunelveli	India	8	N	45	77	E	45
Tirupati	India	13	N	45	79	E	30
Tokyo	Japan	35	N	45	139	E	45
Toranto	Italy	40	N	28	17	E	13
Travancore	India	9	N	20	77	E	0
Trichinopoly	India	10	N	30	76	E	18
Tripolitania	Libya	30	N	56	13	E	30
Trivandrum	India	8	N	31	77	E	0
Tumkur	India	13	N	18	77	E	12
Tunis	Tunisia	36	N	42	10	E	6
Tuticorin	India	8	N	50	78	E	12
Udaipur	India	24	N	36	73	E	44
Udipi	India	13	N	25	74	E	42
Ujjain	India	23	N	9	75	E	43
Vaduz	Lichtenstein	47	N	8	9	E	31
Vaishnava Devi	India	33	N	0	74	W	59
Varanasi	India	25	N	18	83	E	0
Vatican City	Italy	38	N	38	15	E	50
Vienna	Austria	48	N	12	16	E	22
Vijayawada	India	15	N	14	76	E	28
Visakhapatnam	India	17	N	45	83	E	27
Warangal	India	17	N	58	79	E	45
Wardha	India	20	N	45	78	E	39
Warsaw	Poland	52	N	13	21	E	0
Washington	U. S. A.	38	N	50	77	W	0
Waterloo	Belgium	50	N	44	4	E	23
Wellington	New Zealand	41	S	8	176	E	46
Xanthe	Greece	41	N	10	24	E	58
Yemen	Saudi Arabia	15	N	0	44	E	0
Zanzibar	Zanzibar	6	S	2	39	E	20
Zurich	Switzerland	47	N	22	8	E	32

TABLE VIII

Table of Standard Times

Place	Fast (+) or Slow (−) of Greenwich h. m. s.	Date of Adoption
Aden	+ 3 0 0	Recent
Afghanistan	+ 4 30 0	Recent
Africa :		
Cameroons, Fr. Eq. Africa, Tunisia, Angola, Libya,* Nigeria	+ 1 0 0	Sept. 1905
Egypt*, Sudan, Rhodesia, Nyasaland, Union of S. Africa, Mozambique	+ 2 0 0	1930
Ethiopia, Kenya, Uganda, Tanganyka, Madagaskar,	+ 3 0 0	Recent
Zanzibar Islands	+ 2 45 0	Recent
Algeria*, Morocco, Gold Coast, Ivory Coast, French Sudan, Dahoney*, Togoland, Tangier, Sierra Leone	+ 0 0 0	March 1911
Liberia	− 0 45 0	Recent
Port Guinea, Rio-de-oro*, French Guinea*, Mauretanic*, Senegal*	− 1 0 0	Recent
Leopoldville, Coquilhatville	+ 1 0 0	Recent
Africa : Orientale, Kivu, Kasai, Ruanda, Urundi, Katanga	+ 2 0 0	Recent

* Summer Time observed.

Place	Fast (+) or Slow (−) of Greenwich h. m. s.	Date of Adoption
America (U.S.A.) :		
Eastern Time* E.T.‡	− 5 0 0	Nov. 1883
Central Time* C.T.‡	− 6 0 0	,,
Mountain Time* M.T.‡	− 7 0 0	,,
Pacific Time* P.T.‡	− 8 0 0	,,
Alaska :		
Ketchikan to Skagway	− 8 0 0	,,
Skagway to 141° W.	− 9 0 0	,,
141° W. to 162 W.	− 10 0 0	,,
162° W. to Western Tip	− 11 0 0	,,
America (South):		
Equador, Columbia, Peru, Territory of Arc	5 0 0	,,
Veneezuallah	− 4 30 0	Recent
Western Brazil, Bolivia, Argentina*, Chile	− 4 0 0	May 1920
British Guiana & Dutch Guiana	− 3 45 0	Recent
French Guiana : Paraguay	− 4 0 0	Recent
Uruguay	− 3 30 0	May 1920
Eastern Brazil	− 3 0 0	Recent
Australia :		
Victoria, N.S. Wales, Queensland, Tasmania	+ 10 0 0	Feb. 1895
South Australia, N. Terrtory	+ 9 30 0	,,
Western Australia :	+ 8 0 0	,,
New Zealand	+ 12 0 0	,,

* Summer Time observed.

‡ War time (+ 1 hr.) 9-2-1942 to 30-9-1945.

Place	Fast (+) or Slow (−) of Greenwich h. m. s.	Date of Adoption
Austria : Hungary	+ 1 0 0	Oct. 1895
Azores*	− 2 0 0	Recent
Ascension Island	− 0 0 0	,,
Alentian Islands	− 11 0 0	,,
Albania	+ 1 0 0	,,
Bahrein Islands*	+ 3 0 0	,,
Bangla Desh	+ 5 0 0	Oct. 1951
Belgium*	− 0 0 0	Recent
Bermudas Islands	− 4 0 0	,,
Borneo Islands	+ 8 0 0	Oct. 1904
British Honduras	− 6 0 0	,,
Bulgaria	+ 2 0 0	,,
Burma	+ 6 30 0	1906
Canada :		
Newfoundland	− 3 30 0	Nov. 1883
Atlantic Time. A.T.*	− 4 0 0	,,
Eastern Time : E.T.*	− 5 0 0	,,
Central Time : C.T.*	− 6 0 0	,,
Mountain Time : M.T.*	− 7 0 0	Nov. 1883
Pacific Time : P.T.*	− 8 0 0	,,
Canary Islands*	− 1 0 0	Recent
Cape Verde Islands	− 2 0 0	,,
Caroline Islands General	+ 10 0 0	,,
Kasaie, Pinglepag	+ 10 0 0	,,
Truk	+ 11 0 0	Recent
Ceylon	+ 5 30 0	1906

---

* Summer Time observed.

Place	Fast (+) or Slow (−) of Greenwich h. m. s.	Date of Adoption
China :		
Kung Lung (Mountain)	+ 5 30 0	Jan. 1903
Sinyang (Tibet)	+ 6 0 0	,,
Lungtsu (Szchuen)*	+ 7 0 0	,,
Chung Yuan (Central)		
Hong Kong*	+ 8 0 0	,,
Chang Pei (Mountain)	+ 8 30 0	,,
Cocos-Keeling Islands (Indian Ocean)	+ 6 30 0	Recent
Cook Islands (Pac. Ocean)	+ 10 30 0	,,
Corsica Islands (Med. Sea)*	+ 0 0 0	,,
Costa Rica Isls. (Near Panama)	− 6 0 0	,,
Cuba Islands (West Indies)	− 5 0 0	,,
Cyprus Islands (Med. Sea)	− 2 0 0	,,
Czechoslovakia	+ 1 0 0	,,
Denmark	+ 1 0 0	Jan. 1894
Eucador	− 5 0 0	,,
England	− 0 0 0	1880
Estonia : U.S.S.R.*	+ 2 0 0	Recent
Falkland Islands	− 4 0 0	,,
Fiji Islands	+ 12 0 0	,,
Finland	+ 2 0 0	May 1921
Formosa*	+ 8 0 0	Jan. 1896
Fernando Islands	− 2 0 0	Recent
France*	− 0 0 0	May 1911
Gambia	− 0 0 0	Recent

* Summer Time observed.

Place	Fast (+) or Slow (−) of Greenwich			Date of Adoption
	h.	m.	s.	
Germany	+ 1	0	0	April 1892
Gibraltar*	+ 0	0	0	,,
Greece and Crete	+ 2	0	0	July 1916
Grenada Islands (W. Indies)	− 4	0	0	Recent
Greenland : Scoresby Sound	− 2	0	0	,,
Angmagssalik, W. Coast				
excluding Thule	− 3	0	0	,,
Thule	− 4	0	0	,,
Guam Islands	+ 10	0	0	,,
Guatemala (N. America)	− 6	0	0	1883
Haiti	− 5	0	0	Recent
Hawaiin Islands	− 10	0	0	,,
Honduras (Near Panama)	− 6	0	0	Recent
Hungary	+ 1	0	0	May 1892
Iceland*	− 1	0	0	Jan. 1906
India : General‡	+ 5	30	0	1-1-1906
Calcutta (L.M.T.)	+ 5	53	0	
				upto 1-10-1941
Indo-China : Cambodia,				
Laos, Vietnam	+ 7	0	0	1904
Indonesia : Sumatra (North)	+ 6	30	0	Recent
Sumatra (South)	+ 7	0	0	,,
Java, Borneo (Indonesia)	+ 7	30	0	,,
Celebes	+ 8	0	0	,,
Molucca Islands	+ 8	30	0	,,
Iraq	+ 3	0	0	,,
Ireland*	+ 0	0	0	Oct. 1915

* Summer Time observed.

‡ War time (+ 1 hr.) 1-9-1942 to 15-10-1945.

Place	Fast (+) or Slow (−) of Greenwich h. m. s.			Date of Adoption
Israel*	+	2	0 0	Recent
Italy (and Scicily)	+	1	0 0	Nov. 1893
Japan	+	9	0 0	1st Jan. 1888
Jordan	+	2	0 0	Recent
Kamaran Islands	+	3	0 0	,,
Korean Democratic Republic (North)	+	8	30 0	,,
Korea (South)*	+	8	30 0	Dec. 1904
Kuweit (Persian Gulf)	+	3	0 0	Recent
Latvia* (U.S.S.R.)	+	2	0 0	,,
Lebanon (Malayan Archi.)	+	2	0 0	,,
Lithuania	+	1	0 0	,,
Luxemburg	+	1	0 0	,,
Madagascar	+	3	0 0	,,
Madeire* (Brazil)	−	1	0 0	,,
Malaya (See footnote)	+	7	30 0	,,
Malta Islands	+	1	0 0	,,
Mauritius Islands	+	4	0 0	,,
Mexico :				
Centtal Time C.T.	−	6	0 0	Nov. 1883
Mountain Time M.T.	−	7	0 0	,,
Pacific Time P.T.	+	8	0 0	,,
Marianne Islands	+	9	0 0	Recent
Marqueass Islands	−	10	0 0	,,
Martinique Islands	−	4	0 0	,,

---

* Summer Time observed.

Malaya; Upto 31-12-1932 : + 7 hrs.
,,   31- 8-1941 : + 7/20 hrs.
Now : + 7/30 hrs.

	Fast (+) or Slow (−) of Greenwich	Date of Adoption
	h. m. s.	
Monaco	− 0 0 0	Recent
Mozambique	+ 2 0 0	,,
Netherlands*	0 0 0	,,
Netherlands Guinea	− 3 40 0	,,
New Caledonia	+ 11 0 0	,,
Newfoundland	− 3 30 0	,,
New Guinea (British)	+ 10 0 0	April 1911
,, (Netherland)	+ 9 30 0	,,
New Herbrides	+ 11 0 0	Recent
New Zealand	+ 12 0 0	,,
Nicaragua	− 5 45 0	,,
Norfokland	+ 11 30 0	,,
Norway	+ 1 0 0	Jan. 1895
Oman	+ 3 30 0	Recent
Pakistan	+ 6 0 0	Oct. 1951
Panama Canal Zone	− 5 0 0	1911
Papua	+ 10 0 0	Recent
Persia	+ 3 30 0	,,
Peseaderes Islands	+ 8 0 0	,,
Philippine Islands	+ 8 0 0	May 1899
Poland*	+ 2 0 0	Sept. 1919
Portugal*	− 0 0 0	1911
Princess Islands	− 0 0 0	,,
Puerto Rico	− 4 0 0	,,
Reunion Islands	+ 4 0 0	,,
Roumania	+ 2 0 0	,,
St. Lucia	− 4 0 0	,,

* Summer Time observed.

Place	Fast (+) or Slow (−) of Greenwich h. m. s.	Date of Adoption
St. Pierre	− 4 0 0	1911
St. Thomas Islands	G.M.T.	,,
St. Vincent Islands	− 4 0 0	,,
Salvador	− 6 0 0	,,
Samoan Islands	− 11 0 0	,,
Sandwich Islands	G.M.T.	,,
Sarawak	+ 8 0 0	,,
Sardinia	+ 1 0 0	Recent
Saudi Arabia except Dhahran	+ 3 0 0	,,
Dhahran*	+ 4 0 0	,,
Scotland	G.M.T.	1880
Siam (Thailand)	+ 7 0 0	April 1920
Solomon Islands	+ 11 0 0	Recent
Somaliland	+ 3 0 0	,,
Serbia	+ 1 0 0	,,
Seychells Islands	+ 4 0 0	,,
Spain*	G.M.T.	Jan. 1901
Spanish Guinea*	G.M.T.	Recent
Society Islands	− 10 0 0	,,
Sweden	+ 1 0 0	,,
Switzerland	+ 1 0 0	June 1894
Syria*	+ 2 0 0	Recent
Tahiti	− 10 0 0	,,
Tonga (Friendly Islands)	+ 12 20 0	,,
Tunisia	+ 1 0 0	,,
Tasmania	+ 10 0 0	,,
Turkey	+ 2 0 0	,,

* Summer Time observed.

Place	Fast (+) or Slow (−) of Greenwich h. m. s.	Date of Adoption
U.S.S.R.		
Moscow, Ukrain & West	+ 2 0 0	Recent
Black Sea to Caspician Sea*+	3 0 0	,,
Sverdlovsk, West Kazak*	+ 4 0 0	,,
Omsk, East Kazak*	+ 5 0 0	,,
Krasnoyarsk, New Syberia*+	6 0 0	,,
Irkutsk*	+ 7 0 0	,,
Yakutsk, Chitinsk*	+ 8 0 9	,,
Khabarovsk, Vladivostok*+	9 0 0	,,
Magadan, Sakalin Islands*+	10 0 9	,,
Peiropavlosvsk, Kamchatsiky*	+ 11 0 0	,,
Anadyr	+ 12 0 0	,,
Vatican Islands	+ 1 0 0	,,
West Indies' Barbados, Guadeloupe, Leeward Isls., Martinique, Tobago, Trinidad, Windward Isls.,	− 4 0 0	,,
Curacao	− 4 30 0	,,
Dominican Republic	− 5 0 0	,,
Bahamas, Jamaica	− 5 0 0	,,
Wales	G.M.T.	1880
Yugoslovakia	+ 1 0 0	Recent
Yokon	− 9 0 0	Aug. 1900

---

* Summer Time observed.

The Summer Time Bill lays down the following rule :—"The period of Summer Time shall be the period beginning at two o'clock, Greenwich mean time, in the morning of the day next following the THIRD SATURDAY IN APRIL, or if that day is Easter Day, the day next following the Second Saturday in April, and ending at two o'clock, Greenwich mean time, in the morning of the day next following the THIRD SATURDAY IN SEPTEMBER."

The Bill will not be permanent but will be renewable annually.

TABLE IX

Ayanamsa (1891 to 2000 A.D.)

Year	Ayanamsa	Year	Ayanamsa	Year	Ayanamsa
1891	20 53 17	28	21 24 20	65	21 55 22
92	20 54 8	29	21 25 10	66	21 56 12
93	20 54 58	1930	21 26 00	67	21 57 3
94	20 55 48	31	21 26 51	68	21 57 53
95	20 56 39	32	21 27 41	69	21 58 43
96	20 57 29	33	21 28 31	1970	21 59 34
97	20 58 19	34	21 29 22	71	22 0 24
98	20 59 10	35	21 30 12	72	22 1 14
99	21 0 0	36	21 31 2	73	22 2 5
1900	21 0 50	37	21 31 53	74	22 2 55
1	21 1 41	38	21 32 43	75	22 3 45
2	21 2 31	39	21 33 33	76	22 4 36
3	21 3 21	1940	21 34 24	77	22 5 27
4	21 4 12	41	21 35 14	78	22 6 17
5	21 5 2	42	21 36 4	79	22 7 7
6	21 5 52	43	21 36 55	1980	22 7 57
7	21 6 43	44	21 37 45	81	22 8 47
8	21 7 33	45	21 38 35	82	22 9 38
9	21 8 23	46	21 39 26	83	22 10 28
1910	21 9 14	47	21 40 16	84	22 11 18
11	21 10 4	48	21 41 6	85	22 12 9
12	21 10 54	49	21 41 57	86	22 12 59
13	21 11 45	1950	21 42 47	87	22 13 49
14	21 12 35	51	21 43 37	88	22 14 40
15	21 13 25	52	21 44 28	89	22 15 30
16	21 14 16	53	21 45 18	1990	22 16 20
17	21 15 6	54	21 46 8	91	22 17 11
18	21 15 56	55	21 46 59	92	22 18 1
19	21 16 47	56	21 47 49	93	22 18 51
1920	21 17 37	57	21 48 39	94	22 19 42
21	21 18 27	58	21 49 30	95	22 20 32
22	21 19 18	59	21 50 20	96	22 21 22
23	21 20 8	1960	21 51 10	97	22 22 13
24	21 20 58	61	21 52 1	98	22 23 3
25	21 21 49	62	21 52 51	99	22 23 53
26	21 22 39	63	21 53 41	2000	22 24 44
27	21 23 29	64	21 54 32		

TABLE X 267

Proportional Logarithms for finding planets' places

Min.	0	1	2	3	4	5	6	7	8	9	10	11	Min.
				Degrees or Hours									
0	—	1.3802	1.0792	9031	7781	6812	6021	5351	4771	4260	3802	3388	0
1	3.1584	1.3730	1.0756	9007	7763	6798	6009	5341	4762	4252	3795	3382	1
2	2.8573	1.3660	1.0720	8983	7745	6784	5997	5330	4753	4244	3788	3375	2
3	2.6812	1.3590	1.0685	8959	7728	6769	5985	5320	4744	4236	3780	3368	3
4	2.5563	1.3522	1.0649	8935	7710	6755	5973	5310	4735	4228	3773	3362	4
5	2.4594	1.3454	1.0614	8912	7692	6741	5961	5300	4726	4220	3766	3355	5
6	2.3802	1.3388	1.0580	8888	7674	6726	5949	5289	4717	4212	3759	3349	6
7	2.3133	1.3323	1.0546	8865	7657	6712	5937	5279	4708	4204	3752	3342	7
8	2.2553	1.3258	1.0511	8842	7639	6698	5925	5269	4699	4196	3745	3336	8
9	2.2041	1.3195	1.0478	8819	7622	6684	5913	5259	4690	4188	3737	3329	9
10	2.1584	1.3133	1.0444	8796	7604	6670	5902	5249	4682	4180	3730	3323	10
11	2.1170	1.3071	1.0411	8773	7587	6656	5890	5239	4673	4172	3723	3316	11
12	2.0792	1.3010	1.0378	8751	7570	6642	5878	5229	4664	4164	3716	3310	12
13	2.0444	1.2950	1.0345	8728	7552	6628	5866	5219	4655	4156	3709	3303	13
14	2.0122	1.2891	1.0313	8706	7535	6614	5855	5209	4646	4148	3702	3297	14
15	1.9823	1.2833	1.0280	8683	7518	6600	5843	5199	4638	4141	3695	3291	15
16	1.9542	1.2775	1.0248	8661	7501	6587	5832	5189	4629	4133	3688	3284	16
17	1.9276	1.2719	1.0216	8639	7484	6573	5820	5179	4620	4125	3681	3278	17
18	1.9031	1.2663	1.0185	8617	7467	6559	5809	5169	4611	4117	3674	3271	18
19	1.8796	1.2607	1.0153	8595	7451	6546	5797	5159	4603	4109	3667	3265	19
20	1.8573	1.2553	1.0122	8573	7434	6532	5786	5149	4594	4102	3660	3258	20
21	1.8361	1.2496	1.0091	8552	7417	6519	5774	5139	4585	4094	3653	3252	21
22	1.8159	1.2445	1.0061	8530	7401	6505	5763	5129	4577	4086	3646	3246	22
23	1.7966	1.2393	1.0030	8509	7384	6492	5752	5120	4568	4079	3639	3239	23
24	1.7781	1.2341	1.0000	8487	7368	6478	5740	5110	4559	4071	3632	3233	24
25	1.7604	1.2289	0.9970	8466	7351	6465	5729	5100	4551	4063	3625	3227	25
26	1.7434	1.2239	0.9940	8445	7335	6451	5718	5090	4542	4055	3618	3220	26
27	1.7270	1.2188	0.9910	8424	7318	6438	5706	5081	4534	4048	3611	3214	27
28	1.7112	1.2139	0.9881	8403	7302	6425	5695	5071	4525	4040	3604	3208	28
29	1.6960	1.2090	0.9852	8382	7286	6412	5684	5061	4516	4032	3597	3201	29
30	1.6812	1.2041	0.9823	8361	7270	6398	5673	5051	4508	4025	3590	3195	30
31	1.6670	1.1993	0.9794	8341	7254	6385	5662	5042	4499	4017	3583	3189	31
32	1.6532	1.1946	0.9765	8320	7238	6372	5651	5032	4491	4010	3576	3183	32
33	1.6398	1.1899	0.9737	8300	7222	6359	5640	5023	4482	4002	3570	3176	33
34	1.6269	1.1852	0.9708	8279	7206	6346	5629	5013	4474	3994	3563	3170	34
35	1.6143	1.1806	0.9680	8259	7190	6333	5618	5003	4466	3987	3556	3164	35
36	1.6021	1.1761	0.9652	8239	7174	6320	5607	4994	4457	3979	3549	3157	36
37	1.5902	1.1716	0.9625	8219	7159	6307	5596	4984	4449	3972	3542	3151	37
38	1.5786	1.1671	0.9597	8199	7143	6294	5585	4975	4440	3964	3535	3145	38
39	1.5673	1.1627	0.9570	8179	7128	6282	5574	4965	4432	3957	3529	3139	39
	0	1	2	3	4	5	6	7	8	9	10	11	

Proportional Logarithms for finding planets' places—*contd.*

Min.	Degrees or Hours												Min
	12	13	14	15	16	17	18	19	20	21	22	23	
0	3010	2663	2341	2041	1761	1498	1249	1015	0792	0580	0378	0185	0
1	3004	2657	2336	2036	1756	1493	1245	1011	0788	0577	0375	0182	1
2	2998	2652	2330	2032	1752	1489	1241	1007	0785	0573	0371	0179	2
3	2992	2646	2325	2027	1747	1485	1237	1003	0781	0570	0368	0175	3
4	2986	2640	2320	2022	1743	1481	1233	0999	0777	0566	0365	0172	4
5	2980	2635	2315	2017	1738	1476	1229	0996	0774	0563	0361	0169	5
6	2974	2629	2310	2012	1734	1472	1225	0992	0770	0559	0358	0166	6
7	2968	2624	2305	2008	1729	1468	1221	0988	0767	0556	0355	0163	7
8	2962	2618	2300	2003	1725	1464	1217	0984	0763	0552	0352	0160	8
9	2956	2613	2295	1998	1720	1459	1213	0980	0759	0549	0348	0157	9
10	2950	2607	2289	1993	1716	1455	1209	0977	0756	0546	0345	0154	10
11	2944	2602	2284	1988	1711	1451	1205	0973	0752	0542	0342	0150	11
12	2938	2596	2279	1984	1707	1447	1201	0969	0749	0539	0339	0147	12
13	2933	2591	2274	1979	1702	1443	1197	0965	0745	0535	0335	0144	13
14	2927	2585	2269	1974	1698	1438	1193	0962	0741	0532	0332	0141	14
15	2921	2580	2264	1969	1694	1434	1190	0958	0738	0529	0329	0138	15
16	2915	2574	2259	1965	1689	1430	1186	0954	0734	0525	0326	0135	16
17	2909	2569	2254	1960	1685	1426	1182	0950	0731	0522	0322	0132	17
18	2903	2564	2249	1955	1680	1422	1178	0947	0727	0518	0319	0129	18
19	2897	2558	2244	1950	1676	1417	1174	0943	0724	0515	0316	0126	19
20	2891	2553	2239	1946	1671	1413	1170	0939	0720	0512	0313	0122	20
21	2885	2547	2234	1941	1667	1409	1166	0935	0716	0508	0309	0119	21
22	2880	2542	2229	1936	1662	1405	1162	0932	0713	0505	0306	0116	22
23	2874	2536	2223	1932	1658	1401	1158	0928	0709	0501	0303	0113	23
24	2868	2531	2218	1927	1654	1397	1154	0924	0706	0498	0300	0110	24
25	2862	2526	2213	1922	1649	1392	1150	0920	0702	0495	0296	0107	25
26	2856	2520	2208	1917	1645	1388	1146	0917	0699	0491	0293	0104	26
27	2850	2515	2203	1913	1640	1384	1142	0913	0695	0488	0290	0101	27
28	2845	2509	2198	1908	1636	1380	1138	0909	0692	0484	0287	0098	28
29	2839	2504	2193	1903	1632	1376	1134	0906	0688	0481	0284	0095	29
30	2833	2499	2188	1899	1627	1372	1130	0902	0685	0478	0280	0091	30
31	2827	2493	2183	1894	1623	1368	1127	0898	0681	0474	0277	0088	31
32	2821	2488	2178	1889	1618	1364	1123	0894	0678	0471	0274	0085	32
33	2816	2483	2173	1885	1614	1359	1119	0891	0674	0468	0271	0082	33
34	2810	2477	2168	1880	1610	1355	1115	0887	0671	0464	0267	0079	34
35	2804	2472	2164	1875	1605	1351	1111	0883	0667	0461	0264	0076	35
36	2798	2467	2159	1871	1601	1347	1107	0880	0663	0458	0261	0073	36
37	2793	2461	2154	1866	1597	1343	1103	0876	0660	0454	0258	0070	37
38	2787	2456	2149	1862	1592	1339	1099	0872	0656	0451	0255	0067	38
39	2781	2451	2144	1857	1588	1335	1095	0869	0653	0448	0251	0064	39
	12	13	14	15	16	17	18	19	20	21	22	23	

Proportional Logarithms for finding planets' places—/contd.

Min.	0	1	2	3	4	5	6	7	8	9	10	11	Min.
				Degrees or Hours									
40	1.5563	1.1584	0.9542	8159	7112	6269	5563	4956	4424	3949	3522	3133	40
41	1.5456	1.1540	0.9515	8140	7097	6256	5552	4947	4415	3942	3515	3126	41
42	1.5351	1.1498	0.9488	8120	7081	6243	5541	4937	4407	3934	3508	3120	42
43	1.5249	1.1455	0 9462	8101	7066	6231	5531	4928	4399	3927	3501	3114	43
44	1.5149	1.1413	0.9435	8081	7050	6218	5520	4918	4390	3919	3495	3108	44
45	1.5051	1.1372	0.9409	8062	7035	6205	5509	4909	4382	3912	3488	3102	45
46	1.4956	1.1331	0.9383	8043	7020	6193	5498	4900	4374	3905	3481	3096	46
47	1.4863	1.1290	0.9356	8023	7005	6180	5488	4890	4365	3897	3475	3089	47
48	1.4771	1.1249	0.9330	8004	6990	6168	5477	4881	4357	3890	3468	3083	48
49	1.4682	1.1209	0.9305	7985	6975	6155	5466	4872	4349	3882	3461	3077	49
50	1.4594	1 1170	0 9279	7966	6960	6143	5456	4863	4341	3875	3454	3071	50
51	1.4508	1 1130	0 9254	7947	6945	6131	5445	4853	4333	3868	3448	3065	51
52	1.4424	1.1091	0 9228	7929	6930	6118	5435	4844	4324	3860	3441	3059	52
53	1 4341	1.1053	0 9203	7910	6915	6106	5424	4835	4316	3853	3434	3053	53
54	1.4260	1 1015	0 9178	7891	6900	6094	5414	4826	4308	3846	3428	3047	54
55	1 4180	1 0977	0 9153	7873	6885	6081	5403	4817	4300	3838	3421	3041	55
56	1.4102	1 0939	0.9128	7854	6871	6069	5393	4808	4292	3831	3415	3034	56
57	1 4025	1 C902	0 9104	7836	6856	6057	5382	4798	4284	3824	3408	3028	57
58	1 3949	1 0865	0 9079	7818	6841	6045	5372	4789	4276	3817	3401	3022	58
59	1.3875	1 0828	0 9055	7800	6827	6033	5361	4780	4268	3809	3395	3016	59
	0	1	2	3	4	5	6	7	8	9	10	11	

Proportional Logarithms for finding planets' places – *contd.*

Min	12	13	14	15	Degrees or Hours 16	17	18	19	20	21	22	23	Min
40	2775	2445	2139	1852	1564	1331	1091	0865	0649	0444	0248	0061	40
41	2770	2440	2134	1848	1579	1326	1088	0861	0646	0441	0245	0058	41
42	2764	2435	2129	1843	1575	1322	1084	0858	0642	0438	0242	0055	42
43	2758	2430	2124	1838	1571	1318	1080	0854	0639	0434	0239	0052	43
44	2753	2424	2119	1834	1566	1314	1076	0850	0635	0431	0236	0049	44
45	2747	2419	2114	1829	1562	1310	1072	0847	0632	0428	0232	0046	45
46	2741	2414	2109	1825	1558	1306	1068	0843	0628	0424	0229	0042	46
47	2736	2409	2104	1820	1553	1302	1064	0839	0625	0421	0226	0039	47
48	2730	2403	2099	1816	1549	1298	1061	0835	0622	0418	0223	0036	48
49	2724	2398	2095	1811	1545	1294	1057	0832	0618	0414	0220	0033	49
50	2719	2393	2090	1806	1540	1290	1053	0828	0615	0411	0216	0030	50
51	2713	2388	2085	1802	1536	1286	1049	0825	0611	0408	0213	0027	51
52	2707	2382	2080	1797	1532	1282	1045	0821	0608	0404	0210	0024	52
53	2702	2377	2075	1793	1528	1278	1041	0817	0604	0401	0207	0021	53
54	2696	2372	2070	1788	1523	1274	1038	0814	0601	0398	0204	0018	54
55	2691	2367	2065	1784	1519	1270	1034	0810	0597	0394	0201	0015	55
56	2685	2362	2061	1779	1515	1266	1030	0806	0594	0391	0197	0012	56
57	2679	2356	2056	1774	1510	1261	1026	0803	0590	0388	0194	0009	57
58	2674	2351	2051	1770	1506	1257	1022	0799	0587	0384	0191	0006	58
59	2668	2346	2046	1765	1502	1253	1018	0795	0583	0381	0188	0003	59
	12	13	14	15	16	17	18	19	20	21	22	23	